GENDER MEETS GENRE

PUBLICATIONS OF THE UCD FOUNDATION FOR ITALIAN STUDIES

General Editor: John C. Barnes

Dante and the Middle Ages: Literary and Historical Essays, ed. J. C. Barnes and C. Ó Cuilleanáin

Dante Comparisons: Comparative Studies of Dante and: Montale, Foscolo, Tasso, Chaucer, Petrarch, Propertius and Catullus, ed. E. Haywood and B. Jones

Dante Readings, ed. E. Haywood

Dante Soundings: Eight Literary and Historical Essays, ed. D. Nolan

Word and Drama in Dante: Essays on the "Divina Commedia", ed. J. C. Barnes and J. Petrie

J. Petrie, *Petrarch: The Augustan Poets, the Italian Tradition and the "Canzoniere"*

M. Davie, *Half-serious Rhymes: The Narrative Poetry of Luigi Pulci*

T. O'Neill, *Of Virgin Muses and of Love: A Study of Foscolo's "Dei Sepolcri"*

G. Leopardi, *Canti*, with an introduction by F. Fortini and translations by P. Lawton

U. Fanning, *Gender Meets Genre: Woman as Subject in the Fictional Universe of Matilde Serao*

G. Talbot, *Montale's "Mestiere Vile": The Elective Translations from English of the 1930s and 1940s*

Pasolini Old and New: Surveys and Studies, ed. Z. G. Barański

Italian Storytellers: Essays on Italian Narrative Literature, ed. E. Haywood and C. Ó Cuilleanáin

B. Reynolds, *Casalattico and the Italian Community in Ireland*

BELFIELD ITALIAN LIBRARY

Dante Alighieri, *Vita nuova*, ed. J. Petrie and J. Salmons

Lorenzo de' Medici, *Selected Writings*, ed. C. Salvadori

Carlo Goldoni, *La locandiera*, ed. D. O'Grady

Luigi Pirandello, *Il berretto a sonagli*, ed. J. C. Barnes

Eugenio Montale, *Selected Poems*, ed. G. Talbot

GENDER
MEETS GENRE

Woman as Subject
in the Fictional Universe
of Matilde Serao

URSULA FANNING

Published for
The UCD Foundation for Italian Studies

IRISH ACADEMIC PRESS
DUBLIN • PORTLAND, OR

First published in 2002 by
IRISH ACADEMIC PRESS
44, Northumberland Road, Dublin 4, Ireland

and in the United States of America by
IRISH ACADEMIC PRESS
c/o ISBS, 5824 N.E. Hassalo Street,
Portland, Oregon 97213-3644

Website: www.iap.ie

British Library Cataloguing in Publication Data

A catalogue record of this book is available from the British Library.

ISBN 0-7165-2602-6

Library of Congress Cataloging-in-Publication Data

A catalog record of this book is available from the Library of Congress.

Publication of this book was assisted by grants from
The UCD Academic Publications Committee
The UCD Faculty of Arts

Printed and bound by MPG Books Ltd., Bodmin, Cornwall

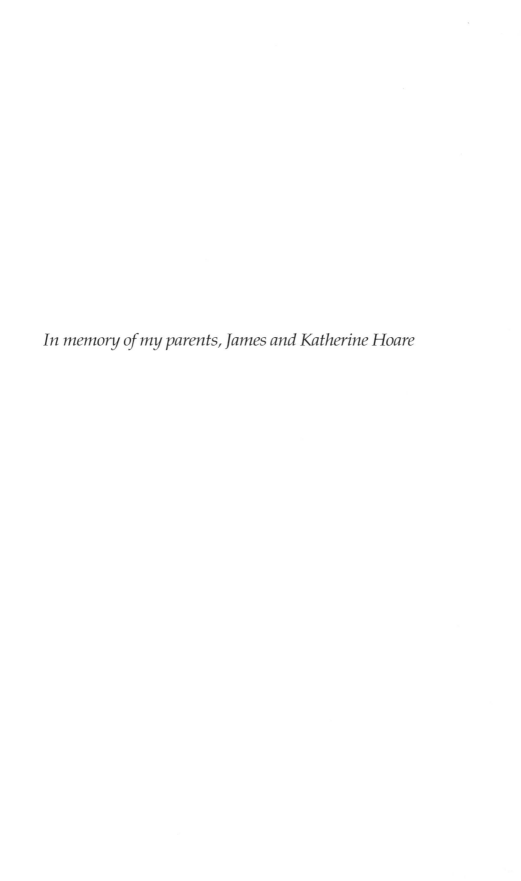

In memory of my parents, James and Katherine Hoare

PREFACE

This book sets out to examine both conventional and radical elements in the writings of Matilde Serao (1856–1927), through a consideration of how she presents female characters in her fiction, how she represents real women in her journalism, and her experimentation with genre conventions in ways which challenge conventional representations of both the feminine and the masculine.

The Introduction provides the context for the analysis which follows. It investigates Serao's peculiar position as a woman writer in the Naples of the late nineteenth and early twentieth centuries, as well as endeavouring to provide an overview of the position of women in Italian society in that period and an analysis of Serao's often contradictory reactions to her preferred subjects.

Part I examines specific roles and images of women offered by Serao: her critical variations on the romance plot, where she presents women as erotic agents, if doomed ones; her ambivalent and highly charged representations of the maternal role and of women as mothers; her representations of working women of different social classes in her realist works, these last riddled with contradictions and uncertainties.

Part II considers two genres adopted by Serao, those of the Sentimental novel and the Gothic novel, for which her views of gender, and her wrestling with issues of gender, have implications. Through a series of close readings of the novels in question, I show how Serao's experimentation with literary forms is itself informed by a surprisingly radical view of gender.

I should like to thank Professor John Barnes for his support, as well as for his painstaking editorial work in bringing this volume to completion.

The book originated as a PhD dissertation presented to the University of Reading in 1990, and I thank Dr Shirley Vinall for her scholarly and ever encouraging supervision of the work in that context. I also wish to thank both University College Dublin and the National University of Ireland for generous grants in aid of publication. A special word of thanks goes to Anne Spillane and to Mai McLoughlin for their excellent secretarial skills. Karen Brown, Patricia Butler and Pat McLean kindly helped procure the photograph for the dust-jacket and permission to reproduce it. The support of my family and friends was at all times invaluable. The book's dedication to the memory of my parents is an inadequate indication of how important their love and support was to the project and to me. Completion of the work would have been far more difficult than it was without the ever present support, conviction and practical help of my husband, Brendan. And the smaller man in my life provided both a sense of perspective and some much-needed humour in the last couple of years of the work—thank you Comhall!

Finally, it remains only to say that any faults or inadequacies in the book are entirely my own.

CONTENTS

INTRODUCTION:
MATILDE SERAO IN CONTEXT

Matilde Serao was an atypical woman of her time in many respects. She was unusual not just in being an Italian woman writer: as a successful southern Italian woman writer she stands out even more. Nor was she successful merely as a writer of fiction: she also carved a place for herself in the cut-throat newspaper world of the South. Her first article, in 1876, was a review for the *Giornale di Napoli*. From there she went on to write for *Il piccolo* and *Cronaca bizantina*, ran the *Corriere di Roma*, the *Corriere di Napoli* and *Il mattino* with her husband, Edoardo Scarfoglio (whom she married in 1884 and with whom she had four children) and ultimately founded two newspapers of her own, *La settimana* and *Il giorno*.[1] She herself felt all the novelty of her position, as she demonstrated in a letter to her friend Gaetano Bonavenia in 1878: "Scrivo dappertutto e di tutto con un'audacia unica, conquisto il mio posto a forza di urti, di gomitate, col fitto ed ardente desiderio di arrivare, senza aver nessuno che mi aiuti o quasi nessuno. [...] Sai che io non do ascolto alle debolezze del mio sesso."[2]

Serao, twenty-one in 1878, was clearly determined, ambitious and industrious. Perhaps more significantly, she indicates in her letter to Bonavenia that she is all these things *in spite of being female*. It is hardly surprising that issues of gender, particularly issues surrounding the acceptable feminine, as I will show throughout this book, are of central importance to her work, as indeed they are to my study of her. Serao is not merely a self-conscious writer but a self-conscious woman writer. And in the formula "woman writer" lies a conflict both for her and, I shall later suggest, for other women who write. This conflict is only to be expected when a woman writes in a world where a respected critic (Ugo Ojetti) defines a "scrittrice" as "un uomo condannato a vivere in un corpo di donna".[3]

At the heart of Serao's self-definition in her letter to Bonavenia, the words "woman" and "writer" clearly conflict with each other. In her own terms, Serao achieves in spite of her sex. Indeed, she sometimes blames her gender for preventing her from achieving what she wishes. As Anna Banti records, towards the close of her life "la vecchia Matilde si lagnava rabbiosamente di quella sua sottana che le impediva di documentarsi di prima mano sulle abitatrici di case chiuse."[4] As we shall see, however, Serao's "sottana" did not altogether prevent her dealing with the subject of prostitution. In the words of Maryse Jeuland-Meynaud, she reveals "un'umana comprensione per quelle disgraziate che vivono del proprio corpo".[5] Her perspective, too, is unusual. It differs from that of male writers like Zola, Maupassant and Huysmans—as Jeuland-Meynaud points out (page 115)—in that in Serao's work such characters are "colte sotto l'aspetto della loro umanità travagliata e mai nell'esercizio della loro *ars amatoria*". In Jeuland-Meynaud's view, this is a defect in Serao's writing. I think it more legitimate to see it as a difference in perspective occasioned by sex and by notions of gender.

Serao's self-definition, then, is conditioned by an awareness of the restrictions placed upon her as a writer precisely because she is a woman. Yet in circumventing those restrictions insofar as it was possible for a woman writer of that period to do so, she placed gender issues at the centre of most of her fictional narratives in a manner which differentiates her from the "great" novelists of the period, both Italian and French. Umberto Eco identifies one of the distinguishing features of Serao's work when he links her with Carolina Invernizio and Liala. He points out: "Non solo sono donne che scrivono, ma scrivono su personaggi femminili e per un pubblico femminile."[6] Wanda de Nunzio Schilardi, too, has identified Serao's public as female, in her journalism as well as her fiction. Serao, she says, "individua il suo pubblico soprattutto nelle lettrici [...]; indirettamente tutta la sua produzione è indirizzata ad un pubblico femminile" (page 36). The centrality of the female protagonist in Serao's work is striking, especially when compared with the cursory delineation of her male characters. It is woman's story which interests her and it is woman's story that she repeatedly chooses to investigate. The various roles open to women of her time are thoroughly examined in her work: woman is seen within the boundaries of the heterosexual love relationship, and in the mother–daughter dyad as both mother and daughter; furthermore, Serao considers the possibilities and limitations of work in female communities, and of female friendship. In her search for a way of writing which will allow her to deal with these matters, she experiments with various literary traditions, with different genres and styles. In this book I shall consider the roles Serao allows her female characters to "try on" and the literary images with which she works and against which she often reacts, as well as her ultimately subversive handling of the genres of both Sentimental and Gothic novel, which illuminates her whole literary enterprise.

Many readers have criticized Serao's writing for its unevenness. Anna Banti claims that "la narrativa di donna Matilde è come una terra da tartufi, non tutti i cani sanno scoprire a fiuto il prezioso tubero" (page 156). Anthony Gisolfi is of the same mind. In his analysis of *Fantasia* (1883), one of Serao's greatest works, he writes about a "contrast between unusual merits and grave defects".[7] Gianni Infusino, for his part, sees "quasi una doppia vena" in Serao's writing.[8] Yet Serao herself was aware of what, in an interview with Ojetti, she called her "stile rotto".[9] She was, she stated, disinclined to change her way of writing, even if she could, as she felt it gave her work vitality. In fact, in my view Serao's mixture of literary styles is one of the most intriguing aspects of her work. She did write works of fiction that fitted broadly into one category or another—Romantic, Realist, Gothic—, yet even in those works traces of other genres are apparent. This in itself differentiates her from those male writers whom she admired and often sought to emulate, and is another of the areas which the present book seeks to analyse and explain.

It is worth pausing at this early stage to reflect on the identity of the writers Serao admired. She read widely in both French and Italian, but not in English. (She had followed only the programme of the Scuola Normale.) She claimed to have read voraciously between the ages of twelve and twenty (Gisolfi, page 36) and we know from her literary reviews in various newspapers that her respect for certain writers increased with time. One writer we know she read and learned from was Balzac; as Martin-Gistucci says, Balzac was "son éternel modèle, sans cesse lu et relu".[10] It is in Serao's use of descriptive detail that Martin-Gistucci correctly finds Balzac's greatest influence on her work. As for Flaubert, Serao wrote a review of his letters to George Sand, in which she stated her belief that he was a great writer and expressed the judgement that "la critica fu sempre con Flaubert di una severità eccessiva."[11] Of

Zola she wrote, in his obituary, that he had "sollevato un mondo di idee" and that he was "un confratello, [...] un maestro che [...] venerammo" (de Nunzio Schilardi, pages 187–88). When Serao spoke to Ojetti about her own work she classified herself with other Italian writers, referring to "noi quattro (intendo Verga, de Roberto, me e un po' Capuana" (Ojetti, page 237). She also knew the work of d'Annunzio well; he was Scarfoglio's close friend and enemy, a witness at their wedding and later the faithless lover of her dear friend Eleonora Duse,[12] besides which she and Scarfoglio provided a platform for d'Annunzio's writings in their newspapers. While she was familiar with d'Annunzio's work, however, any literary influence seems to have gone from her to him: as Jeuland-Meynaud says (page 26), "Circa i debiti del pescarese nei confronti della Serao, ci sarebbe un grosso capitolo da aprire." On another level, Paul Bourget was a friend of Serao's who to some extent certainly influenced her work, though she moved increasingly away from his influence; paradoxically, she was distancing herself from his style by the time she dedicated *Suor Giovanna della Croce* to him (1901).[13] Mastriani, too, exerted an acknowledged influence on Serao, though she did not overestimate his ability: as she pointed out amid her praise for his work in her obituary of him, "Aveva torto di volersi misurare con Emilio Zola" (de Nunzio Schilardi, page 175).

In my analysis of Serao's work, which involves inevitable comparisons with other writers, I shall give greater consideration to those of the above-mentioned authors whose fame has endured. The work of Bourget and that of Mastriani, while undeniably important for Serao, remains different in kind and stature from that of Balzac. I wish to measure Serao against the writers she respected, and who remain important in any consideration of the literature of the period. I would argue that Serao herself has an important part in this literary history. Eco, too, despite his decision to consider the three writers in one volume, makes a qualitative distinction between her work and that of Invernizio and Liala: although he tends to gloss over this distinction, he nonetheless acknowledges that "quanto a Matilde Serao, [...] a buona ragione viene presa in considerazione da quelle storie della letteratura che abitualmente trascurano le altre due autrici del nostro trittico" (page 5). Serao, like Mastriani, Invernizio and Liala, is a writer of the *romanzo popolare*, but she is also part of the mainstream of Italian literature, and her work was highly valued in her own time. Consequently, I also wish to measure her work against that of other women writers of stature in both a European and an American context.

It is noticeable in the foregoing, as well as in Serao's writings, that she rarely measures herself against other women writers; indeed she rarely refers to other women writers at all. When she does so she is often disparaging. In her article on Flaubert (mentioned above) she refers in passing to George Sand, and particularly to her heroine Lélia in the novel of that name: Lélia, she says, "è una amara e odiosa filosofante" (de Nunzio Schilardi, page 166). In an article entitled "Novità letterarie" (1876), she reviews among other works Neera's *Un romanzo*. She appears to intend no malice in this analysis and yet the review, while on the whole positive, is somewhat patronizing: "Le scene di un Romanzo [*sic*], anche a chi nol sapesse, rivelano la mano gentile e delicata di una donna" (de Nunzio Schilardi, page 152). This leads her to generalize about how women's analytical talents are best suited to the art of the novel, where women writers can indulge their thirst for in-depth portraits, showing how "esse vanno al fondo di ogni gesto, di ogni parola" (de Nunzio Schilardi, page 152).

This approach to women writers raises a number of interesting questions which I will address in this book: How is it that a writer who chooses to locate female characters at the centre of her narrative, and to explore particularly female dilemmas in her fiction, appears so ready to criticize other women writers who are engaged in a similar exercise? Why indeed does Serao so often ignore her creative sisters? What is the precise nature of the conflict which, as we have seen, she perceives between the terms *donna* and *scrittore*? What is her approach to the feminist movement of her time and how can it be reconciled with her writings on women? Finally, does writing as a woman, and writing of women, affect her literary style?

In posing these questions, and in searching for answers to them, I have inevitably found myself drawing on recent work in feminist literary criticism. This is, in essence, what differentiates my approach to Serao from that of literary critics who have previously analysed her works in any depth. While many of those critics have recognized that Serao's perspective on her literary world is definitively female and concerned with female problems, few have chosen to make this the central point of their analysis,[14] with the notable exception of Nancy Harrowitz in her recent comparative work on Serao. In the present study my analysis centres on a close re-reading of a wide range of Serao's writings within a critical framework which is beginning to be used increasingly in relation to the work of Italian women writers. There is much more to be done in this field.

Before analysing Serao's literary production in detail, and before situating her work in its literary context, I shall locate her writing, both fiction and journalism, in the precise historical and ideological framework to which it belongs. It is especially important to consider Serao's work in a historical and ideological framework, because of her peculiar status as a woman writer and journalist in that period of Italian, and particularly Neapolitan, history. Her (resultant) ambiguity towards the role of women in society is, at least in part, conditioned by that experience. The ideological shifts in her writing have led to scores of negative and patronizing critical judgements in relation to both her and her work. Such negative comments are as prevalent in current critical analysis as they were in her own day. Antonio Ghirelli, for example, in his comprehensive study of post-Unification Neapolitan society, while identifying the unique situation in which Serao found herself, nonetheless repeats many of the old stereotypes in his analysis of her work. He refers to Serao with a mixture of admiration, wonder and contempt: "La bruttezza fisica è pari in lei al fascino, all'arguzia e alla vivacità della rappresentazione, una miscela che è resa ancor piú esplosiva dalla stupefacente capacità di lavoro e da un livello di emancipazione che, pur essendo assolutamente superficiale, non è per questo meno inconsueto in una donna italiana di fine secolo."[15] As a woman, she is constantly judged in terms of her appearance, and invariably found wanting. She is also repeatedly judged in terms of her femininity, or lack of it. Ghirelli follows his nineteenth-century predecessors in this respect too, referring to her "temperamento ardente, estroso, quasi virile seppur teneramente materno" (page 111).

The nature of Serao's work, her position in the masculist Scarfoglio–d'Annunzio circle, her obsession with acceptable femininity, and her interest in women and their situation in society, explored repeatedly in both her fiction and her journalism, all made Serao something of a fascinating enigma to her contemporaries. She is still an interesting figure and I would argue that this is due, at least in part, to the way in which she both reflects and challenges the views on women prevalent in her time, in her political analyses and in her reflection and reworking of traditional literary representations of women.

In order to contextualize Serao's work, I shall examine the position of women in the period in question, together with the prevailing attitudes towards woman's role, with particular reference to the situation of Neapolitan women.

WOMEN'S POSITION IN ITALIAN SOCIETY, 1860–1930

In the 1860s, the period of Matilde Serao's childhood in Italy, Italian women had few legal rights, especially after marriage. The Codice Civile of 1865 ensured that the newly unified Italy would follow French law in denying married women financial independence. This decision was reached despite the fact that Giuseppe Pisanelli, who had drafted the original version of the Codice, was against it.[16] As Fiorenza Taricone and Beatrice Pisa summarize it, the law in question would act, for women, as a disincentive to marriage: "Si precludevano in definitiva alle donne le donazioni [...], le ipoteche, le cessioni o riscossioni di capitale, le relative transazioni e azioni giudiziarie, e di conseguenza anche, come ribadí la legislazione successiva, l'autonoma gestione dei conti bancari" (page 29). As late as 1910 Sibilla Aleramo rails against the fact that this law is still in existence, drawing attention to the campaign for its repeal conducted by the Associazione per la Donna (of which Serao was a member). Aleramo writes:

> Oggi la donna maritata non può disporre in Italia dei propri averi senza la firma del marito. Un progetto di legge per questa abolizione è allo studio del parlamento, ma è quasi certo che esso non sarà per ora votato, perché i deputati, i quali rappresentano l'opinione e l'interesse maschile del paese, trascureranno tranquillamente la questione di giustizia per mantenersi il proprio privilegio.[17]

The issue of women's suffrage (one index of the status of women in society) is one which Serao repeatedly mocked. This may seem somewhat negative at first, but when it is realized that even as late as 1900 only 6% of the Neapolitan population were eligible to vote her cynicism is less surprising.[18] Her most caustic treatment of the issue occurs in "Votazione femminile", included in her *Pagina azzurra*;[19] I shall discuss it in some detail in Chapter 3. Her judgement is based ultimately on class as well as on gender.

Whereas women in other European countries experienced improvements in their legal lot, matters became progressively worse for Italian women until the end of the Second World War. Repeated petitions for female suffrage (in 1904 and 1908) met with no success; only widows and unmarried women enjoyed anything like the legal rights of men; marriage remained a condition in which women had no control over money, property, or even their children (Taricone–Pisa, page 31). And although after 1873 women were, for instance, permitted to work in the Post and Telegraph Office (in itself not much of an achievement, as we shall see), Giuseppe Pennisi could confidently claim in 1905 that "il patrimonio intellettuale della società è dovuta agli uomini."[20] The limited suffrage theoretically granted to women in 1925 was exceedingly restrictive in its exclusion of the poorer classes and, in the words of Camilla Ravera, "riduce l'eleggibilità femminile a una concessione umiliante".[21] Serao thus witnessed a relatively static phase in the history of the status of Italian women. This phase was soon to be followed by one of erosion of the few rights then enjoyed. In 1927, the year of Serao's death, and again in 1938, the female workforce was drastically cut by the Fascist government: in 1927 women were forbidden to teach *lettere* and philosophy in *licei*, and in 1938 female employment was forcibly limited to 10% of the national total (Ravera, pages 128–29). The writing had been on the wall for some time. Mussolini's desire that Italian women remain at home and produce sons for the fatherland, and specifically for his bellicose undertakings, was clearly incompatible with any improvement in women's lot as employees. In Ravera's words again, "il progresso della donna [...] è nel nostro paese violentemente stroncato dall'avvento del fascismo" (page 127). Women in Italy were not finally admitted to suffrage until 1946, at least twenty years later than most of their European counterparts. The climate in which Serao wrote, then, was one of legal repression of women, which became still more severe in the years immediately following her death.[22]

In any period of economic difficulty such resistance to women working is perhaps unsurprising. Indeed, Evelyne Sullerot postulates a direct relationship between economic growth (or lack of it) and the employment of women.[23] She draws specifically on the Italian situation to support her thesis: "En Italie, avec la démographie galopante que le pays connut au début du xxᵉ siècle, et des difficultés économiques énormes par manque de matières premières, on verra le taux de femmes au travail faire un plongeon spectaculaire" (pages 134–35). In view of the official disapproval we should hardly be surprised that Serao's attitude to women working is highly ambivalent.

Ambivalent though she was about women's role in the workforce, Serao was no less uncertain about their role in the family. She was aware that whatever their social class women were at a legal and economic disadvantage there; yet she was also influenced by the propaganda around her, and paradoxically by the enactment of the Christian—and especially Roman Catholic—ideals consonant with this propaganda that she must have witnessed. One example of the type of propaganda disseminated during Serao's childhood is found in the work of Antonio Rosmini, *Filosofia del diritto* (1841–45).[24] Rosmini, a controversial theologian, had founded his Congregazione dei Rosminiani, also known as the Istituto della Carità, in 1828. During his lifetime and after his death the Congregazione's influence in Italian schools was widespread at all levels.[25] Rosmini, according to Gigliola De Donato, expressed the view that "essendo la donna rivolta al patire in virtú della sua debolezza può rovesciare in positiva tale sua menomazione cosicché [...] tale patire è oltre modo fecondo di virtú e di meriti."[26] The ideology here is of course Roman Catholic; yet, as we shall see, attitudes and prescriptions for women in the Catholic faith and in Catholic schools did not differ markedly from those of the post-Unification secular model.

In Serao's fiction we see many wives of the ideal Rosminian type—passive and prepared to suffer—; yet interestingly Serao, while faithfully portraying the ideal wife of such propagandist literature, cannot let her be. She is compelled either to transform her, as she does with Luisella Fragalà in *Il paese di Cuccagna* (1891), or to show how utterly fruitless such an existence is, as she does with Caterina in *Fantasia* (1883).[27] In fact Caterina is especially interesting when directly compared with Rosmini's type of the ideal wife. Rosmini describes the duties of the ideal wife as being "di soggiacere e di compiacere al marito, aiutandolo, onorandolo, amandolo, servendolo, e di riceverne in cambio tutela, onore, felicità" (*Filosofia del diritto*, I, 29). Caterina is exactly this type of bourgeois wife. Serao writes of her: "L'incarico suo era di trovar saggio e onesto quanto suo marito faceva" (*Fantasia*, page 112). Yet she receives anything but happiness for her pains; indeed her unhappiness culminates in suicide, which in Rosmini's terms could only be seen as subversive. Thus Serao clearly does not wholly accept the mood of the times, which involved an exaltation of the ideal that, as De Donato puts it (page 58) "la società in tutti i suoi strati (ma la lezione è riferita sostanzialmente ai ceti inferiori e alle donne di tutte le classi) sacrifichi il principio del piacere a quello del dovere".

The characterization of working-class women, too, in *Il paese di Cuccagna*, indicates both an awareness of, and a sense of impotent rage about, the fact that "these women continued the self-sacri-ficing, self-exploitative work [...] characteristic of the peasant or household economy."[28] Generally speaking, Serao's middle- and working-class female characters work harder than their male counterparts and contribute more to the family's well-being, such as it is. This is not merely a reflection of male-centred propaganda about how things should be but a factual representation.[29]

While considering the historical family and its literary representations, it is interesting to look, albeit briefly for now, at how Serao deals specifically with motherhood. Massimo Livi Bacci, together with other demographers, is categorical about the existence of some form of birth control in certain areas of Italy even prior to Unification;[30] and Serao's representations of the different family patterns in the upper and lower classes would seem to indicate a knowledge of this on her part. Those of Serao's upper-class female characters who have children are very much a minor-ity, reflecting Livi Bacci's observation that "durante il diciannove-simo e all'inizio del ventesimo [secolo], mentre le categorie privi-legiate apprendevano a controllare in maniera efficiente la loro fecondità, il peso delle famiglie numerose passò sulle spalle dei piú poveri, con le conseguenze che è facile immaginare" (page 281). It is often in fact these consequences of a high birth rate in the working-class population which hold Serao's attention, in works such as *Il ventre di Napoli*.[31] She is also aware of, and saddened by, the predicament of young, unmarried, working-class mothers, as she reveals, for example, in the closing chapters of *Suor Giovanna della Croce*. Many of these young female characters in her work act according to a sense of traditional family values, based on love and marriage, unaware of the different social context in which they find themselves in the city of Naples, and thus the results of their liaisons with men are unfortunate. Scott and Tilly discuss the rise of illegitimate birth rates in many European cities in the nineteenth century, stressing the causative factors of loneliness and isolation, together with the conditions of domestic service, which often demanded that servants be unmarried (page 169). It was likely that a young girl alone in a city (as many of Serao's characters are) would seek comfort in a romantic liaison, expecting a conventional solution (marriage) which often proved elusive. As Scott and Tilly point out, once away from their own families these girls were also removed from the traditional context which enforced moral behaviour (page 170). The ensuing dilemma arouses Serao's compassion—and of course her ambivalence, because although she is aware of the constraints placed upon women by the traditional family structure, she cannot see the impoverished and desperate lifestyle of these young girls as a viable alternative.

The rather bleak picture of women's lives which I have painted here is not the whole story. The feminist movement was active in Italy during the post-Unification period, as in other European countries, drawing attention to the situation of Italian women and encouraging them to organize and improve their lot. Nonetheless, the Italian feminist movement was itself rather less organized than most of its European equivalents, and somewhat restricted in its appeal. Camilla Ravera points out: "In Italia […] giunge soltanto di riflesso in ristretti circoli intellettuali. Le donne nella loro grande maggioranza vi rimangono estranee; né potrebbero comunque collegarlo con la reale situazione in cui si svolge la loro vita familiare e sociale" (page 15). To begin with, at any rate, the feminist movement's appeal was largely confined to the middle class and to the North of Italy. Middle-class working women were the first group to begin to be conscious of themselves as disadvantaged in the workplace on the basis of their sex, and, as Ravera notes, it was through them that feminism became a more active force in Italy: "Nasce […] in questi strati femminili—come manifestazione di malcontento, e come rivolta contro l'ingiustizia di cui sono vittime—un primo interesse verso i movimenti femministi che già si sono sviluppati negli altri paesi" (page 66). Gradually (the period referred to by Ravera is that of the First World War) feminism became relevant to at least some sections of the female population in Italy, though theoretical and intellectual debates on the nature of feminism raged.

Two of the most significant protagonists and debaters of feminism in Italy were Anna Maria Mozzoni and Anna Kuliscioff. The former was strongly in favour of extra-domestic employment for women, and Ravera describes her as one of "le prime donne italiane a capire il socialismo, a fare della questione femminile un aspetto del movimento operaio" (page 73). She translated many of the "bibles" of the European feminist movement into Italian, bringing feminist doctrines within the reach of many more Italian women.[32] Yet despite her significance she was, as Gigliola De Donato puts it, a "voce isolata" (page 43).

Kuliscioff, too, was something of a "voce isolata" within the Italian Socialist Party. She reacted violently in 1910 when the Party refused to make female suffrage part of its platform. As Ravera says, she was "in amara polemica con il suo partito, che sembrava respingere o ignorare la specificità della questione femminile" (page 75). Indeed, the PSI was never very sure of its stance on female suffrage. Both it and in later years the Italian Communist Party were anything but allies in the struggle to improve the status of Italian women, as Franca Pieroni Bortolotti indicates when discussing the Third International of 1919: "Non tutti quei socialisti che parlavano di eguaglianza, infatti, erano poi davvero disposti a tradurla in azione politica e legislativa, e quasi tutti avevano creduto che la 'rivoluzione' dovesse 'cogliere' intanto il voto alle donne del ceto medio (quando pur ce l'avevano) e talvolta neppure darlo alle 'arretrate', alle operaie e alle contadine."[33]

In fact the whole issue of the vote seems to have been for most Italian women—as indeed for Serao—a purely academic question. As Ravera notes, the majority of Italian women were simply not interested, in the face of other, more pressing needs: "In Italia, le operaie, le contadine, le impiegate lottano strenuamente per il pane e per i loro diritti sul lavoro" (page 108). So although several attempts were made by concerned women's groups to persuade the government to introduce female suffrage,[34] there was a general sense of its irrelevance to the majority of Italian women. Mussolini later capitalized on this apparent irrelevance when, in 1925, he made his proposals for (very) limited female suffrage, for women over twenty-five who had received medals for special duties in military or civilian life, or had made great contributions to public health, or in teaching, or in times of national disaster; women who were mothers or widows of war heroes, who could read and write, or who paid taxes of 100 lire per annum—a true "voto alle signo-re"![35] In any case these proposals were soon rendered useless by the abolition of administrative elections.

Despite the apparent indifference of Italian women to their political rights, however, their political awareness and organizational capacity were increasing. In any event, political rights were only one issue: there were many other battles to be fought. As Scott and Tilly stress in relation to all European countries, "There was little relationship between women's political rights and women's work. The right to vote did not increase the size of the female labour force" (page 146). In Italy various *unioni femminili*, even in the South, had by 1911 embarked on ambitious programmes of female education, setting up nurseries, libraries, summer schools for women workers, evening classes and hospitals (Taricone–Pisa, page 77). Such initiatives were boosted with the onset of the First World War, when women, employed in greater numbers, really did become part of the Italian working class, involved in its unions and its strikes (Ravera, page 92). Italian organized feminism made gradual if slow progress until the advent of Fascism.

As I have indicated, from its earliest stages Italian feminism had to contend with the ideals of the nascent Italian state. I shall now examine those ideals in greater detail and consider how they worked against the formation of a self-conscious feminist movement. It is also interesting to note how, up to the Fascist period, attacks on the feminist movement became more specific as it grew stronger. At the same time it is important to bear in mind the position of a woman writer like Serao—very much part of the establishment, with a vested interest in the status quo but also a keen awareness of the inadequacies and problems of women's existence.

From the Risorgimento onwards, as is shown by Fiorenza Taricone, a subtle connection was made between the terms *donna* and *patria*. It seems that the task of creating a new, morally upright nation was to rest squarely on the shoulders of Italian women; the bourgeoisie, at any rate, was to devote its energies to bringing up its children in a proper and moral manner. The moral nature of the task was consonant with Roman Catholic ideology. I quote Taricone on the Italian woman's role as envisaged by the exemplary texts of the early 1880s: "La sua missione si conferma [...] nella famiglia, altrimenti chiamata santuario, fuoco sacro, focolare e cosí via; a misura che la famiglia umana si estende, la missione della donna si va anch' essa trasformando e ampliando, rimanendo illeso il principio fondamentale; la felicità dell'uomo, l'educazione dei figli, il perfezionamento del proprio ascendente basato sulle qualità morali."[36] This vision of ideal family life is one which seems to have had some effect on Serao, given her regret, frequently expressed in *Il ventre di Napoli* and elsewhere, that women should have to work, to be away from their families and most especially from their children.

It was repeatedly stressed that, as well as being an exemplary moral educator, woman must be prepared to sacrifice herself for others. As Taricone shows, the *cataloghi* are peppered with phrases like "la santa virtú del sacrifico" and (the duty to) "apparire sempre serena, sempre fidente, sempre forte" (page 60). The Church helped diffuse these ideas through works aimed specifically at women readers.[37] Serao, as we have seen, although infected by such views, could not wholly agree with them.

Above all, women were required to be essentially passive. As De Donato says, "una società cosí disgregata e arretrata [...] ha bisogno [...] delle virtú 'passive' della donna" (page 17). And, as Serao herself was to discover, "l'ideologia dominante non mostra eccessiva simpatia per la donna intellettualmente qualificata, guardandosi con ammirazione piuttosto dubbia di donne 'virili' dedite a pubbliche attività" (De Donato, page 37). De Donato's judgement on the attitudes of Serao's contemporaries might equally well apply to Ghirelli's recently expressed views on Serao, quoted earlier. (The tendency to view intellectually able women involved in public life as somehow less than feminine was not confined to the nineteenth century.) With hindsight, however, it is obvious that Serao could more easily get on with her day-to-day work, her journalism, on which her very existence and that of her family depended, if she remained uncontroversial and simply toed the conservative line in relation to women. Indeed, as De Donato points out in her analysis of the journalistic writings of the period, newspapers and magazines were "il termometro piú sensibile delle opinioni e delle ideologie dominanti circa la donna e i suoi interessi".[38] And, she reveals, the opinions and ideologies conveyed by the press were largely conservative, and fearful of women's independence. How could Serao have survived in that climate, as one who earned her living primarily through journalism, had she not fitted in? Subtle subversion was less likely to be noticed in her fiction, and indeed, as I shall demonstrate throughout this book, that is where her more ambivalent and perceptive analyses of women and their situation in society are found. In any case Serao was never politically inclined to the left, and if even the left was opposed to women's intellectual emancipation in its early years she was doubly unlikely to be controversial in that regard. Feminists such as Mozzoni and Kuliscioff, as we have seen, were clearly isolated.

The isolation became more pronounced, and feminists more open to virulent attack, when the question of female suffrage arose. Other prominent Italian women besides Serao openly expressed their disapproval of the proposal. One such woman, as tightly enmeshed in her social world as Serao, was Gina Lombroso, the daughter of Serao's friend Cesare Lombroso, the latter a figure of significance in scientific and social circles. (Typical of his work in the field of criminal anthropology is the study *La donna delinquente*, in which he outlined the likely physical characteristics of criminal female types.)[39] Gina Lombroso was not, on the whole, a reactionary figure; she inclined towards democracy. And yet on the question of female suffrage she was adamantly negative:

> Le donne in genere non s'interessano di questioni politiche […]. La donna in questo momento vuole il voto perché l'hanno persuaso che il voto […] è decoroso di possedere […]. Dal punto di vista femminile il voto non ha alcun vantaggio, e può avere […] molti svantaggi; allontanare l'uomo dalla donna, diminuire matrimoni e natalità, diminuire la coscienziosità della donna, diminuire il suo interesse familiare, prevalere delle donne anormali sulle normali.[40]

Reactionary though these thoughts are, we must recognize that Gina Lombroso's point of view is dictated by fear of change: it reflects the prominence of the ideal female figure we have already observed in earlier propaganda. Equally, her words could be Serao's: the concerns voiced are those which she too expressed. As late as 1924 women were voicing the same concerns, but at that stage in more malevolent tones, influenced by Fascism and its ideals. Teresa Labriola was more viciously anti-feminist than Serao had ever been: "Io penso che se all'incuria e al vizio degradante delle donne del popolo si venisse ad aggiungere il femminismo esaltato delle borghesi, qualunque paese precipiterebbe presto nell'anarchia [...]. Non protesti la donna italiana per la sua 'schiavitú' che non è tale, e resti sempre l'angelo."[41] As I shall show in my opening chapter, Serao had little patience with the figure of the "angelo".

The foregoing gives a general Italian perspective on the legal status of women in the period, their role in the family, the state of feminism and the nature of anti-feminism. Italy, however, was not united in its stance on these issues, and the case of the South, and of Naples in particular, differs in many ways from that of the North. To begin with, the economic situation of the South was far worse than that of the country as a whole. Naples was a city of extremes of wealth and poverty; there was gross economic mismanagement, widespread illness with repeated cholera epidemics, and a serious emigration problem in the late 1880s. Agriculture was in crisis throughout Europe, and thus the agricultural South of Italy suffered badly.[42] As I have already indicated, an economic situation in itself has an effect on women's position in the community. Gigliola De Donato makes a direct connection between the economy and the status of women in the early nineteenth century, referring to the South as that part of Italy where "mancano ancora le grandi industrie che creano [...] interessi collettivi, e la donna non ha potuto maturare la coscienza di alcuni diritti" (page 81).

By 1884, when Serao published *Il ventre di Napoli*, her forthright attack on the government for its lack of action to remedy the city's ills, Naples was on the verge of self-destruction. There was a serious housing problem, detailed by Ghirelli (page 17), and the problem of class division was a grave one, creating a situation ripe for social unrest. As Ghirelli says, "I signori, le belle dame, i buoni borghesi, i poeti e gli innamorati scivolano piú leggiadramente che mai in mezzo agli stracci [...] della plebe" (page 37). Writers such as Serao, Jessie White Mario and Renato Fucini struggled to interest members of their own class, and above all the government, in the plight of the poor.[43]

Thus Serao was more socially concerned and aware than many of her class. Yet in other respects she remained within the confines of Neapolitan intellectual parochialism. As Ghirelli points out, "L'intellettuale napoletano ripiega frequentemente [...] sull'apologia della sua angusta provincia anziché spaziare sui temi fondamentali che la società capitalistica va proponendo all'umanità piú avanzata: il riscatto delle plebi, l'emancipazione femminile, il tramonto dell'imperialismo, l'audace ricerca intorno all'inconscio individuale" (page 90). While Serao certainly considered these themes, in her journalism she never did so in a manner that could be termed progressive—with the single exception of her attitude to the poor and the demands she made on their behalf. Much of her journalism is rather superficial in tone. She wrote *cronaca mondana* and advised her women readers on matters of etiquette. She did occasionally become involved in social issues (with, for instance, *Il ventre di Napoli*, a collection of articles originally published in a newspaper), and she wrote some interesting book reviews. Her literary works, however, are wholly different. As I intend to demonstrate fully in Chapter 1, she does not share what Ghirelli sees as the attitude typical of the Neapolitan artist, the "concezione sessuofobica della vita [...] in cui l'angelo del focolare ruota come un satellite intorno al capo di famiglia, paga di riscaldarsi al calore del suo affetto e della sua potenza virile" (page 93). Ghirelli does see Serao as nothing more nor less than a typically Neapolitan character and writer, even identifying her with the city itself: "La sua commozione e la sua furberia sono le stesse con cui i napoletani si compromettono ogni giorno [...]. Matilde Serao, la piú grande narratrice di Napoli, è il capo d'accusa piú schiacciante contro la città" (page 117). His analysis may well be correct, but not in the terms in which he conceives it. He equates Serao with Naples in terms of self-indulgence and weakness. In my view she acts, on the contrary, as an accuser of Naples: as a writer greatly influenced by the conventions of her environment, though fully aware of the complexities elided—all of which she transports into, and battles with in, her literary writing.

The ambivalence and complexities in Serao's work arise in several areas coloured especially by her awareness of the special circumstances of Naples. Primarily, her work is an analysis of the place of women in Italian society and in Italian literature, and that is the subject of this book. Here I propose to look briefly at three areas which must have coloured her perception of the role of women in society, because of her experience of them in a specific-ally Neapolitan context. They are motherhood, employment and education—all, as it happens, interconnected.

Motherhood was almost bound to be an area which Serao explored in some detail, partly, of course, because of her status as woman writer and mother, but also because of the high birth rate in the South. Mothers and children surrounded her in abundance—except, as I have indicated, in the higher social echelons; and that difference in itself interested her. During her lifetime she would see little or no change in the pattern of large working-class families, as Livi Bacci implies: "Nel mezzogiorno, dove la popolazione è [...] piú omogenea nelle sue caratteristiche economiche e sociali e [...] meno differenziata dal punto di vista culturale, l'adozione del controllo della fecondità è stata non solo piú tarda ma non ha nemmeno creato importanti differenze territoriali" (page 224). And no doubt Fascism eventually slowed down any tendency to limit family size that may have begun: "Gli effetti indiretti della politica demografica del fascismo hanno rafforzato tutte quelle forze che agivano per frenare la diffusione del controllo della fecondità" (Livi Bacci, page 345). Hence, as a Neapolitan writer who was interested in the role of women in society, Serao could scarcely avoid the dynamics of mother–child relationships in her narratives.

I have already mentioned the ambivalence in Serao's writings over the role of women workers. I suggest that this attitude, too, is a response to the peculiar situation of women workers in the South and especially Naples. While at the national level women were beginning to make an impact on the workforce and this was causing much debate, in Naples the growth of female employment was much slower because of the economic situation, and there was greater resistance to it. Women's employment was also particularly exploitative. Marcella Marmo shows how the slow process of industrializaton in Naples from 1870 to the early 1900s militated against female employment: "Lo sfruttamento femminile e minorile è nel suo insieme molto inferiore a quello di altre aree e delle medie nazionali, grazie all'assenza del settore tessile" (page 39). There was in fact an unemployment problem in Naples, as Marmo stresses, because "alla disgregazione lenta delle strutture artigiane si accoppia una debole espansione della fabbrica" (page 29). And, as we have seen, this kind of climate both militates against female employment and promotes a negative view of it. By 1911 the picture had not improved overall. Despite an increase of 18–24% in female employment in the new textile industries, food preservation, and tobacco factories, there was, according to Marmo (pages 447–48), an overall decrease in female employment. Thus for Serao the notion of female employment outside the home is on the whole an alien one (even though she is herself part of the new trend). Yet she was not merely concerned in her journalism with fostering the notion of an idealized role for women in the family: she was also aware of the exceedingly poor pay and general conditions of employment of women workers, and knew that the situation was unlikely to improve in the foreseeable future since there was no effective organization to represent workers, least of all women workers. In any case, as Marmo says, "la scoperta dell'organizzazione sindacale non serve perché non può [...] modificare un dato strutturale, la dipendenza del posto di lavoro dalla spesa pubblica e l'insicurezza [...] della condizione operaia" (page 456). Unemployment was a problem, and there were many desperate people willing to work; those who had jobs feared losing them.

Furthermore, the standard of education in the South was inferior to that of the country as a whole, and a matter of grave concern. Attempts were made to enforce education in the South as a means of encouraging a sense of national unity,[44] but this coercive approach was unlikely to work. In any case, too little money was invested in education in the South to enable the government's objectives to be achieved. Dina Bertoni Jovine considers the conditions in which schools were expected to be run: "Difficoltà gravissima, nelle province meridionali, era quella degli edifici scolastici—le scolaresche erano ospitate in locali di fortuna quasi sempre non rispondenti alle piú elementari norme di igiene" (page 259). It is hardly surprising, then, that even in 1907 "l'obbligo scolastico restava inoperante" (page 244). And, as Bertoni Jovine points out, the situation as regards female education was more problematic still:

> Anche per l'istruzione femminile, l'Italia meridionale si trovava in condizioni di speciale difficoltà; per le donne del popolo l'istruzione era stata ritenuta, per molti secoli, del tutto inutile; per la borghesia era molto radicata la tradizione degli educandati, nella quasi totalità retta da suore. La sorveglianza statale su questi educandati era ancora piú difficile di quella sui seminari; ed era ancora piú facile, per il clero, trasformarli in centri di propaganda anti-governativa. (page 174)

Serao must have been aware of the difficulties involved in organizing a sound basic education for women, such as she herself had had, inadequate though that now seems. Thus she knew that the likelihood of a significant proportion of the female population attaining a relatively decent job with a reasonable salary was minimal. Her ambivalence towards women's employment is all the more comprehensible on that account.

In this Introduction I have focused on how Serao represented contemporary society and how she reacted to the ideological tracts of the period. My intention, however, has not been to belittle the importance of her personal views or of literary convention in her writing. In the chapters that follow I shall analyse the literary conventions and genres within which she worked, considering how she at first adhered quite faithfully to them and then gradually moved away from them, ever guided by her desire to achieve more varied modes of being for her female characters while reflecting women's position in society—all this with a predominantly female reading public in mind.

The conditioning to which she was subject was nonetheless significant and should not be minimized. It may perhaps best be summed up by Pieroni Bortolotti's analysis of the ten commandments for women published in the *Giornale della donna* of 12 January 1926. These commandments centred on respect for God, femininity and motherhood; they advocated dependability and sweetness in marriage; they exalted love in a spirit of sacrifice; they established the house and home as of primary importance for women and the value of silent work, duty fulfilled and the sanctity of life. Pieroni Bortolotti comments: "Tutte le volte che qualche illustre personaggio si meraviglia dell'arretratezza femminile, o dell'irrazionalità femminile ecc., dovrebbe leggersi sistematicamente e ripetutamente decaloghi come questo, che sono stati irradiati sistematicamente e ripetutamente nella testa della donna italiana" (*Femminismo e partiti politici*, page 369).

The wonder, then, is not that Serao was at times conservative and often ambivalent, but that she managed to achieve what she did and to be as progressive as we shall see she was.

NOTES

1   A thorough account and analysis of Serao's journalism is provided by W. de Nunzio Schilardi, *Matilde Serao giornalista* (Bari, Milella, 1986).

2   Quoted by G. Buzzi, *Invito alla lettura di Matilde Serao* (Milan, Mursia, 1981), p. 22.

3   Quoted by G. De Caro, *Matilde Serao aneddotica* (Naples, Berisco, 1977), p. 28.

4   A. Banti, *Matilde Serao* (Turin, UTET, 1965), p. 270.

5   M. Jeuland-Meynaud, *Immagini, linguaggio e modelli del corpo nell'opera narrativa di Matilde Serao* (Rome, Edizioni dell'Ateneo, 1986), p. 115.

6   U. Eco, *Tre donne intorno al cor: Carolina Invernizio, Matilde Serao, Liala* (Florence, La Nuova Italia, 1979), p. 5.

7   A. M. Gisolfi, *The Essential Matilde Serao* (New York, Las Americas, 1968), p. 46.

8   G. Infusino, *Matilde Serao tra giornalismo e letteratura* (Naples, Guida, 1981), p. 20.

9   U. Ojetti, *Alla scoperta dei letterati* (Milan, Dumolard, 1895), pp. 236–37. It is hardly coincidental that Serao is the only woman *letterato* interviewed in this collection. She was the only one who had made an overwhelming impression on the literature of her time, on contemporary critics and on other writers, as well as on her public, while succeeding in outwardly respecting the status quo.

10   M. G. Martin-Gistucci, *L'Œuvre romanesque de Matilde Serao* (Grenoble, Presses Universitaires de Grenoble, 1973), p. 148. This study contains an extensive bibliography of the critical literature which preceded it.

11   Quoted from an anthology of Serao's journalism included in W. de Nunzio Schilardi, *Matilde Serao giornalista*, p. 63.

12   These and many other events of Serao's life are fully detailed in Banti's helpful biography.

13   M. Serao, *Suor Giovanna della Croce* (Milan, Treves, 1901). In this novel Serao overtly rejects Bourget's Romantic portrayal of his female characters in favour of a Realist approach.

14   The other most significant studies of Serao's work include M. Jeuland-Meynaud, *La Ville de Naples après l'annexion (1860–1915)* (Aix–Marseille, Editions de l'Université de Provence, 1973), which devotes much space to Serao and her *œuvre*; G. Infusino, *Matilde Serao: vita, opere, testimonianze* (Naples, Polisud, 1977); T. Pinto Wyckoff, *Realism and Romanticism in the Presentation of Female Characters in the Works of Matilde Serao* (unpublished PhD dissertation, University of Washington, 1983); V. Pascale, *Sulla prosa narrativa di Matilde Serao* (Naples, Liguori, 1989); N. A. Harrowitz, *Antisemitism, Misogyny and the Logic of Cultural Difference: Cesare Lombroso and Matilde Serao* (Lincoln, Nebr., University of Nebraska Press, 1994).

15   A. Ghirelli, *Napoli italiana: la storia della città dopo il 1860* (Turin, Einaudi, 1977), p. 105.

16   F. Taricone and B. Pisa, *Operaie, borghesi, contadine nel XIX secolo* (Rome, Carucci, 1985), p. 28.

17   S. Aleramo, "Appunti sulla psicologia femminile italiana" [1910], in *La donna e il femminismo: scritti 1897–1910*, edited by B. Conti (Rome, Editori Riuniti, 1978), pp. 133–58 (pp. 156–57).

18   M. Marmo, *Il proletariato industriale a Napoli in età liberale (1880–1914)* (Naples, Guida, 1978). Marmo gives the figure 6% on p. 233.

19   M. Serao, *Pagina azzurra* (Milan, Quadrio, 1883).

20   G. Pennisi Badalà, *La donna nella vita pubblica: studio critico* (Acireale, Donzuso, 1905), quoted in F. Taricone and B. Pisa, *Operaie, borghesi, contadine*, p. 33.

21 C. Ravera, *Breve storia del movimento femminile in Italia* (Rome, Editori Riuniti, 1978), p. 128.

22 For further information see L. Caldwell, "Reproducers of the Nation: Women and the Family in Fascist Policy", in *Rethinking Italian Fascism: Capitalism, Populism and Culture*, edited by D. Forgacs (London, Lawrence and Wishart, 1986), pp. 110–42.

23 E. Sullerot, *Histoire et sociologie du travail féminin* (Paris, Gonthier, 1968). She writes: "Un pays où l'homme ne trouve pas aisément du travail, ou risque de le perdre facilement sera un pays de bas niveau d'emploi féminin" (p. 134).

24 A. Rosmini, *Filosofia del diritto* [1841–45], 2 vols (Naples, Lauriel–Rossi Romano, 1856).

25 A detailed analysis of Rosmini's beliefs and philosophies may be found in the *Enciclopedia italiana di scienze, lettere ed arti*, 35 voll (Rome, Istituto dell'Enciclopedia Italiana, 1925–36), xxx, 123–26.

26 G. De Donato, "Donna e società nella cultura moderata del primo Ottocento", in *La parabola della donna nella letteratura italiana dell'Ottocento*, edited by G. De Donato (Bari, Adriatica, 1983), pp. 11–96 (p. 49).

27 M. Serao, *Il paese di Cuccagna* [Milan, Treves, 1891], in her *Opere*, edited by P. Pancrazi, 2 vols (Milan, Garzanti, 1944–46), i, 105–529; M. Serao, *Fantasia* [Turin, Casanova, 1883], in her *Opere*, ii, 5–274.

28 J. W. Scott and L. A. Tilly, "Women's Work and the Family in Nineteenth-century Europe", in *The Family in History*, edited by C. E. Rosenberg (Philadelphia, University of Pennsylvania Press, 1975), pp. 146–78 (p. 173).

29 J. W. Scott and L. A. Tilly, "Women's Work", quote extensively to this effect from F. Le Play, *Les Ouvriers européens*, 2 vols (Paris, Imprimerie Impériale, 1855–78).

30 M. Livi Bacci, *Donna, fecondità e figli: due secoli di storia demografica italiana* [1977] (Bologna, Il Mulino, 1980), p. 7.

31 M. Serao, *Il ventre di Napoli* (Milan, Treves, 1884).

32 John Stuart Mill's *La soggezione della donna* was published in 1870, Ibsen's *Casa di bambole* in 1879 and Bebel's *La donna e il socialismo* in 1891.

33 F. Pieroni Bortolotti, *Femminismo e partiti politici in Italia, 1919–1926* (Rome, Editori Riuniti, 1978), pp. 86–87.

34 Such attempts included Anna Maria Mozzoni's petition of 1877, the Alleanza Femminile Italiana's propaganda and its inclusion on the agenda of the Congresso Nazionale delle Donne Italiane in 1904. All these initiatives are detailed in F. Taricone and B. Pisa, *Operaie, borghesi, contadine*, p. 25.

35 See C. Ravera, *Breve storia del movimento femminile*, pp. 127–28. Mussolini also said, "La donna italiana merita il voto perché non si è agitata per averlo" (p. 128).

36 F. Taricone, "I cataloghi femminili dell'Ottocento", in F. Taricone and B. Pisa, *Operaie, borghesi, contadine*, pp. 11–25 (pp. 13–14).

37 For example, those of Tommaseo which extol "la virtú del patire" (see G. De Donato, "Donna e società", p. 51).

38 G. De Donato, "Donna e società", p. 87. De Donato discusses in this light the attitude of Cattaneo, who is not ashamed to "esibire […] tutto intero il suo malanimo verso la emancipazione intellettuale della donna" (p. 38).

39 C. Lombroso, *La donna delinquente, la prostituta e la donna normale* (Turin, Loescher, 1893).

40 F. Pieroni Bortolotti includes this quotation on p. 54 of *Femminismo e partiti politici*. It comes from G. Lombroso, *Il pro e il contro (riflessioni sul voto alle donne)* (Florence, Associazione Divulgatrice Donne Italiane, 1919).

41 This quotation, too, is found in F. Pieroni Bortolotti, *Femminismo e partiti politici* (p. 209). It is taken from *Il giornale della donna*, 7 Dec. 1924.

42 A. Ghirelli, *Napoli italiana*, studies the city's fortunes after 1860, and chapter headings like "L'economia strozzata" and "La città del colera" speak for themselves.

43 J. White Mario, *La miseria di Napoli* (Florence, Le Monnier, 1877); R. Fucini, *Napoli a occhio nudo* (Florence, Le Monnier, 1877).

44 D. Bertoni Jovine, *Storia dell'educazione popolare in Italia* [1954] (Bari, Laterza, 1965), p. 142.

Chapter 1

WOMEN IN LOVE: ROMANCE REVISITED

The theme of love is the most central to Serao's work, and therefore merits close examination. While sexual love is not the only emotion Serao depicts her female characters as feeling (the emotions of maternal love and of female friendship are also highly significant), it is undeniably the emotion to which she devotes most space in the greater part of her writing.[1] It is also the emotion which most of her female characters are depicted as feeling—in fact it is common to almost all of them.

Serao's view of love itself, and of the part it plays in the lives of her female characters, does not greatly alter during the course of her literary career. She perceives love, almost exclusively, as a negative force in the lives of most women: she depicts it as causing them pain, suffering and loss of dignity. The image she uses most frequently to describe love is that of a dream or illusion. It is, for her, an essentially deceptive force. This may be seen repeatedly in *Fior di passione*, an early collection of short stories.[2] The view of love as a dream is also to be seen in *Tre donne* (1905) and in the story "Sogno di una notte d'estate", included in *Le amanti* (1894).[3]

A truly positive view of love is not found anywhere in Serao's work. There is always something to mar the relationships of her protagonists, even if the two characters concerned love each other deeply. An example of this is the love we are told about in *Mors tua* (1926), Serao's final work.[4] There Carolina Leoni, who we are told looks aged beyond her years, is described as having had a loving marriage—but now her wedding ring is "il ricordo di lui che era stato il suo unico amore e che, adorandola, era morto troppo presto" (page 50). Love is therefore a source of pain even for this character. This is also an example of Serao's tendency to describe the positive aspects of love in past tenses, while pain caused by love is conveyed in the present tense of the narrative. The implication is that the only positive love possible resides in idealized memories, and one member of the couple must be missing or dead to allow such memories to exist. The process of idealization is seen as necessary to romantic love.

This depiction of love as a negative force is not in itself particularly unusual. What makes Serao different in attitude, for example, from Realist writers dealing with the same subject is the total exclusivity of her view. She is unable to see love as a positive force at any stage. She diverges from both Romantic and Realist writers in her concentration on the female point of view: for Serao the female protagonist is the focus of the narrative. The aristocratic male protagonist who suffers as a result of love and violent passion is a stereotype—he is found in the work of such writers as Balzac, Flaubert, Verga and d'Annunzio.[5] Serao, however, invests her female protagonists (especially those of the aristocracy) with emotions and actions (such as suicide) which had more typically been the prerogative of the aristocratic male. She might seem to be attempting to create a new type of Romantic heroine. It is, indeed, strikingly difficult to categorize those novels in which Serao's subject-matter is romantic love. The very term "Romantic novel" seems, of necessity, to imply that the protagonist is male and is in any case (in Italy after the early nineteenth century) anachronistic. The focus on the female protagonist in these novels may initially lead the reader to identify them as more akin to the Sentimental novel. Yet they are, in a sense, not novels of manners but novels of adventure, of growth and development (albeit, as we shall see, of a debatable type). Perhaps Serao is attempting not so much to create a new Romantic heroine as to fuse the genres of *Bildungsroman*, Romantic novel and Sentimental novel.

There is, indeed, an important element in Serao's depiction of her female characters in love which reinforces the suggestion that she has not totally broken away from traditional depictions of women. She tends, in the manner of male writers from Dante to d'Annunzio, to polarize her female characters, and it is worth remembering that in Serao's time the most valued literary works were those of male writers. One obvious and very influential example of this type of polarization is found in the Biblical presentation of the figures of Eve and Mary, where Mary is, even in function, the diametrical opposite of Eve.[6] As in the works of writers such as Milton, Goethe, Flaubert and Verga, some of Serao's female characters represent positive forces while others have a more mysterious, sinister function.[7] Serao portrays, in essence, the "angel in the house" versus the monster outside.[8] The monster figure is a female character who is firmly located outside the idyllic sphere of domesticity and gradually impinges on it as an invading force, functioning as a challenge to the angelic figure.[9] Another significant negative image of woman on which Serao draws is that of the *femme fatale*, extensively cultivated by nine-teenth-century male writers.[10] As we shall see, Serao's treatment of these figures is exceedingly complex. Annis Pratt, in her study of romantic fiction written by women, identifies certain common traits. She finds that "authorial ambivalence in combination with the necessity for drowning out the nature of her hero's true feelings creates a labyrinthine twisting of attitudes in this genre, most often manifest in the author's encoding of self-doubt and blame into the hero's consciousness [...]; the hero of this fiction is, like her author, a victim of both external, societal structures and self-flagellation" (Pratt consistently uses the term "hero" to refer to the female protagonist).[11] Self-doubt, blame, self-flagellation: all these traits are manifest both in Serao's angels and in her monsters. I shall examine first her stereotyped *donne angelicate* and secondly her stereotyped evil women, indicating the points where Serao strains against, and to some extent reworks, those stereotyped figures.

THE ANGELIC WOMAN IN LOVE

In this section and the next I shall concentrate on the four main works of Serao's early period: *Cuore infermo* (1881), *Fantasia* (1883), *La conquista di Roma* (1885) and *Addio, amore!* (1890), as each of these works contains an angelic female figure who suffers, as well as a female figure who acts as a destructive, negative force. Each of these novels uses the structure of the love triangle, with the *donna angelicata* and the *femme fatale* apparently revolving around the primary male character (though in only one of these novels is he the protagonist).

Even Serao's choice of name for her heroine in *Cuore infermo* is indicative of the type of woman she is intended to represent— Beatrice could not be associated with any literary role-model other than the beloved of Dante. The resemblance between the characters, however, is confined to the most basic structural level: Serao's Beatrice, for example, has no associations with the abstract concepts of grace or theology. On the other hand, she does conform to a certain stereotype of femininity.[12] Like Dante's Beatrice (and indeed Verga's La Longa and Mena),[13] she is kindly, good, chaste, passive, and religious—the perfect "angel in the house". At the beginning of the novel Serao's Beatrice even appears to share the detached, austere other-worldliness of Dante's creation. We first glimpse her when she is with her friend Amalia:

> La lasciava parlare [...] sorridendo un poco, senza turbarsi; la sua bella figura posava in una calma sicura, in una tranquillità riflessiva [...]; lo sguardo era limpido, freddo, chiaro, mai vagante [...]; il profilo fine, diritto, ma non severo [...]; il mento di disegno fermo [...] dando al volto un'ovalità intelligente e pensierosa [...]. Tutto il volto era chiuso, silenzioso, sereno, nell'indifferenza, immobile [...], perfetto nell'unica [...] espressione della calma; il corpo [...] quieto, senza moti disordinati.[14]

Given this description of Beatrice Revertera and her resemblance to her more famous literary predecessor, it does not at this stage surprise the reader to learn that she begins her married life in a state of supreme indifference to her husband, Marcello Sangiorgio. Yet Serao uses *Cuore infermo* to convey an extremely negative view of love, and the reader soon learns that Beatrice's indifference is studied, not real. The motivation Serao gives her character for this attitude casts a powerful shadow of ill omen over the story from the beginning. We learn that Beatrice's mother died of the combination of an excess of passionate love and her own physical weakness, and for Beatrice love is associated with the motif of fear from the time she learns she has inherited her mother's physical disability—which is, significantly, a weak heart.

Serao shatters the Dantesque stereotype when she describes the awakening of Beatrice's passion for Marcello, and the jealousy and insatiable curiosity she feels towards the other woman in his life. But Serao has rejected one stereotype to use another. Here we see what is to become a familiar portrait in Serao's gallery of female characters: the loving martyr who is prepared to suffer in silence. The idea of martyrdom and suffering as means of self-improvement, purification and elevation to a higher state is one common to many women writers.[15] Serao toys with it but, as we shall see, ultimately rejects it. In Serao's works such women always use religion as a prop. One of many examples of this in *Cuore infermo* is the scene where Marcello is absent from home late at night. The use of the imperfect tense in this passage describing Beatrice effectively conveys the notion of continual suffering:

> Si gittava come disperata sul letto, torcendosi le braccia, soffocan-do i singulti [...]; a poco l'idea fissa appariva, assidua, fatale: "Non tornerà piú; è partito, è partito." Per rifugio, pregava; s'indirizzava alla Vergine, che doveva comprendere il grido di un cuore femminile, "Madonna Addolorata, fatelo ritornare! [...] Madonna santa, non me lo togliete! Vergine santa, rendetemelo!" Poi tendeva di nuovo l'orecchio, sperando nel miracolo della buona Signora degli afflitti. (page 242)

This is the stereotyped Catholic female martyr, sure of her unworthiness, suffering deeply; and for Serao the source of such deep pain is always the same—love. It is, however, interesting that Beatrice's actual avowal of love to Marcello should be made in a way that is both humble and demanding: "'Marcello, io non voglio che tu parta' disse ella, rizzandosi in piedi [...]. 'Te ne supplico, non andartene. Se parti, ti seguo [...]. T'amo, non lo comprendi? Sei mio, non ti lascio, non ti cedo.' E gli si avvinghiò al collo, con una stretta frenetica" (pages 201–02). (Serao, writing largely for a female readership, was well aware of the appeal of melodrama.)[16] In a sense the depiction of Beatrice enters a new phase with this declaration: she is now seen as aware of her own needs. For a short time love is presented in glowing and very positive terms; for example: "Beatrice e Marcello vivevano in un raggio di sole, circonfusi di luce; un raggio di sole che penetrava nel cuore, portandovi l'ardore [...]. Chiudevano gli occhi, sorridenti, abbagliati [...]; ne provavano il calore sulla pelle, nei capelli, sulle palme brucianti delle mani [...]; rimanevano uniti da una forza unica" (pages 263–65). Yet Beatrice still acts as a martyr: she refuses to seek medical help for her quickly deteriorating body, and when she does seek it she does so in the name of love, as she fears disruption of their idyllic existence.

Ultimately love is a totally destructive force for Beatrice: her death may be directly attributed to it—she is killed by the physical disruption caused by the literal and metaphorical strain on her heart. She dies as a martyr, in pain and suffering. The elusive and undependable quality of even this deep love is also stressed by the denouement as she dies in mental torment, suspecting her husband of betrayal: "'Marcello, vieni!' gridò una voce soffocante. Nulla. Silenzio profondo. 'Marcello, Marcello!' fu il supremo grido d'angoscia" (page 316). This case of romantic heterosexual love is a distinct failure, and Serao intends it thus.

The second stereotype of an angelic woman in Serao's work is Caterina Spaccapietra-Lieti in *Fantasia.* In her depiction of this character Serao no longer focuses on a Dantesquely austere concept of womanhood. Caterina is human and loving from the start, though cast in the mould of virtue to an even greater extent than Beatrice. Serao's inspiration here is probably religious: the name she chooses is reminiscent of St Catherine of Siena, who, appropriately, was a martyr (though Serao's view of St Catherine is restrictively one-dimensional).[17] The fact that Caterina loves her husband is clear at the very beginning in her welcome to him when he returns from hunting: "'Sei venuto... sei venuto' mormorava lei, tutta ridente col pettine che le cadeva e certe macchie rosse che le apparivano vive sulla pelle."[18] Caterina's role as martyr is also defined at a very early stage in the novel: "L'incarico suo era trovar saggio e onesto quanto suo marito faceva" (page 112). Caterina is portrayed as having no sense of her own needs as an individual (except in the important area of her intense friendship with Lucia: see Chapter 4); she wholly subordinates her own needs to those of her husband, as the typical "angel in the house" must: "[Andrea] sapeva che se si fosse alzato e fosse uscito al balcone, dopo poco, Caterina senza far rumore sarebbe scivolata dal letto e sarebbe venuta [...], ombra bianca, ombra piccina, fedele e amorosa, a vegliare con lui, poiché egli non poteva dormire" (page 201). Caterina's relationship with her husband is never depicted as passionate (in the way that Beatrice's was), yet the extent of her love, the narrator states, is never in doubt: "Nel matrimonio, essa era stata sempre un po' riservata, facendosi piccola piccola innanzi a suo marito, non trovando frasi o pensieri eleganti o idee politiche, per dirgli che gli voleva bene. Ma forse egli doveva intenderlo, perché ella, dalla mattina alla sera, si occupava del suo benessere" (page 257). Caterina's inability to express herself verbally is all the more interesting when compared with the dramatic loquaciousness of Lucia (the other woman of the triangle), who is in a sense her *alter ego.* In this novel Serao proceeds to damn any possibility of happiness within the framework of calm love, just as she earlier showed the defeat of a passionate love. As the plot unfolds, Caterina is deceived as a direct result of her trusting love.

Caterina has a physical reaction to her betrayal: "Il capogiro crebbe, i mobili girarono attorno a lei, gli orecchi le fischiarono, una luce abbagliante le colpí gli occhi" (page 242). The shock is so great that it penetrates her physical being; as in the case of *Cuore infermo*, Serao links the emotional with the physical. This sense of deep shock is carried over into her death: "Gli occhi di questa piccola morta erano spalancati, ma vitrei, come nella stupefazione di qualche spettacolo incredibile" (page 273). Caterina's solution to her heartbreak is also physical, final and violent. Although she is calm prior to committing suicide her crutch is—appropriately for one of Serao's good women (though oddly, given the Roman Catholic attitude to suicide)—religion: "Non piangeva, non singhiozzava, non sospirava neppure [...]; era una preghiera muta, lunga, tranquilla" (page 273). This act of suicide indicates the supreme martyrdom of a female character. Caterina punishes and annihilates herself; rather than express her anger, she turns all negative emotions in on herself. Her reaction is extreme and violent, but in taking her life in a bloodless and comparatively decorous manner (self-suffocation by fumes) she is enshrined as an exemplary passive female. This sacrifice, too, is presented as a direct result of love.

Fantasia, then, conveys an extremely negative view of love, through a female character in some respects more stereotyped than her predecessor. Caterina, unlike Beatrice, demands nothing from her husband, and yet the novel is subversive in its very stereotyping. In this novel, as in its predecessor, Serao chooses to kill the the angel; in both works it is the grasping, passionate female character who is allowed to survive. This suggests, I think, a vengeful reworking of the literary stereotype discussed by Gilbert and Gubar. In their words, "When women did not turn into male mimics [...] they may have attempted to transcend their anxiety of authorship by *revising* male genres [...], enacting a uniquely female process of revision and redefinition that necessarily caused them to seem 'odd'" (page 73).

By the time Serao wrote *La conquista di Roma* she was slowly redefining the passive, virtuous and angelic stereotype. Although the protagonist of this novel is male, there are two women in his life who play important parts and exemplify the polarization of female characters which I am discussing. As the story unfolds, Contessa Elena Fiammanti is shown to be good, kind and affectionate. Interestingly, though, she is the first such character of Serao's who is involved with a man in an extra-marital relationship. Nor is Donna Elena a virgin when she begins her relationship with Sangiorgio: she is a mature and experienced woman who has been married before. This character is therefore a much more balanced creation than her predecessors: she is not an angel. Yet she is firmly placed in the position of "angel in the house". It is she, not the other woman, who has access to Sangiorgio's living quarters. She even leaves some of her property there, thus in a sense laying claim to them. In the structure of the text, then, she occupies the position of the wife.

Love is here still depicted in a negative light: in Serao's world-view extra-marital relationships, too, are doomed to failure. As with Beatrice's love, there is a shadow over Elena's love from the beginning. Her view of love in the abstract is negative, as is stressed in the first words given her: "L'amore è una vecchia farsa, di cui nessuno ride piú. Vi par viso di pianto, il mio?"[19] Elena is here jokingly refuting the possibility that she might fall in love.

It is Elena, and not the male protagonist Sangiorgio, who initiates their sexual relationship; this is a departure from the previous, rather passive, behaviour of Serao's good female characters. It is also Elena and not Sangiorgio, however, who falls in love. She is tender and kind to Sangiorgio, who reacts with indifference. Once Sangiorgio becomes interested in the other woman, Elena disappears. Perhaps the most interesting thing about Elena, however, is the way in which Serao disposes of her: she does not commit suicide like Caterina, or allow herself to die like Beatrice; she is simply expunged by the author—she ceases to exist. Within the framework of the text the other woman takes precedence over her and annihilates her. This is an indication of Serao's increasing interest, at this point, in the "monster" figure.

The final female protagonist cast in the role of "angel in the house" is Anna Acquaviva in *Addio, amore!* Like Beatrice, Anna is passionate, but she represents a further development in Serao's presentation of "good" women characters insofar as she is an active character throughout the text. Like Elena, Anna initiates her relationships with men. She is the driving force in her relationship with Giustino Morelli, and she strives hard to set the tone of her second romance, with Cesare Dias, but fails in this because of his stronger character (he is in fact one of Serao's strongest and most unusual male characters).

In her depiction of Anna, Serao shows more clearly than ever before how love is the focal point of these aristocratic women's lives. In the three novels already considered, Beatrice's only function apart from her role as wife is that of society hostess/guest, Caterina is clearly bored with her role of officiating on committees and Elena admits to Sangiorgio that without company she is literally lost. That unbalanced approach to life reaches its peak with Anna. In her first relationship, with Giustino, she says: "La passione mi consuma […]. Io non sento né il freddo, né la notte, né il pericolo, né nulla. Non sento che te, non voglio che l'amor tuo, non voglio che vivere con te, sempre sino alla morte, e di là anche, sempre con te, intendi, sempre."[20] It is because of this passionate exclusivity that Anna falls ill when her relationship with Giustino ends: because all her energy and interest are concentrated on this relationship, when it ends it is as though her life has ended. In her suffering, like Beatrice and Caterina, she turns to religion. Specifically, like Beatrice, she prays to her mother: "una preghiera indistinta, un'invocazione senza impeto, monotona, continua […]. La Vergine nel cielo e lo spirito della madre […] si confondevano nella sua mente" (page 152). Anna cannot fully recover from her illness until she has found another man to idealize. The circumstances of the second relationship, however, are different; whereas Anna won (and, paradoxically, lost) Giustino by strength and passion, she must win Cesare by being passive and suffering intensely. This is a pointer to her role as martyr in the rest of the novel. Anna's two love relationships are paralleled by Serao, with a wealth of trivia differentiating them, in order to reveal the emptiness of her life. Because of this emptiness the fruitlessness of her second relationship, coupled with her sense of betrayal, culminates in her suicide.

Yet Anna does not give in to suicide passively like Beatrice or Caterina: she has the strength to confront both the woman and the man who are betraying her. This marks a real development in Serao's portrayal of her female characters: this woman's love does not blind her to the faults of the man she loves, and she is unwilling passively to erase herself from his life. In her final confrontation with Cesare she says: "Tu sei veramente un uomo senza cuore e senza coscienza, un'anima senza grandezza e senza entusiasmo [...]; tu appartieni alla grande classe degli uomini putrefatti, tu mi fai ribrezzo e pietà, intendi?" (page 281). Yet despite Anna's development as a character she still retains a link with the "angel in the house", as she berates Cesare for destroying the life of her sister Laura, who has also betrayed her; in the midst of her suffering she still thinks of others. One of the most interesting aspects of her most intense period of suffering is that she no longer seeks solace in religion but takes control of events herself; and this detaches her from Serao's earlier stereotype of the good, religious woman. Anna's suffering, like Caterina's, is physical as much as emotional; thus the idea of a physical resolution to her dilemma seems appropriate: "Non faceva un passo, temendo istintivamente di crollare al suolo. Restò cosí, quasi facesse allontanare, a poco poco, l'impressione di un dolore tutto fisico" (page 288). This physical resolution is not, however, achieved in the same way as Caterina's (or, indeed, in the same way as that most famous literary female suicide, Emma Bovary); there is no passive feminine waiting for something (poison or carbon fumes) to take effect. Anna's resolution is violent, active and quick (she shoots herself); this act is the suicide of a typical Romantic hero, so once again Serao has transposed a sex role.

Serao developed the role of the stereotyped good woman to a new degree; even at the most superficial level of character description this is revealed by the differences between Caterina and Anna. By 1890 Serao's good female characters were portrayed in a more balanced fashion. As we shall see, however, still more interesting developments were taking place in the subtexts of these novels. Each of these four "good" female characters is shown, throughout the novel to which she belongs, to feel a sense of both identification with, and curiosity about, the other woman. While this is less developed in *La conquista di Roma*, in the other three novels the attraction/repulsion between the two female characters, the manner in which their stories parallel each other, the reciprocal curiosity of the angelic woman and the *femme fatale*, the ultimate emargination of the male character, and the way in which the female characters seem to offer two distinct modes of existence, lead me to conclude that in these novels Serao works with the motif of the double.[21]

Serao's use of the double motif is especially interesting as it appears to be linked to the dichotomy which she sensed between her role as a woman and her role as a writer. Indeed, many women writers, especially in the nineteenth century, have felt a need to explore issues of duality. Elaine Showalter highlights the use of the female double in the works of Charlotte Brontë and George Eliot.[22] Gilbert and Gubar, too, consider these writers' use of the motif, as well as its presence in the works of Jane Austen, Christina Rossetti, Elizabeth Barrett Browning and Emily Dickinson. It seems that in using the double device women writers have found a way to portray a complete female character, splitting it into two very different female types, one socially acceptable, the other unacceptable. Clare Rosenfield, discussing the implications of the double device in general, makes a point which adds credence to this idea. She says: "The novelist who consciously or unconsciously exploits psychological doubles may either juxtapose or duplicate two characters; the one representing the socially acceptable or conventional personality, the other externalizing the free, uninhibited, often criminal self."[23] What we see, then, in the portrayal of the female double in nineteenth-century literature written by women is the acceptable feminine self, the angel, struggling against the monstrous independent other self. Having stepped outside the boundaries of the conventional feminine, this latter self mobilizes those aspects of the female which are unacceptable.

THE MONSTROUS WOMAN OR *FEMME FATALE*

The female characters I intend to analyse in this section are the direct counterparts of those I examined in the last. Once again they are all set in the aristocratic mould. They too suffer during the course of their romantic relationships, but probably the greatest difference between them and their angelic sisters is that they refuse to be martyrs.

In depicting these women Serao was combining (and, ultimately, trying to break away from) two stereotypes, that of the *femme fatale* and that of woman as monster. The monster figure, as I have indicated, is that of a female character firmly located outside the idyllic sphere of domesticity, who gradually impinges on it as an invading force, functioning as a challenge to the angelic figure. Eve, the Harpies and the Gorgons, archetypes of the monster tradition (all much used by male writers), for the male character symbolize both temptation and destruction. The *femme fatale* is something of a nineteenth-century commonplace, found, for instance, in Chateaubriand's *Martyrs*, Flaubert's *Salammbô*, Mérimée's *Carmen* and Gautier's *Mademoiselle de Maupin*. The figure is used repeatedly in the works of both Swinburne and d'Annunzio. Essentially, such female characters are mysterious, sensual, and often sickly in appearance, while there is an aura of danger about them, especially for the male character. In the first of her portrayals of such women, that of Lalla d'Aragona in *Cuore infermo*, Serao includes both the mystery and seductiveness of the *femme fatale* and the destructive intent of the monstrous woman. Even as early as this, however, her own understanding of the female psyche was visible through the stereotype, as she tried to give Lalla *reasons* for her behaviour and also depicted her as suffering.

In keeping with the tradition of the *femme fatale*, Lalla has a dark, mysterious past: she is a widow whose husband died, it is rumoured, because of their passionately unhealthy love. This makes her seem not only mysterious but also threatening and lethal (in keeping with the tradition of the monster woman). Again, like the conventional *femme fatale* she is at once sensually attractive and very sickly; there is an irresistible allure and, equally, an odour of decay about her. The first detailed description of her underlines both these elements:

> I grandi occhi neri, dalla incassatura troppo profonda che accresceva la lentezza voluttuosa dello sguardo, erano sottolineati da un semicerchio bruno; tutto il volto di un pallore caldo, uguale, di avorio fiorentino, un volto scarno, dai pomelli salienti; la bocca grande, dalle labbra sottili, troppo vivide, dipinte forse, aveva quel sorriso un po' stirato, che scopre con un fremito i dentini superiori, che pare voglia mordere; il corpo magro si perdeva nelle pieghe di velluto grigio dell'abito [...]; si abbandonava sulla seggiola di ferro come stanco ed abbattuto. (page 93)

The repeated use of the word *troppo* here, together with the apparent evil intent of her teeth, underlines the abnormal (monstrous) and threatening aspect of this character. Yet alongside this the sensuality of the figure is stressed.

Lalla's monstrous capacity for evil is seen throughout the text, as she simultaneously taunts Marcello and hurts Beatrice. Her position as the monster *outside* the house is stressed along with her strength as a divisive force, as she tries to persuade Marcello first to introduce her into his home, and finally to take her away with him. Serao is most explicit about the monstrous nature of her creation at the end of the novel when she describes Lalla's attempt to lure Marcello away from his mourning of Beatrice: "Ritta col gesto largo che pareva volesse dilatare l'orizzonte, col volto acceso da una fiamma, gli occhi seduttori, la persona quasi ingigantita, ella rassomigliò un momento al Gran Tentatore che offre a Gesú tutt' i beni della terra" (page 338). The link with the stereotype of the *femme fatale* is also made here with the use of the noun *tentatore*.

Yet Serao differs from other writers (such as d'Annunzio, who is preoccupied with the effect of such women on the male prot-agonist) in her painstaking analysis of such a character's motiva-tion. Lalla's past may be mysterious, but her present is not: Serao examines her emotions in minute detail, and she is shown to feel intense pain at the memory of her husband. She is frank with Marcello—an honesty that does not coincide with the *femme fatale* stereotype. She says to him: "Siete innamorato; ma colei che non vi ama in casa vostra, venite ad amarla qui, in casa mia. Non è bella la verità, duca: né per voi, né per me" (page 119). Another aspect of Lalla's character which does not conform to the literary stereotype is her identification with Beatrice. From the first encounter be-tween these characters, their mutual curiosity is evident. They first see each other at the railway station when Beatrice and Marcello are leaving on their honeymoon. In accordance with the general presentation of the double as Keppler has characterized it,[24] it is Lalla, the second self, who appears the more curious: "Ella fissò uno sguardo nero e lungo nella vettura degli sposi; per un sol momento quei tre personaggi si guardarono" (page 46). At this stage the fascination is common to all three characters, but Marcello, despite his affair with Lalla, is about to be excluded from the more significant relationship between the two women.

A little later (pages 67–68) we find the normally reserved Beatrice avidly questioning a friend about Lalla. Since this occurs before Lalla's liaison with Marcello has begun, it is clear that Serao is focusing on the relationship between her two female characters from the beginning of the novel. When Lalla first meets Marcello she similarly questions him about Beatrice. As the Lalla–Marcello affair unfolds, the empathy between the two female characters grows, as does their fear of each other.[25] Lalla pursues Beatrice, seeking opportunities to meet her. Serao insists on Lalla's obsession with Beatrice: "Era lei la prima a pronunziare il nome di Beatrice, a condurre la conversazione su di lei" (page 175). Beatrice at first avoids Lalla, but soon comes to pursue her just as obsessively as she has been pursued. She follows the lovers by playing music that they can hear, in a manner described by Serao as threatening. Lalla recognizes this as persecution: "Beatrice [...] ci cruccia col suo lume; la fuggiamo, ella ci riprende colla sua musica" (pages 182–83). Yet Lalla also reveals empathy with her *alter ego*: "Udite [...] quanta maliniconia in questo ritmo! [...] Tua moglie è triste, Marcello" (page 182). Marcello does not in fact grasp the emotional significance of Beatrice's music, and he therefore neither understands nor accepts Lalla's analysis. He thus stands outside the relationship between the two female characters. Serao also suggests that Lalla and Beatrice may be blood relatives, half-sisters, corresponding perhaps to the half-brothers common in male writers' presentations of the double.

Serao's analysis of Lalla hinges on her concern to provide her with motives and feelings—to make her, in some way, an "alternative" *femme fatale*. She is not depicted as the *femme fatale* who is supremely self-confident and monstrously indifferent to her rival. On the contrary, she is occasionally intimidated by Beatrice's strength: "[Beatrice] si voltò con tutta la persona, e determinatamente si rivolse verso il palchetto di Lalla, sbarrandovi i suoi grandi occhi: la vide scuotersi, farsi indietro come si arrestasse davanti ad un pericolo [...]. Continuava a guardare là. La mano di Lalla, abbandonata, in grembo, stringeva convulsivamente il fazzoletto" (pages 252–53). Serao points out that it is Lalla's distress following this incident that leads to her attempt at destructiveness in asking Marcello to leave Beatrice; she shows us her character's motivation.

In this novel a classically angelic female character is compelled to recognize her other self, her passionate, potentially monstrous essence. This recognition kills her, but she has grown as a character.[26]

The depiction of Lucia Altimare (a namesake of Manzoni's Lucia) in *Fantasia* is fascinating partly because of Serao's entrenchment in the stereotype of the *femme fatale* and partly because of her attempt to break away from it. Lucia is more mysterious than Lalla, and this quality in her is studied. As a child she cultivates an aura of mystery around herself which fascinates all those who come into contact with her. Her strange appeal is more far-reaching than was Lalla's. While Lalla was attractive to many men, Lucia's fascinating influence extends to women too, and her first serious conquest is that of Caterina, who adores her. It is this relationship which frames the novel: the narrative begins and ends by highlighting their friendship.[27] Lucia's attempted suicide at an early stage in the text adds greatly to the air of mystery she projects. The physical description of Lucia also conforms to the *femme fatale* stereotype: she is thin and pale with large magnetic eyes—rather like Lalla.

Lucia's sickliness, together with the monstrous sense of decay which surrounds her, is stressed rather more than Lalla's. From her schooldays, Lucia is depicted as causing a stir through her physical frailty, for example at the ball in Chapter 2: "Diventò pallidissima, respirò forte, poi scivolò dal divano a terra svenuta" (page 60). The monstrous element of her sickliness intensifies throughout the text; towards the end she is more violent than ever in her illness:

> Un giorno [...] cadde per terra, in preda a una convulsione nervosa [...]; si contorceva tutta, le braccia fendevano l'aria, la testa balzava sul pavimento [...]; le battevano i denti come per tremore febbrile, l'orbita scompariva sotto le palpebre. Balbetta-va parole [...], apriva gli occhi, guardava la gente attorno, ma li richiudeva subito, come inorridita, dava in un altissimo grido, e ricadeva convulsa, dibattendosi. (page 216)

Lucia's monstrously evil nature and her power as a *femme fatale* are stressed throughout the depiction of her relationship with Andrea. There is never any doubt that it is she who is in control: "Ella *si lasciava* attirare, *si lasciava* soffiare nel volto come magnetiz-zata, ma a un tratto si staccò bruscamente [...]. 'Voglio andarmene, voglio andarmene' disse battendo i piedi nervosamente [...]. 'An-diamo pure' disse lui, chinando il capo *domato, incapace di avere altra volontà che quella di Lucia*" (pages 168–69; italics mine). She repeatedly points out to him that they are doing wrong and compels him to accept responsibility for his actions. Yet she is also fully aware of her role and of her evil nature, and her creator reminds us that she is conscious of her use of the stereotype of the seductive *femme fatale* and that of the lethal female monster-cum-witch when she has Lucia say, "Io sono una donna fatale; ti recherò sventura" (page 175), and again: "Bada che io ti ho dato un filtro. Non risanerai mai piú: io sarò la tua malattia, la tua febbre, il tuo malore inguaribile" (page 209). Lucia's power as a *femme fatale* is highlighted by the denouement—she succeeds where her predecessor failed. In this respect the denouement of *Fantasia* seems to serve as a corrective to that of *Madame Bovary*,[28] a novel referred to several times in the text. Lucia and Emma are similar in many respects: both nurtured on Romantic novels, they are both self-conscious heroines. Lucia, however, is allowed to overturn Emma's tale in her relatively positive denouement; on one level the moral of the tale seems to be that adultery does not consign woman to hell-fire and a painful death. Annis Pratt holds that "in women's love fiction […] the *liebestod*, or love death, traditionally dealt out in medieval fiction for extra-marital love, often replaces survival" (*Archetypal Patterns in Women's Fiction*, page 75). This literary commonplace is undone by Serao: *Fantasia*'s conclusion is clearly unorthodox.

Donn' Angelica Vargas in *La conquista di Roma* represents a considerable development in Serao's use of the *femme fatale*. As a character Angelica functions on more than one level: she is both a female figure in her own right and a symbol of Rome (indeed, of Rome's fatal attraction).

At the beginning of the novel she is described in the manner of the stereotypical *donna fatale*, as a very beautiful, unknown woman who commands homage from men. In fact her first appearance in the text is reminiscent of Lalla's in *Cuore infermo*: she is surrounded by a group of entranced men (page 287). She also reminds us (in her deeds as well as her name) of the Angelica in *Orlando furioso*, a pre-eminent *femme fatale*.

The deceitful and evil aspects of Donn' Angelica are not fully revealed until the text closes (as is also the case with her two predecessors). It is she who, through the medium of her husband, orders Sangiorgio to leave Rome (thus knowingly destroying his political career) and destroys him emotionally by refusing to see him again. As a monstrous woman/*femme fatale* she, like Lucia, is successful, in that she achieves what she intends.

Yet Donn' Angelica represents a departure from the *femme fatale* stereotype in a number of ways. To begin with, there is the question of her name: Angelica would hitherto have been a more appropriate name for one of Serao's angelic female characters; Serao, then, inverts the stereotype in the act of naming. She continues the inversion when describing Angelica's nature: it is repeatedly stressed that she is good and virtuous. Angelica's appearance, too, involves a departure from one attribute of the *femme fatale*: she is indeed beautiful, but there is nothing sickly or suggestive of decay about her. (One could argue that the full destructiveness of her nature is therefore more powerful when the author chooses to unleash it.)

Serao does not give us the same gradual insight into the development of Angelica's emotions and motives as she did with her predecessors. Rather, she restricts us to Sangiorgio's point of view and allows us to see and interpret the character's actions as he does. It is when he finally discovers that Angelica is "la donna che non sapeva amare" (page 512) that the reader learns this too. Given Angelica's reputation for virtue, her modest reserve (which is demonstrated throughout her relationship with Sangiorgio) and her husband's equanimity about her relationship with Sangiorgio, it seems reasonable to argue that Serao is here portraying the first unsensual *femme fatale* in Italian fiction. I cannot think of any *femme fatale* who resembles Angelica in the coldness of her destruction. Emma Bovary, for instance, is not just a romantic idealist, she is also physically passionate. D'Annunzio, whose work abounds with *femmes fatales*, finds the sexual, passionate demands of his characters threatening. Charles Klopp refers to "the sexually insistent 'Superfemmina'" in d'Annunzio's work, "whose personal potency and impatience with any restrictions on her animal appetites make her as dangerous as she is alluring" (page 88). Certainly those Italian writers with whom Serao most closely associated herself (Verga, De Roberto and Capuana) did not create any character like Angelica,[29] who represents a complete departure from the stereotype.

The question of Angelica's emotional motivation is dealt with eventually; Serao's sense of fairness to her female characters seems to demand this. The defence of Angelica's emotional manipulation of Sangiorgio is entrusted to Don Silvio, her husband, who says to Sangiorgio: "Angelica è bella, è giovane, è intelligente, avrebbe bisogno di una persona giovane, come lei, tutta a lei dedicata, che la sapesse apprezzare in tutte le sue belle e buone qualità, che vivesse con lei la vita in comune, la vita dello spirito e del cuore: invece ha un vecchio inaridito" (page 510). Angelica is the *femme fatale* who comes closest to being exonerated for her destructive actions in Serao's work up to this point. Her actions are seen as being dictated by circumstances, so Serao is moving away from unreserved condemnation such as she expressed previously, and such as male writers have characteristically expressed in respect of this kind of female character. Verga, for instance, seems to condemn Eva through the words of both his male characters; d'Annunzio, as Klopp has pointed out (page 13), takes pleasure in punishing *femmes fatales*.

The depiction of Laura Acquaviva in *Addio, amore!* is similar to, but goes even further than, that of Angelica. The stereotyped elements in Laura's character more or less replicate those in Angelica's. She too is depicted as beautiful and mysterious; and it is only at the end of the text that Serao considers the character's motivation. Since the tale is told from Anna's perspective, Laura's emotions are thus a mystery to the reader for most of the text. From the beginning she is presented as an enigma: she never shows any emotion. The first description of her is as follows:

> La bellissima fanciulla, dai capelli biondo fulvi [...] sulla fronte, dall'ovale roseo purissimo, dai bigi occhi metallici, dalla piccola e fiera bocca, era seduta sul letto e leggeva quietamente [...]; la tacita fanciulla dal mobile e niveo volto verginale non ruppe il suo silenzio, non cambiò di colore, non cessò di sorridere altamente, come se tutto l'umano fango dell'amore non giungesse a macchiare la candida stola del suo cuore glaciale. (page 27)

The language here is straight from the love lyric. The reader's discovery, towards the end of the text, that Laura is not in fact as cold as she seems but actually sensual, seductive and passionate, merely serves to increase the aura of mystery surrounding her:

> Laura aveva preso dalla sua cintura [...] il fascetto di bianche rose [...] sempre guardando Cesare e sempre sorridendogli; due o tre volte, con uno scherzo d'amore, aveva battuto con le rose sulla spalla di Cesare. Poi aveva portato le rose alla faccia chinandosi sovra esse, volendo assorbire [...] tutto il loro [...] profumo [...]. E sorridendo, guardando Cesare con un'intensità amorosa profonda, gli aveva offerto le rose da baciare [...]. Laura aveva ribaciato le rose, con un movimento convulso, arrovesciando la testa. (page 242)

In terms of the plot, Laura's negative, evil qualities are seen in her destruction of Anna's marriage and her contribution to the events which lead Anna to commit suicide. Laura's own words to Anna, when she betrays her, show her to be cruel in the tradition of woman as monster: "Riprendilo, se ne hai la forza. Ma tu non l'hai avuto, mai" (page 263).

Many of the elements that differentiate Laura from the literary stereotype are similar to those which differentiated Angelica from it. Laura's name, like Angelica's, is significant. This *femme fatale* must primarily be associated with Petrarch's Laura: Serao's Laura is reminiscent of Petrarch's in her appearance, and as we have seen, Serao borrows the language of the love lyric to describe her. Like her Petrarchan namesake, this Laura is a more complex character than she initially seems. Apparently cold and unemotional at first, she soon reveals that she is in fact sensual, seductive and passionate. Like Angelica, Laura is strong and healthy; there is no air of sickness or decay about her. In some ways, then, Serao's character does not conform to the stereotyped *femme fatale* figure. We have noted the Dantesque reference in the name Beatrice, the reference to Ariosto in the name Angelica, while Lucia must remind us of, as she contradicts, Manzoni's Lucia; and now we see the Petrarchan Laura. One cannot help feeling that Serao sets up a gallery of the most famous female characters in Italian literature and then sets about presenting them in a different light—indeed, that she completely subverts them.

Serao explores Laura's motives for her actions in great detail towards the end of the text, and allows her to express them herself. Thus for the first time the reader is permitted to see things from Lucia's point of view: "Io amavo Cesare da prima: tu mi hai tradita" (page 257), she says to Anna, and later, "Il mio sangue è simile al tuo, i miei nervi sono simili ai tuoi nervi, il mio amore è ardente come il tuo, la mia anima inebbriata di passione come la tua, noi siamo figlie di Francesco Acquaviva e di Caterina Acquaviva— ebbene, Cesare ha affascinato te, e Cesare ha affascinato me" (page 260). Again we have typical doubling elements here: Laura's perspective on events (betrayal by her sister) is exactly the same as Anna's; it is as though they were the same character. Yet while here using the double device Serao departs radically from the angel/ monster stereotype. Neither character could be described as an intruder on the life of the other; both occupy, in structural terms, the position of "angel in the house". Neither, though, as we have seen, is presented in wholly angelic terms. Anna has no monopoly of pain; Laura too is shown to suffer: "Ebbe un minuto di pallore intenso, vedendosi inginocchiata, davanti e plorante, quella donna che aveva offeso cosí crudelmente; e chiuse gli occhi come se svenisse" (page 261). It is stressed that Laura is incapable of ending her relationship with Cesare: in reply to Anna's pleas she says three times, "Anna, non posso" (pages 261–62). In this text Serao's ultimate rehabilitation, as it were, of the *femme fatale* consists of the latter's being forgiven by her victim. Anna refers to Cesare as "una mummia di gentiluomo" who has destroyed "mia sorella, la creatura purissima, l'adorata figura di castità della mia casa" (page 281). Here the blame is completely removed from the *femme fatale* and placed on the male protagonist. For the first time in Serao's work a female character is permitted to criticize openly the actions of a male character (and one who, as I have indicated, is unusually strong when compared to other Serao males). The two female characters in this novel, then, eventually unite against the male (and against his perception of them as diametrically opposed) in such a way that despite his strength he is practically negated in the text.

Yet Serao's attempt to make Laura credible does not end there. In *Castigo* (1893),[30] a sequel to *Addio, amore!* extending the story of Laura and Cesare, her character is transposed into that of a good victim while she has to face another woman, Hermione, who is a complex blend of *femme fatale* and good woman. Ultimately Laura too loses Cesare and is thus as much a victim as Anna. In a sense she becomes Anna.

Serao's real interest in her female characters shows itself most clearly in her analysis of the *femme fatale*. She moves from a stereotyped male view of that figure to a more comprehensive female view, which is far removed from, for example, d'Annunzio's superficial interest in his *femmes fatales*. D'Annunzio was primarily interested in such characters for their effect on his male characters; he had no interest in their possible motives or emotions. Serao, on the other hand, at a relatively early stage in the developing presentation of woman in Italian literature, was concerned with reworking the old stereotype.

Serao's most revealing juxtaposition of the *donna angelicata* with the *femme fatale*, however, occurs not in an analysis of either one of them but in a strange combination of the two. It is found in the collection of short stories *Fior di passione* (1888), and specifically in the story "La donna dall'abito nero e dal ramo di corallo rosso".

Here we have a dramatic presentation of the "manifest double".[31] This analysis of how one (ordinary, rather than angelic) woman is possessed by another (monster) woman relates precisely to Gilbert and Gubar's analysis of the difficulties facing the woman writer in her attempt to create a credible female character. These critics state that "a woman writer must examine, assimilate and transcend the extreme images of 'angel' and 'monster' which male authors have created for her [...]; until quite recently the woman writer has had (if only unconsciously) to define herself as a mysterious creature who resides behind the angel or monster or angel/monster image" (*The Madwoman in the Attic*, page 17).

Interestingly, the short story in question is written in the first person, which is relatively unusual for Serao; and thus, I think, a certain amount of authorial identification with the character is implied. The character is also anonymous and so, in a sense, may represent Everywoman. She says she has a horrendous secret: "L'ho *taciuto* sinora per l'*orrore* della mia *mostruosità*."[32] The use of the term "monster" here is crucial, as is the difficulty the character has in speaking. Gilbert and Gubar have analysed the difficulties which woman writers have in breaking the silence imposed on them by the culture they live in. The difficulty Serao's fictional character experiences in verbalizing the secret (her dual nature) is crucial: it may be seen as a symbol of the problems experienced by women generally in relation to self-expression. (Indeed all Serao's angelic women have great difficulty in expressing themselves.) This, I think, exemplifies precisely the difficulties analysed by Gilbert and Gubar. As Annis Pratt points out, "We are the heirs [...] of centuries in which women, like words, have been considered symbolic objects of use in a masculine structure, linguistic tokens rather than wielders of words in our own right. When a woman sets out to manipulate language [...] she transgresses fundamental social taboos in that very act" (*Archetypal Patterns in Women's Fiction*, page 11). The *femme fatale* Lucia, however, is the only one of Serao's female characters capable of easily expressing herself. She does so, in her diary, through the written word. The narrator of "La donna dall'abito nero e dal ramo di corallo rosso" ultimately transcends the opposites angel/*femme fatale*, and also writes her story in order to convey her experiences.

In the short story the purpose underlying the character's eventual decision to write is "perché si sappia la verità del caso mio" (page 130). It appears that Serao here wishes to deal with the difficulties she has as a woman writer. The concept of madness surfaces, and is negated six times in the text. This is interesting because the prevailing nineteenth-century view was that women writers were at worst unfeminine, irrational creatures, and at best merely trivial and frivolous.[33] The narrator states clearly, "Non è vero che io sia pazza; io vivo, sento, ricordo e ragiono" (page 130). This underlines Serao's view of women as essentially rational. Yet the apparently rational character then describes a strange experience of duality: "Dentro l'anima mia vi è un'altra anima. Dentro la mia volontà vi è un'altra volontà. Dentro la mia ragione vi è un'altra ragione" (page 131). Serao here makes overt the female experience of duality.

The story of the character's possession or psychic split is then told. While out one day she comes across "una donna di mezza statura, col volto pallido e allungato, sciupato dall'età, dalle sofferenze; ma in quel volto consumato ardevano gli occhi neri, bruciavano di sangue le labbra" (page 132). This character of the second self clearly corresponds in appearance to the stereotype of the *femme fatale*. The first self feels compelled to follow her and to behave as she does—which is soon revealed to be not in character, as it were. She finds herself involved in a relationship which is antipathetic to her: "Avvinghiata ad essa che rappresentava la bugia e il tradimento, io sono stata la bugia e il tradimento" (page 137). The effect of this *femme fatale* transforms the protagonist. When at last she is involved in a positive relationship with a man, "vidi comparire fra noi la donna dall'abito nero [...]; i soavi occhi lampeggiavano malignamente, le sue labbra di garofano sogghignavano" (page 138). It appears, in fact, that the first self's relationship with the male character is what calls the second self into being. Serao seems to imply that the romantic male–female relationship leads to a sense of duality and ultimately of crisis for the female.

At this stage the character no longer seeks the *femme fatale*, rather the *femme fatale* imposes herself upon the narrator. At the story's dramatic climax it suddenly seems to the narrator that her lover's words are addressed not to her but to the other female figure, seated next to her, and so she accuses him of loving this ghostly female figure, describing her in detail. To her horror, he agrees and states that she has just described herself. He leads her to the mirror and she describes what she sees as follows: "Vidi nel cristallo una faccia smorta, consunta dall'età, dalla sofferenza, due occhi neri, ardenti, due labbra brucianti [...]. Vidi la sua figura, che era la mia figura; urlai come una bestia: 'Non sono pazza [...]; il fantasma si è messo nell'anima mia [...]; siamo due'" (pages 140–41).

The act of looking in the mirror is frequently used in the literature of the double as a symbol of the final recognition of one's true self. Serao, however, by making the male character lead the narrator to the mirror, and thus to a different perception of herself, appears to be claiming that woman is compelled to perceive herself, with distress, in the light of man's perception of her. As Gilbert and Gubar state, with reference to the artist's literary self-definition, which they say must precede self-assertion, "The woman writer acknowledges with pain, confusion and anger that what she sees in the mirror is usually a male construct [...], a glittering and wholly artificial shield" (pages 17–18). Serao's short story may thus be read as an analysis of the dilemma of the woman writer who is finally compelled to see herself, against her better judgement, as a monstrous being. Yet, in Serao's terms, it is man who has presented woman with this incomprehensible image of herself. The short story makes explicit what has been implicit in the other works discussed: that the heterosexual romantic relationship is doomed to failure in Serao's world-view, because of the constrictions placed on the women enclosed within it.

VARIATIONS

Serao does not confine her investigation of the romantic love relationship to the sphere of the aristocracy: she is also increasingly interested in both middle- and lower-class women in love. Here too she presents certain literary novelties. Because of the enormous number of such characters in Serao's *œuvre* I shall be very selective in my consideration of them.

Perhaps the most typical of Serao's presentations of the middle-class woman in love is that of Luisella Fragalà in *Il paese di Cuccagna*. At first we are shown Luisella's happiness and the extent of her love for her husband. Serao's use of free indirect speech indicates her detachment from her character's illusions: "Oh, giammai, giammai suo marito Cesare avrebbe fatto nulla senza consultarla: l'aveva sposata per amore, senza un soldo, contro la volontà di tutti [...]; la bruna madre, dal volto fresco e piacente, sottovoce benedí la piccola creatura dormiente, e la pregò che facesse benedire dal Signore i disegni di suo padre e le speranze di sua madre."[34] Luisella's trust in her husband is also shown here.

Continuing the pattern of these works, Serao then shows the character's introduction to reality, followed by her reaction. By the time Luisella discovers that her husband has been ruinously gambling, she has also realized that she is the stronger of the couple, and accordingly she is shown as having the strength to take charge of their lives. Her love for her husband changes from that of a wife to a maternal love, protective, guiding and stern: "Prometti di lasciare in mia mano tutti gli affari del nostro commercio, debiti e crediti, compera e vendita? [...] Prometti che nessuno varrà piú di me, prometti che mi ubbidirai, *come a tua madre*, quando eri fanciullo?" (pages 376–77; my italics). Here Serao portrays a female character who has the courage to confront and remonstrate with the man she loves, and the strength to assume what is traditionally the male role within the family.

Yet Serao does not see Luisella as a sort of superwoman; she shows that although she can cope with a difficult situation it does not come easily to her. Luisella is still a martyr, albeit a strong one. She endures great emotional suffering, and her solace and source of strength is that very religion which demands that she be a martyr. This is revealed even before she has to face the truth:

> Seduta in un angolo della chiesa [...] —credeva profondamente; tanto che nella piccola convulsione, che cresceva nei suoi nervi di creatura pietosa e religiosa, le lagrime già le scorrevano su le guance, in silenzio: e nella oscura previsione di una sventura che ella sentiva avanzarsi [...] ella chiedeva a San Gennaro la forza che egli ebbe nel suo atroce martirio, per sopportare il misterioso cataclisma che le sovrastava. (page 307)

The use of the word "martirio" here is significant, as it indicates that this is precisely what Serao has in mind for her character. Furthermore, what Serao describes as Luisella's natural female inclination to martyrdom is a vital part of what gives her strength in the face of the actual disaster: "Ella non provava che un infinito desiderio di abnegazione... *Sparite le grettezze che potevano* [...] *restringere il suo spirito femminile*, la sua anima si elevava alle altruistiche altezze del sacrificio [...]. Ella [...] si spiritualizzava, lasciando che tutta la parte nobile del proprio carattere signoreggiasse" (page 374; my italics).

Here Serao makes a direct, overt and precise link between femininity, religion and martyrdom. She again claims that suffering in romantic love is woman's destiny. Religion exalts woman's passive suffering by making her a martyr. Religious ecstasy then replaces sexual love: in other words, one illusion replaces another. Neera mapped out the same process in *Teresa* (1886). In the words of Christine Maxfield, "As Neera analyses Teresa's sentiments, she is aware of a relationship between human passion and religious ecstasy."[35] Despite this view of woman as martyr, however, Serao here depicts development in the role of woman in love. Whatever her inner feelings, Luisella is outwardly impassive and strong. She is, then, a figure of compromise, a capable female character who, in spite of herself, eventually controls the family purse-strings (and a business as well). Yet Serao cannot allow her to be this type of character in a straightforward manner. She frees her financially, and even emotionally, as her love for her husband dies, but retains elements of martyrdom in the graphic portrayals of her pain and in keeping her fettered to a debilitating religion which—yet another paradox—is one of the sources of her strength.[36]

The role of love remains one of destruction and pain in Serao's view of middle-class women in love. It is interesting, however, to note how she allows her characters to develop and become stronger in dealing with its undeniably negative force. Their increasing emotional strength, and often their role as controlling agents in their relationships with men, distances them from their literary precursors.[37]

Also interesting is the fact that Serao is not as fond of repeating this plot with her middle-class female characters as she is with her aristocratic characters. Perhaps the middle-class woman does not lend herself to the role of Romantic heroine. Yet despite this, where Serao does use the "women in love" theme in the novels she sets in a middle-class milieu, it is developed in an unrelentingly negative manner which is similar to its working-out in her aristocratic novels. Equally, in these novels Serao moves tentatively towards a new definition of female self-sacrifice. What Patricia Meyer Spacks says of *The Mill on the Floss* is true, I think, of much of this work by Serao: "She makes this version of an ancient [...] male argument seem a dignified rather than merely submissive position."[38]

For working-class women just as for aristocratic and middle-class women, love is, according to Serao, a destructive, negative force. One significant difference between Serao's working-class characters and her characters from other classes is, however, that working-class women in her writing are always aware from the beginning of the realities of their position. From their first appearance in Serao's work to their last, they are not prone to deception by men. They may make allowances for their men's shortcomings, but they are fully aware of what those shortcomings are. Another element in Serao's portrayal of these women, as opposed to her portrayal of women of other classes, is her concentration on how financial factors often affect their relationships with men. There is some development in her view of these women during the course of her writing career, but on the whole she sees them in a realistic way, recognizing that—as we have seen in the Introduction—working-class women were in no position to be the stronger or more independent partners in their relationships with men. (In fact, these women tend to be the ones who are *always* seen as martyrs—in Serao's view they have no alternative.) Their strength had to be conserved for survival. What mainly differentiates Serao from many earlier, and indeed later, writers is her very concentration on, and intense interest in, working class *women* as a group.

Some of Serao's working-class women in love, though by no means all, are prostitutes. Examples are Maddalena in *Il paese di Cuccagna*, Carmela in *La ballerina* and Gelsomina, whom I shall briefly consider here, in *Storia di due anime*.[39] Gelsomina's reasons for becoming a prostitute are explained: her lover has left her, there is no way for her to return to respectable society, and poverty now dictates her actions. Her continuing pain is expressed: "Sparita, per sempre, da quegli occhi grigiastri e grandi la espressione maliziosa di dolcezza infantile e l'altra, anche infantile, d'improvviso smarrimento: un avvicendarsi, invece, di una rassegnazione passiva, di una tristezza torbida, di una curiosità dolente, di uno stupore dolente" (page 761). At this point it is indicated that Mimi, her first love, may deserve some of the blame for her situation. To his offer of help her response is: "'È troppo tardi' [...]; aprendo le braccia, con un gesto desolato, non volendo aggiungere altro [...] vi era tanta espressione di rammarico inconsolabile, di un lungo rimpianto antico, senza conforto, tanta evocazione di un passato che era stato dolce e che avrebbe potuto essere felice, che egli, ottuso, sordo e cieco, intese il rimprovero" (page 763). Serao is scarcely complimentary about the weak Mimi here. Next, Gelsomina as a prostitute is given a symbolic function by her creator; her pain and desperation are made to stand for that of many women in her position: "Tante altre, come me, tante altre poverette, hanno pregato, hanno fatto voti [...] e nulla hanno ottenuto [...]; certe non pregano piú" (page 763). This character is a more cynical version of Maddalena in *Il paese di Cuccagna*.

Eventually, when Mimi threatens to kill himself, Serao reveals Gelsomina's motivation for becoming a kept woman, allowing her to express real anger:

> "Tu vuoi ucciderti" gli gridò nel viso tenendogli le mani, brucian-
> dolo coi suoi sguardi, ove ardeva la vampa della disperazione.
> "...E che avrei dovuto fare io? Cento volte, avrei dovuto ucciderm-
> mi, io! Ero una fanciulla buona, ti volevo bene, mi hai respinta,
> non mi hai voluta, ed io mi sono lasciata prendere, da uno
> qualunque, cosí, per debolezza, per tristezza, per non aver piú
> che fare di me [...]. Don Franceschino Grimaldi mi ha lasciata; e
> io, abbandonata, già perduta, ho rotolato sempre piú giú." (page
> 798)

Serao, then, sees Gelsomina's unrequited love as the main cause of her degeneration into the role of kept woman, and society's intoler-ance as the reason for her prostitution. This is love at its most destructive in Serao, and it is important to remember that in the author's eyes Gelsomina is not an isolated case—there are "tante altre" (page 763). Despite her pain, however, Gelsomina is strong enough to terminate the relationship. The notion of strength as a feminine attribute, and weakness as a masculine one, is striking.

Two interesting facets of Serao's handling of prostitutes are her sympathetic presentation of them and her explanations as to how they became prostitutes. To some extent her sympathetic portrayal must have challenged received notions of the nature of the prosti-tute. As Mary Gibson points out in her study of prostitution in Italy during the period in question, "members of the ruling classes held continuously, from unification until World War I, an image of the prostitute diametrically opposed to that of 'honest' women who made up the majority of the female population."[40] This is, of course, the familiar polarization of women, in both life and literature, as angel or evil (if not monstrous) woman. It appears that Serao, in her representation of the prostitute, generally tries to undo this polar-ization, to present the prostitute as an "ordinary" female character who is in effect the victim of circumstances. In some respects,

Serao's work is part of a general literary movement described by George Watt in his study of the fallen woman. In his words, "a sympathetic approach to fallen women in the nineteenth century, an approach which encouraged a revaluation of popular misconceptions, really begins in the novel."[41] Yet, as the discrepancy between Watt's view and Mary Gibson's indicates, this sympathy seems to have been manifested first in England and only later in continental Europe. Serao's handling of prostitutes may be akin to Mrs Gaskell's, for instance, but is not so close to Verga's.[42] Serao differs from Gaskell, however, in her emphatic imputation of blame to romantic love and/or the male character. Ironically, there may have been a grain of reality in this view; Gibson writes, "High rates of male migration and emigration may have increased prostitution because many women were left behind by their fiancés" (page 99). Economics, as Serao also implies, played its part: Gibson notes that "women supplemented their income by practising prostitution after working hours or when work was scarce" (page 109).

Serao, then, presents working-class prostitutes both positively and sympathetically. Victims of men, and of circumstances, they are morally exonerated by their creator, and do not contrast strikingly with the "honest" women of the narratives.

In *Mors tua* (1926) Serao analyses many working-class characters, but only one working-class woman in love, Mariuccia Pietrangeli, whose love is seen in negative terms from the start. Like Tommasina, the servant in "Terno secco",[43] she is an impoverished mother. She is also under immense pressure because her husband has to go away to war. Serao describes the strain she is under, again in physical terms: "Muta e sempre piú cupa Mariuccia Pietrangeli stringeva la bocca, come per reprimersi" (page 78). Her love for her husband also causes her great pain: "'Cesare, Cesare!' ella gridò, come se si fosse sciolto il nodo che l'affogava, buttandoglisi sul petto e lasciando, infine, sgorgare tutte le sue lagrime" (page 84). One might think that Mariuccia was a perfect candidate for loyal martyrdom, but in fact she is a somewhat more complex character. Her sense of self-preservation is stronger than any conscious inclination to martyrdom. She falls in love with another man and deserts her family for him while Cesare is away. When she meets Cesare again her explanation is: "Ho mancato, migliaia di donne hanno mancato, e i mariti non le hanno ritrovate piú. Che vuoi? La donna è di carne" (page 288). The desertion is, then, explained in terms of female sexual needs. Yet Serao is keen to stress that although Mariuccia's new love has given her a degree of prosperity it is not to be viewed in a wholly positive light. Mariuccia hurries away from Cesare, explaining that she will be late home: "Avrò una brutta scena, rientrando. Se si accorge di qualche cosa, piovono gli schiaffi" (page 288). On the one hand, then, Serao asserts this character's right to a kind of sexual self-definition; but, on the other, this assertion of female sexuality disrupts the text as Mariuccia's choice of love object ultimately brings her more pain. Her bid for independence thus comes to nothing, and she is simply involved in another negative love relationship; she has exchanged one state of martyrdom for another.

Women of the lower classes are thus seen by Serao as inexorably doomed to martyrdom. There can be no improvement in their lives because they are subject to many kinds of pressures, mainly financial, which do not impinge in quite the same way on the lives of women of other classes. Yet it is their realistic acceptance of the inevitable negativity of their lives, especially in the realm of love, that gives them the strength and dignity which only martyred women can have in Serao's work. Despite her obvious pity for, interest in, and sympathy with such women characters, she is here concerned—perhaps not surprisingly—with description rather than Utopian prescription.

The narratives I have analysed in this chapter replay the drama of romantic love from different perspectives but have in common an unremittingly negative view of the heterosexual romantic relationship. Through these portrayals Serao also "tries out" different versions of the female character, with varying degrees of success. Some characters are presented sympathetically, many are well thought out; others exist only on the most superficial levels of the narrative and scarcely deserve to be defined as characters at all. All of them, however, have the same function: to highlight, from the female perspective, the unsatisfactory nature of the plot of Romantic and Sentimental novels.

In rethinking and reworking these genres, and the roles they allot to the female character, Serao considers the various polarizations of the female character and re-forms these as well. By exploring female dualities she also explores female creativity and the role of the woman writer itself. Her conclusions are sometimes surprisingly revolutionary. Shirley Foster points out that although George Eliot is often considered an unorthodox woman writer she presents the "vindication of the ultimate sanctity of matrimony. Alternatives are inconceivable."[44] Serao's fiction, on the other hand, upholds neither the institution of matrimony nor the bond of romantic love. As we shall see, she searches for alternatives in every possible location. The next chapter explores one of the bondings offered in Serao's writing as an alternative to romantic heterosexual love: the maternal bond.

NOTES

1   Her interest in the depiction of heterosexual romantic love waned somewhat in her later years.

2   M. Serao, *Fior di passione* (Milan, Galli, 1888).

3   M. Serao, *Tre donne* (Rome, Voghera, 1905); *Le amanti* (Milan, Treves, 1894).

4   M. Serao, *Mors tua* (Milan, Treves, 1926).

5   The eponymous protagonist of *Albert Savarus* (H. de Balzac, *Albert Savarus* [1842], in his *Œuvres complètes*, vol. III, edited by M. Bouteron and H. Longnon [Paris, Conard, 1912]) is one example of this type; interestingly, in this novel Balzac's maiming of Rosalie seems to be an act of revenge for his male protagonist. Frédéric in Flaubert's *L'Education sentimentale* [1869] (Paris, Flammarion, 1985) traffics in idealistic Romanticism, with his images of Mme Arnoux. The two male characters in Verga's *Eva* [1873] (in his *Opere*, edited by L. Russo [Milan, Ricciardi, 1965]) suffer agonies at Eva's hands. In d'Annunzio's *Giovanni Episcopo* [1891] (G. d'Annunzio, *Prose di romanzi* [Milan, Mondadori, 1953]) the suffering hero is presented in a slightly different manner: as Charles Klopp says, "The hero derives masochistic satisfaction [...] from the inhuman treatment to which [the heroine] subjects him" (C. Klopp, *Gabriele d'Annunzio* [New York, Twayne, 1988], p. 80).

6   See M. Warner, *Alone of All Her Sex* (London, Picador, 1976), especially Ch. 4, for one of the many useful studies of the Mary/Eve dichotomy.

7   Milton uses the angelic female figure in his "Methought I saw my late espoused saint" (c.1658); his portrayal of the evil female figure is found in his presentation of Eve in *Paradise Lost* (1667). Goethe's *Faust* (1808 and 1832) contains both evil prostitutes and angelic virgins. Flaubert uses the manipulative female character in *Madame Bovary* (1857) and the angelic female in *L'Education sentimentale*.

8   Virginia Woolf first used the term "angel in the house" in "Professions for Women" [1931], included in her *The Death of the Moth and Other Essays* (London, Hogarth Press, 1942), pp. 236–38. She was inspired by Coventry Patmore's poem *The Angel in the House* (London, Bell, 1885).

9   Prototypes of the monster figure (for example, in the works of Pope and Spenser), as well as of the angelic figure, are studied in an enlightening

manner by S. Gilbert and S. Gubar, *The Madwoman in the Attic: The Woman Writer and the Nineteenth-century Literary Imagination* [1979] (London, Yale University Press, 1984).

10 M. Praz, in *La carne, la morte e il diavolo* (Milan, La Cultura, 1930), gives an interesting study of these figures in the chapter "La Belle Dame sans merci".

11 A. Pratt, *Archetypal Patterns in Women's Fiction* (Brighton, Harvester Press, 1982), p. 75.

12 The use of a character named Beatrice conforms to the view expressed by Z. G. Barański in "The Power of Influence: Aspects of Dante's Presence in Twentieth-century Italian Culture", *Strumenti critici*, new series, 1 (1986), 343–76. He writes about the effort of twentieth-century authors "to achieve some kind of integration between the directions of their own vision and the paternal authority of Dante" (pp. 350–51). This paternal authority becomes, I think, even more important when viewed from the perspective of a woman writer, especially a woman writer whose fiction, however subtly, as we shall see, was to challenge literary conventions.

13 G. Verga, *I Malavoglia* [1881], in his *Opere*, pp. 175–404

14 M. Serao, *Cuore infermo* (Turin, Casanova, 1881), pp. 9–11.

15 J. Calder, *Women and Marriage in Victorian Fiction* (London, Thames and Hudson, 1976), pp. 145–49, for instance, finds in George Eliot's fiction the notion of martyrdom as seductive for the female character.

16 The continuing appeal of melodrama for the female reader/spectator is interestingly analysed by T. Modleski, *Loving with a Vengeance: Mass-produced Fantasies for Women* (New York, Routledge, 1988).

17 M. Serao, *La Madonna e i santi nella fede e nella vita* (Naples, Trani, 1902). In this text Serao reveals that the aspect of St Catherine that most impressed her was her martyrdom.

18 M. Serao, *Fantasia* [Turin, Casanova, 1883], in her *Opere*, edited by P. Pancrazi, 2 vols (Milan, Garzanti, 1944–46), II, 5–274 (p. 44).

19 M. Serao, *La conquista di Roma* [Florence, Barbera, 1885], in her *Opere*, II, 277–514 (p. 338).

20 M. Serao, *Addio, amore!* [Naples, Giannini, 1890] (Rome, Edizioni delle Donne, 1977), p. 19.

21 For a detailed analysis of the double motif in these novels, see my essay "Angel vs. Monster: Serao's Use of the Female Double", in *Woman and Italy: Essays on Gender, Culture and History*, edited by Z. G. Barański and S. W. Vinall (London, Macmillan, 1991), pp. 263–93.

22 E. Showalter, *A Literature of Their Own* [1977] (London, Virago, 1982).

23 C. Rosenfield, "The Shadow Within: The Conscious and Unconscious Use of the Double", in *Stories of the Double*, edited by A. J. Guérard (Palo Alto, Stanford University Press, 1967), pp. 313–22 (pp. 313–14).

24 C. F. Keppler, *The Literature of the Second Self* (Tucson, University of Arizona Press, 1972).

25 In the standard presentations of the double by male writers, fear is an emotion normally restricted to the first self. See U. Fanning, "Angel vs. Monster", p. 272.

26 "In the vast majority of cases the harm done to the first self by the second is [...] as catastrophic as harm can be [...]; it may and usually does kill him [...] but it [...] compels self-awareness" (C. F. Keppler, *The Literature of the Second Self*, pp. 194–95).

27   See Chapter 4 for more on this friendship.

28   G. Flaubert, *Madame Bovary* [1857] (Paris, Garnier, 1966).

29   A. Banti, *Matilde Serao* (Turin, UTET, 1965), p. 216, cites these writers as important for Serao in the sense that she read and commented on their work. She also recognizes the same kind of importance for Serao of Zola, Flaubert, Balzac (p. 29) and d'Annunzio (at several points in her biography).

30   M. Serao, *Castigo* (Turin, Casanova, 1893).

31   This term comes from R. Rogers, *A Psychoanalytic Study of the Double in Literature* (Detroit, Wayne State University Press, 1972). Rogers asserts that there are two kinds of double: the obvious double, which he calls the manifest double, and a double of whose existence the reader only gradually becomes aware and who is never overtly identified as such; this he calls the latent double. Serao, as we have seen, for the most part uses latent doubles. This clear case of the manifest double indicates her awareness of precisely what she was doing with the double device.

32   M. Serao "La donna dall'abito nero e dal ramo di corallo rosso", in her *Fior di passione*, pp. 129–41 (p. 129).

33   For a detailed analysis of this view see E. Showalter, *A Literature of Their Own*, especially Ch. 3, "The Double Critical Standard and the Feminine Novel".

34   M. Serao, *Il paese di Cuccagna* [Milan, Treves, 1891], in her *Opere*, I, 105–529 (p. 137).

35   C. Meredith Maxfield, *"Valorose donne": The Emerging Woman in the Nineteenth-century Novel* (unpublished doctoral dissertation, Cornell University, 1977), p. 102.

36   The other, perhaps even more significant, source of Luisella's strength is her experience of motherhood, which I investigate in the next chapter.

37   Emma Bovary, for example, is never in control of her relationships with men; she is at their mercy, as well as at the mercy of her own demanding passions. Nor do Balzac's middle-class heroines control their destinies.

38   P. Meyer Spacks, *The Female Imagination* (London, Allen and Unwin, 1976), p. 46

39   M. Serao, *La ballerina* [1899], in her *Opere*, I, 3–101; *Storia di due anime* [1904], in her *Opere*, I, 675–799.

40   M. Gibson, *Prostitution and the State in Italy, 1860–1915* (New Brunswick, Rutgers University Press, 1986), p. 95.

41   G. Watt, *The Fallen Woman in the Nineteenth-century English Novel* (London, Croom Helm, 1984), p. 11.

42   *Ruth* and *Eva*, for example, are very different in their approaches to the figure of the fallen woman.

43   M. Serao, "Terno secco" [in her *All'erta, sentinella!*, Milan, Treves, 1889], in her *Opere*, I, 991–1024.

44   S. Foster, *Victorian Women's Fiction: Marriage, Freedom and the Individual* [1985] (Totowa, Barnes and Noble, 1986), p. 222.

Chapter 2

MOTHERS AND MOTHERING:
ICONS SHATTERED

In order to appreciate Serao's portrayal of motherhood it is necessary to consider how the character of the mother is presented in the works of her predecessors and contemporaries. I shall return to this topic in the concluding chapter, but at this stage I wish to make some preliminary observations. I am particularly interested in the views of male novelists who were predecessors and contemporaries of Serao, because it is they who are still regarded as the great writers, as was the case in her own lifetime. As a woman writing within the framework of a male tradition, it is to male writers that Serao must have looked for ideas and by male writers that she must have been most influenced. In many of their works, however, ideas on motherhood were sadly lacking. For writers such as d'Annunzio and Flaubert to depict a woman in the role of mother would have detracted from the female character's main function in their works, that of sexual being. In *L'Education sentimentale*, for example, Flaubert's Mme Arnoux is, for Frédéric, and possibly for Flaubert, much less a mother than a sensual woman. At her first appearance in the novel she is presented in splendid isolation, and Frédéric's point of view is clearly expressed: "Jamais il n'avait vu cette splendeur de sa peau brune, la séduction de sa taille."[1] Her relationship with her child, although important for the structure of the text, is referred to rather than described. Those male writers who dealt more fully with the character of the mother (such as Balzac, Mastriani, Verga and Di Giacomo) presented the character in an extremely monotonous and stereotypical manner: happy in motherhood, very possessive (especially about male offspring), frequently tyrannical, thus invested with power in the eyes of the child, yet often destined to suffer in later life for the pleasure experienced in early motherhood—mother as victim.[2]

It is the sense of the mother as primarily a tyrant that marks the viewpoint of such writers as specifically masculine—even Verga's long-suffering Maruzza in *I Malavoglia* stunts her son's growth.[3] In this novel Verga seems to express the resentment and dependence of the male child in relation to the mother, frequently commented on by psychoanalysts.[4]

In nineteenth-century Italian novels written by women, however, I can find no overt trace of such resentment. Perhaps there is no need for it because of the relatively clear-cut nature of the female role at that time. It is with women's increasing struggle for independence, and a sense of individuality, coupled with their desire for a role different from that enacted by their mothers, that one finds such resentment openly creeping into women's writing. The theme is prevalent in twentieth-century literature by women.[5] Serao differed from male writers in her understanding of motherhood, and this comes across clearly in her fiction. Most striking is the difference in her use of narrative point of view. Never does she present the figure of the mother through male eyes (for example, son, husband or lover), as male writers have tended to do. Frequently, and especially in her earlier work, the mother is presented through the sympathetic female eyes of a sister, friend or daughter. The opinions voiced in relation to the character are expressed by women (though they are not always positive, as Serao does not idealize the role of mother). Often, in her later work, she presents the narrative from the point of view of the mother character herself.

It is also significant that while male writers tend to deal extensively with the theme of fatherhood in their works, Serao has little interest in that theme.[6] Where she does introduce male characters who happen to be fathers, they are either inadequate or cruel. There are three examples of this in *Il paese di Cuccagna* alone: Annarella's husband, who is cruel to his wife and children, Cesare Fragalà, who is incapable of supporting his family either emotionally or financially, and Marchese Cavalcanti, who is responsible for ruining his daughter's health, her emotions and ultimately her life.[7] These three characters all represent different social classes. Thus Serao's presentation of them indicates that she sees inadequate fathering as a phenomenon found in all classes.

Yet perhaps the most striking point to be made about Serao as a woman writer dealing with the portrayal of the mother figure, and with the theme of motherhood in general, concerns the very frequency in her writing of the focus on the mother. The figure of the mother is one which becomes increasingly important, to the extent that it supersedes the writer's interest in the dilemmas of romantic love. I think it is legitimate to see Serao as representative of women writers in her focus on the theme of motherhood. Indeed, the way in which she deals with the theme of separation from the mother (which, as we shall see, is caused by the precedence of the romantic love relationship in our society) reflects a pattern in women's writing commented on by Gilbert and Gubar, who stress that "women writers from Mary Shelley [...] to [...] Toni Morrison [...] have described female sexual initiation in terms of the myth of Persephone, with its themes of abduction [...] and sorrowful separation from female companions."[8]

In my analysis of Serao's presentation of motherhood I shall first trace the development in her treatment of the theme. Secondly, I shall examine an important elaboration of it: the mother–virgin dichotomy or Madonna complex. Finally I shall analyse the significant apparent absence of the theme in certain areas of her work. Ultimately, for Serao the Madonna figure is linked, as we shall see, to the figure of the mother in general. Both are viewed ambivalently, and for the same reasons. The absent mother theme turns out, in terms of the subtext, to be an inescapable presence, and the inevitable nature of the mother figure, and of the act of mothering, is itself one of the causes of Serao's ambivalence.

PROGRESSION AND DEVELOPMENT

In this section I shall consider Serao's use of motherhood as a central theme in both her journalism and her fiction, and how her presentation of it, spanning these very different modes of writing, is strikingly consistent.

The first notable presentation of a mother occurs in *Dal vero*, an early collection of Serao's short stories. One of these stories, entitled "Silvia", deals specifically with the experience of first-time motherhood. It was first published in 1879, the year in which Serao's own mother (whom she loved and idealized) died. The author was twenty-three, and it was six years before she was to become a mother herself. For this reason it is hardly surprising that at this stage she should look on motherhood in a semi-idealistic way—and more surprising that at the same time she should be keenly sensitive to its negative possibilities.

"Silvia" is one of Serao's best-constructed, best-written and most striking short stories. It is divided into two parts: the first analyses the character's existence prior to pregnancy while the second explores the effect of impending maternity and ultimately of maternity itself.

The introduction vividly conveys the harsh, closed atmosphere in which Silvia has grown up; the very countryside is described in terms of stillness and impenetrability. The story opens thus: "La cittaduzza era silenziosa e deserta in quel lunghissimo pomeriggio estivo; [...] i balconi delle sue case, alti [...] dalla incurvatura profonda, erano tutti chiusi; le porte brune massiccie, costellate di chiodi [...], erano anche esse sbarrate."⁹ Serao begins this tale with a description of the village at siesta time, in order to create an atmosphere of closed unfriendliness. She then moves on to describe Silvia, seated behind her window. Silvia is shown as a stiff, lifeless character: "Era venuta là per abitudine [...], una fredda e indifferente abitudine" (page 285). Serao partially explains Silvia's indifference by revealing that she has had a childhood without love (not coincidentally, a motherless childhood). Here the figure of the father is introduced, and even at this early stage in Serao's work we glimpse her interest in paternal ineptitude: we are told that Silvia remembers "la ciera pallida e noncurante di un padre egoista che non la baciava mai" (page 287). At the same time the importance of the figure of the mother in the narrative also becomes clear: we read that Silvia has never had "qualcuno che le parlasse della madre, morta troppo presto" (page 287). Like Anne Elliott in *Persuasion*, Silvia clearly "misses the support of a loving female influence."¹⁰

From this background information, Serao moves on to a physical description of the character and, as we might expect, her emotional aridity is reflected in her appearance: "Era una figura alta e magra, vestita di grigio o di nero invariabilmente [...], gli occhi neri senza splendore, i capelli oscuri, tirati e stretti sulla nuca" (page 288). Serao repeatedly emphasizes Silvia's complete emotional aridity. This culminates in the description of a serious illness suffered by her father, during which "la figliuola lo vegliò [...], gli prestò le cure piú minute [...], ma la premura dolce e affettuosa [...], il sorriso di affetto [...] mancavano in lei" (pages 290–91).

Next the reader is told of Silvia's marriage of convenience, at the age of twenty-nine, to a forty-five-year-old who is cold and ugly. Silvia is indifferent to this as to so much else: "Era una persona di piú a cui doveva rispetto ed obbedienza, erano nuovi doveri, ma aridi e secchi come tutti gli altri" (page 295). She is repeatedly presented as a kind of automaton, "camminando a passi cheti e moderati, dritta nelle pieghe rigide, quasi monacali, del suo abito nero [...], parlando poco, sorridendo molto meno, pensando pochissimo" (page 296). Having built up the character in this way, Serao surprises the reader at the end of Part I by describing an initially unexplained change in Silvia's character: "Sentí un grande calore scorrerle per la persona, un senso benefico e piacevole [...]; ecco i forti ed onesti palpiti del cuore [...], l'intelligenza che si dispiega, la fantasia che sorge [...]; una gioia insolita le folgorò dagli occhi" (page 297).

In Part II Serao immediately explains this change, and in so doing gives an indication of how at twenty-three she may have viewed older childless women: "La donna di prima, lettera morta, pagina bianca, era scomparsa [...] ed era subentrata la donna completa, viva, forte e buona: la madre" (page 297). It is possible that Serao at this early stage regarded women without children as incomplete. Such a view, however, also accords with literary, cultural, and religious stereotypes which reiterated the belief that woman is fulfilled only in motherhood. Jeuland-Meynaud's analysis of the role of the mother in Italian literature, for instance, extends as far as Pirandello, who she says sees motherhood as "capable de purifier la femme de toutes les souillures antérieures à la maternité" (page 242). Silvia, at any rate, now changes for the better, and Serao continually expresses a positive and admiring view of motherhood: "La persona parve formarsi e completarsi [...] mentre alle tempia si scorgeva quell' ombra leggiera che è il segno sacro della maternità" (page 298).

The most significant change which pregnancy brings about in Silvia's life is happiness: "Obbliò tutto [...], le cure di casa, il marito, il padre [...]. Rivolgeva attorno sguardi di amore; spesso le venivano agli occhi lagrime di consolazione, che la soffocavano in una gioia infinita" (page 298). Part of her joy includes the relegation of the two commanding male figures in her life to relative absence; indeed Serao allows the instrument of the pregnancy, the husband, to disappear from the narrative at this point. Marianne Hirsch, in her excellent study of mother–daughter relationships in fiction, claims that "the feminist family romance of the 1970s de-emphasizes the role of men: the retreat to the pre-Œdipal as basis for adult personality, the concentration on mother-daughter bonding and struggle, and the celebration of female relationships of mutual nurturance leave only a secondary role to men."[11] It seems to me that this kind of "feminist family romance" is discernible in women's writing well before the 1970s, and that Serao's fiction provides several examples of it.

The idealized portrayal of motherhood continues. For the first time Silvia is shown to exercise her imagination, becoming creative on two levels, the simple, biological level and the mental level. She becomes a kind of artist, a kind of storyteller, rather like her creator: "Silvia volava con la fantasia ai paesi immaginari" (page 299). In her mind's eye she sees a son grow from babyhood to childhood, inventing all sorts of childish adventures for both of them. Then, equally happily, she turns her attention to the image of a daughter and a second fictitious scenario (this too is indicative of the author's sex—only the male child tended to be fit subject-matter for the pens of male authors). Serao repeatedly stresses, however, that this is happening strictly within the realms of fantasy.

Another surprise is introduced when Silvia is described as physically failing: "Una fiamma continua le imporporava le gote, una fiamma che le consumava nel suo ardore; i polsi le batteano frequenti, il corpo si dimagrava, le mani si assottigliavano" (page 304). The experience of labour is not described in the text, but it is alluded to in wholly negative terms after the reader has become aware that both Silvia and her baby are to die: "Silvia dormiva di un sonno affannoso ed irregolare, coi lineamenti contratti, col viso diminuito, quasi divorata dalla lotta combattuta" (page 305). Serao seems to be saying, then, that pregnancy and birth can be totally futile—takers of life rather than givers. The reader's expectations are overturned. Yet this shift in perspective should not wholly surprise us. As Margaret Homans points out:

> The thought of the event of childbirth itself would have had highly ambiguous connotations for any pre-twentieth-century woman. In the nineteenth century, giving birth was not unlikely to be fatal to the mother or to the child or to both, and to fear childbirth or associate it with death would have been quite reasonable [...]. Women who become mothers in novels tend to die physically if they do not die literally [...]. Within the conventions of fiction, childbirth puts an end to the mother's existence as an individual.[12]

Although the end of the story is so crushingly negative, it does also keep motherhood in the idealized, hallowed place it occupied in the body of the text. At the moment of her death Silvia feels close to the mother she never knew: "'Dimmelo, papà, te ne prego. Era molto dispiacente di morire?' 'Sí, perché lasciava in terra una figlia' […]. 'Essa sel sapeva' riprese lei lentamente 'essa sel sapeva. I figli non possono restare senza madre sulla terra'" (page 306). Here we have a complete negation of the role of the father; he is seen as useless. Serao indicates that motherhood is wonderful in theory and might well be wholly fulfilling; but she also subverts that message by warning that the fulfilment may be dangerous, painful and even elusive. Silvia precisely replicates the experience of her mother (as we have seen other of Serao's female characters do), and Serao here creates a martyr to mother love, contrasting with her female martyrs to sexual love.

An analysis of Serao's use of a different medium reveals how she became increasingly realistic about the trials and tribulations of motherhood, especially in relation to the poor. The most interesting example of this occurs in her writings about poverty in Naples, published in book form as *Il ventre di Napoli* (1884).[13] Her presentation of motherhood in the lives of working-class women shows that there is complete conformity between her fiction and her journalism. The theme is here presented in the same way as in "Silvia", again from a distinctively female angle rather than as a wholly objective sociological enquiry. The omniscient female journalist frequently filters point of view through the eyes of women observing other women, in the form of brief sketches. The female bias in the work is strong.[14] The nine articles, originally written for the Roman *Capitan Fracassa*, here appear as nine chapters, each dealing with a different aspect of Neapolitan working-class life.

None of the chapters is specifically devoted to the problems of motherhood, but the theme of motherhood runs through the work with a unifying force. Chapter 2, entitled "Quello che guadagnano", which is ostensibly about the working classes' low wages, concentrates no less on poverty itself than on the strain poverty puts on the role of the mother. Serao points out that poverty leads many women to try and play a dual role: "E come la miseria incombe, la donna, la moglie, la madre, che ha già molto partorito, che ha allattato, tutti quelli che dovrebbero lavorare in casa, cercano lavoro fuori" (page 17). Here Serao reveals an awareness that motherhood is in itself a difficult and painful business; having to work as well (without having the means to arrange satisfactory child care) could well make life unbearable. For women in such a situation Serao sees marriage as the beginning of the end, because it inevitably leads to child-bearing and thence to poverty and suffering: "Ebbero un minuto di bellezza e di gioventú, furono amate, si sono maritate: dopo, il marito e la miseria" (page 19). She states baldly that for these women children are "una cura di piú, una pena materna, una sorgente di lacrime e di fame" (page 21). Certain characters sketched here will later be incorporated into her fiction and further developed (for example, Annarella in *Il paese di Cuccagna*). This chapter, then, while on one level dealing with work, on another is concerned with the pains of motherhood.

Chapter 4, "Gli altarini", ostensibly deals with Neapolitans' religious habits (focusing on the women as the most religious and superstitious group). Yet here again there are several specific references to mothers, both positive and negative. In Chapters 5 and 6 it is made clear that if women gamble in the *lotto* (the subject of both chapters) it is for their families, specifically their children, rather than through addiction, as in the case of men; thus this is a relatively stereotypical presentation. Such women are particularly at the mercy of usurers, as Serao indicates in Chapter 7.

The ninth chapter, "La pietà", centres mainly on the pity of lower-class women for suffering children. Serao here describes many instances of what could be termed maternal instinct. She shows that these women want to be mothers, and if they are incapable of bearing children themselves they adopt. Yet despite Serao's awareness of this desire for children, she is careful not to gloss over the tasks of motherhood. Bearing children and giving birth to them are evidently not the only maternal trials: "Questa creaturina, non sua, ella l'ama come se l'avesse essa messa al mondo; ella soffre di vederla soffrire" (page 89). Serao here indicates that her concept of mothering is broader than the biological. She presents, too, a kind of maternal solidarity: she states that if a child's natural mother is unable to breastfeed, somebody else will do it for her. In such cases the natural mother is described as "sommessa, umile, riconoscente" (page 92), while the wet-nurse "finisce per mettere amore a questo [...] bimbo, e allo svezzamento ci soffre di non vederlo piú" (page 92). She also describes another aspect of this maternal solidarity, a kind of informal baby-sitting system for the mother who must work. The maternal warmth extends as far as self-sacrifice: "Nessuna donna che mangi, nella strada, vede fermarsi un bambino a guardare, senza dargli subito di quello che mangia" (page 94). The conclusion of this chapter hinges on the experience of childbirth, with a brief sketch of a woman giving birth in the street: "Ella taceva, ma per pietà [...] molte altre donne strillavano e piangevano" (page 99). I quote Marianne Hirsch again: "Women's basic and continued relatedness and multiplicity, the mirroring of mothers and daughters, influence women's writing in important ways" (page 20). Examples of multiplication and interrelatedness between women, especially in the maternal role, abound in this text, and in Serao's fiction. So the "pietà" referred to in this chapter is of a maternal nature: it is motherhood and children that produce the strongest reaction in the characters described.

In fact the prevalence of the theme of motherhood in this collection makes its title particularly apt: not only does Serao discuss "il ventre di Napoli" in the sense of the centre of Naples, she also focuses on the collective maternal "ventre", forever giving birth to more children who are destined to grow up in poverty and suffering. The portrayal of motherhood in this text is on the whole negative, if sympathetic. It is considerably more negative than in "Silvia" because Serao here deals very much with the general rather than the particular, and thus the impression of negativity, pain and suffering is overwhelming. The sympathy may well be linked to Serao's personal experience of pregnancy and miscarriage in this period in her own life. In essence, both "Silvia" and *Il ventre di Napoli* are marked by ambivalence. Serao oscillates between positive and negative representations of maternity.

To return to Serao's short stories, a particularly telling analysis of both pregnancy and motherhood is found in "Terno secco".[15] This story was originally published in 1889, a few years after *Il ventre di Napoli*, and Serao's presentation of her subject is even subtler here than in the earlier text. The theme is ostensibly a win in the *lotto* for various people (while the character who is the source of the winning combination of numbers loses). Beneath the surface, however, maternity (with its effects) is once more Serao's primary consideration.

The pregnant character is Tommasina, a servant. Serao introduces her pregnancy in the first paragraph, thus giving it promin-

ence. Her description of Tommasina is interesting: "Era una creatura alta e sottile, scarna scarna, con un volto assai giovanile, lungo
e bruno; ma la persona gracile [...], la persona di giovanetta fine e
malaticcia era sproporzionata da una grossa pancia che il grembiu-
le di cotonina azzurra disegnava precisamente" (page 125). Here
already pregnancy is seen as negative; it distorts Tommasina,
altering her grotesquely. A little later in the text Serao conveys
Tommasina's feelings about the impending birth: "Voltò il capo,
impallidendo: sempre che le parlavano di questo figlio, la cui
nascita era imminente e per cui non aveva pronto ancora nulla [...],
si turbava, rabbrividiva, già madre, già fremente di amore e di pietà
per la sua creatura" (page 132). As in *Il ventre di Napoli*, this is a
description of how poverty exacerbates the stresses of motherhood. Again Serao illustrates a kind of maternal solidarity, this
time one which crosses the divide of social class, between Tommasina and her employer: "Guardò in viso la sua signora e le due
madri s'intesero, tacitamente, tanto era il turbamento della giovane, tanto era l'affettuosa compassione della piú vecchia" (page
132). Not only mental anguish, however, awaits Tommasina: Serao
is again explicit about the physical anguish of motherhood. Tommasina is shown performing her chores "penosamente, per il
fastidio della gravidanza" (page 134), the use of the word "fastidio" colouring the reader's attitude towards this pregnancy.

While tidying the bed, Tommasina finds a piece of paper with
the *lotto* numbers written on it and decides to play, thus becoming
the fictional embodiment of Serao's observations in *Il ventre di
Napoli* about women who will gamble to provide for their child. As
with many of Serao's women characters, Tommasina must do this
because her husband will be an inept father: he is depicted as
lacking in loyalty to his family, and, while he has money to lend to
his friends, "lasciava che sua moglie crepasse di fatica, incinta, mal
vestita, malaticcia" (page 160). As the story unfolds, the physical
inconveniences of Tommasina's pregnancy become clearer: "Abbattuta dalle scale, dai pesi che aveva portato, dalla fatica [...],
sonnecchiava, col capo sul petto, presa da un gran torpore" (page
161). Eventually she gives birth in great pain. Serao uses Tommasina's unsympathetic husband Francesco in her narration of this
event: "Tommasina strillava come un'anima dannata," he says
(page 175), and "Che volete signori miei, quando la donna sta in
quello stato, le pare sempre di morire" (page 177). Through Tom-

masina, then, Serao conveys a view of motherhood as physical pain and mental anguish, beyond the comprehension of her male characters.

The tale of Tommasina's pregnancy may seem like a subplot, unrelated to the main events (the failure of the other mother to win in the *lotto*), yet this is not the case. What really links Tommasina and her employer is their shared bitter-sweet experience of maternity.

The *signora*, unlike Tommasina, represents Serao's view of the ideal mother. The third-person narrator unfailingly presents this character in a positive light. Often, too, point of view is manipulated so that we see the *signora* through the eyes of her adoring daughter, while at other times we share the *signora*'s perspective. This is hardly surprising as this mother figure was created from Serao's idealized memory of her own mother, as is generally recognized by Serao critics.[16] Caterina, the daughter, is based on Serao herself.

From her first appearance Caterina's mother is described in idealistic terms: according to Serao she is a model of femininity. She has a "voce velata femminile" and "un profilo purissimo, con un paio di occhi bigi molto dolci, a mandorla, con certe mani cosí candide che pareano quelle di una giovinetta" (page 127). She has "lunghi capelli biondi, una meravigliosa chioma che si mescolava appena appena di bianco" (page 127). From the beginning she is described as a tender, loving mother who is entirely positive about her role. When Caterina is slow to awake she encourages her: "'Su, piccola, su', rispondea la mamma, carezzevolmente, come se parlasse con una bimba di quattro anni" (page 130). Although this character is clearly better off than the servant she lives in genteel poverty, and she too makes sacrifices for the sake of her child: "Per scrupolo non faceva colazione e stava sino alle cinque, senz' altro che quell' uovo" (page 131). Yet she harbours no resentment at the demands made on her by her daughter: "'O mamma, tu mi porti' diceva, scendendo le scale. 'Ma tu mi sostieni, piccola' rispondeva la madre" (pages 133–34). Even on her return from work (for this is a working mother who wears herself out teaching to support her child), when she is described as extremely tired, it is on her daughter that she concentrates: "La madre, ogni tanto, si fermava, guardandola mangiare, intenerita" (page 164). Mother and daughter discuss their day, revealing their closeness; theirs is a relationship of solidarity. When the mother hears that the numbers were successful in the *lotto* she reacts with shock: "'È uscito?' domandò la signora fattasi bianca come un cencio di bucato" (page 166). She claims she forgot to place a bet. When she is in the presence of others she is composed, but when alone with Caterina she reveals her true feelings: "Con la bocca sui capelli della figlia, tenendone il capo stretto sul petto, la madre singhiozzava profondamente, senza rumore, con un sussulto cupo, senza lagrime, scossa da tale un'emozione che parea il cuore le si spezzasse" (page 168).

So far, then, what we have seen is an intense mother–daughter relationship. At the end of the story, however, Serao has a shock in store for her reader. The closing sequence takes the form of a dialogue between mother and daughter, in which Caterina asks her mother:

> "Hai dimenticato o non avevi denaro? La verità, mamma", "… non avevo denaro." "Come non avevi denaro? Non ti ho chiesto una lira per i miei cartoncini di disegno e me l'hai data?" Nulla disse la mamma, non proferí parola, non fcce atto. Ma come uno straccio le cadde ai piedi, la figliuola, con le braccia aperte, battendo la testa sulle ginocchia materne, gridando: "Perdono, mamma…" E fiocamente la madre diceva: "Piccola, piccola figlia…" (pages 178–79)

The reason why the mother has not won the money is thus her self-sacrifice for her child, and the extent of her consequent suffering is clearly shown. The identification between mother and daughter here could well be seen as excessive: the daughter literally enacts the mother's despair. In a sense, the positive, idealized relationship is split asunder by the daughter's overwhelming guilt, coupled with the mother's saintly forgiveness. This is not, perhaps, altogether surprising when considered in the light of current psychoanalytic theory. Nancy Chodorow speaks of the intensity, ambivalence and boundary confusion inherent in the mother–daughter relationship. The daughter, she claims, is preoccupied with her mother and "experiences a continuation of the two-person relationship of infancy" (page 96). For Chodorow, the father functions in the family structure as a kind of safety net, a provider of respite from a potentially dangerous, intense and stifling mother–daughter relationship. In this story the father is absent; there is no safety net. Hence, perhaps, the excessive sense of claustrophobia and mutual guilt in the situation.

The common experience of mothering, regardless of class difference, is one important general concern of this story's subplot; mothering daughters in particular is another. The story is concerned as much with this as with the overt theme of the *lotto*. It is interesting to wonder why the mother in this short story is never referred to by name but always as either "la madre" or "la signora". I think it is possible that, although Serao presents this character as the ideal, albeit dangerous, mother in terms of her appearance, attitudes and character, she also presents her, in a sense, as everymother, whence her anonymity. Everymother is here shown to live a life of sacrifice for the sake of her offspring, and she "enjoys" a virtually symbiotic relationship with her female offspring.

Il paese di Cuccagna, Serao's novel of 1891, is one of her most interesting works. There are many themes in this text, the most significant of which is undoubtedly the *lotto* and its effect on the lives of Neapolitans, irrespective of social class. Another interesting theme in the novel is love, and yet another is motherhood. Serao's presentation of her female characters here, in a frame overshadowed by images of maternity, and in the shadow of motherhood, is striking.

There is in this text an interesting example of the significance, from the child's viewpoint, of the *absence* of the mother figure, a theme suggested at the close of "Silvia" and here developed. Bianca Maria Cavalcanti, an impoverished aristocrat, is motherless. Like Silvia, not only is she without a mother, she is also very much at the mercy of an inept father, Marchese Cavalcanti. From the moment these two characters are introduced it is obvious that they are extremely dissimilar in temperament and that, despite Bianca's peace-loving nature, they frequently disagree. One of the first scenes in which they feature as protagonists shows how clumsy the Marchese is as a father figure: "'Pazze ed egoiste, le donne!' urlò lui, esasperato da quella mancanza di resistenza, da quella dolcezza [...]. 'Ingrate e perfide, le donne!' Ella abbassò il capo, si mordeva le labbra per non scoppiare in singhiozzi" (page 169).

It soon becomes clear that the Marchese is concerned only with winning money in the *lotto*, while Bianca Maria is religious and retiring by nature: "Né si poteva abituare a quegli sfoghi di passione che facevano trasalire e sussultare la sua anima innamorata di pace e di silenzio" (page 171). It is the Marchese who, with his talk of divine inspiration (connected merely with *lotto* numbers), frightens Bianca into illness: "La fanciulla, che tutto aveva inteso, fu presa da tale invincibile paura che fuggí, tenendosi la testa fra le mani, con gli occhi chiusi [...]; folle di terrore, senza che un grido potesse uscire dal petto, crollò per tutta la sua altezza sul pavimento e giacque come morta" (page 180). He is also responsible for her failure to recover; he rejects her doctor's advice to move her to the country: "Piú forte di ogni convincimento e di ogni collera, era la ostinazione dell'indurito giuocatore, che considerava la sua figliuola come la spirituale sorgente dei numeri e che la metteva alla tortura" (page 403). Furthermore, he causes the destruction of the relationship between Bianca and the doctor, Antonio Amati. In her attempts to persuade her father to support her desire for marriage, Bianca invokes the figure of her dead mother, who is clearly important to her: "'Mia madre era una santa donna e vi ha amato' osservò ella" (page 407). Even this plea does not affect the Marchese, who curses her desire for marriage: "Guai alla fanciulla che preferisce le volgari laidezze della passione umana, alle purissime altitudini della vita spirituale!" (page 407). It is Bianca's story which closes the text; and in her deathbed agony she finally chooses to turn her back on her inadequate father: "La mano faceva un cenno continuo, sempre quello, ostinato, scorante, quello di allontanare suo padre" (page 507).

Yet it is clear that Bianca must turn to someone, and it is not surprising (especially given Serao's attitude to the mother figure in the earlier, and similar, "Silvia") that this character should be that of her dead mother: "Bianca Maria si metteva a gridare. 'Mamma, non voglio morire, non voglio, non voglio, mamma cara!'" (page 528). These are her last words, and thus show the depth of her preoccupation with the absent mother figure. Serao uses these characters not only to illustrate male ineptitude (and, in this instance, cruelty) in fatherhood but also—and more importantly— to illustrate how powerful the mere notion of the mother figure can be. Bianca Maria's mother, although never described and never even named, has an important function. Her absence in the text contrasts with her presence in Bianca's mind. She is such a powerful figure that she can reach from beyond the grave. Serao here develops the theme she touched on in "Silvia", to allow a different perspective on motherhood, as something which can somehow transcend the normal barriers of time and place (both in real life and within the constraints of fiction). This is her most powerful presentation of motherhood so far.

Inevitably, there is also a negative portrayal of motherhood, this time from the perspective of a mother within the text, and, as is often the case with such descriptions, Serao concentrates here on a lower-class character. Annarella is one of three sisters, and Serao associates the theme of motherhood with all three of them, initially by explaining that they have just lost their own mother and that each of them feels the loss keenly. Thus they are seen first in the role of daughter and only later in that of mother. (For an analysis of how Serao uses the theme of motherhood in relation to Maddalena and Carmela, Annarella's sisters, see the section entitled "The Maternal 'Negative'" later in this chapter.)

To begin with, Serao describes Annarella as the mother of three children. She is married to a man who is not only an inept father but also a cruel one. Desperate for money with which to gamble, he beats both his wife and his children to take their earnings from them. The pain caused Annarella by her children's suffering is shown to be far greater than any distress she might feel for herself:

> Al sabato sera, quando tornavano a casa, i ragazzi portavano le tracce delle busse paterne e trovavano la madre che aveva dimenticate quelle toccate da lei, e piangeva sulle teste dei poveri figliuoli, domandando loro: "Quanto ti ha portato via?" "Quattordici soldi" rispondeva Teresina, malinconicamente. "Mi ha levato mezza lira", diceva Carmine, rabbioso. "Oh Gesú, oh Gesú" esclamava la madre, piangendo. (page 344)

The sadness and anger of the respective children is as nothing compared to the anguish of the mother. Yet Serao is intent on showing that the experience of motherhood can be more painful still: "Quello che non le poteva uscire dalla mente, era il suo bambinetto di due anni e mezzo, che era morto per cattivo latte [...]; nulla poteva levarle dalla mente che il vizio del marito avesse ucciso il piccolo figlio" (page 344). Serao here takes up a theme she had previously outlined in *Il ventre di Napoli*. The earlier episode in the text where Serao describes Annarella's discovery that her milk has killed her son is even more heart-rending: "Sola, chinando gli occhi sul suo bimbo, ricominciò a piangere, e la ricetta nella sua mano tremava, tanto le era insopportabilmente amara, l'idea di aver avvelenato il suo figliuolo col suo latte" (page 191).

In this novel Serao explores motherhood from a number of different angles. Firstly, she suggests that for a child to be mother-less has all kinds of negative consequences. In the case of Luisella

Fragalà, another significant character in this work, motherhood is shown as a positive strengthening experience. In the Annarella episode, although motherhood is seen in a negative light (the earliest description of Annarella in the novel is: "Annarella, col suo passo molle di donna che ha fatto troppi figli", page 126), both poverty and the influence of the husband are seen as factors contributing to its negativity. It is almost as though Serao were trying in this text to redress the mainly negative portrayal of the experience of motherhood with which she had presented her reader hitherto. If that is so, however, the description of Annarella's character is so poignant and negatively structured that she did not succeed.

Serao's perspective on motherhood is at times revealed in rather unexpected places. She has a (sometimes irritating) tendency in both her journalism and her more contemplative writings to lecture to her readers. She was especially inclined to address her female readers, often specifically in the context of their role as mothers. Two somewhat unexpected instances of this are found in volumes of her writings about war, *Evviva la guerra!* and *Parla una donna*.[17] The first of these books, concerned with the Libyan War, is a collection of journalistic writings dated 1911 and 1912 and originally published in *Il giorno* and *Il giornale d'Italia*, together with a lecture (the title piece) which Serao gave repeatedly all over Italy to groups such as the Associazione della Stampa in Rome. *Parla una donna* is a collection of contemplative writings on the First World War which, although patriotic, are much more pacifist in tone.

One of the most interesting elements of *Parla una donna* is the way in which, in the preface, Serao regards herself as a representative of the creative female mind. She speaks of female writers and poets, whom she clearly views in a different light from other women. It gradually becomes clear that she views war as something which unifies all women and bridges the gaps which exist between them as individuals by appealing to what could be termed a maternal instinct: "E le scrittrici, le poetesse? [...] Esse sono balzate fuori dal forte, dal soave sogno che tenea la loro anima [...]; una freccia mortale ha trafitto il loro cuore [...]. Tutte sono ridiventate delle donne, delle semplici oscure donne [...] nella loro tenerezza [...], in tutte le loro viscere materne" (page xii). The maternal sensibility thus becomes a focal point of this work; indeed Serao sees it as her inspiration: "Io, ultima fra tutte queste mie grandi sorelle, ho fatto [...] un silenzioso e tenace esercizio [...] che [...] aveva una duplice possente spina: l'amor del mio paese, l'amor dei miei figli, come migliaia di altre madri" (pages xii–xiv).

Serao's consciousness of other women writers, and of the link between her and them, effectively illustrates a point made by Elaine Showalter: "Women writers were united by their roles as daughters, wives and mothers [...]. On the whole these are the implied unities of culture, rather than the active unities of consciousness. From the beginning, however, women novelists' awareness of each other and of their female audience showed a kind of covert solidarity that sometimes amounted to a genteel conspiracy."[18] Not only does Serao here openly indulge in this kind of conspiracy (the very title suggests it), she admits that the work was prompted by maternal feelings; thus the conspiracy becomes even more closed. According to Gilbert and Gubar, "the patriarchal notion that the writer 'fathers' his text just as God fathered the world is and has been all-pervasive in Western literary civilization" (page 4); it is therefore interesting that Serao here sets up an image of "mothering" the text and indeed of producing it through a maternal process. Not only is mothering compatible with literary production: it becomes essential. This is an aspect of the presentation of maternity which is confined to Serao's contemplative writing, having no overt parallel in her fiction. Indeed, *Parla una donna* is a strikingly maternal text: it contains scarcely a chapter that lacks a reference to the figure of the mother. Given the work's title, its bias towards the feminine experience (as opposed to the masculine) is hardly surprising. What is striking is that Serao chooses to focus primarily on the experience of the mother figure, rather than on that of the wife, sister or lover (though she does not neglect these).

The presentation of war in *Parla una donna* is thus slanted towards the feminine/maternal principle rather than the masculine/warlike, and the same is true of the earlier *Evviva la guerra!* By virtue of this perspective these works stand out amid the plethora of literature on war in contemporary Italy.

At this point I shall return to Serao's fiction, where the themes discussed in relation to her journalism and contemplative writings are reflected and developed. In her fiction, too, she focuses on the position of the mother in time of war, and affirms the maternal principle as creative, concerned with life, rather than destructive, concerned with war and death.

Serao's final work, *Mors tua* (1926) is concerned with the First
World War in retrospect. It reveals her stance as entirely and
committedly pacifist, no longer complicated by a conflict between
pacifism and patriotism.[19] The work was consequently viewed
unfavourably by the Fascist regime, and this is generally believed
to be the reason why Serao did not win the Nobel Prize for
literature in 1926.

The novel deals with a number of issues: the misfortunes of
soldiers at the front, the effect of war on the love relationship, the
role of the religious in time of war; but, strikingly, its main theme
is motherhood, specifically the reaction of the mother figure to the
loss of her child and to the danger surrounding both her and her
child. Many of Serao's works, particularly those earlier writings
concerned with heterosexual romance, have a "daughterly" focus;
her later writings, however, shift to a wholly maternal perspective,
and in this she is most unusual.

Motherhood frames the text, which opens by depicting a group
of mothers and closes (very negatively) by showing the pain
suffered by one mother in particular. The work is dedicated to the
"madre ignota", which underlines Serao's view of the mother
figure as central. Throughout the novel Serao again filters the
narrative through the eyes of different female characters. Each of
them watches and analyses the others, thus maintaining the text's
female perspective.

From the beginning, the author's interest is focused on how the
war impinges on the character of the mother. The mothers gathered
together have a common fear: the onset of war. Their worries make
the beauty of the afternoon fade into nothingness: "Discorrendo
teneramente [...] di quello che era il centro della loro vita, cioè i loro
figliuoli, quell' incanto primo era infranto" (page 9). It is clear from
this that they define themselves primarily as mothers and see
themselves first and foremost in relation to their children. The
novel thus opens with what seems like an idealization of the
mother–child relationship.

Among these mothers worrying about their sons, Serao homes
in on the character who is depicted as the group's focal point, Marta
Ardore. The name may well have Biblical significance. From the
start of the text this woman is described as suffering greatly:
"Gemeva sangue, quell' anima di madre" (page 10). She is the
mother of two sons, of whom the elder, Fausto, is described as very

patriotic and pro-war. From the beginning this causes conflict in the mother–son relationship. Unusually for Serao, this division is depicted as extremely deep: Marta's anti-war convictions are so strong that her relationship with her son ultimately becomes cold. Having heard Fausto speak to the crowds, inciting them to fight, she reacts with shock and disgust: "Si abbatté in una poltrona col volto chiuso fra le mani, senza piangere, senza singhiozzare, piegata in due, quasi spezzata in due" (page 12). She tries to explain to Fausto the extent of her hatred of war: "La mia anima è vincolata dal mio sangue materno. Io non sono libera. Io sono schiava del mio amore per te, per Giorgio" (page 13). This is not one of the brave, smiling maternal figures common in *Evviva la guerra!* and present in *Parla una donna*: this is an independent spirit reacting politically on the basis of maternal considerations.

As the text unfolds it becomes clear that Marta's greatest fear is for the future of her younger son, Giorgio, who follows in Fausto's footsteps. She naturally disapproves of his idolization of Fausto, indeed this disapproval hardens her attitude towards her first-born. Predictably, the crisis centres on Giorgio, who joins the army and is killed. Marta's first reaction is one of intense anger and hatred directed at her elder son, who brings her the news. We learn of this only much later in the text, from Fausto's narrative: "Madre, finché io viva, ovunque io vada [...] io udrò il tuo urlo che mi accusava, vedrò il fulgore del tuo sguardo, che mi volea fulminare" (page 325). This reaction is atypical of Serao's mother figures; this mother, clearly the subject of the novel (whereas in "Terno secco", for instance, the mother is the idealized object), is allowed to express openly her anger at the futility of war, and also her negativity towards her son. Furthermore, Serao here clearly shows her own views on war. She has Fausto, previously the spokes-person for war, admit he was wrong: "Tu avevi ragione, nel tuo infinito sgomento e nel tuo infinito ribrezzo della guerra [...]. È vero che sono Caino" (page 326).

Marta, however, accentuates a trend visible in Serao's earlier characters: that of intense suffering. She is so grief-stricken that she is incapable of living in the present, and maintains her youngest son's bedroom as a shrine. She still speaks to him as though he were alive: "'Mia creatura, mio fanciullo, mio fiore' [...] lo saluta, dispe-ratamente" (page 318). Such is her pain that she is incapable of rebuilding her badly fractured relationship with her elder son. Her

awareness of the gap between them is revealed in her words to him
near the close of the text: "Fausto, io ho vinto e sono perduta" (page
327). And Marta ends the novel by revealing the extent to which her
life has been devastated: "A un tratto, un sobbalzo e un grido
lacerante: 'Signore, quanto tempo ancora ho da vivere cosí? Signore, quanti anni, quanti giorni, quante ore?'" (page 328). The war is
seen as responsible for her negative existence, through the pain
caused her as a mother.

Another of the many suffering mother figures depicted in the
same novel is that of Antonia Scalese. She is the only mother figure
in the text who is described as trying to be brave about the war; in
other words, she is the only mother figure in the same position as
Serao's characters in *Evviva la guerra!* Yet Serao again decides to
depict even this response to war as completely destructive, in
sharp contrast to the earlier texts.

Antonia Scalese stands out for another reason: she is the only
unmarried middle-class mother depicted in *Mors tua*, which contains no sense of shame in relation to this or any authorial judgement on it. Antonia herself is initially presented as proud of and
positive about motherhood: "Tutti i nostri figli sono buoni per noi
[...]. Noi sole, le madri, conosciamo tutto l'animo loro", she says
(page 4). She is shown to reject the possibility of war, and from the
beginning is presented as unable to bear even the thought of the
loss of her son: "Io [...] ho detto [...] se dovessi perdere mio figlio,
il mio unico bene [...] io lo seguo subito, nella morte" (page 8).
Although her inclination is to oppose war, she is also aware that her
son is unhappy. Gianni explains this unhappiness in terms of his
sense of guilt at not fighting and his sense of obligation to his
country. This is unacceptable to his mother. Serao here reveals the
potential extent of maternal dependence and possessiveness: "Ella
afferrò Gianni [...] e se lo tenne stretto, da soffocarlo, e [...] gridò:
'Figlio mio, bene mio, amore mio [...], unico amore mio [...],
nessuno mi ti deve togliere, nessuno mi ti deve toccare, colpire,
ferire, uccidere [...]; ti ho procreato fra i dolori [...]; ho tutto
sofferto, per te'" (page 55). This mother–son relationship is clearly
stifling and unhealthy for both characters.

Typically of Serao's maternal figures, however, it is Antonia
who must make sacrifices within the relationship: she must sub-
merge her own feelings for the sake of her son's happiness, letting
him go to war. On leaving, Gianni instructs her to be happy, and

this she pitifully tries to be, always wearing on her face a "bizzarro riso di obbedienza" (page 100). By the close of the text, Gianni has disappeared and Antonia is presented as a madwoman, holding conversations with her absent son through the floorboards in a manner reminiscent of Bertha Mason.[20] She is, in Gilbert and Gubar's terms, another "madwoman in the attic". Serao describes her as "povera, abbandonata orfana di suo figlio" (page 321). The thwarting of her maternal love and her unbalanced attempts to be happy have resulted in lunacy. This, Serao seems to say, is what happens to the mother whose dependence on her child is excessive: she cannot exist as an individual. We remember too that, inheritance of mental illness aside, Bertha Mason is in a state of wholly isolated dependence on Rochester; a foreigner in a strange country, she is certainly made more vulnerable by this. Antonia, because of her status as an unmarried mother, is also in a sense a vulnerable foreigner in a strange country. Her madness, Ruth's cholera and Tess's hanging may all perhaps be read as an unwilling acknowledgement of conventional morality on the respective parts of Serao, Gaskell and Hardy, despite the obvious sympathy of each author for her/his creation.[21]

Examples of women characters who suffer for their sons abound in the text; the ones I have mentioned are simply the most important ones in the overall plot. There is, however, one such mother in the text who is interesting because of her anonymity. She is, in a sense, everymother, the "madre ignota" to whom the work is dedicated. This character has lost her son in the war and has just heard of the armistice. Her grief is all the more unbearable when contrasted with the happiness of others. She has lost "tutto il bene della sua vita, l'unico bene" (page 224); her life is described as completely empty. She is seen in terms of her lack of resources: "E non ha piú lacrime, non ha piú preghiere, non ha piú parole, questa madre ignota" (page 224). The anonymous mother is the subject of three literary comparisons: she is seen as being like Ovid's Niobe, who turned to stone as a result of her maternal distress, and also like the Biblical Rachel, who was inconsolable for the loss of her sons; ultimately, she is compared to the supreme Biblical mother figure: "Ella porta, come la Nostra Donna dei Dolori, sette spade che le trafiggono il cuore" (page 224). Serao here puts the end of the war very much in perspective. Although it was a source of joy to many, she does not take refuge in the easy option of glorifying those who had fought, or those mothers who had loaned their children to the motherland (as she calls Italy in *Evviva la guerra!*). Rather, she dwells on both the positive and the painful aspects and, once again, chooses to present them from a maternal perspective.

In *Mors tua* Serao does not confine herself to describing the mother–son relationship: she also considers the relationship between mother and daughter. Here her presentation of the mother figure develops more than it does elsewhere in the novel. In all the mother–son relationships I have analysed it is the circumstance of war, together with male patriotism, that causes the mother pain. In the case of the mother–daughter relationship, although war ostensibly causes its breakdown the issues are more complex. Serao here describes a basic difference and incompatibility between mother and child which ultimately breaks the mother's heart.

From the beginning of the text Carolina Leoni's worry is that her daughter Loreta will follow her beloved Carletto to the front, leaving her behind. It is also clear from the beginning that the mother has the role of subordinate in this relationship: she is afraid to argue or remonstrate with her daughter. She makes a subtle attempt to prepare Loreta to find consolation for her fiancé's departure in her religion, offering her medals, "con atto gentile, ma quasi timido" (page 47). She is shocked at Loreta's harsh and negative reaction, but stifles her emotions: "Abbassò le tenue palpebre per celare le lacrime, di cui erano velati i suoi occhi amorosi" (page 48). Throughout the text she is also humiliated by her daughter's overtly sexual relationship with her fiancé: "Si levò di scatto, fuggí via [...] confusa e vergognosa" (page 52). Loreta's departure with Carletto leaves her "come una inferma" (page 76). It is the daughter's heterosexual love relationship, as much as the war, that ends this mother–daughter relationship.

Towards the end of the text Carolina reappears after an absence of some two hundred pages. She openly confesses her shame at the dishonourable life her daughter is leading, and now feels that the gap between herself and her child is unbridgeable. The maternal resentment towards Loreta is powerful: "Se fosse morta, pura, casta e intatta come era, l'avrei pianta, ma mi sarei rassegnata al volere di Dio. Ma ella vive, disonorata, nel peccato" (page 270). Moral and ideological conflicts have undone this relationship. One of the most interesting statements relating to motherhood in all Serao's work is to be found here. Carolina blames herself for loving her child too much, and says, "Questo è il destino delle madri folli, come me" (page 271). Indeed, it could well be stated that Serao sees motherhood itself as a condition which induces a sort of madness (and is thus clearly akin to sexual love). It seems, then, that this kind of intense love must always involve sacrifice and pain. The bitterness depicted in Carolina, however—and indeed in Marta Ardore—, indicates a development in Serao's view of the mother character. She here attaches blame to the child, and her sympathy is directed solely towards the mother. For the first time in her fiction, we see ideological and emotional clashes between mother and child leading to a disintegration of the strong relationship which binds them together. Again, the mother is the subject of the narrative, with the child in the position of object.

What Serao analyses in this text is not simply the mother–child relationship but, more significantly, the process of its breakdown. The relationship may end for many different reasons: death, absence, different political/moral convictions; but the effect of its end on the mother is always devastating, because of the undeniable bond that exists between mother and child. *Mors tua* contains Serao's most negative analysis of the role of the mother and its problems. The perspective remains sympathetic, but leaves the reader in no doubt that motherhood is potentially as destructive an experience as Serao also showed romantic heterosexual love to be.

Is there, in Serao's fiction, any alternative for the mother character? Does motherhood have to mean self-immolation on the altar of love for the child? Not always; in fact, in this very text there is one mother who does not allow herself to be sacrificed for her children. This is Mariuccia Pietrangeli, a working-class woman. At the start of the text she is shown in the role of the traditionally "good" wife and mother; by the end the War has changed her so greatly that she has left her family and set up home with another man. Although Serao is interested in this character primarily from the point of view of the love relationship, she is also interested in her as a mother.

Mariuccia is never described as being especially affectionate towards her children, which immediately differentiates her from the other mother figures in the text. Yet Serao is not wholly unsympathetic towards her. Mariuccia's reasons for putting her sick baby in a home are clearly explained (she wanted him to be properly looked after and lacked the financial means to take care of

him). Equally, her reason for seeking work is financial, and it is
through her work that she meets the man with whom she falls in
love. When Serao describes her meeting with Cesare at the end of
the text, she dwells on her reaction to the fate of each of her children.
Interestingly, the keynote of this reaction is bitterness: the mother
has not simply left her family, it is clear that in some sense she felt
unwanted by them. Her response to Bettina, who has taken the
same path as Loreta Leoni, is expressed thus: "'Se fosse stata
angelo, non si perdeva' ribatté, amara, Mariuccia" (page 287). In
relation to the fate of her imprisoned son "è sempre acerba" (page
287). Her sense of being unwanted is most obvious when she
speaks of Bicetta, her youngest daughter: "'Quella non ha piú
bisogno di me. Ha la sua mamma Tuta' conchiude sdegnosamente
Mariuccia" (page 287). It is only in connection with the death of her
baby that she covertly reveals actual pain ("La donna abbassa un
istante gli occhi", page 287), yet pain clearly underlies her relationship with all her children. Circumstances have separated them and
she is shown living with the hurt of this separation, despite her
ability to lead a new life. Mariuccia is not one of Serao's self-
sacrificing characters, and yet clearly pain still attaches to her role
as a mother. This presentation of a mother is far removed from
d'Annunzio's in *Il trionfo della morte*, which Valeria Finucci has
described as a "moving acount of a mother's inexhaustible love
and almost sacred dedication to the family".[22] In *Il trionfo della morte*
d'Annunzio romanticizes and glorifies the mother's self-abnega-
tion, the perspective being that of the son: "Un'onda di tenerezza
impetuosa gli gonfiò il petto [...]. Le impronte della sofferenza
erano [...] indelibili sul caro volto ch'egli aveva veduto tante volte
chinarsi verso di lui, con tanta bontà."[23]

It emerges from her work that Serao's view of motherhood
developed in one sense particularly: by the end of her life she had
come to see it in an almost wholly negative light. In *Mors tua* the
idyllic elements of motherhood which were present in early works
(such as "Silvia"), the mutual love and support of mother and child,
and the mother's pride in the child are eroded. Serao's own
experience of motherhood had clearly increased her negative
perception of the role. The bond between mother and child is still
seen as unbreakable (the mother will always suffer from the loss of
her child), but it is no longer seen, in itself, as a good thing. Most
striking of all is the presentation of the mother attempting to break
this unbreakable bond, either because she is too hurt to bear any

more or because she feels, paradoxically, too far removed from her child.

The tendency towards a negative perception of motherhood which is present in Serao's work from the beginning thus grows at the expense of the positive aspects which she originally saw in the role. Her perception of it at the end of her life is essentially as negative as her perception of women in the love relationship. As her female characters in the love relationship become more assertive in her later writing, however, so too do her mother figures. They are portrayed as unable to avoid the suffering which Serao sees as part of their role, but they are no longer willing to be the passive victims of their children (in the same way as her women in love cease to be the passive victims of their husbands/lovers). It is a sense of the need for self-preservation (as opposed to self-sacrifice) that impels Serao to allow mothers in her last work to stand back and distance themselves from their offspring in a quite deliberate way. Her judgement of mothers who are incapable of doing this is to be found in her portrayal of Antonia Scalese: that way lies madness.

The fact that Serao always presents examples of mothering which may be regarded as "bad" (in *Piccole anime*, for example) as well as those which may be seen as "good" (to use a simplistic and moralistic terminology) provides evidence of her tendency to avoid glorifying the role of the mother, and also of her attempt to avoid stereotyping in her presentation of female characters.[24] Her move towards a female, maternal perspective, in both her fiction and her journalism, indicates the increasing importance for her of rewriting the experience of motherhood, of presenting it from a female point of view. The increasingly negative, if almost empathetic, presentation clearly implies a non-celebratory attitude towards her subject, and thus sharply differentiates her work from that of writers such as d'Annunzio and Verga. Yet the bleakness of this portrayal offers another kind of stereotype: the victim mother, who is revolutionary only insofar as hers is the subject position in the narrative. These mothers are in a sense figures of dire warning.

MADONNA, VIRGIN/MOTHER

In this section I shall consider the important role played by the figure of the Madonna in Serao's work. I shall examine firstly the

didactic writings and then the fiction, in which certain aspects of
the contemplative writings are reflected. In both genres Serao
draws parallels between the figure of the Madonna and that of the
mother in general. She draws attention to the significance of the
Madonna as role model for her female characters, hinting, too, at
her significance for Italian women of that period. Yet she also
indicates that as far as she is concerned this role model is suffused
with negativity.

Despite an open admission of religious doubts,[25] Serao's work
shows that her faith was deeper than she may have realized. Even
when voicing her doubts she placed her question mark over the
dogma, ritual and rules attached to religion rather than over the
essence or spirit of faith itself: "Non intendo dire [...] che io sia
cattolica apostolica romana, come il Fogazzaro [...]. Io non posso
accettare tutti i dogmi" (U. Ojetti, *Alla scoperta dei letterati*, page
240); "La religione non basta piú [...]. L'amore ci unisca, secondo
i dettami di Cristo, che furono dettami d'amore" (page 241). I
therefore find Maryse Jeuland-Meynaud's moral indignation at
Serao's religious writings unjustified. Jeuland-Meynaud implies
that because of her lack of blind faith Serao simply ought not to
have indulged in religious writing: "Dans ces conditions il fallait
avoir la pudeur de se taire [...], exclure de son œuvre des recueils
comme *Preghiere* [...]. C'était là l'imposture majeure et la trahison
non seulement de toute verité mais des lecteurs eux-mêmes auxquels
on s'adressait" (*La Ville de Naples*, page 341). She accuses Serao of
using religion to pacify her readers. My argument, on the contrary,
is that Serao's rejection of dogma enabled her to investigate the
workings of religious symbols, and that this is an integral part of
her complex portrayal of the Madonna.

Serao's religious writings are overtly consolatory but they also
have a second function, and to my mind an equally significant one.
They reveal above all else that part of Serao's unorthodox faith was
the fact that her religion was woman-centred and her deity essentially female. Although in her religious works she undoubtedly
pays homage to the theoretically paramount figures of God and
Jesus Christ, she concentrates far more on the Madonna. It is to
Mary that her contemplative *io* addresses most of her prayers, and
it is to this same figure that she has most of her female characters
address theirs. When she is considering religion in the abstract it is
again the Virgin who is foremost in her mind. She considers the

various faces of the figure of Mary, but the two most important to her are that of the Madonna Addolorata and that of the Virgin Mother. It seems to me that Serao may be attracted to the figure of the Virgin Mother because it is in itself contradictory to our notions of motherhood. As Marina Warner says:

> If on one plane the perfection of Mary is defined as the conquest of the natural laws of childbearing and death, then the prevailing idea of perfection denies the goodness of the created world, and of the human body, and postulates another perfect destiny where such conditions do not obtain. This is dualistic, and the Virgin Mary is a symbol and an instrument of that dualism.[26]

Serao was not the first to make literary use of the Madonna Addolorata: she took her directly from Verga's *I Malavoglia*, where Maruzza, through the tragedies in her life, is gradually associated with this Madonna figure and eventually represents suffering motherhood: "D'allora in poi fu presa da una gran devozione per l'Addolorata […]; si sentiva fitte nel cuore tutte quelle spade d'argento che ci aveva la madonna. Ogni sera le donnicciuole […] la vedevano […] accasciata sui ginocchi, e la chiamavano anche lei la madre addolorata" (page 124). What is new about Serao's use of this figure is the central position it occupies in her work. Whereas Verga used it once and did not allow it to infiltrate his other works, Serao uses it repeatedly and develops its significance. Ultimately, there is a fusion in her work between this figure and that of the Virgin Mother. Warner suggests that "under her aspect of Mater Dolorosa, Mary most resembles the fertility goddesses of antiquity" (page 221) in that the son is sacrificed, while she remains the principle of the abiding earth. This further complicates Serao's use of the Madonna Addolorata alongside the Virgin Mother.

Two of Serao's works in which the Virgin Mother is central are separated by nineteen years, indicating that the figure did not lose its significance for her. They are *La Madonna e i santi* (1902) and *Preghiere* (1921),[27] both somewhat didactic and contemplative in tone. The earlier text is as much an analysis of traditional religious, semi-superstitious customs in Italy as it is a moral pamphlet, and it gives an insight into how Serao herself saw Mary the Virgin Mother. The overwhelming impression left by the text is not that of a remote being but of a maternal, martyred, ambivalent figure, reminiscent of many of Serao's fictional creations. No less importantly, Serao does not see the appeal of this figure as something personal to her. She assumes that Mary is important to all women and sees her as a focal point for the female characters she sketches in this text.

In the preface to her later *Preghiere* Serao continues to elaborate on Mary's importance as a maternal figure: "Tutti gli appellativi della verginità di Maria [...] cedono innanzi al suo miglior nome, quello di Madre di Gesú" (page ix). In this text too, then, Mary reflects maternity. Again she is presented, through constant, forceful references to her, as a role model for women in general. Again the central significance of the figure for those who are mothers is stressed: "Maria, madre di Gesú [...] è, per chi è madre, il piú limpido fra gli specchi dell'anima" (page x). It must be to Mary, then, rather than to any other image of religion that the mother in Serao's fiction naturally turns.

Preghiere may be seen as a series of short stories told in first-person narrative, in the form of prayers. In the introductory prayer Serao refers to "Maria madre del Divino Amore!" (page 22), thus announcing that her preoccupation throughout the text will be with her subject's maternal role. In the same prayer she identifies Mary as the source of the figure of the female martyr in her work. This is relevant not only in relation to the suffering of her maternal characters: it may also be linked to her portrayal of the love relationship and to female suffering on a broader scale. Serao considers precisely what significance Mary might have for her female characters. Her subject has thus changed slightly; Mary is no longer a figure of isolation, rather her function as role-model for other women is under consideration. Serao's acknowledgement that this figure has special importance to women is interesting: presumably, her attraction resides precisely in her femininity. Christianity proffers no comparable female role-model for women. On the one hand, Mary is a particularly positive role-model/image for Roman Catholic women—adored, beautiful, powerful and benevolent—; on the other, she is destined to suffer and to obey. She is the image of the conventional feminine and thus restrictive and frustrating. These aspects of Mary are recognized by Marina Warner:

> The Virgin Mary, a polyvalent figure who appears under many guises, is the Church's female paragon, and the ideal of the feminine personified. But, in the Church's attitudes to women,

the oscillation between regarding them as equal in God's eyes
[...] and yet subject and inferior to the male in the order of
creation and society [...] has never ceased, and provides continual background interference to any discussion of the Virgin,
the model of the sex, who accurately reflects this perennial
ambivalence. (page xxiv)

Serao also considers the traditional Roman Catholic view of
Mary as redemptress, the antidote to Eve: "È la rivendicazione di
Eva, è la eletta che schiaccia la testa di quello stesso serpente, che
tentò la prima genitrice" (page 66). It is interesting that she chooses
to use the word "rivendicazione", thus stressing the closeness and
duality between these two female figures, rather than difference
and opposition. She sees Mary as Eve's double rather than her
opposite. This is therefore a more unorthodox view than the reader
might at first think: what interests Serao here is the possible bond
between two different images of maternity. The Eve/Mary dichotomy has of course conditioned literary portrayals of women
throughout the centuries, as I mentioned in the previous chapter.
Generally, this has involved presenting Eve and Mary as polar
opposites, but, paradoxically, Serao is interested in the continuity
between them, as similar images of femininity. Mary, in Serao's
text, vindicates Eve and is important precisely because of the
revenge she takes on the figure of the serpent, here the ultimate
tempter. In a sense Serao subverts the Biblical text as she is
interested in these figures not from the perspective of humankind
(in which Mary redeems us and simply corresponds to Eve as
Christ does to Adam) but for the dynamics of the interaction she
constructs for them as dualistic images of the feminine.

In one of the more interesting prayers, the "Preghiera di una
fanciulla innamorata", the Virgin is addressed in her maternal role.
The girl regards Mary as a maternal protector: "Io vi chieggo di
proteggermi maternamente [...], di difendermi contro qualche
periglio oscuro che mi minaccia" (page 54). This "periglio oscuro"
is caused by a man, and it is interesting that Serao has the girl turn
away from him towards a feminine maternal power. The conflict
between the man (representative of heterosexual bonding) and the
mother figure exists on an emotional level. The move towards
heterosexual love seems to threaten—certainly to contrast sharply
with—the mother–daughter bond. Paradoxically, however, the
heterosexual coupling is the way towards a personal creation of the

mother–child bond for the female character in becoming the mother.
This is an outcome both desired and feared. (I discuss this point
later in the present chapter and again in Chapters 4 and 5.) Such a
convoluted plot structure mirrors the findings of Nancy Chodorow
in relation to the mother–daughter relationship: Chodorow (*The
Reproduction of Mothering*, page 140) identifies a conflict between
the heterosexual relationship and the mother–daughter bond. Both
Helene Deutsch and Chodorow conclude that "women experience
heterosexual relationships in a triangular context"—that is, a context in which the woman's relationship with her mother is ever
present.[28]

One prayer in this collection is addressed to the figure of the
Madonna Addolorata. The reader might expect it to be that of a
suffering mother (certainly Serao's Madonna Addolorata is often
used in connection with textual mothers), but in fact it is that of a
prostitute in despair at the life she is living—again, Serao's understanding of such a broad spectrum of female characters differentiates her from male writers. Although the prostitute relates to
Mary primarily as maternal ("Madre dei Dolori", page 78; "Madre
mia cara", page 79), the writer intentionally turns Verga's symbol
upside-down by relating it not to the Maruzza-type figure but to
the character recalling Verga's banished Lia. The language used
here is strongly reminiscent of the passage from Verga quoted
above: "Madonna Addolorata, Voi portate nel santo cuor Vostro,
sette spade che lo trafiggono e io tutte sette me le sento nel cuore,
e le mie ferite sanguinano" (page 77)—though of course the image
ultimately derives from the liturgy. Serao's interest in the figure of
the prostitute and in her relationship with religion was something
on which she concentrated increasingly with the passing of time.
Her sympathetic way of looking at such characters divorced her
from male authors and linked her with such female writers as Mrs
Gaskell.

Not surprisingly, all the *preghiere-novelle* indicate, and indeed
emphasize, difficulties and problems encountered by the characters in even approximating to the Virgin's role. Serao presents
Mary as a wonderful ideal, separated by an abyss from those who
would emulate her. This is the crux of the text: on the one hand,
Serao acknowledges the admirable strength of the figure while, on
the other, uncovering the dismal "realities" faced by her characters
and, presumably, by their flesh-and-blood equivalents.

La Madonna e i santi and *Preghiere* show why Serao portrays the figure of Mary as she does in her novels. Through these works we may see that for Serao Mary is a model of femininity: the loving mother, beautiful and caring, with a darker side of suffering and martyrdom. We also understand why Mary is a central and significant figure for Serao's fictional female characters: as the only relatively positive exemplar of womanhood in the Christian, and especially Roman Catholic, tradition she must be a role-model to some degree. This encourages an analysis of some significant examples of the role of Mary in Serao's fiction proper.

Just as in the *Preghiere* sketches Serao tends to fuse the role of natural mother with that of spiritual mother, so too she tends to merge the two roles when portraying the mother figure in her novels. This happens mainly because of the author's idealized view of her own mother, as we have already seen it in "Terno secco". It is hardly surprising that she gives her female characters the same view of their mothers; yet the mother figures are generally placed safely beyond the reach of criticism, enshrined in death.

This tendency does not appear in Serao's later works, where, as I stressed earlier in this chapter, she was more interested in portraying mothers as strong individuals taking control of their relationships with their offspring; it is most evident in her earlier fiction. There she seems to find it difficult to portray mother figures realistically. They are either cruel and bad, as in *Piccole anime*—and she chose not to (was perhaps afraid to) examine this character-type in detail at that stage—, or they were good... and are dead. Serao's early novels, as we shall see in both this chapter and Chapter 5, prefigure women's novels of the twentieth century in that, like later novels defined in Judith Kegan Gardiner's words ("A Wake for Mother", page 146), they "trace the coming to adulthood, that is, to individual identity, of a daughter who must define herself in terms of her mother". Yet for these early Serao characters co-existence with the mother is impossible; as a general rule in these novels only a dead mother can be idolized. (The novels also tell of the—doomed—struggle of the adolescent female character who tries to avoid becoming a mother.) Dead mothers, like the Madonna, function as desirable ideals—the imitation of which nonetheless leads to suffering and ultimately self-annihilation.

The first of these portrayals occurs in *Cuore infermo* (1881),[29] which Serao dedicated to her own mother, underlining the importance of the experience of maternity in the text as a whole (see below, "The Maternal 'Negative'"). Here Beatrice is profoundly affected by the figure of her dead mother: she has inherited her weak heart and, although determined to be different from her predecessor, falls prey to the same illness. At first she is almost indifferent to religion (as she appears to be to the memory of her mother). There is certainly no passion in her praying: "Diceva le sue orazioni non molto lunghe [...] e si addormentava del suo sonno felice e leggiero" (page 148). But her attitudes to religion and to her mother (both poses of deliberate detachment) are destined to undergo radical, simultaneous changes. When she finally realizes that she cares for her husband, while he appears to care for someone else, she rushes to her bedroom, adopts a position of prayer and prays fervently, not to the Madonna but to the figure of her mother, which now coincides with that of the Virgin: "Ella andò a cadere presso il letto, sul tappeto [...] alzando verso il ritratto di Luisa Revertera le sue mani [...] e gridando con la voce del fanciullo disperato: 'Mamma mia, Mamma mia'" (page 195). The figure of the mother here has all its symbolic significance, and Beatrice is at last compelled to admit its importance. In the first place, the mother acts as a role-model for the (reluctant) daughter, and secondly she becomes the most powerful female figure in the text, as idol and source of strength, fused with the figure of the spiritual mother/Madonna. Ultimately Beatrice, in becoming (like) her mother, is destroyed. Again it is at a moment of crisis in heterosexual love that the bond with the mother is brought sharply into focus: Beatrice's relationships are clearly situated in the triangular context mentioned earlier.

The mother figure is equally powerful in *Addio, amore!* (1890).[30] From the beginning Anna Acquaviva sees the figure of the Madonna as her source of strength and help. A mere two pages into the text, during a depiction of her rather childish encounter with her first love, Anna calls on this figure for help: "'Madonna mia, Madonna mia' diceva fra sé, angosciata" (page 17). While she is ill, following her first betrayal, a portrait of the Madonna Addolorata hangs in her room and, picked out by the lamplight, acts as the room's focal point. Later, while in love with Cesare Dias, Anna turns for help once again to the figure of Mary: "Ogni tanto, fra sé, mentre aspettava Cesare Dias, andava dicendo, monotonamente: 'La Madonna mi deve aiutare'" (page 112). She prays before an image of the Virgin, but also before that of her dead mother. Serao's language indicates that the relationship between mother and daugh-

ter is in some way mystical: "A Sorrento [...] Laura e Anna
Acquaviva celebravano la religione delle memorie materne [...]
con un persistente rimpianto della loro giovinezza senza i baci
della madre, rammentando la cara figura e adorandola nella imma-
ginazione" (page 143)—the mystical quality attaching to the mother
figure is conveyed by the words "religione" and "adorando". Both
girls habitually pray before an image of the Madonna in their
mother's church, but for Anna the mother's role takes on a more
overt symbolism: she is obsessed by the need to go to her mother's
house, and as soon as she arrives "si era subito buttata sull'inginoc-
chiatoio di legno scolpito [...] e innanzi alla Madonna della Seggio-
la, innanzi alla piccola e gentile miniatura di sua madre [...] aveva
abbassato il capo sulle mani guantate" (page 131). The fusion of
mother and Madonna appears to have taken place for her. Serao
analyses the powerful place occupied by these two female figures
more closely here than in the earlier text:

> "Madonna mia, mamma mia." Ella balbettava in sé stessa, i due
> nomi, egualmente dolci [...]. La Vergine nel cielo e lo spirito della
> madre, nelle celestiali sfere [...] si confondevano nella sua mente
> [...]; si levò e baciò, con le fredde, aride labbra, la immagine della
> Madonna e la delicata miniatura di sua madre, salutandole quasi
> fossero persone vive, promettendo loro di ritornare subito a viver
> con loro, in quella stanza che era il tempio della gioventú,
> dell'amore, della morte. (page 152)

It is clear that at all stages Anna sees these two figures as the
focal point of her life. It is also evident that the mother who died
young is here, as in the earlier text, a role-model for the unfortunate
daughter. During her final quarrel with Cesare (another time of
crisis in the heterosexual relationship), Anna again invokes, alternately, both her mother and the Virgin: "'Ti giuro sulla memoria di
mia madre' gridò ella, 'che niente è piú importante!'" (page 272);
"'Oh Madonna mia!' ella disse, sottovoce, vacillando" (page 275).
Although Anna seems to move away from both these figures
immediately before her suicide, their importance in her story as a
whole is clearly conveyed. Anna, however, like Beatrice, can find
no real solace in them at the time of greatest crisis, because they are
not "persone vive"; but their power is no less real. In fact it could
be argued that in death Anna, too, joins with/becomes her mother,
thus destroying herself in the ultimate imitation. Marianne Hirsch
(*The Mother/Daughter Plot*, page 34) suggests that in the nineteenth

century "women writers' attempts to imagine lives for their heroines which will be different from their mothers' make it imperative
that mothers be silent or absent in their texts, that they remain in the
prehistory of plot, fixed both as objects of desire and as examples
not to be emulated." This is true of Serao's earlier novels, but she
departs from Hirsch's pattern in that, even in her early works, for
her protagonists imitation/emulation of the mother on some level
is unavoidable.

Serao describes a similar situation in *Il paese di Cuccagna*, which
I have already touched on in my discussion of the character Bianca
Maria Cavalcanti. Earlier I dealt with the importance of the (absent)
mother figure in relation to Bianca Maria; here I shall outline the
inevitable parallel between the figure of the mother and that of the
Madonna. The first time Serao introduces the reader to Bianca she
is described in an attitude of prayer. Again the figure of the
Madonna—specifically the Madonna Addolorata—is the focus of
the character's attention. In the first paragraph describing the
character and her surroundings, Bianca's name occurs twice while
that of the Virgin occurs three times. Throughout this scene in the
chapel the figure of the Madonna continues to dwarf that of Bianca,
and it is stressed that the Virgin is the focal point of the chapel as
far as Bianca is concerned: "Guardando fra le dita la faccia dolorosa
della Madonna, parea che continuasse a meditare, a pregare, come
se nulla la potesse strappare a una infinita preghiera" (page 163).
As in the earlier texts, Serao uses light to pinpoint the Virgin's
centrality: "Quella sera, stranamente, ardeva una sola lampada,
innanzi alla Vergine" (page 164). Later in the same chapter it is
stated that Bianca's preferred prayer is the Rosary (the prayer most
closely associated with Mary) and that this is the prayer from
which she succeeds in deriving comfort: "Cosí, fra la mistica
attenzione della preghiera e la emozione naturale che le suscitava-
no quelle consuete ma sempre poetiche orazioni [...] la fanciulla
dimenticava per un poco il grande dramma paterno" (page 175).
When Bianca falls ill it seems natural that Serao should show her
turning to Mary for relief: "Ella [...] guardò disperatamente la
Madonna" (page 277).

In most of the crises Bianca faces her inspiration is not the figure
of her dead mother but that of the Madonna. It is not until she enters
the love relationship that she begins, as I showed earlier, to see
parallels between her own life and her mother's. Again the context
is triangular. Interestingly, whereas in Serao's work the figure of

the Madonna is generally shown teaching female characters to be resigned and to accept a life of martyrdom, for Bianca Maria the figure of her mother has that function. Bianca refuses to marry Amati, as her father wishes her to, and one of her reasons for this is: "Mia madre mi maledirebbe dal cielo" (page 428). Gradually Serao shows how the more this character suffers the more significance her mother acquires. Bianca calls on her mother at the hour of her death (when, as a Roman Catholic, she should call on the Virgin, according to her beloved Rosary prayer), and also throughout the agony preceding her death: "Nelle lugubri convulsioni [...] ella aveva lungamente delirato, lungamente gridato, chiamando sua madre, mamma, mamma, come il fanciullo in pericolo" (page 510). It is also significant that Bianca, like Beatrice, fights hard not to become her mother—she does not want to die. Once she is dead, however, Serao again links the mother with the Virgin, restoring the latter to prominence. Bianca, having repeatedly called on her mother, is depicted lying with a peaceful expression: "Con le ceree mani dalle dita livide, congiunte per mezzo di un rosario" (page 529). She is seen in death, as in life, with the figure of the Madonna at the centre of her being.

The experience Serao describes in all these texts is a peculiarly female one. Without exception, the female characters most devoted to the Virgin Mother are those who lack the all-important maternal figure in their lives. There can be no substitute: fathers are incapable of successfully occupying this uniquely female position. Hence Serao shows how for these female characters the mother becomes someone to adore, someone awesomely spiritual in her greatness and other-worldliness. It is little wonder, then, that she presents the absent mother figure as allied to the uniquely spiritual being whom such characters, through prayer, would have referred to as their mother from babyhood: the Madonna. More than anything else, Serao's use of the Virgin Mother symbol reveals her view of how important it is that women should have some kind of female role-model. The male figure is both inappropriate and inadequate. The tragedy of Serao's view (and thus the tragedy of her female characters) is that the Madonna is inevitably seen in her Addolorata guise and the mother, being dead, is also an image of sorrow and suffering.

Serao's conflation of the two figures of mother and Virgin Mother deliberately offers them as role-models while simultaneously and systematically deconstructing this function. Both images make impossible demands and both are ambivalent: socially sanctioned and admirable in their other-centredness, yet terrifying because of the negation of self implied in that other-centredness. The adolescent, Serao implies, must find her self but dreads the possible discovery that her self is her mother. As Ellen Moers says of mothers in the works of Willa Cather, Gertrude Stein, Virginia Woolf and Colette, "these mother figures are dangerously seductive" (*Literary Women*, page 236). Becoming one's/a mother is a dangerous but, Serao implies, inevitable undertaking. Chodorow would not, I think, be surprised at this covert drama being played out in much of Serao's work, for she claims that mothers experience their daughters "as an extension or double" (*The Reproduction of Mothering*, page 109). It takes mature and perhaps strong characters in Serao's fictional universe fully to face up to the role of mother/mothering. Even for them it is a painful role, but some control is possible, Serao suggests as she herself becomes more mature.

THE MATERNAL "NEGATIVE"

Many of Serao's female characters, even when married, are childless. The reasons for this, I think, are complex. One of the most interesting aspects of such a presentation of the female character is that it occurs mainly in Serao's early work, that is, at a time when she was concentrating rather more on portraying women in love (see Chapter 1) than on the mother figure; there are far fewer childless women in Serao's later work. In her earlier work, then, Serao reflects in part Hirsch's proposal (page 14) that "the nineteenth-century heroine, determined to shape a different plot for herself, tends not only to be separated from the figure and the story of her mother, but herself tries to avoid maternity at all costs." Yet it is not simply a question of Serao's perspective changing over the years:[31] she also appears to consider the subject from a class-related point of view. In general it is her aristocratic female characters who are married and childless (though this does not mean they are indifferent to the prospect of motherhood).

Why should this be so? Apart from anything else, such a presentation of childlessness in the upper classes and motherhood in the lower classes is realistic: in Serao's time contraception was far more easily available to the wealthy upper classes than to impoverished working people.[32] Serao is clearly aware of this, and discusses it openly in *Parla una donna* (pages 133–34). Since she found the conscious rejection of motherhood unpalatable, however, at that stage she chose to distance it by regarding it as a primarily non-Italian phenomenon: in *Parla una donna* she discusses female sterilization in France. She begins by considering the motives of women who take this step, making it clear that she is focusing on the upper classes, "le dame francesi". The main reason she can see for sterilization is to preserve a feminine appearance: these women, "per conservare intatta la loro perfezione estetica, rinunziavano spontaneamente alla maternità". Apparently she is not insensitive to this reasoning, seeing such women as incarnations of "le prime cose belle della vita, la grazia, la seduzione, l'amore". The motivation she attributes to these women accords precisely with the type of character she delineates in her early fiction, where her characters sacrifice the possibility of maternity to preserve the exclusivity of the love relationship.

Even while describing characters in this restricted role, however, Serao often allows them to consider maternity, to be confronted with it in some way, though not necessarily in relation to themselves. Some of her characters are clearly opposed to motherhood while others appear to hanker after it, and a third group display an initially puzzling indifference.

An early example of this variety of views is found in *Cuore infermo*, where Serao presents a group of upper-class women discussing the recent birth of a baby to a mutual friend. Most of the young women are either opposed to motherhood or highly pragmatic about it. Only one of them is positive about the prospect of maternity: "'La contessina deve essere contenta. Un primo figlio dopo un anno di matrimonio, e maschio' sospirò la Fanny [...]. 'Fastidi e null'altro' osservò la Filomarino. 'Per me, almeno per adesso, non amo i bimbi. Mi darebbero noia. Piú tardi, forse.' 'Piú tardi, è vero' approvò la padrona di casa" (page 199). Serao here presents a different reason for these characters' avoidance of motherhood from that outlined in *Parla una donna*: motherhood is not regarded as something which spoils a woman's appearance and femininity but as a nuisance, an irritation, an interference with her normal life. Beatrice, the protagonist, ventures no opinion on the subject. She seems indifferent to the possibility of motherhood, because her whole existence is centred on a man and on passionate sexual love. Later in the text, when Fanny, Beatrice's closest friend, becomes pregnant Beatrice reacts positively to the news, but Serao does not present anything resembling envy in Beatrice's response, which is solely one of gladness at her friend's happiness. That Beatrice's reaction is prompted solely by their mutual affection, rather than by a positive response to the idea of a child in itself, is shown by the language used: "Ed involontariamente, per uno spontaneo moto di affetto, le due amiche si abbracciarono" (page 279).

It becomes clear on several levels of the text that Beatrice's indifference to motherhood is solely a result of her passion for Marcello. When other characters discuss babies she does not even consider the subject but thinks of her husband: in terms of the structure of the text, he takes the place of a baby in her life. Most interesting of all in this connection is the section of the text where Beatrice begins to realize she is falling in love with her husband. Her reactions are strangely similar to those of Silvia, in the story of the same name, when she becomes pregnant. Firstly, Beatrice, like Silvia, desires solitude and peace: "Nella camera sua faceva sempre abbassare le cortine bianche, come un grande ed ermetico sipario, teso fra lei e la vita del mondo esterno" (page 216). Then, like Silvia, she begins to have food fads: "La prendevano certe voglie segrete ed indefinite, di qualche camangiare piccante, nuovo, che le desse una sensazione piú forte" (page 226). Here, then, the experience of passionate love is portrayed in terms akin to those used to describe pregnancy. Beatrice's physical deterioration after the birth of her passionate relationship with her husband is also described in an unusual way. Her attacks of illness are rhythmic and have an unmistakable similarity to childbirth: "Sbalzava da un periodo all'altro, con un sussulto crudele che faceva crescere il suo male" (page 284). Serao even uses the same metaphor for Beatrice's illness as she used to describe Silvia's labour, that of a battle: "Egli la vedeva pallida, stanca dalla sua lotta, con le labbra aride e striate, col volto quasi cinereo, chiuso" (page 286). Beatrice's love for Marcello, then, takes the place of pregnancy and childbirth: yet there is something fruitless about this and the "childbirth" scene must be repeated over and over again, with no tangible result. This is linked with Beatrice's fear of becoming her/a mother. In the end she dies of this repetitive agony.

In *Fantasia*, published two years after *Cuore infermo*, in 1883, Serao depicts a rather similar situation.[33] One of the two protagonists, Caterina, is married to Andrea, whom she loves dearly, though in a manner overtly different from the way in which Beatrice loves Marcello (see Chapter 1). There is, however, less difference in their modes of loving than might at first be supposed. Caterina does have a more passive and subdued way of loving than her predecessor but her attitude towards her husband is essentially the same: he is her child. The text makes no mention of children in relation to Caterina: she does not need them because she fulfils all her maternal impulses in her relationship with her husband.

From the start of the text she treats him as a child and watches over him as a mother would. When he returns from hunting she is on her way to oversee the evening meal "ma ritornò subito, e stette a origliare presso la porta se egli la chiamasse" (page 45). This is the act of a mother with a sleeping child, not that of a wife with an adult husband. She also sees her role as including maternal tasks: "'Non la trovi la cravatta, Andrea? Vengo io?' chiese lei" (page 45). Even the first evening of their married life described in the text reveals that Caterina thinks of her husband in a maternal way. She reads while he sleeps, but the scene is presented in such a way that she is like a mother reading her child a bedtime story: "Quando ebbe finito di leggere, guardò suo marito: dormiva sempre, come un grande fanciullo, bello e buono nella sua forza, nella dolcezza infantile dell'uomo che ama" (page 50).

Further on in the text Caterina's maternal impulses are continually pointed up. Like a devoted mother she is incapable of resting at night if she senses restlessness in her husband-child: "Appena sentiva scricchiolare un po' il letto, Caterina si svegliava e domandava: 'Vuoi qualche cosa?'" (page 201). She views her husband with a favourably prejudiced eye. When he is merely polite she sees his behaviour as extremely virtuous, looking on him as a mother might a spoiled child: "Andrea si sacrificava senza mormorare [...]; non si lasciava piú andare in quelle collere subitanee che la sgomentavano. Andrea arrivava sino all'estrema cortesia di non addormentarsi piú sul seggiolone, nell'ora della digestione" (page 185). She is, in effect, proud that he no longer throws tantrums!

Andrea himself is sometimes portrayed in childlike terms, as where he laments the fact that he cannot get close enough to Lucia, whom he loves: "Quando Caterina si frapponeva, egli avrebbe strillato, pestando i piedi in terra, singhiozzante come un fanciullo a cui la madre toglie un balocco: le convulsioni interne rassomiglia-vano alle terribli nervosità dei bambini cocciuti, che muoiono di un capriccio non soddisfatto" (page 197). Here we see not only Andrea as a child but also that he regards Caterina as a mother figure. This view of Caterina from his standpoint is repeated later: "Oh lui la conosceva Caterina, e misurava tutto l'affetto calmo, profondo, previdente, quasi materno, che era in quella piccola anima" (page 201). Caterina's role as mother of her husband acquires added poignancy towards the end of the novel. When he has left her she is unaware of what is happening and simply thinks, with typical maternal concern for his well-being: "Andrea non viene [...]; ho fatto proprio bene a dirgli di prendere il paletot: queste sere si fanno fredde" (page 240). It is hardly surprising that Caterina never discusses children: she is indifferent to them because she is already, in a sense, a mother. She has a particularly demanding, if beloved, child to contend with; the birth of a real child would disrupt her relationship with her husband, and so cannot be contemplated.[34]

In both *Cuore infermo* and *Fantasia*, then, Serao presents an aristocratic female character who appears indifferent to mother-hood but in fact sublimates her desire for motherhood by mother-ing her husband.

In 1884, the year after *Fantasia* appeared, Serao published a somewhat ironic sketch of the life of a bourgeois woman entitled *La virtú di Checchina*.[35] Although motherhood is not one of its themes, Checchina's reaction to the idea of maternity is briefly touched on in a conversation with her friend Isolina. The scene is strongly reminiscent of some of the descriptions of Beatrice in *Cuore infermo*. Isolina has noticed that Checchina is somehow different from her usual self and comments on this. Checchina explains that she is somewhat unwell and Isolina instantly jumps to a logical conclu-sion, only to have her theory rejected with disdain: "'Da qualche giorno patisco disturbi, non so perché'... 'Sarai gravida forse, Checca mia'. 'Ma che!...'" (page 905). Checchina scornfully rejects the notion that she might be pregnant, and the reader already knows the reason for her ailment: as with Beatrice it is love for a man that has brought on her symptoms. Checchina recalls both Beatrice and Silvia in reacting to the onset of love with ailments that suggest pregnancy: "Provava certi lenti brividi di freddo per la persona, con una pesantezza vincente della testa [...]. Aveva una voglia grande di sdraiarsi in una poltrona [...] affondando i piedi in un tappeto caldo e molle [...]. Una scossa nervosa la fece trasalire [...]; tremava dal freddo" (page 879). To some extent she sees both the main male characters as children. The Marchese, with whom she is falling in love, speaks (it seems to her) with "una esse infantile, molto dolce" (page 873). With Toto, her husband, she has the same problem as Caterina in *Fantasia*: like a child, "egli aveva bisogno di dormire un'oretta, dopo il pranzo" (page 874); and like Caterina she watches him sleep, though without affection: "Si alzò per vedere quello che faceva suo marito. Dormiva, russava sopra un grosso libro, con la bocca socchiusa e storta, la testa china sopra una spalla, il panciotto sbottonato" (page 885). Her relationship with Toto is like that of a mother with a troublesome, petulant, demanding child, while the relationship she would like to have with the Marchese would be one of maternal love. Checchina, then, oddly conforms to Serao's stereotype of the aristocratic married woman, apparently indifferent to motherhood and yet cast in the role of mother figure to the man in her life. She departs from the stereotype, however, in that she resents playing this role for her husband and views him with a pragmatic eye more typical of Serao's bourgeois women.

Most of Serao's lower-class women characters who are married have children (see "Progression and Development" above). Even those lower-class women who are unmarried, however, are de-picted in a maternal light. They often share with her (married) upper-class women a tendency to mother the men they love.

Carmela and Maddalena, the two sisters in *Il paese di Cuccagna*, are perhaps the best examples of this tendency. Quite early in the text Carmela speaks of Raffaele as though she were his mother, discussing the possibility of his conscription with repugnance: "È una infamità del governo, prendersi un bel figlio di mamma" (page 186). It is repeatedly stated that she supports him financially, as a mother might her son. Her pride in Raffaele is most clearly de-scribed as maternal in the episode of the carnival, where Serao also presents Raffaele as a childish figure: "Raffaele le aveva volute, a forza, quaranta lire [...] perché si disperava di far cattiva figura con i compagni" (page 214). Carmela sells various utensils to obtain this money for him and thus allow him to dress up for the carnival. The fact that it is household goods she sells highlights her maternal aspect. The scene culminates with Carmela in the crowd watching Raffaele pass by in uniform: "Ella sopportava l'urto di quel pomeriggio carnevalesco, a cui non prendeva parte, perché era assorta nella buddistica aspettazione dell'amor suo" (page 215)—which prefigures Serao's later sketches of real mothers and sons in *Evviva la guerra!* and *Parla una donna*. Towards the end of the novel, although Carmela knows Raffaele to be unfaithful, her primary emotion is one of maternal protectiveness: "Ella vedeva salire e crescere nell'anima sua un solo desiderio, quello di scendere di lí, di prendere pel braccio Raffaele e di portarselo via, con sé, lontano, dove non lo raggiungessero ne camorristi ne guappi" (page 455).

Serao devotes less space to describing Maddalena's maternal relationship with the same male character; nonetheless the nature of Maddalena's love is clear. Firstly, like Carmela, she too supports Raffaele financially. Secondly, Serao explicitly describes Maddalena's maternal protection of him: "Ella andava accanto a lui, pallida, poiché tutto il rossetto si era dileguato sotto la pioggia, con la camiciuola intrisa di acqua che le si attaccava alle spalle e i capelli che le s'incollavano sulla fronte, andava, abbassando maternamente l'ombrello dalla sua parte" (page 381). This is a typical portrait of maternal self-sacrifice.

In *Il paese di Cuccagna* there is another female character who has a maternal love for her partner, Luisella Fragalà. Here the situation is more complex in that Serao is describing a married bourgeois woman who is already a mother. Initially her love for her husband is not at all maternal. As he becomes increasingly childish and irresponsible, however, in his dedication to gambling and his abdication of family responsibility, she is compelled to become more responsible and maternal in her view of him. Ultimately she has to acknowledge that their relationship can no longer be a partnership, and he too accepts this: "'Prometti che nessuno varrà piú di me, prometti che mi ubbidirai, come a tua madre, quando eri fanciullo?' 'Come a mia madre, obbedirò'" (page 377). In this case, as in that of Annarella, it is the real child who brings solace to the mother while the child-husband is the source of pain and distress.

In this presentation of the dual role of her characters as wife/mother or lover/mother with one object for these contradictory emotions, Serao shows that maternity, in whatever form, is inescapable for them. If they are childless their husbands become their children and thus, in the aristocratic cases, even preclude the need for literal children. Bourgeois and lower-class characters, however, are sometimes compelled by circumstances to have, as it were, two groups of children. This role of mother/lover is not presented in terms of maternal instinct: more often it is a source of frustration and stress and reveals as much about the male characters as the female ones. It is also eloquent in relation to women's social expectations: these characters cannot get away from their nurturing role.

This view of the female character, as I suggested earlier, is far more prevalent in Serao's early work, and as her career progresses it becomes less frequent until it finally disappears. This is because in later life Serao became interested more in motherhood *per se* than in mothering within the love relationship. She became correspondingly less interested in the role of the adult male in the lives of her female characters and more interested in relationships between women and their children, especially their daughters, and how best to portray those relationships.

This chapter has explored the essential elements of Serao's presentation of motherhood. Even her rather romantic early view of this female role is tempered by awareness of a potentially dangerous and sinister element latent in it ("Silvia"). Subsequently all romantic elements gradually disappear from her portrayal of motherhood, to the point where her view of it is overwhelmingly negative (*Mors tua*) because it causes pain, suffering and even madness. In the course of this development there is also a shift in sympathy: from a sympathy divided between mother and child she moves to a wholly woman-oriented (feminist?) position. Marianne Hirsch (*The Mother/Daughter Plot*, page 163) has suggested that even today's "feminist writing and scholarship, continuing in large part to adopt *daughterly* perspectives, can be said to collude with patriarchy in placing mothers into the position of object—thereby keeping mothering outside of representation and maternal discourse a theoretical impossibility". Serao, in her careful positioning of mother as subject, as narrative explicator of the mother-child relationship and often of its breakdown, and in her representation of the mother's increasingly angry, resentful voice, which rejects enclosure in the stereotype of angel or victim, could not be accused of keeping mothering "outside of representation", nor even of wholly objectifying the mother figure.

Equally interesting is Serao's presentation of the Madonna as mother, an image of martyrdom for her female characters and simultaneously an indication of how important the figure of the mother is to the female child, even when that child becomes adult. The Madonna, like the mother, is a dangerously seductive figure. Although madonnas and mothers are both beloved and admirable, to imitate them threatens a loss of individuality and promises only a future of suffering. Most interesting of all, perhaps, is the way in which Serao ultimately presents motherhood as something which no woman can escape. Motherhood is covertly present in her early work, where she ostensibly deals with the love relationship but as something of a camouflage for what is really a maternal relationship. This is not to say that in Serao's view all women have a basic maternal instinct (she often illustrates a complete lack of it, especially in *Piccole anime*). Rather, her characters find themselves experiencing motherhood as a direct result of the positions or attitudes they are obliged to adopt in their relationships with men because of the latters' weakness. Thus in her analysis of motherhood Serao continues to analyse the love relationship, and *vice versa*. The themes are fundamentally connected in a way that the reader might not at first suspect. It is thus the prevalence of motherhood throughout her work that differentiates Serao from male writers, and indeed from many female writers.[36] She felt compelled to examine and re-examine many different aspects of motherhood: as a source of joy, and of pain (both physical and emotional), as an ideological role, and in terms of women's relationships with men. The overall and overwhelming impression created by her writings on motherhood is one of disillusion and disappointment: it is seen as a crippling experience with which only the strong can cope. Like romantic love, it often destroys her characters. Thus, according to Serao, the two prescribed roles for women in her day (lover/wife, mother) both cause personal devastation. She in fact presents a critique of the feminine roles that were socially acceptable in contemporary society, and her negative view of them is clear. It will be interesting to consider next how she presents the then *pro*scribed role for women, that of worker.

NOTES

1   G. Flaubert, *L'Education sentimentale* [1869] (Paris, Flammarion, 1985), p. 51.
2   An interesting analysis of the mother figure in the works of Mastriani and Di Giacomo may be found in M. Jeuland-Meynaud, *La Ville de Naples après*

l'annexion (1860–1915) (Aix–Marseille, Editions de l'Université de Provence, 1973). Jeuland-Meynaud finds that "Mastriani célèbre le culte de la mère comme divinité tutelaire du foyer" (p. 241). His mothers, then, are significant in their location at the centre of the family: they are more important in what they do for others than they are as individuals. Mothers in Di Giacomo, too, have this role. In Jeuland-Meynaud's words, the mother is the "pole d'attraction de la vie familiale" (p. 253).

3   G. Verga, *I Malavoglia* [1881], in his *Opere*, edited by L. Russo (Milan, Ricciardi, 1965), pp. 175–404. It is Maruzza who pleads with 'Ntoni to remain at home, in the restrictive circle of the family, and strives to prevent him from making his way into the outside world. Her death is what liberates him.

4   Freud discussed the threat of castration emanating from the mother: S. Freud, *On Sexuality* (London, Penguin, 1981), p. 381. Nancy Chodorow points out that "for children of both genders, mothers represent repression and a lack of autonomy. A boy associates these issues with his gender identification [...]; a boy must reject dependence [...]; [he] rejects and devalues women and whatever he considers to be feminine": N. Chodorow, *The Reproduction of Mothering: Psychoanalysis and the Sociology of Gender* (Berkeley, University of California Press, 1978), p. 181.

5   Ellen Moers identifies resentment of the mother as a theme specific to the twentieth century. She says: "In our own time there has been no clearer index to the revival of a specifically female impetus to literature than the return of women's fiction to this crucial scene, the maternal deathbed, and of the character of ageing female tyrant": E. Moers, *Literary Women* [1963] (London, The Women's Press, 1978), p. 239.

6   Judith Kegan Gardiner finds this approach in the works produced by English and American women writers between 1927 and 1975. She underlines the importance of mothers there when she states that "the fathers in these fictions are relatively unimportant. They are neither role models for their daughters nor are they primary objects of love, whereas the mothers are both": J. Kegan Gardiner, "A Wake for Mother: The Maternal Deathbed in Women's Fiction", *Feminist Studies*, 4 (1978), 146–65 (p. 159).

7   M. Serao, *Il paese di Cuccagna* [1891], in her *Opere*, edited by P. Pancrazi, 2 vols (Milan, Garzanti, 1944–46), I, 105–529.

8   S. M. Gilbert and S. Gubar, *The Madwoman in the Attic: The Woman Writer and the Nineteenth-century Literary Imagination* [1979] (London, Yale University Press, 1984), p. 504.

9   M. Serao, "Silvia", in her *Dal vero* [1879] (Milan, Baldini and Castoldi, 1905), pp. 285–306 (p. 285).

10   J. Austen, *Persuasion* [1818] (Oxford, Oxford University Press, 1926); S. M. Gilbert and S. Gubar, *The Madwoman in the Attic*, p. 178.

11   M. Hirsch, *The Mother–Daughter Plot: Narrative, Psychoanalysis, Feminism* (Bloomington, Indiana University Press, 1989), p. 133.

12   M. Homans, *Bearing the Word: Language and Female Experience in Nineteenth-century Women's Writing* (London, University of Chicago Press, 1986), pp. 88–89.

13   M. Serao, *Il ventre di Napoli* (Milan, Treves, 1884).

14   It is interesting that where Serao discusses work she deals not, as one might expect, with the work of the men but with that of the women. I shall deal with this in the next chapter.

112   *Chapter 2*

15 M. Serao, "Terno secco" [in her *All'erta, sentinella!* (1889)], in her *Opere*, edited by P. Pancrazi, 2 vols (Milan, Garzanti, 1944–46), I, 991–1024.
16 A. Banti, *Matilde Serao* (Turin, UTET, 1965), p. 14; T. Pinto Wyckoff, *Realism and Romanticism in the Presentation of Female Characters in the Works of Matilde Serao* (unpublished doctoral dissertation, University of Washington, 1983), p. 200.
17 M. Serao, *Evviva la guerra!* (Naples, Perrella, 1912); M. Serao, *Parla una donna* (Milan, Treves, 1916).
18 E. Showalter, *A Literature of Their Own* [1977] (London, Virago, 1982), pp. 15–16.
19 M. Serao, *Mors tua* (Milan, Treves, 1926).
20 C. Brontë, *Jane Eyre* [1847] (London, Norton, 1987).
21 E. Gaskell, *Ruth* [1853] (Oxford, Oxford University Press, 1985); T. Hardy, *Tess of the d'Urbervilles* [1891] (Oxford, Clarendon Press, 1983).
22 V. Finucci, "The Search for the Mother in G. d'Annunzio's *Il piacere*", *Journal of the Association of Teachers of Italian*, 47 (Summer 1986), 4–17 (p. 5).
23 G. d'Annunzio, *Il trionfo della morte* [1894], in his *I romanzi della rosa*, 2 vols (Milan, Mondadori, 1949), I, 651–1049.
24 M. Serao, *Piccole anime* [1883] (Naples, Libreria Economica, 1907).
25 Serao expressed these doubts in an interview with Ugo Ojetti, reproduced in U. Ojetti, *Alla scoperta dei letterati* (Milan, Dumolard, 1895), pp. 236–37.
26 M. Warner, *Alone of All Her Sex: The Myth and the Cult of The Virgin Mary* (London, Picador, 1976), p. 254.
27 M. Serao, *La Madonna e i santi* (Naples, Trani, 1902); M. Serao, *Preghiere* (Milan, Treves, 1921).
28 N. Chodorow, *The Reproduction of Mothering*, p. 193; H. Deutsch, *The Psychology of Women*, 2 vols (New York, Greene and Stratton, 1944), vol. I, where the notion of triangular relationships recurs frequently.
29 M. Serao, *Cuore infermo* [1881] (Florence, Salani, 1914).
30 M. Serao, *Addio, amore!* [1890] (Rome, Edizioni delle Donne, 1977).
31 The idea that Serao's viewpoint changed as she herself aged and moved from being a young, romantically inclined wife to an older woman, concerned mainly with her children, is put forward by T. Pinto Wyckoff, *Realism and Romanticism*, p. 25.
32 M. Livi Bacci, *Donna, fecondità e figli: due secoli di storia demografica italiana* [1977] (Bologna, Il Mulino, 1980). Livi Bacci states: "Durante il diciannovesimo e all'inizio del ventesimo [secolo] [...] le categorie privilegiate apprendevano a controllare in maniera efficiente la loro fecondità" (p. 281).
33 M. Serao, *Fantasia* [1883], in her *Opere*, II, 5–274.
34 As we shall see in Chapter 5, however, another aspect of this relationship is that Caterina too often functions as a child within it while Andrea is the father figure. The family structure that Serao weaves here is highly complex.
35 M. Serao, *La virtù di Checchina* [1884], in her *Opere*, I, 863–908.
36 There is still more to be said, however, about Serao's representation of the mother–daughter relationship. See Chapter 5.

Chapter 3

WORKING WOMEN:
ENTERING NEW TERRITORIES

There are many different ways of analysing the issue of work in general, and women's work in particular. The critic may consider work, for instance, from a Marxist perspective, a Roman Catholic perspective (relevant for Serao, given the prevailing ideology of the period in which she wrote) or a Feminist perspective. There are, of course, potential conflicts inherent in at least the Feminist perspective, with some feminists being distinctively pro-career while others would argue for an acceptance of women's work in the home along with remuneration from the state, which would valorize the role of houseworker (rather than housewife) and mother. The nature, value and place of work are not wholly straightforward in any of these philosophies, however, and if this is borne in mind the ambivalence detectable in Serao's writing is unsurprising and perhaps ultimately positive, in that it does not represent a simplistic approach.[1]

As we shall see, Serao appears to have been partly imbued with the Roman Catholic attitude towards women's work, in which woman's place is (ideally) in the home, caring for and educating her children, while she is in turn supported by a caring husband and father. Yet, as was seen in the Introduction, the Socialist approach to women's work was not very different: in the view of most socialists of Serao's time, good socialist women should stay at home and raise good socialist children. But in any case Serao was no socialist. Nor did she openly align herself with the feminist demands for increased women's rights in the workplace voiced, as we have seen, by Kuliscioff and Anna Maria Mozzoni. Yet beneath her concern with women as workers outside the home lies a deep disquiet at the nature of their working conditions. As we saw in the Introduction, women workers were discriminated against in terms of salary, their employment was restricted to certain "suitable" areas, and middle-class women (teachers or workers in the telegraph office) lost the right to work when they married.

When I refer to work in this chapter I mean work—however badly paid—outside the home/family structure. On the other hand, I do draw attention to Serao's complex and correct view of women's work as (at least) two-dimensional. She is seldom concerned simply with "women at work": she always follows them out of the workplace proper to the other workplace known as home. Her awareness of the dual nature of the woman worker's role embraces all social classes.

Much of my analysis of woman as home-worker/mother is located in the preceding chapter. Here my interest centres both on Serao's writing about women's work as defined above and on the relationship of her fiction to the reality of working women's lives in Italy in the late nineteenth and early twentieth centuries. While wishing to avoid any simplistic correlation of women's lived experience and the manner in which Serao represents it in her fiction, I think it is important to point out that her portrayal of the different experiences of both working-class and middle-class women in the workforce is remarkably accurate.

A large proportion of Serao's fictional characters are women who work. The proliferation of such characters, together with their creator's evident interest in the minute details of their work, is in itself surprising. Women who work are not generally central to the narratives of male writers. Of the writers I have judged to be particularly appropriate as points of comparison in a study of Serao, few depict women as workers in any detail. Balzac, for instance, is not particularly interested in the minutiae of Cousine Bette's work. He chooses to refer to its nature in asides, for example: "Lisbeth travaillait à la terre, quand sa cousine était dorlotée; aussi lui arriva-t-il un jour, trouvant Adeline seule, de vouloir lui arracher le nez."[2] For Balzac, Bette's work and her impoverished status function only as a catalyst for her jealousy and her machinations—and these are the aspects of her character which interest him. She may be "la plus habile ouvrière de la maison Pons" (page 29), but we see her at work only rarely. As Anna Krakowski points out, the only safe place for women in Balzac's writings is in the framework of marriage: "Balzac […] n'hésite pas à dire que la femme représente un danger social qu'il faut supprimer par la réclusion."[3]

Nor is Flaubert particularly interested in women as workers outside the home. Indeed, I tend to agree with Krakowski when she claims that in spite of Emma Bovary "Gustave Flaubert n'a pas beaucoup de temps à consacrer à la femme, ni à ses problèmes particuliers" (page 239).

D'Annunzio, too, reveals no particular interest in women who work. As heroines (insofar as such characters exist at all in d'Annunzio's fiction) working women of the proletariat or the bourgeoisie would be unfitted for the role of fantasy figure/catalyst for the emotional and sexual neuroses of his heroes.

Verga certainly writes about women who work, and he writes about their work in considerable detail. From *Nedda* to *Mastro-don Gesualdo* they proliferate in his fiction, and he views them with sympathy.[4] He registers, too, the inequality of men's and women's work, referring in *Nedda* (without comment) to the fact that in the fields men earn thirty *soldi* a day while women earn only twenty. Even so, he is not interested in the role of the woman worker *per se*, or in the special dilemmas created for women by their work. Male workers, like Padron 'Ntoni, young 'Ntoni and Gesualdo occupy more narrative space than women do.

Zola is perhaps closest in his narrative approach to Serao. Like Verga, he identifies the problems of the workforce in general— inadequate working conditions, poor wages and so on—; and like Verga he is concerned with men's problems as well as those of women. Yet he is rather more concerned than Verga with the specific nature of the exploitation of women. In Krakowski's words, he tries to "dénoncer la situation précaire et injuste de la femme" (page 203). In *La Terre* we have a detailed view of the hard work undertaken by Lise Mouche and Fanny Fouan.[5] Zola, however, evinces no sense of solidarity between women who work, even within a single family. In *Germinal* mother and daughter are at odds.[6] La Maheude turns on Catherine: "Elle l'accable, elle se soulagea [...]; il fallait être la dernière des filles dénaturées [...]; une mère n'oubliait jamais un pareil tour" (page 191). In this respect, as we shall see, his portrayal of women workers contrasts sharply with that of Serao. This type of rancour between women also marks his portrayals of women in domestic service, who frequently hate the bourgeois women they serve, whereas this is another area where Serao overwhelmingly represents solidarity between women. Ultimately, however, Zola differs most from Serao in his view of the consequences of women's work. To borrow Krakowski's words again, he proves in his narratives that "une femme vivant de son travail peut se suffire" (page 218). Serao, on the other hand, shows that women may survive, but stresses the cost of that survival; her characters cannot "se suffire": they are too poorly paid and too badly treated.

Ellen Moers, in her exhaustive study of nineteenth- and twentieth-century women writers, has the following to say about George Eliot:

> Her aim as a novelist was not to argue for a diminishing of the social inhibitions and a widening of the options that affect the lives of ordinary women; instead, like Madame de Staël, George Eliot was always concerned with the superior, large-souled woman whose distinction resides *not in her deeds*, but in her capacity to attract attention and arouse admiration."[7]

Such a presentation of the female character recurs throughout nineteenth-century literature by women. Serao too, as we have seen in earlier chapters, created many such women characters. We shall see here, however, that she also sketched a gallery of female characters whose work-related deeds are central to the narrative: the fact that these characters work affects their roles as lovers, wives and mothers.

Nevertheless, Serao's use of such characters does not imply a revolutionary or feminist view of the role of work in the lives of nineteenth-century women. It is still true of women writers (of this period at least) that, as Patricia Meyer Spacks puts it, "women have not created important fictional heroines, who find gratification through doing something in the world."[8] Serao created important fictional heroines whose lives are not entirely circumscribed by home and family or by their relationships with men, but the fact that they work and are financially independent (indeed often the sole financial support of their families) does not mean their work is a source of gratification.

In fact the key to Serao's manipulation of these characters is her ambivalent attitude towards them and their work. This ambivalence is in turn often centred on her consciousness of class as a force which constructs society and sharply differentiates the experiences of women. In a sense, she makes two kinds of division in her work, one based on gender and the other on social class. She is not particularly interested in men's work, and in this sense her writing is radically revisionist, as she primarily defines work, in her fiction, as something that is done by women. She looks at men's work in only two novels, *La conquista di Roma* (1885) and *Vita e avventure di Riccardo Joanna* (1887).[9] In the first she explores the southerner's attempt to conquer the big city, the story being in part her own, though she distances it by making the hero, Sangiorgio, a politician (and therefore necessarily male). The second novel deals with a closer counterpart to Serao, in that Joanna is a journalist. (If her fictional journalist had been female, attention would have been overtly drawn to her own unusual status as a woman journalist, which was something she constantly tried to avoid.) In both these novels, then, Serao confronts her own dilemmas, as an outsider in the one and as a journalist in the other. Since the dilemmas are highly personal I do not think these novels may be described in exclusive terms as simply novels about men's work.

Regardless of what social class she is dealing with in representing the working lives of women, Serao evinces an understanding of, and sympathy with, the difficulties women face in dovetailing the two main areas of their lives, family and employment. Paradoxically, though, as we shall see, she is also keen to distance herself from the characters she creates.

If gender is the basis of the primary division in Serao's analysis, class is nonetheless extremely significant. Overall, she shows that society exploits its women workers, and, consistently with this view, she frequently laments the fact that women of certain classes are compelled to work. Her representations of working women are founded in reality: exploitation, as we saw in the Introduction, was a constant in the lives of women who worked—the lower classes and unmarried middle-class girls and women—, and Serao represents this exploitation faithfully in her fiction. Yet despite her concern at the exploitation she seems to have been aware that there were certain psychological and personal gains to be had from the world of work. This accounts, I suggest, for the sense of emptiness she creates in the lives of her aristocratic female characters. We might have expected her (and them) to exult in their freedom from the workplace, but she does not: she frequently indicates that they have no outlet for their (sometimes quite considerable) intelligence and talents, and that theirs is another negative state of existence. Women like Serao herself who earn their living with their pens are on the whole strikingly absent from her writing: women writers are represented covertly rather than overtly.[10] Where such characters do exist, or, more accurately, are discussed, they are seen as oddities who are possessed by something greater than themselves and therefore cannot help themselves. As Spacks has pointed out, "relatively few women have asserted themselves unambiguously as shaping artists in the act of writing about themselves" (page 181).

Ambiguity and ambivalence, then, mark Serao's presentation of women as workers. The nature of this ambivalence is most clearly visible when such characters in her fiction and journalistic sketches are considered in the context of their social class. I shall therefore look first at her working-class characters and secondly at her middle-class women who form part of the workforce. Finally, I shall offer an explanation of her conflict-ridden approach to women workers, which I find to be rooted in her view of herself as a woman writer.

WOMEN OF THE PROLETARIAT: VISTAS OF POVERTY

What sort of work was done by women of the working classes in the period before the turn of the century when women's employment was expanding? In the country women did heavy agricultural work while in the cities (such as Serao's Naples) there existed, in the words of Beatrice Pisa, "un vasto esercito femminile di servizio".[11] Women worked as domestic servants and in factories. Factory owners actually preferred to employ women for a variety of reasons: they cost less than men and were more willing to work long hours without complaint (Pisa, page 200). Neapolitan women contributed to the family income "attraverso tutta una serie di attività che le tenevano quanto più possibile lontane dalle spoglie e umide mura domestiche" (page 129). Such are the women characters who populate works like Serao's collection of articles *Il ventre di Napoli* (1884) and her novel *Il paese di Cuccagna* (1891).[12] Many of those characters' occupations reflect the type of work undertaken by real women of their class. Pisa's study speaks of the "grossa quantità di donne che si offrivano come 'serve': lavandaie, squattere, bambinaie, nelle case benestanti cittadine" (page 160), and even Serao's later, Gothic, novels reflect this reality, with their sinister *balie*. In *Il ventre di Napoli* and *Il paese di Cuccagna* Serao portrays many impoverished women as wet-nurses—the reader might find the number improbably high, but Pisa speaks at length of "il lavoro di allattamento, diffusissimo nella sua forma piú povera" (page 190).

Il ventre di Napoli is a series of nine articles written for the Rome newspaper *Capitan Fracassa* and subsequently published in book form. Although the overall tone of the work is journalistic, Serao included various pen-portraits which bear the mark of the novelist. Indeed, many of them were later amplified and converted into fiction in *Il paese di Cuccagna*.

The point of departure for this work was the cholera outbreak which shook Naples in September 1884, claiming many lives, even in its earliest stages, and occasioning a series of debates in local and national newspapers on the condition of Naples.[13] King Umberto visited the city on 7 September, and while he was there Depretis, the Prime Minister, made his famous statement, "Bisogna sventra- re Napoli."[14] This provided Serao with the title of her collection of articles, though it also pays homage to Zola's novel about working-class Paris, *Le Ventre de Paris*.[15] While the terms she uses are second-hand, however, she soon reshapes them to her own highly polemical ends, rejecting both the vocabulary and the intentions of the government: "Sventrare Napoli? Credete che basterà? [...] Vedrete, vedrete [...]; bisogna rifare" (page 9).

Not only does Serao wish Naples to be totally reconstructed, she also proposes to reshape the way in which it is presented in both the literature and the journalism of her contemporaries: in a sense, she herself begins the reconstruction. In the opening article, addressing herself primarily to the government, she alerts her readers to the differences they will find between her style and that of her predecessors and contemporaries: "Non son fatte pel gover- no [...] le descrizioncelle colorite di cronisti con intenzioni lettera- rie [...]. Tutta questa minuta e facile letteratura frammentaria, serve per quella parte del pubblico che non vuole essere seccata con racconti di miserie" (page 2). Her approach will be avowedly more realistic: "Al diavolo la poesia e il dramma!" (page 7). Although these articles were written for a newspaper Serao is very pre-occupied with style. Indeed, the eighth of them, entitled "Il pittore-sco", launches a full-scale attack on literary and artistic depictions of Naples. As so often in this collection, Serao fixes her gaze on the street markets and exclaims with mock lyricism: "Che quadri di colore acceso, vivo, cangiante, che bella e grande festa degli occhi, che descrizione potente e carnosa potrebbero ispirare a uno dei moderni sperimentali, troppo preoccupati dell'ambiente!" (page 72). The homage she may have seemed to pay Zola becomes dubious in the light of a statement about the Pignasecca area: "Qui il romanzo sperimentale potrebbe anche applicare la sua tradizionale sinfonia degli odori, poiché si subiscono musiche inconcepibili: l'olio fritto, il salame rancido, il formaggio forte, il pepe pestato nel mortaio, l'aceto acuto, il baccalà in molle" (page 81). Thus style seems to be of the essence in this work, which, although it was initially intended as journalism, Serao clearly does not divorce from her literary production.

Perhaps the single most striking feature of this work is the fact that Serao chooses to focus almost exclusively on the lives and work of women rather than on those of men. For her it is the lives of women who work that are most indicative of the degradation of their class, the poorest members of society. This is one respect in which her narrative differs sharply from that of Zola. Zola does consider the lives of working women in *Le Ventre de Paris*, but his narrative is framed by the characters of Florent and Claude. First we see Florent, a figure of pity: "Il était lamentable [...], un visage dur et tourmenté" (page 8); Claude, whose anger is directed against two women representatives of the Gras, closes the narrative, "pris de colère à les voir si bien portantes [...] avec leurs grosses gorges" (page 502). Serao's representatives of the Gras, on the other hand, are the male members of the government, whom she criticizes for their inadequate knowledge of the situation in Naples. Her attitude seems to have been fully justified given that law 2892, "la legge per il Risanamento della città", was passed only in January 1885 and that, in the words of Ghirelli, "non si riferisce ad alcun piano specifico di opere"—not to mention the fact that no work took place to clean up the city for a further four years.[16] At the very start of this series of articles Serao signals that her concentration on women is to be part of her recreation of Naples: she points out that the government is unaware of "quante femmine disgraziate, diciamo cosí, vi esistano" (page 2).

She begins her analysis of working women in the second article, "Quello che guadagnano", with an expression of pity for those (especially mothers) who are obliged to work: "E come la miseria incombe, la donna, la moglie, la madre, che ha già molto partorito [...], tutte quelle che dovrebbero lavorare in casa cercano lavoro fuori" (page 17). This pity appears to be based on the fact that in effect such women are compelled to do two jobs. The choice is not between leisure and work, but between work in the home and work outside. Serao also indicates that there are different kinds of work to be found outside the home, some preferable to others: "Fortunate quelle che trovano un posto alla fabbrica del tabacco, che sanno lavorare ed arrivano ad allogarsi, come sarte, come cappellaie, come fioraie" (page 17). These occupations, especially that of tobacco-factory worker, will be analysed in her later fiction, and in *Il paese di Cuccagna* she will show all the distress inherent in even that occupation, described in relatively positive terms in *Il ventre di Napoli*. She claims, however, that most women will end up as servants. She sketches one such character, Annarella (who will later be more fully developed in *Il paese di Cuccagna*): "Faceva tre case al giorno, a cinque lire: alla sera era inebetita, non mangiava, morta dalla fatica, talvolta non si svestiva per addormentarsi subito" (page 18). From this brief sketch of the servant's experience she moves on to catalogue other possible female employment and highlights the generally unhealthy conditions involved: "tutti gli altri mestieri ambulanti femminili [...], mestieri che le espongono a tutte le intemperie, a tutti gli accidenti, a una quantità di malattie, mestieri pesanti o nauseanti" (page 19). All the unpleasant jobs mentioned have one thing in common—they are shockingly badly paid: "Le povere donne, sedute sullo scalino del basso, ne comprano e cenano, cioè pranzano, con questo soldo di pizza" (page 24). These women's lives are determined entirely by financial misery; their only hope of escape is in the *lotto*: "La venditrice di frutta, che sta sotto il sole e sotto la pioggia, giuoca [...]; la moglie del sarto che cuce sulla porta [...], la lavandaia che sta tutto il giorno con le mani nella saponata, la venditrice di castagne che si brucia la faccia [...] al calore del fornello [...], tutte queste donne [...] giuocano fedelmente [...] al lotto" (page 48).

Il ventre di Napoli often departs from its sparse journalistic prose to offer a rhetorical evocation of female friendship and support that reminds the reader of many of Serao's short stories: a semi-romantic female solidarity, if not a solidarity of workers in general, is one of the keynotes of the collection.[17] All the more noticeable, then, is the intermittent breakdown in the carefully constructed solidarity between the author and her characters. Serao seems to be aware of the literary balancing act she is performing here. I suggest that the text's precariousness originates in Serao's consciousness of class, her sense of being in some way detached from the women about whom she writes so sympathetically. Cora Kaplan states, "If texts by women reveal a 'hidden' sympathy between women, as radical feminist critics often assert, they equally express positive femininity through hostile and denigrating representations of women."[18] She suggests that it is difficult if not impossible for middle-class women to write with complete empathy about the experiences of working-class women. Women's writings may well show solidarity based on gender but that solidarity is threatened by the equally important division of class. Serao is rarely hostile towards her female characters but she is occasionally denigrating. Even at a relatively early stage in the text her use of the verbs *insegnare* and *salvare* indicates her privileged, superior stance in relation to her subjects: "Per levare la corruzione materiale e quella morale […], per insegnar loro come si vive […], per dir loro che essi sono fratelli nostri, che noi li amiamo efficacemente, che vogliamo salvarli, non bisogna sventrare Napoli: bisogna in gran parte rifarla" (page 11). Later, when she moves on to physical descriptions of these women, her denigration becomes more overt and her sense of superiority increases: "Sono esseri mostruosi, la pietà è uguale alla ripugnanza che ispirano" (page 18); "Sono brutte […], si trascurano […], fanno schifo, talvolta" (page 19). She seems consciously to struggle against her own perception of these women when she declares, "Non è una gente bestiale […], non è cupa nel vizio" (page 12), or, "Non è dunque una razza di animali che si compiace del suo fango" (page 14). In a later article, however, she makes a precise connection she has earlier denied when she compares "la pettinatura delle donne e la spulciatura del gatti" (page 83). She even suggests that there is a "natural" vice in these women: "Sono naturalmente rissose e brutali: vi dànno a bere l'acqua per forza, litigano ogni minuto fra loro, rubandosi gli avventori" (page 84); she thus allows the solidarity and friendship between her characters, of which there are numerous examples, to break down entirely.

Why this evident ambiguity and why this struggle with sympathy/identification and pity/detachment? Kaplan provides a clue when she states, referring to the writings of Mary Wollstonecraft, Elizabeth Barrett Browning and Virginia Woolf, that "the difference between men and women in the ruling class had to be written so that a slippage into categories reserved for lesser humanities could be averted [...]. These fragmented definitions of female subjectivity [...] were shaped by the ways in which women of the middle and upper classes understood and represented their own being" (page 167). Kaplan claims that the need for middle-class women to differentiate themselves from women of an inferior social class led to a displacement of negative "feminine" attributes onto the latter where they were represented in the fictions of middle-class women. The tension between gender allegiance and class allegiance is certainly evident in both Serao's fiction and her journalism, whether she writes about the sub-proletariat, domestic servants or factory workers.

The overall impact of this text is that of a radical blueprint for social reform, and this makes its class consciousness all the more problematic. *Il ventre di Napoli* is in essence an overtly political document which warns of the potentially dire consequences of a superficial approach to a serious problem. On balance, Serao's sense of gender solidarity outweighs the occasional lapses which threaten to unbalance her thesis. Her almost frantic attempts to negate the politically questionable elements of her own discourse (her sense of social superiority, her attempt to appear more authentically feminine) indicate unease on her part with certain generalizations she makes in relation to working-class women. The sense of conflict and paradox in this work is fascinating.

The same ambivalence may be detected in parts of *Il paese di Cuccagna*, which, as I have suggested, amounts to a fictionalization and expansion of *Il ventre di Napoli*. In *Il paese di Cuccagna* she analyses in some depth three types of women's work, that of servants, factory workers and usurers, and focuses on one representative of each of these groups. She also includes brief sketches of working women in other occupations.

One of the first in-depth portraits of working women in this text is that of Annarella, transferred from *Il ventre di Napoli*. Serao instantly reveals both her sympathy for the character and her sense of distance from her: "Era una donna poverissamamente vestita [...]; faceva pietà e disgusto" (page 123). Annarella's position as a servant is clearly inadequate to feed her family, especially in view of her husband's addiction to the *lotto*: "Mangiamo ogni tanto, cosí, quando porto io un pezzo di pane a casa" (page 125). Serao is interested in Annarella primarily as a mother figure, all of whose energies are devoted to the welfare of her children. Annarella is unfortunate, Serao implies, not so much because she must leave her children to find work as because she cannot find *enough* work to support them: "Non trovo neppur modo di dar pane ai figli" (page 190). Having barely recovered from the birth of her last child she is desperate to find work: "Ora che era svezzata ella avrebbe trovato un altro mezzo servizio, se la Madonna l'aiutava" (page 237). After finding it she soon loses it again, which worsens an already bad situation: "Dei due mezzi servizi che faceva, ella ne aveva perso uno, dieci lire" (page 344). Serao stresses once more through this character how working women are exploited. Workers like her may be disposed of at the whim of the more powerful classes. Resentment at the situation is the reaction which Serao allows her character at first, and the resentment is expressed not by Annarella alone but also by her sister, Carmela (the factory worker): "Quando poi Carmela e Annarella si trovavano insieme per la via [...] era un lungo sfogo di dolori, era un racconto alternato, dove scoppiavano tutte le amarezze fisiche e morali della loro triste esistenza" (page 348). Their pain is seen as equal and equally devastating. Annarella, however, is more pragmatic than her sister and eventually her attitude is marked primarily by resignation. When Carmela induces her to go to a *fattucchiera* she has no faith in the enterprise: "Annarella [...] avendo già curvate le spalle alla fatalità del suo destino, sentendo una sfiducia crescente in qualunque mezzo di salvazione [...] non provava altro, attraverso la sua malinconia che una impressione sempre più distinta di spavento" (page 353).

In terms of the plot her fear proves justified since she is murdered by her husband. As Annis Pratt points out, "When women writers turn to the description of conditions among the proletariat, they deal with the way the relationships between men and women are damaged by economic forces beyond individual control. One of the principal difficulties that their heroes face is victimization at the hands of angry husbands frustrated by economic and social impotence."[19] In *Il paese di Cuccagna* it is onto Annarella's husband that Serao deflects much of her personal hostility towards the working class. Her sense of solidarity with the female character and her awareness of the difficulties women such as Annarella must face in real life account for the displacement of so much authorial hostility onto the working-class male character. An example of this is shown through Annarella's view of Gaetano: "Ella glielo aveva letto, negli occhi inferociti, [...] l'indomabilità di quel vizio; ella lo aveva visto maltrattare i suoi figli, con quella rabbia compressa di chi è capace anche di maggiore brutalità" (page 356). Throughout the novel the reader's perception of Gaetano is filtered through either Annarella's point of view or Carmela's equally negative one. In this text the displacement of authorial hostility onto the brutalized and animalized working-class male character allows Serao to maintain, for the most part, her position of solidarity with her female characters.

Serao locates Carmela in a different kind of working regime, that of the newer, more industrialized society: Carmela in fact works in one of the two tobacco factories which existed in Naples at that time. This permits the writer to inveigh against the conditions which the mainly female workforce was obliged to endure. Carmela is presented from the beginning as a character whose very physical appearance is conditioned by pain and hard work: "il volto pallido e attraente di Carmela, quella seduta sul macigno, volto sfiorito, dai grandi occhi stanchi e addolorati" (page 112). Although unmarried and childless, she has, like her sister, the responsibility of caring for a whole family, whence her addiction to the *lotto*. She says to Annarella: "Tu lo sai che vorrei vedervi tutti contenti [...]; tu lo sai che la vostra croce è la mia croce [...]. Cosí, tutto quello che mi resta di quello che guadagno, lo giuoco. Un giorno o l'altro, il signore mi deve benedire" (page 125). Such hope on Carmela's part is shown to alternate with deep despair, some of which centres specifically on her work: "Oh non bastava che ella lavorasse in quel nauseante mestiere alla fabbrica dei tabacchi, per sette giorni alla settimana. Non bastava che non avesse né un vestito decente, né un paio di scarpe non rotte, tanto che alla fabbrica non la vedevano bene; non valevano né la fatica, né la miseria, né la fame" (page 128). Serao indicates that the working conditions in such factories were dreadful, the hours too long and the pay insufficient; and we have seen in the Introduction that this was indeed the case. This is a fairly damning indictment of the new, technologically more advanced Naples.

The power of the factory owners and their exploitation of their female workforce is further emphasized when Carmela is under still more stress (in that her mother has died and Raffaele no longer wants anything to do with her): "Ella smarriva la testa [...], lavorava cosí distrattamente [...] che la multavano" (page 342). In the Introduction I have already mentioned the fines harshly levied by employers: workers were fined for eating, for not producing enough and for producing work of "inferior" quality.[20] Serao ensures that her reader knows Carmela is not atypical of working-class women working in industry when she describes the group exodus from the factory: "Le povere donne che venivano dalla Fabbrica con le facce pallide dalle esalazioni cattive della foglia e le mani macchiate sino ai polsi, comperavano qualche cosa per portare a casa, per dar da mangiare, dopo la giornata di lavoro, alla loro famiglia" (page 347). Carmela thus symbolizes many women of her class and in her position. The negativity of her existence is fully conveyed when Serao describes the close of her day: "Stanca, abbattuta, senza un centesimo in tasca, dopo la giornata di lavoro, ella tornava a invidiare sua madre che era morta" (page 347). Most striking of all in Serao's portrayal of Carmela is the lack of authorial ambivalence: here all Serao's sympathy and support is given to her character. This is not so surprising as it may at first seem, however, since in Carmela Serao creates an almost archetypal female victim.

In this novel, then, the negative aspects of Serao's ambivalence towards working-class women are deflected firstly onto male characters and secondly onto the social system, and specifically onto the government, against which the text contains much invective. This allows her to express her sense of solidarity with lower-class women more effectively and more comprehensively than was the case with *Il ventre di Napoli*.

In *Napoli* (1906) Serao reprinted her earlier text on Naples and added a further seven articles on the poverty which, as she had predicted, the *sventramento* had failed to eradicate. All these articles are taken from her own newspaper, *Il giorno*, in which she was at comparative liberty fully to express her opinions, without the censorship of her critical husband, Scarfoglio.[21] Her tone here is much angrier than in *Il ventre di Napoli*, and she seems less concerned with the projection of her own image.

The same kind of sketches as we have seen in her earlier journalistic writings abound here too, polished with the careful touches of the writer of fiction. In the newer articles Serao concentrates not specifically on employment but on the mismanagement of Naples by those who are in charge of it. While appealing, however, for better education for working-class Neapolitans (in "Pane dell'anima", 1904), she pauses to consider the kind of work done in Naples; and again it is on the women that she chooses to focus. What concerns her specifically is the arrangements made by these women for the care and education of their children while they are out at work: "Vi è ancora tra il popolo, una istituzione strana e caratteristica; una specie di piccola scuola tenuta da qualche donnetta [...]; altre donnette, operaie, serve, lavandaie, stiratrici, vi portano i loro figlioli e le loro figliuole [...] prima di andare al lavoro e pagano [...] le più facoltose, diciamo cosí, venti soldi" (page 187). Here one may detect again a combination of sympathy for these impoverished women and a sense of detachment (note the diminutive—and diminishing—"donnetta/e"). Serao goes on to stress that from the educational point of view this arrangement is unproductive; she now concentrates, in a manner that is both sympathetic and detached, on the figure of the over-burdened teacher: "La donnetta [...] non insegna nulla a tutte quelle creature: le tiene raccolte un poco: [...] le sgrida, sempre [...]; pianti, strilli, singhiozzi: ma infine, è responsabile, per [...] due centesimi, di ogni bimba, di ogni bimbo, sino alla sera" (page 187). Then Serao injects a very personal note into her account, reminiscing over her own days as a student teacher. She stresses the difference between her ambition ("questa missione di dare il pane dell'anima alle figlie del popolo": page 187) and the reality, which was that she found herself teaching only the children of the bourgeoisie. Her anger is unmistakable as she focuses on one working-class child: "La scuola non era fatta per essa" (page 187). Serao criticizes the educational system and those who manage it for its lack of direction towards the real needs of the poor. Her use of the word "missione" clearly indicates again, though, that she is distancing herself from the working class.

Yet the biting anger and irony she directs at the bourgeoisie in general is openly directed at herself in the very next paragraph, which leads us to assume that she is not wholly unconscious of this distancing process in herself: "Non vi sono scuole, e altre dame della Società Margherita e io con esse [...] organizziamo, conferenze, recite, gite per aiutare ventidue [...] ciechi, a domicilio, comprando loro un pianoforte o un fonografo o una bicicletta! Non vi sono scuole a Napoli, e le maestre muoiono di fame e le ragazze e i ragazzi del popolo vanno al vizio" (page 188). Also evident here is the fact that she seems to privilege the necessity of educating women, always placing them first; and of course it was women whom she saw it as her "missione" to aid and educate.

Serao's anger at herself as in some ways a typical member of her class may well underlie the vitriolic anger she expresses towards the bourgeois members of the Neapolitan *comune*: "Costoro che siedono al municipio di Napoli, sono i nemici di Napoli" (page 203). This anger is expressed throughout the text but particularly in "I nemici di Napoli" (1905). She goes on to lament all Naples's ills (unemployment, lack of education, a rising crime rate and a lack of hygiene) and asks, furnishing her own devastating answer: "Che fanno, dunque costoro? Niente: non sanno far niente: non possono fare niente: non vogliono fare niente" (page 204). She concludes by describing them as "i nullatenenti dell'ingegno [...], i peggiori nemici di Napoli" (page 205). In this text particularly, then, it seems that Serao is acutely conscious of where she stands as a representative of her class and where she stands as a representative of her sex. She sees clearly the conflict between the two and endeavours to foreground her gender allegiance.

The deflection of authorial distaste for working-class characters onto male representatives of that class continues in "Terno secco".[22] In this short story Serao's working-class female character, Tommasina, is almost saint-like. A servant devoted to the woman for whom she works, she scrimps and saves to support the child she is due to have. Her husband Francesco, meanwhile, comes in for virulent criticism from the author: "Fingeva sempre da persona rispettabile autorevole [...] di non occuparsi della miseria familiare: e mentre aveva sempre la mezza lira in saccoccia per offrire un sigaro o un bicchiere a un amico [...] lasciava che sua moglie crepasse di fatica, incinta" (pages 139–40). One could develop the displacement idea by noting that in this recognizably autobiographical story, where the angelic mother is a version of Serao's own mother and the intelligent, mercurial daughter Caterina a version of Serao herself, the only father is this inadequate one, Francesco, who shares his name with Serao's father. Francesco seems to bear the weight not only of Serao's disapproval of the working class but also of her resentment at her own father's inadequacies. The female servant in the bourgeois household, though, remains a figure of empathy.

In these works, both fictional and journalistic, Serao's ambivalence centres on the very nature of working-class women. She feels pity for the dilemmas of her (female) characters of both the proletariat and the sub-proletariat, and anger at those in power, who appear to have no will to improve such women's living conditions. Yet her pity is severely circumscribed by her attempts to construct herself differently from these women. She must, as a middle-class woman, distance herself from them, and she chooses to do so by de-feminizing and sometimes even dehumanizing them, particularly in her earlier works. As her writing on this social class develops, she distances herself from it by representing the victimization of these women at the hands of denatured, brutalized and brutalizing men. These may be writings located in the domain of realism, but the strategies of authorial distancing make them complex versions of lower-class life which may not be defined simply as realist.

WOMEN OF THE MIDDLE CLASS: REALITIES AND FICTIONS

It is unsurprising that Serao reveals ambivalence over the idea that women of the middle class should work. As a working member of the bourgeoisie she was scarcely in a position to castigate others like herself. Yet she must have been aware of the frequent expressions of disapproval in nineteenth-century society towards such women. Certainly her fiction realistically registers several instances of discrimination against middle-class working women. Society's attitude towards working women of this class may explain her uncertainty in handling these characters, and it may also be relevant in a consideration of how relatively few examples of this type of female character occur in her fiction.

How does Serao's representation of middle-class women workers relate to the real experiences of such women in this period? In practice, it is largely restricted to two categories, teachers and telegraph operators. Not coincidentally, I think, Serao herself had belonged to both these categories and so writes in part from personal experience. My concentration here will be on her representation of women telegraph operators in "Telegrafi dello Stato", and on women teachers and student teachers in "Scuola normale femminile".[23]

In "Telegrafi dello Stato" (1885) Serao presents a whole gallery of young female characters. As in the case of most of the lower-class working women she describes, few of them are (at first) shown to enjoy their work. Another common factor of their existence is that they too are exploited. Both these facts are communicated through Serao's presentation of the character Maria Vitale, one of those on whom she dwells in some detail. Discussing her work with a friend, Maria says: "Il lavoro mi è piaciuto sempre anche per portare a casa quei quattrini, per sollevare papà, che ha l'asma, dalla soverchia fatica; per confortare mammà che ha perso la salute coi figli, ma questa è una vita troppo dura. [...] Se cadiamo ammalate e manchiamo all'ufficio, ci trattengono le giornate alla fine del mese [...]; questa è la schiavitú" (page 929).

It is not the work that Maria complains of but the exploitation attached to it. Of course she and the other female employees are exploited not because of their class but because of their sex: they receive less money than their male counterparts and are more closely supervised, Serao says, because they are not trusted to work well on their own.

The general tone of the office when work is about to begin is rendered as follows: "Si vedevano le faccie assonnate di quelle che avevano troppo poco dormito, le faccie smorte di quelle colpite dal freddo, le faccie scialbe di quelle malaticcie; e da tutte si diffondeva un senso di pacata rassegnazione, di noia indifferente, di apatia quasi serena" (page 921). Some of the young women are described as whiling away the time until marriage, like the rich Adelina Markò, "una delle due o tre felici signorine, che lavoravano solo per farsi i vestiti, per comperare la biancheria del corredo" (page 916). The difference between her status and that of her co-workers is that the latter must work in order to support themselves, until an appropriate marriage comes along. Serao, however, in the course of the narrative, reveals one of the reasons why all her characters will cease to work when they marry. The story of the female assistant manager is used to indicate both the limitations placed on women workers and the ambition of most of the telegraphists as they speculate about which of them might be promoted. Rumour has it that the assistant manager is to marry the male manager (who is, of course, the superior of the female manager in charge of the women's section). This prompts gossip: "La discussione era: la vice-direttrice può conservare il suo posto, maritandosi? Le ausiliarie, secondo il regolamento, non potevano; ma il regolamento si estendeva alla direttrice e alla vice-direttrice?" (page 935). In fact, as Serao reveals, the rule applied to all women workers at that time.

It is scarcely surprising, then, that most of her female characters in this short story see work in terms of a stage in their lives which will end when they marry.

One of them, however, does not. This is the female character who occupies the most senior position, the *direttrice*. Serao highlights her perennial single status from her first appearance in the text: "Tutto il volto aveva la grassezza molle, il pallore di avorio delle zitelle trentenni" (page 919). The *direttrice* takes the responsibility of her work very seriously, but Serao's representation of her speech gives the impression that she could be a teacher addressing a class of unruly schoolgirls rather than a manager addressing her subordinates. Her frame of reference is essentially moralistic: "Signorine ho creduto sempre di esser qui a dirigere un ufficio di fanciulle serie, di impiegate solerti, che dimentichino in questo luogo, la storditaggine e l'imprudenza giovanile. Vedo di essermi ingannata [...]; se non mettete giudizio, le cose andranno male [...]. Siamo intese per un'altra volta" (page 924). Serao explains this character's attitude by stressing her sense of inferiority. She, like her subordinates, is aware of being mistrusted: "Tremava continuamente che la sua sezione sfigurasse innanzi ai superiori" (page 925). Clearly, where their work is concerned all these women feel as though they are on trial.[24] Even the rather serious and saintly *direttrice*, however, is not immune to resentment at exploitation, especially when working on Christmas Day: "Scriveva una lettera a una sua compagna [...]; pure la lettera era malinconica [...]. Levava la testa e guardava tutte quelle ragazze immobili [...], e non le sgridava piú [...]; le nasceva in cuore una pietà profonda di loro, di sé medesima" (page 927). This combination of resentment and self-pity leads to a sense of solidarity with her subordinates: again, gender allegiance is shown to overcome social restrictions.

Eventually Serao introduces a note of drama into the descriptive narrative. An election is about to take place, and over the weekend the volume of telegraph messages is expected to increase enormously. The management of the telegraph office therefore suggests to the female staff that they sign up for extra hours—"che tutte quelle che volessero dare una prova di amore al lavoro, si firmassero [...], che si lasciava, per questo, intera libertà, non volendo obbligare nessuno" (page 938). The use of the word "amore" here is to be of considerable significance. In the first place, Serao uses this event to reiterate more clearly the conditions under which these women worked, and to inform the reader of their awareness of their exploitation and resentment at it. Hence the characters' first reaction is wholly negative:

> Il fermento di ribellione nacque subito [...]. No, non volevano prestar servizio straordinario [...]. Perché, per chi? Le trattavano come tante bestie da soma, con quei tre miserabili franchi al giorno, scemati dalle tasse, dalle multe [...], e invece, esse avevano quasi tutte il diploma di grado superiore e al telefono prestavano servizio come uomini [...] che avevano duecento lire il mese. [...] Non avevano da aspettar pensione [...]; se avevano la disgrazia di restar telegrafiste sino a quarant' anni, il governo le metteva sulla strada [...] consumate nella salute e senza un soldo. (page 939)

Here Serao again mentions aspects of the discrimination which faced even the most qualified of women workers: low pay and no prospects. Yet, curiously, she then goes on to relate (without any explanation of this twist) that all the workers agree to work the extra hours requested. The scenes she now describes reveal the workers at their best, busiest and most committed: "Le ausiliarie erano tutte svelte, tutte intelligenti, quel giorno: quell' ambiente, quell' eccitamento avevano sviluppato in loro qualità nuovissime. Si soccorrevano [...]. Alle otto di sera [...] le ausiliarie [...], senza aver fatto colazione, senza aver pranzato, seguitavano a trasmettere" (page 944). The women do in fact give "proof of their love", sacrificing themselves without pay. While choosing not to examine why, Serao implies that out of this loving self-sacrifice comes good for all concerned. We see here her acceptance, and even valorization, of certain "feminine" traits. Problematically, in spite of Serao's awareness of the exploitation involved in this work, she suggests that in great sacrifice is to be found great joy. She once again presents stereotypical feminine victims who on some level find joy in their victimization. Thus ambivalence again rears its head, and it is only partly offset by the concomitant claim that through work the women succeed in experiencing a sense of unity with others and become conscious of themselves as a social group, clearly divided from others of the same social class by virtue of their sex; nor is it eliminated by Serao's insistence that the women's most positive and supportive relationships are formed in their working environment, in sharp contrast with their often negative and demanding family and romantic ties outside the world of work.

Between 1881 and 1901 the proportion of teachers in Italy who were women increased from 55% to 68%.[25] This was no doubt partly due to teaching's relative social acceptability as an occupation for middle-class women. If educated women of the bourgeoisie were waiting to be married, or were unfortunate enough to be unable to marry and therefore had to support themselves, according to conventional wisdom teaching was by far the most respectable option, believed to be, as Perugi puts it, "la carriera piú consona al temperamento e piú compatibile con le esigenze delle donne".[26] Women were thought to have certain natural inclinations fulfilled in teaching; they were felt to possess, in Gigliola De Donato's words, "doti di educatrice civile che potrebbero utilmente trovare impiego nell'insegnamento e nell'assistenza sociale".[27] Serao's concentration on middle-class women as teachers reflects the increasing employment of women in the profession, but she also draws on her own experience to explode certain myths surrounding this form of employment.[28]

In "Scuola normale femminile" Serao begins by presenting her characters' training and moves on, in the final section, to an overall view of them at work. The first section, detailing their own education as trainee teachers, is revealing in its negative comment on both what was studied and the manner in which it was taught. Serao describes the students in a frenzied process of learning by rote before the examinations: "Si chiedevano e si davano certe ultime spiegazioni, di lettere italiane, di geometria, di chimica, finendo di stordirsi […]; quelle che ascoltavano, assorte, come in sogno, ripetevano, balbettando, la spiegazione" (page 976). The fragmentary and superficial nature of the education described corresponds to the curriculum outlined by De Donato in her study of women's education in nineteenth-century Italy: Italian language and literature, science, history, studies of exemplary lives, geography, basic physics and philosophy, all disseminated in a hasty and superficial way. Serao emphasizes that this training is inadequate.

She also highlights the poor pay and conditions attaching to this work. One cause of the increase in the percentage of women teachers in this period was a simultaneous decrease in the number of men attracted to teaching due to its economic inadequacy. In

Bruna Conti's words, "Lo stipendio del maestro superò di rado quello di un operaio o di un artigiano, anche se il costo di formazione era molto superiore. L'opportunità di accedere a professioni piú remunerative per gli uomini che avevano ricevuto una certa formazione dalla scuola ebbe un ruolo determinante per l'aumento relativo della presenza femminile" (page 18).

Women teachers were, of course, paid even less than their male counterparts. Camilla Ravera discusses at length the position of middle-class women entering the workforce, and underlines their financial problems: "La minore retribuzione femminile ne facilita l'assunzione [...]; gli stipendi delle impiegate sono forse ancora piú 'da elemosina' dei salari delle operaie."[29] In "Scuola normale femminile" Serao depicts a constant economic struggle for her female characters once they have begun their work as teachers. Several of her newly qualified female teachers die far from home as a result of penury which has led to hunger, cold and illness: "Non si può bene accertare il giorno della sua morte, avendola poi ritrovata quasi nera sul letto in una stanza senza mobilio [...], un lume spento, per terra, in un angolo" (page 963). Beatrice Pisa's study reveals, in terms akin to those of Serao's narrative, that "il misero stipendio percepito, la diretta dipendenza dalle autorità locali per licenziamenti e traslochi, la lontananza dalla propria casa e dal proprio ambiente rendeva queste pioniere dell'autonomia femminile facili prede del pregiudizio e della rapacità di biechi personaggi di provincia" (page 257). Duties tended not to be confined to the classroom: teachers were "on call" for the entire community. Female teachers sometimes became the sexual prey of rapacious men, as in the case of Italia Donati prior to her notorious suicide in 1883.[30] One of Serao's fictional teachers, too, commits suicide. In this short story the author is clearly reacting to factors which certainly shaped her own decision to reject the option of working as a teacher, and keen to bring the most unacceptable aspects of this work into sharp focus.

As we have explored it up to this point, Serao's representation of the lot of women teachers is compassionate, even empathetic, itself an act of female solidarity in its highlighting of inadequacies and its exploding of the conventional view of this kind of work. Yet here again we find a tension in the text, an ambivalence at its core. Serao is unreservedly sympathetic towards those of her characters (the vast majority) whom she locates in situations of poverty, deprivation and unhappiness, and whom she presents as victims; but her sympathy does not extend to two characters, Giustina Marangió and Isabella Diaz, who are allowed to succeed and even excel in their work. Both these characters are depicted as extrinsic to Serao's typically supportive group during the training process, both being consciously excluded by their companions, though for very different reasons. Giustina is described in negative terms from the beginning: "quella testolina viperea che sapeva sempre e tutte le lezioni, che non le spiegava mai a nessuna compagna, che non prestava mai i suoi quaderni e i suoi libri, che rideva quando le sue compagne erano sgridate, che i suoi professori adoravano, che non aveva amiche, e che rappresentava la perfidia somma" (page 955). She retains these characteristics as a successful teacher: "È riuscita una delle prime, insegna [...], e ha ottenuto finanche che la direttrice della scuola fosse traslocata [...], assumendo lei la direzione [...]. È lei che inventò un nuovo metodo [...] per non fare tardare le alunne alla scuola: [...] a chiunque arriva dopo le otto, sequestra la colazione implacabilmente" (page 985). Giustina, then, comes across as aggressive, ambitious and harsh, achieving success at the price of affection and indeed of personal development.

The first description of Isabella Diaz, as a new pupil, is as follows:

> Era una faccia piatta, senza linee precise, con un colorito giallastro [...], gli occhi erano chiarissimi, le labbra violacee e macchiate dalla febbre, i denti guasti. Ma quello che impressionava era l'assenza totale delle ciglia e delle sopracciglia, non un pelo, non un'ombra; con una brutta e malfatta parrucca rossastra [...] che discendeva troppo giú sulla fronte [...]. Ella era orrenda. (page 959)

Eventually, however, Isabella is the most successful of the characters. She has intelligence, initiative and organizational ability, and is sympathetic towards her pupils: "La prima riuscita nel concorso, passata subito a insegnare in quarta classe [...]. Risultati eccezionali. Semplificato il modo di sillabazione, modificato l'insegnamento della geografia, in meglio. Fondato un giardino d'infanzia [...]. Sempre orrenda. [...]. Direttrice della scuola piú popolosa di Napoli; da lei parte la prima abolizione dei vecchi metodi punitivi" (page 988). Despite all these achievements Serao cannot resist a reminder of Isabella's physical anomalies.

Why does she feel the need to defend the ambitions of the two characters who are most intelligent and most successful at their work and simultaneously to make them personally unattractive? I think Serao is making the controversial point that the only women who can be truly successful in their chosen careers are those for whom marriage is not, for whatever reason, an option—which is interesting in view of women's obligation in that period to terminate their careers when they married. Yet the reason why these characters are unlikely to marry is troubling: they are, in different ways, repulsive. This in itself indicates a degree of ambivalence on Serao's part when she deals with working women of her own class. In a sense, "Scuola normale femminile" performs a deconstruction which is diametrically opposed to that of its predecessor. Here Serao at first seems to be supportive of her characters and positively disposed towards the idea that they should be educated for the purpose of obtaining work which brings a degree of social standing and for which a rather "unfeminine" intelligence is required (though she is also justifiably negative about certain aspects of both the education and the work itself). The idea of success, however, with the concomitant rejection of the traditionally feminine role at the heart of the family, appears to have deeply troubled her, leading her to undermine and negate the positive achievements of her most capable characters. Both Giustina and Isabella are made unfeminine: one harsh and aggressively masculine, the other the epitome of physical ugliness.

Serao seems here to respond to a specific debate on the issue of women's work. The exemplary texts of the early 1880s, to which she was undoubtedly exposed in the course of her own education, prescribed a specific role for women. As Fiorenza Taricone says in her study of these texts, woman's mission "si conferma [...] nella famiglia, altrimenti chiamata santuario, fuoco sacro, focolare e cosí via" (*Operaie, borghesi, contadine*, page 73). Above all, women were required to be essentially passive: in Gigliola De Donato's words, "l'ideologia dominante non mostra eccessiva simpatia per le donne intellettualmente qualificate, guardandosi con ammirazione piuttosto dubbia da donne 'virili' dedite a pubbliche attività" (page 37). As we saw in the Introduction, Serao herself was constantly judged in her own time in terms of her appearance (where she was found wanting) and of her femininity (or lack of it). It is perhaps hardly surprising, then, that her response to middle-class women teachers is ambivalent.

All the texts Serao chooses to people with middle-class women workers present them as intelligent, capable, responsible and successful.[31] Sometimes the characters are even ambitious for success, and it is then, as we have seen, that Serao feels unable to be totally positive about them: a fear of unacceptable female success leads her to represent them as in some way flawed. Serao's novels, like those of Gaskell, Woolf and Welty, express—as Meyer Spacks puts it in relation to the three non-Italian writers—"a qualified faith in the possibility of an individual female self-assertion" (*The Female Imagination*, page 261). Serao also points out that society clearly opposes middle-class women who work: exploitation and discrimination are spectres which haunt almost all these characters. Ambivalence towards middle-class women's work, then, is the keynote of her literary production which deals with this topic, and the ambivalence is obviously formed, at least in part, through her awareness of the censures imposed by the society in which she lived.

ALTERNATIVE ACTIVITIES

Sometimes Serao treats middle-class and aristocratic women characters no less ambivalently even though they are located either outside the world of paid work or on its fringes. The most obvious vocation/location of such characters is within marriage (inevitably, as was noted in Chapter 1, unhappy marriage)—this is, after all, what most such women are trained for. If characters do not wish to marry or are unsuccessful in the competition (for so Serao sees it, no less than Jane Austen), the alternative Serao allows them is often the convent. Sometimes the convent is presented in a wholly negative light (the predictable escape from the world), sometimes in a wholly positive one (as a means of creating for oneself a new, much less restrictive existence and an identity in community).[32] By and large, however, Serao's aristocratic women characters in particular (with whom she is often impatient) are portrayed as unsatisfied. Often they demand more from their world than it seems able to provide. Virginia Woolf identified precisely the same tendency in George Eliot's heroines, a "demand for something—they scarcely know what—for something else that is perhaps incompatible with the facts of human existence".[33] For Serao this "something else" seems to be more correctly definable as incompatible with the facts of *female* existence. The demand for it has been described by Nancy Miller as "the extravagant wish for a story that would turn out differently".[34] Such extravagant wishes may be found both in Serao's convent novels and in her more conventional romantic novels, and provoke further ambiguity and ambivalence in their telling.

I think Serao's careful yet ambiguous distancing of herself from her successful middle-class female characters is underpinned by a combination of conditioning and defensiveness that is as deeply rooted as the class consciousness which underlies her distancing of herself from her working-class female characters. The whole of Serao's representation of women workers is linked to, and conditioned by, her view of herself as a woman writer. It is clear that she took her role as a women writer very seriously indeed. In the introduction to *Suor Giovanna della Croce* (1901) she is explicit about the potential influence of what she writes—about the relationship she sees as existing between literature and society. She there outlines a change in her mode of writing and a still more serious approach to her subjects:

> Rinunzio a piacere e a sedurre coloro che chieggono, nelle opere d'arte, la bellezza delle linee e dei colori [...]; rinunzio a lusingare coloro che domandano il rinovellamento di quella eterna storia di amore che tutti hanno raccontato [...]. Vi sono anime malinconiche [...], che niuno vede [...]: vi sono ombre, nella via [...] e se le mie mani di lavoratore e di artefice, di altro scrivessero, dovrebbero essere maledette. (pages 536–37)

These very lines, however, in which Serao writes so openly about her concept of her own work, reveal a degree of ambivalence about her fitness for the task. She refers to her hands as those of a "lavoratore" and an "artefice", two masculine nouns which presumably indicate their appropriateness for a masculine task. This is typical of Serao's approach to her own work and is connected with the ambivalence we have seen in her portrayal of women and their relationship to work in her writing as a whole. Anne Stevenson says of Sylvia Plath that she "implies all the way through that the roles of 'writer' and 'woman' are in some way incompatible".[35] Serao, like Plath, conceives of writing in male terms. As late as 1906, when she was the editor of her own newspaper, *Il giorno*, she envisages the figure of the editor in masculine terms: "Un giornale fermo [...] sotto la direzione di un uomo che è pronto a tutto perdere per tutto guadagnare, può fare tutto il bene e tutto il male."[36] Even the figure of the ideal journalist, which she imagines at the close of the same essay, is male: "Bisogna che nel giornalista nasca un uomo nuovo [...]. Noi sogniamo un uomo, di noi piú forte" (pages 42–43). As Gilbert and Gubar state, "inalterably female in a culture where creativity is defined purely in male terms, almost every woman writer must have experienced [...] gender conflicts."[37] Serao clearly experiences gender conflicts, and one way in which she tries to resolve them (for other women writers as well as for herself) is by her insistence that in writing women enter another state of being. Her claim that she writes involuntarily is reminiscent of the attitude of Charlotte Brontë, another woman writer who was wont to ascribe her most creative moments to a force beyond herself.[38] Serao sees the woman writer as somehow different from all other women. Thus whenever she mentions women writers overtly—and it is noticeable that she never does so in her fiction—she is at pains to highlight that difference, and hence their overwhelming need and right to write.

Apart from the introduction to *Suor Giovanna della Croce*, there are two other texts where Serao refers to women writers.[39] Both date from the later period of Serao's life, indicating her increasing concern with the function of her writings in her later years, and both were originally published in article form. *Parla una donna* is a collection of articles on the First World War dating from 1915–16, while *Ricordando Neera* is an article written in commemoration of Anna Radius Zuccari after her death in 1918. Another feature common to these works is Serao's clear sense that women writers are not only different from other women, but also form a group with a sense of its own identity.

In the preface to *Parla una donna* Serao discusses the aim of her writing and of that of other women. She claims that in times of stress, such as war, women writers become similar to other women (which indicates the difference she sees between them in normal circumstances): "Con profonda devozione [...] esse hanno preso e tenuto un posto qualsiasi di donna nella immensa folla muliebre, e hanno dato le loro energie a un lavoro qualsiasi [...]: e hanno messo ogni loro ingegno, a essere consimili a tutte le altre donne" (page xiii). Serao clearly sees this as part of the war-effort: the sacrifice made by women writers involves placing themselves on the same level as other women. Serao also here reiterates her conviction that women writers cannot help doing the work they do because they exist on some different level from the ordinary mortal: they are (under normal circumstances) in some way possessed. As a result of the War, however, "esse sono balzate fuori dal forte, dal soave sogno che tenea la loro anima, e ogni visione della loro mente è stata abolita" (page xii). To write as a woman, she hints, is to enter into this "soave sogno", which she is powerless to resist. She implies, as she had in the introduction to *Suor Giovanna della Croce*, that in some mysterious way writing removes femininity from women writers—it is only under stress that "tutte sono ridiventate delle donne" (page xii). Writing, we must assume, not only transports women into a different, ethereal realm, it also desexes them. All this—the desexing of women writers, the implication that when writing they have no will of their own, their separation from mere "ordinary" women—combines to reveal the deep-seated unease Serao clearly felt about her role as a woman writer. She goes to some lengths to emphasize that in writing this collection of articles she is writing as a woman, not as a writer: "Questo libro [...] non è uscito dalla penna di una scrittrice: in esso, parla una donna" (page xv). Before this, however, she has highlighted her sense of community with other women writers, mentioning her "grandi sorelle" in literature (page xiii). In denying her difference from "ordinary" women she reiterates it; in asserting her identity as a woman she alternately denies and asserts the special nature of her role as a woman writer. Clearly, although the issues of femininity and writing were ones which she strove to separate in her mind, she nonetheless felt at one with other women involved in the process of literary creation.

Exactly the same traits surface in *Ricordando Neera*. Serao here reveals great admiration for the work of Anna Radius Zuccari (Neera), referring to her "laboriosa carriera di narratrice" (page 15), and her "ultimi magnifici romanzi" (page 15). She reveals the same sense of identification with this woman writer as she did with women writers at large in the preface to *Parla una donna*: "Io avevo seguito [...] tutta la grande fatica letteraria della mia amica e della mia sorella lombarda" (page 16); she also calls Neera "la mia sorella in arte" (pages 24 and 27). But with this sense of unity comes the same process of desexualization. She refers to their exchanges as having occurred "fraternamente" (page 16), and three sentences later praises in Neera "la elevatezza della virtú virile" (page 17). It seems that the more she praises this other woman writer, and the more she allows herself to identify with her, the more masculine Neera must become.

Serao describes a meeting with Neera in the aristocratic salon of Countess Clara Maffei. According to Serao the two women writers naturally gravitated towards each other to talk about their work. Neither of them, she says, fitted in with the beautiful, elegant, aristocratic women who surrounded them. She is keen to stress their difference from other women: "Né la mia cara Neera né io facemmo alcuna figura, in quel salone" (pages 23–24). Both, when exposed to society, seemed to take refuge in withdrawal and silence: "Neera, con un vestito di seta nera e un filo di coralli al collo, se ne stette seduta, tacita, immobile, presso un balcone, io malgrado i miei bollenti spiriti non osai aprir bocca" (page 24). The common denominator linking the two individuals is this un-willingness to express themselves, this self-consciousness about the act of self-expression. The fear of self-expression is something Serao, who refers to Neera as a "creatura di possedente silenzio" (page 53), seems to see as peculiar to the woman writer. It is, I think, linked with her desire to abdicate responsibility for her writing, seen in her assertion that she cannot help writing, that it is in some sense involuntary. When she does eventually speak (and then only to Neera), she discusses writing as a mystical process: "Chi non sogna, non scrive" (page 25).

In the closing section of the essay Serao considers the role of literature, specifically from the viewpoint of the woman writer. She begins with an analysis of the particular (Neera), using it to deconstruct the general concept of female virtue. She describes Neera as "un documento preclaro della virtú muliebre e quando parlo di virtú, voglio dire, coscienza, coraggio, elevazione" (pages 37–38). There is no mention here of the traditional notions of female virtue such as modesty and self-sacrifice. Serao appears to address herself to a kind of intellectual and moral virtue which she sees as peculiar to women. She states that in her writing Neera displayed "un superbo ingegno" (page 38), and this idea of "ingegno" also runs counter to the traditional feminine ideal. From this particular instance of writing as a woman, Serao moves on to the general, and for the first time in her work admits the possible existence of a specifically female dimension in writing. She uses an exclusively female metaphor to make her point about the significance of literature to its female creator, that of maternity: "Chi ha un figlio [...] si consola lentamente di declinare [...], il suo sangue si perpetua in quelle giovani vene" (page 40). Even more important than one's children, however, are one's writings: "Chi potette in un libro [...] esprimere quanto di piú intimo ha il cuor suo [...], chi potette creare delle immagini e fissare delle visioni: [...] costui, costei, non muore tutto [...]; la miglior parte di sé, la piú degna di vivere, resta sulla terra, impressa, ma vivente in quei caratteri" (page 41). Having established the significance of writing to the writer, Serao uses the childbirth metaphor again to convey the difficulty, specifically for a woman, of producing such work; she implies that while writing is a difficult undertaking for anybody it is much harder for a woman: "Quante dure fatiche, quanti diuturni travagli, quanti aspri sacrifici costa fare un libro, specialmente a una donna" (page 41). Thus *Ricordando Neera* becomes as much a meditation on the process of women's writing as a tribute to a specific woman writer.

Serao here overtly analyses the ambitions and difficulties of the woman writer; indeed she stresses the latter rather more than the former. This is the only place in her writings where she openly considers this topic. In her earlier fiction, however, she covertly creates women characters who write, and the degree of subterfuge she uses when dealing with them is of considerable interest. Never does she create a woman protagonist who works as a writer: rather her literary women write, as she herself would claim to do, in a covert and involuntary fashion. The fact that they write is treated by their creator as peripheral—it is never overtly presented as central—; and yet when one looks at these (rare) characters it is evident that writing, although a difficult, traumatic process rather than a purely involuntary act, is essential for them: without writing they certainly cannot express themselves. The two writing characters I shall analyse are Lucia Altimare in *Fantasia* and the anonymous woman writer in "La donna dall'abito nero e dal ramo di corallo rosso".[40]

Lucia Altimare, the *femme fatale* of *Fantasia* (1883), is Serao's earliest female character who writes. Lucia's writing is a subject of the novel from a very early stage (pages 15–16), where we read about her melodramatic school essays, the products (it is suggested) of an over-active and unhealthy imagination. With an ambition to lead a more active life than the average young woman of her social class, Lucia has the "extravagant wish" for "something else". One indication of what she hopes to do is provided by a scene in the opening chapter of Part III. A local fête takes place and various journalists are present. Lucia and Andrea discuss them, and during this exchange she asks: "'Anche quella lí è una giornalista?' 'Credo, non ne so il nome.' 'Io la invidio se è intelligente. Ha almeno un'ambizione.' 'Bah; preferite sempre essere una donna.' 'La gloria è bella'" (page 119). I cannot dismiss this conversation as Lucienne Kroha does:[41] it seems to me to embody Lucia's need to write, which has already been revealed in the essays and in letters to her friend Caterina and will be further developed in the concept of the novel/diary. It also clearly restates, from a male point of view, the dichotomy between the terms "woman" and "writer". Incidentally, this cameo figure of the female journalist is the only portrait in the whole of Serao's fiction of a female character who earns a living through writing.[42]

The next indication of Lucia's need to write hinges precisely on the "novel" she is supposed to be writing, and which eventually turns out to be a diary. (Although at the end of *Fantasia* Lucia's script is presented as a diary, up to that point the reader is led to see it as a novel.) In my view it functions as both diary and novel. It might be said that Lucia creates her own melodrama, which she has already plotted from quite an early stage in the text—that she creates herself as an anti-heroine. This is suggested in the scene where she warns Andrea of the inevitable denouement: "Io sono una donna fatale: ti recherò sventura" (page 175). In a sense she here functions as the opposite of the successful female journalist: prevented by social restrictions from working as she wishes, in order to "work" at all and justify the act of writing she must fictionalize her own life. There is fiction on two levels here: the fictional female character recreates herself by creating another fiction.

The fiction of Lucia's writing of the novel/diary is closely analysed. At first the activity of writing is covert: "Quando non si usciva, Lucia si ritirava in camera sua un'ora prima del pranzo. 'Che farà in quest' ora?' domandò una volta Andrea a sua moglie. 'Non so'" (page 152). It is her husband who eventually discovers that she is writing, and he tells the others how she works:

La sua Lucia era dietro a un altro lavoro importante. Nessuno doveva saperne niente, zitti dunque: Lucia lo aveva pregato di non dirne nulla a nessuno […]; nientemeno che Lucia stava scrivendo un romanzo, un grande romanzo, tutto di fantasia, tutto di creazione [...]. Lucia ci lavorava dopo la mezzanotte: lui, Alberto, se ne andava a letto: Lucia disponeva la lampada in modo che non gli ferisse gli occhi [...], si prendeva la testa fra le mani, meditando prima di scrivere. Poi si curvava a scrivere lungamente senza fermarsi mai. Talvolta, sotto l'impeto della ispirazione, ella si alzava, passeggiando, agitata, contorcendosi le mani. (page 182)

This description highlights several elements of the creative process in the female writer: the desire for secrecy (the basic unacceptability of the enterprise, which in fact is never discussed by the group as a whole since Andrea and Caterina refrain from comment), the effort and strain involved, and the paradoxical process of inspiration which, in this sketch, does not lessen the difficulty of the work.

It is through writing, then, that Lucia, as it were, creates her story. It is also often through the written word that she communicates with other characters; for example, she writes long, poetic letters to Caterina when they are separated and short, intense notes to Andrea when she wishes to communicate with him in a crowded room. Writing is clearly essential to her: although it is not easy for her to write, it is only through the written word that she can really express herself—often she is silent and detached when the spoken word is required. Although Serao attempts to hide or marginalize the references to writing (distracting the reader by surrounding them with a wealth of detail which is relevant to the acceleration of the plot), when one looks at them in isolation they acquire significance and indeed centrality in Lucia's character. Thus these episodes help explain Serao's ambivalence towards Lucia, whom she clearly dislikes and yet makes much more interesting than Caterina. Serao is unable totally to dissociate herself from the woman writer she creates, even though she also casts her as a *femme fatale*.

In "La donna dall'abito nero e dal ramo di corallo rosso" (1888) Serao's protagonist writes about how she has sensed a duality in herself and how she is threatened by the character of the title. One of the main themes of this story, though a covert one, is the difficulty the woman writer experiences in expressing herself. The main device used in the story is that of the double, and the tone is undeniably Gothic.[43] Again, though, the melodramatic elements in the text combine to distract the reader from the central issue of writing.

The process of self-definition is initiated early in the text when the narrator states that she has a horrendous secret: "L'ho taciuto sinora per l'orrore della mia mostruosità" (page 129). It transpires that the monstrosity to which she here refers is her dual nature. The difficulty she experiences in verbalizing the secret is crucial; speech, however, here functions as a symbol of self-expression. The real problem is that of writing, since that is what the character ultimately does in order to convey her experience. This difficulty, first with speech and then with writing, exemplifies the difficulties women writers face in breaking the silence imposed on them by the culture around them. It mirrors the difficulty experienced, for instance, by Serao and Neera.

The purpose behind the character's eventual decision to write is "perché si sappia la verità del caso mio" (page 130). What she narrates is the story of a psychic split. First she sees the character of the title and subsequently she perceives (on seeing herself in a mirror) that she is that same character. What is most striking about her is her physical description. Repeatedly she is referred to in almost the words of the short story's long title (pages 132, 133, 138 and twice on page 140). Her physical appearance is clearly significant; inevitably one thinks of the much later description of Neera quoted above: "Neera, con un vestito di seta nera e un filo di coralli al collo" (*Ricordando Neera*, page 24). Serao's physical descriptions of Neera and of her anonymous 1888 character are not dissimilar. The latter is sketched as follows: "una donna [...] col volto [...] sciupato [...] dalle sofferenze; ma in quel volto consumato ardevano gli occhi neri" (page 132). This, on the other hand, is the 1920 Neera: "Ecco i suoi occhietti nerissimi [...], la sua bocca [...] senza un sorriso [...], la sua profonda e tacita tristezza [...], quelle labbra serrate, il suo portentoso segreto di malinconia" (pages 4–5). I do not wish to suggest that the anonymous "donna" is intended to be Neera in disguise. The similarities, however, beg comparison and some thought as to what this "donna" represents. She is, after all, responsible for overcoming the difficulty of self-expression; it is she who causes the act of writing to take place. If the conclusion (where the two characters, narrator and "donna", merge in the mirror) is to be trusted, it is she who is really the woman writer. This is in fact what I think she may symbolize: the woman writer saddened by her long experience of silence (Neera is described as "tacita" while the 1888 narrator has "taciuto" her story) and by her

unpleasant appearance to the world as a whole, finding it extremely difficult to express herself, to accept that she can and must write,
that she must define herself.

What Serao indicates in this short story and in her other
fictional and journalistic analyses of women writers is the difficulty
of combining the roles of woman and writer. She clearly cannot
conceive of being "feminine" (as defined by the culture in which
she lived) as compatible with writing. We have seen that she was
not alone in this: the same ambivalence about women's writing
(sometimes overt, often covert) is detectable from the eighteenth
century onwards. Patricia Meyer Spacks says that "most women
writers [...] neglect to specify the significance of their literary
activity" (page 315). Serao is one of those who do register the
significance of their writing in and through the writing itself. As I
have shown, however, it is a topic which surfaces rarely in her
work. She allows herself to discuss women's writing openly and
seriously only in her journalism; in her fiction representations of
the woman writer are always covert. Yet I think it is this ambivalence about her own role as a woman who writes that conditions,
and may go some way towards creating, her sense of ambivalence
towards the work of all women, of all classes.

Serao's ambivalent approach to the whole question of women's
work automatically prevents her from presenting it positively in
either her fiction or her journalism. Undecided as to how fit women
were to become involved, on any level, in politics, concerned about
the exploitation of both lower- and middle-class women workers,
paradoxically irritated by the frivolous attitude which she knew
was encouraged in upper-class women and, most of all, unable to
reconcile the terms "woman" and "writer" in relation to herself
and other women like her, she displays an attitude to the whole
area that may be described as a mass of contradictions.

Clearly she sees that potentially the world of work has something to offer women—financial independence, self-respect, sometimes an alternative to the crushing existence of marriage or the
romantic heterosexual relationship. Yet almost invariably something (society, men) impinges on the potentially positive scenarios
she herself sets up, and deconstructs them. Annis Pratt would
probably define many of Serao's novels as novels of social protest,
and in that case I would agree with her generalizations about such

texts: "In the novel of social protest [...], authors treat the family and marriage as enclaves within a wider enclosure, as individual prisons bounded by the walls of a wider community. Since modern society itself is the object of awareness and target of satire in these novels, authors censure impersonal economic and social forces as responsible for the oppression of women" (*Archetypal Patterns in Women's Fiction*, page 59). Serao's is, however, a factual representation as well. As we have seen in the Introduction, for most women of her time the experience of work was not a positive one. Serao never plots or envisages a revision of the patriarchal structures which oppress her female characters, but her very dissent from the traditional restrictions she represents indicates a repressed desire for a different kind of social structure. Most significant, and I think ultimately most interesting, is the prominence (the sheer amount of space) Serao gives to the question of women's work; she is truly unusual in paying it so much attention. She strives to depict the experiences of her working women characters as realistically as possible: she fully intends to draw attention to the appalling conditions in which both working- and middle-class women were compelled to eke out a living. But although her works may certainly be read as documents of social analysis, they are also literary constructs which explore ideological confusions. It is here that perhaps their greatest interest lies.

NOTES

1   Much of my discussion of the ambivalence of Serao's approach to her working women characters is drawn from my article "Writing Women's Work: The Ambivalence of Matilde Serao", *Italian Studies*, 48 (1993), 62–70.
2   H. de Balzac, *La Cousine Bette* [1846] (Paris, Garnier, 1962), p. 28.
3   A. Krakowski, *La Condition de la femme dans l'œuvre d'Emile Zola* (Paris, Nizet, 1974), p. 235.
4   G. Verga, *Nedda* [1874] and *Mastro-don Gesualdo* [1890], in his *Opere*, edited by L. Russo (Milan, Ricciardi, 1965), pp. 89–113 and 497–800.
5   E. Zola, *La Terre* [1887], in his *Œuvres complètes: Les Rougon-Macquart*, 5 vols (Paris, Cercle du Livre Précieux, 1960–67), IV, 363–811.
6   E. Zola, *Germinal* [1885], in his *Œuvres complètes*, III, 1131–1591.
7   E. Moers, *Literary Women* [1963] (London, The Women's Press, 1978), p. 194 (italics mine).
8   P. Meyer Spacks, *The Female Imagination: A Literary and Psychological Investigation of Women's Writing* (London, Allen and Unwin, 1976), p. 318.

9   M. Serao, *La conquista di Roma* [1885] and *Vita e avventure di Riccardo Joanna* [1877], in her *Opere*, edited by P. Pancrazi (Milan, Garzanti, 1944–46), II, 277–514 and 517–740.

10   Lucia Altimare in *Fantasia* [1883] (M. Serao, *Opere*, II, 5–274), for instance, writes. Both later in this chapter and in Chapter 5 I discuss in greater detail this covert representation of the woman who writes.

11   F. Taricone and B. Pisa, *Operaie, borghesi, contadine nel XIX secolo* (Rome, Carucci, 1985), p. 182.

12   M. Serao, *Il ventre di Napoli* (Milan, Treves, 1884); M. Serao, *Il paese di Cuccagna* [1891], in her *Opere*, I, 105–529.

13   Three hundred people had already died by 6 September according to the essay by G. Infusino, "I mali antichi di Napoli", in M. Serao, *Napoli* [1906], edited by G. Infusino (Naples, Quarto Potere, 1977), pp. 9–32. By the end of the cholera outbreak 6,852 people had died while a further 12,224 had been infected (p. 18).

14   *Il pungolo*, year 25, no. 245, 12/13, ix (1884), p. 1.

15   E. Zola, *Le Ventre de Paris* [1873] (Paris, Livre de Poche, 1969).

16   A. Ghirelli, *Napoli italiana* (Turin, Einaudi, 1977), p. 58.

17   It is through the proximity occasioned by work that many of Serao's characters form friendships. Even the women who work in the street, Serao's sub-proletariat, evince a form of solidarity in their role as mothers who work, looking after each other's children and identifying with each other's experiences of pregnancy and labour (pp. 92–99).

18   C. Kaplan, "Pandora's Box: Subjectivity, Class and Sexuality in Socialist Feminist Criticism", in *Making a Difference: Feminist Literary Criticism*, edited by G. Greene and C. Kahn (London, Methuen, 1985), pp. 146–77 (pp. 166–67).

19   A. Pratt, *Archetypal Patterns in Women's Fiction* [1981] (Brighton, Harvester Press, 1982), p. 65.

20   M. Marmo, *Il proletariato industriale a Napoli in età liberale* (Naples, Guida, 1978), pp. 165–70.

21   Serao founded *Il giorno* in 1904, just after her separation from Scarfoglio. All these articles were written between the middle of 1904 and late 1905.

22   M. Serao, "Terno secco" [in her *All'erta, sentinella!* (1889)], in her *Opere*, I, 991–1024.

23   M. Serao, "Telegrafi dello Stato" [1885] and "Scuola normale femminile" [1886], in her *Opere*, I, 911–50 and 951–88.

24   A sense of resentment related specifically to the male attitude to their work is often evident, especially among the telegraphists themselves. An example of this is the scene early in the text where Ida Torelli complains about working on the Avellino line: "Io con quel vecchione del corrispondente non posso lavorare: figurati […] una mummia […] che non può soffrire la sezione femminile. […] È irascibile, cocciuto e insolente" (p. 918). Serao indicates that the younger female characters are less tolerant of such discrimination than their superior.

25   See Bruna Conti's introduction to S. Aleramo, *La donna e il femminismo* (Rome, Editori Riuniti, 1978), pp. 3–31 (p. 18).

26   G. Perugi, *Educazione e politica in Italia, 1860–1900* (Turin, Loescher, 1978), p. 104.

27   G. De Donato, "Donna e società nella cultura moderata del primo Ottocento", in *La parabola della donna nella letteratura italiana dell'Ottocento*, edited by G. De Donato (Bari, Adriatica, 1983), pp. 11–96 (p. 40).

28 These myths sought to link the pedagogical and the maternal, seeing the woman teacher as a mother-substitute. Fiorenza Taricone writes of "la nebbia di un certo misticismo [...] particolarmente fitta nell'identificazione della maestra con una madre-martire" (*Operaie, borghesi, contadine*, p. 58).

29 C. Ravera, *Breve storia dell'movimento femminile in Italia* (Rome, Editori Riuniti, 1978), p. 32.

30 D. Bertoni Jovine, *Storia dell'educazione popolare in Italia* [1954] (Bari, Laterza, 1965), p. 288. On the Donati case see also F. Taricone and B. Pisa, *Operaie, borghesi, contadine*, p. 257. Donati repeatedly repelled the sexual advances of an important citizen in the Pistoia area, where she had been sent to work. As a result he blackened her character and, unable to bear the shame, she committed suicide, leaving her body as proof of her virginity.

31 Such characters are found in works other than those discussed here. The *signora* of "Terno secco" is another capable, if sad, female character who works and supports her family single-handed. Luisella Fragalà, who in *Il paese di Cuccagna* takes the family business in hand when her husband fails to run it properly, also supports her family single-handed (and sadly).

32 The negative view is most clearly shown in M. Serao, *Storia di una monaca* (Catania, Giannotta, 1898), while the positive one is found in *Suor Giovanna della Croce* [1901], in M. Serao, *Opere*, I, 533–674.

33 V. Woolf, *The Common Reader* [1925] (London, Hogarth Press, 1929), p. 217.

34 N. K. Miller, "Emphasis Added: Plots and Plausibilities in Women's Fiction", in *The New Feminist Criticism: Essays on Women, Literature and Theory*, edited by E. Showalter (London, Virago, 1986), pp. 339–61.

35 A. Stevenson, "Writing as a Woman", in *Women Writing and Writing about Women*, edited by M. Jacobus [1979] (London, Croom Helm, 1986), pp. 159–77 (p. 160).

36 M. Serao, *Il giornale* (Naples, Perrella, 1906), pp. 30–31. This is the published version of a lecture Serao gave in Turin in 1905 to the Associazione della Stampa.

37 S. Gilbert and S. Gubar, *The Madwoman in the Attic: The Woman Writer and the Nineteenth-century Literary Imagination* [1979] (London, Yale University Press, 1984), p. 66. The authors devote a chapter of this book to what they define as the anxiety of female authorship.

38 Several instances of Brontë's tendency to do this are found in W. Gérin, *Charlotte Brontë* [1967] (Oxford, Oxford University Press, 1987), e.g. p. 512.

39 These are M. Serao, *Parla una donna* (Milan, Treves, 1916) and M. Serao, *Ricordando Neera* (Milan, Treves, 1920).

40 "La donna dall'abito nero e dal ramo di corallo rosso" first appeared in M. Serao, *Fior di passione* (Milan, Galli, 1888), pp. 129–41, and later became the title piece of another collection of short stories (Naples, Chiurazzi, 1892). My references are to the earlier edition.

41 L. Kroha, "Matilde Serao's *Fantasia*: An Author in Search of a Character", *The Italianist*, 7 (1987), 45–63.

42 Indeed I am tempted to see this as a self-portrait because only four pages earlier, at the start of the same chapter (p. 115), Serao has used the word *gibus*, one of her journalistic pen names. I think this is a signpost to her appearance in the text, in which case this passage must be of considerable significance.

43 See my article "Angel vs. Monster: Serao's Use of the Female Double", *The Italianist*, 7 (1987), 63–89.

Chapter 4

SENTIMENTAL SUBVERSIONS:
FEMALE FRIENDSHIP

The theme of friendship is one constantly reworked in a variety of literary settings and in the literature of many countries. It is important in folk literature and in the Italian *novella*. In both, however, the issues of friendship centre solely on men. Rotunda, in his study of motifs in the Italian *novella*, records many instances of male friendship,[1] though these are also interesting for the light they cast on the role of women. In the tales in question women often temporarily interrupt true friendship between men; ultimately, however, men choose each other over women, recognizing their bond of friendship as primary.[2] Another feature of such *novelle* is the swearing of brotherhood between men—a further sign of the centrality of male bonding in these tales.[3] Boccaccio is one of those who privilege male friendship in his narratives. In *Decameron*, IV. 9, for example, the men are the focus of interest while the woman is an object of contention;[4] frequently in Boccaccio she is the cause of tragedy. We see this, too, in Marguerite de Navarre's *Heptaméron*.[5] Other elaborations of the theme include Boccaccio's celebration of male friendship in Ciceronian terms in *Decameron*, X. 8, where the woman is an impediment to male friendship.[6]

The same themes are repeated throughout European literature. Montaigne glorified male friendship and even doubted that friendship between women was possible.[7] Male characters in nineteenth- and twentieth-century fiction by men often have, if not true friends, then at least understanding male acquaintances. Charles Bovary is understood by Homais, while Emma is isolated from female companionship.[8] Zola's male workers toil in both friendship and animosity, but solidarity, as we saw in the previous chapter, is not a feature of his female characters' existence. Verga's characters, both male and female, are often isolated in their society, but he shows groups of men gathered socially to do mutually profitable work more often than such groups of women.[9] D'Annunzio elevated male bonding to a quasi-erotic level and correspondingly degraded male–female bonding, while bonds between women interested him only on a voyeuristic level. In *Il trionfo della morte*, for instance, the relationship between Giorgio Aurispa and his uncle Demetrio is of paramount importance, while the play *La fiaccola sotto il moggio* is a story of powerful *negative* reciprocal female passion (between Gigliola and Angizia).[10]

Female friendship, on the other hand, is a theme on which Serao focuses throughout her writing, from her earliest novel (*Cuore infermo*, 1881) to her last (*Mors tua*, 1926). She explores various modes and manifestations of female friendship in all social classes, and sometimes, as we shall see, even depicts such friendship as something capable of transcending otherwise insurmountable social divisions. She does not confine her exploration of this theme to her fiction but also incorporates it in her journalism, in her sketches of groups of women, some of which have been considered in Chapters 2 and 3.

She was, however, not alone in writing about female friendship; in fact she was thereby continuing a literary tradition which had its roots in the two centuries before she began to write. As Janet Todd points out, "Female friendship is a literary given of the eighteenth century."[11] But while in that century female friendship is frequently described in such a way as to appear incidental, for Serao it is of central importance. The position the theme occupies in her writing is unusual, whether we compare it to early narrative forms, to eighteenth-century narrative or to that of the nineteenth century.

On the whole, male writers tended to present female friendship as a bond which was clearly secondary in importance to the heterosexual romantic love relationship. Often their depiction of such friendship was confined to the earliest stages of the plot, prior to the formation of that central love bond.[12] Female writers, however, tended to privilege women's friendship rather more, though in their writings too it may eventually appear to take second place, for instance to marriage—which is often the denouement of the nineteenth-century woman writer's novel.[13] Serao, on the other hand, accords female friendship a highly privileged place. Her novels do not (as we have seen) end in marriage; rather, marriage is often posited as the starting-point for negative observations about the romantic love relationship.

One possible reason why women writers in general, and Serao in particular, foreground relationships between women is that by depicting female friendship they can create a further version of the intense mother–daughter bond.[14] Elizabeth Abel identifies this tendency, though her focus is on more recent women's writing.[15] She applies to the mother–daughter relationship Chodorow's use of object-relations theory, which argues that the child's social relational experience from earliest infancy is central to personality formation, highlighting how the asymmetric organization of parenting affects our unconscious psychic structure.[16] Abel observes that "because of the identification between mother and daughter, the female child has difficulty establishing ego boundaries", and that "men are particularly ill-prepared to satisfy the deep and complex relational needs of women, who retain both the desire and capacity for fusion and the more specific desire for union with the mother, a bond that heterosexual love can partially restore only for men." Therefore "other women [...] offer the best solution to the need for identification that originated in relation to another woman" (pages 417–18). Abel, however, sees the working-out of such psychological dilemmas in fiction as being confined to recent women's writing; she says, "Recent fiction by women points to the alternative that Chodorow slights: women friends [...] play a crucial role in relaxing ego boundaries and restoring psychic wholeness" (page 418).[17] But the practice of foregrounding such relationships as psychologically significant existed at least as early as 1881, when *Cuore infermo* was published. The intense and often passionate relationships between Serao's women characters, especially in her fiction, are often reminiscent of the intense mother–daughter relationship also present in her work, which I analysed in Chapter 2. A factor common to these two types of relationship is their ultimate exclusion of the male character.

Linked to the desire to replicate the intense mother–daughter relationship is the equally intense, and paradoxical, need to break away from the mother. As we have seen in earlier chapters, nineteenth-century women writers, including Serao, were locked in a painful struggle for self-definition. One way in which female self-definition in general is attained seems to be through an intense attachment to a woman or girl other than the mother.[18] Helene Deutsch stresses the need for independence of the mother, particularly in adolescence. At that stage in her life the girl will often gravitate towards another girl who functions as an *alter ego* for her, becoming "an extension of the girl's own ego, identical with her in respect to age, interests and desires".[19] This leads the girl to a sense of being "doubled" (page 13) and therefore more secure in her own concept of identity. The whole issue of the double device in women's fiction, especially that of Serao, is one on which I shall concentrate later in this chapter. Serao uses it extensively and, I think, in a very significant way.[20] Moreover, it appears that Serao was aware of this tendency in women long before Deutsch theorized it, since, as I shall also show, she frequently analyses adolescent female characters and their tendency to form couples who intensely and passionately identify with each other. The essence of such friendships as Serao presents them, however, is not the similarity between the girls so paired but the differences.[21] Thus Serao's characters define themselves through intense relationships of similarity and opposition, while she in turn seems to define herself through writing about this process of female self-definition achieved through relationships with other women.[22] Abel is right when she asserts that in the fiction of women writers "friendship becomes a vehicle of self-definition for women" (page 416); in fact her assertion seems to be true on more than one level.

THE LOCATION OF WOMEN'S FRIENDSHIP IN SERAO'S NOVELS

There are two main areas in which Serao locates her female characters when she presents them locked in intense same-sex pairings. In the first place, such pairings can be contemporaneous with and contingent on the romantic heterosexual relationship. In such instances the latter seems on the surface to take precedence but on closer analysis this is not the case: the central, and certainly the formative, relationship in the development of the female characters concerned is that between the women. Sometimes Serao considers such relationships using a triangular structure, with one male character often supposedly desired by both women; the subtext, however, subverts the whole idea of the traditional love relationship. The use of this structure would not surprise Janet

Todd, who remarks in relation to Rousseau's *Julie* (1761): "We face the inevitable triangle, it seems, for literary female friendship is rarely allowed to exist in a pair" (page 132).

Serao's nineteenth-century canvas is not quite so circumscribed, however, as she frequently considers such female friendships, secondly, as contemporaneous with but apart from the hetero-sexual romantic involvement. At times this variation involves concentration on adolescent women who form part of a female group, or community, and create subdivisions within it; alternat-ively, Serao sometimes groups together nuclei of adult women who exist precisely as a community of women. The first such grouping she describes is that which takes place in the (generally sex-segregated) workplace. Here her approach to the setting is entirely realistic: as she knew, women who worked in industry, business and education were segregated from their male counter-parts. It is therefore hardly surprising that women's friendship is an overtly central issue. The other grouping is that of a community of women who have chosen to situate themselves outside patri-archal society, in the convent. I disagree with Maryse Jeuland-Meynaud's assertion that Serao's attitude to the cloistered female existence is wholly negative. Jeuland-Meynaud speaks of "la tacita omologazione posta dalla scrittrice tra presa di velo e soppressione di sé".[23] While Serao is sometimes crushingly negative about the taking of the veil, once it has been taken she is wholly positive about the supportive female environment to which it leads. Supportive-ness is what most clearly defines the female environment, in sharp opposition to the patriarchal world outside. And when Serao presents the opposite move, from the female environment back to the patriarchy, as she does in *Suor Giovanna della Croce* (1901), the female supportiveness is unable to survive.[24] It is the move back to society that is seen in wholly negative terms.

Hence in Serao's representation of female friendship there are two basic plot structures. The first involves an apparent privileging of the heterosexual relationship with female friendship as a sub-plot; this type may be subdivided into two structures, one triangu-lar, the other based on an adolescent female community. The second uses the female group as its base; this type too may be divided into two subsets, one situated in the workplace and the other in the female community *par excellence*, the convent.

HIDDEN MEANINGS: WHAT THE SUBTEXT SAYS

As I have suggested, it is the subtext that reveals the importance Serao ascribes to the whole area of female friendship. There are, however, two potentially contradictory elements in many (though not all) of Serao's subtexts. The first significant device she uses is that of the female double, most frequently in her earlier writing. It is more often latent than manifest and thus forms part of the subtext.[25] Through the portrayal of two female characters (who are often, though not always, friends) she presents elements of complementarity and difference which indicate a degree of identification between them. She seems to suggest that many of her female characters, especially those who are writers, tend to be fragmented, split into two aspects of "womanhood". The "double" texts which I shall examine here follow the typically male-oriented genre of the *Bildungsroman*, but in inverse form (the degree of development, in the male sense, achieved by the female heroine being questionable). The *Bildungsroman* is traditionally a male genre in more senses than one: typically it is written by a male author, has a male protagonist and tells a tale of male progress in which, learning from mistakes, the young protagonist is educated and finds his true profession. Elizabeth Abel, Marianne Hirsch and Elizabeth Langland have drawn attention to the existence of a female *Bildungsroman*, in which the different gender of the protagonist modifies every aspect of the genre: "its narrative structure, its implied psychology, its representation of social pressures".[26] The title of their study, *The Voyage In*, emphasizes the inverse, inward development of the heroine of the female *Bildungsroman*. Hence, as Annis Pratt says about inversion of the novel of development (she here refers specifically to female madness, whereas I wish to extend her point to one of literary structure), "One might [...] postulate that the double bind underlying the structure of the *Bildungsroman*, derived from the contrary forces of a girl's desire for authenticity and her society's desire for her femininity, [...] mimics the type of 'split' in the personality clinically defined as schizophrenic."[27] The female *Bildungsroman*, then, strives towards the form of its male originator (education, outward progression) while recognizing the inapplicability of this plot structure to the life of the nineteenth-century woman, and woman character. Pratt therefore identifies a structural "split", a dualism in the text, which she connects with the dualism often presented by female authors in the female protagonists of these very texts. The split of Serao's ideally unified character into two distinct entities is also, it seems to me, dictated by the conflict between autonomy and femininity set up by society, and has much to do with the divided structures and fragmented tone of the texts as a whole.

There is, however, another latent significance in Serao's descriptions of female friendship, which recurs still more frequently than the double motif but is arguably present even within those texts which contain the latter. Many of the dialogues between Serao's female characters are reminiscent in tone and language of those which ordinarily take place between male and female characters in the traditional romantic novel; and the relationships between Serao's female characters are at least as passionate as those she creates between a male and a female protagonist. Hence, given the frequent centrality of the female relationship in Serao's novels, it seems reasonable to propose the possible existence of a (very) latent lesbian subtext. The critic must, however, explore this possibility with care, developing a new approach which Ann Rosalind Jones characterizes thus: "to listen 'otherwise', to read between the lines for desire or states of mind that cannot be articulated in the social arena and the languages of phallocentrism".[28] To quote Jones again, "Resistance to official discourses, the breaking of taboos and the exploration of homosexual or otherwise anti-patriarchal relationships are often perceived in the interstices of single texts or of collections of texts" (page 99). In the present chapter I shall explore this subtext in order to decide whether it may be legitimately defined as lesbian or whether it functions more as an asexual but nonetheless anti-patriarchal and female-centred discourse, equally challenging to the hierarchical structure of the society Serao lived in.

As well as being awake to the possible presence of lesbian subtexts, one must be careful what one reads into them if one finds them. After all, we cannot be sure how consciously Serao may have intended them to be part of her narrative: they may derive directly from her subconscious. Alternatively, she may have employed increasingly subtle strategies to hide the lesbian themes in her work in the wake of negative attitudes to female friendship spread by the work of sexologists from the late 1890s onwards. I shall discuss this possibility in some detail. I think the lesbian subtext is in any case intimately linked with (though not confined to) Serao's use of the double. A "double" reading and a lesbian reading of a text may be potentially contradictory, insofar as the latter would seem to require two separate female characters, thus precluding the notion of a split character. Yet since on the surface Serao's doubles may generally be seen as two separate characters (both duality and lesbianism are latent and therefore reside only in the subtext), the two readings are only potentially contradictory and do not have to be mutually exclusive. The whole notion of dualisms is significant for what might be termed lesbian feminist criticism, as well as for women's writing at large. As Bonnie Zimmerman says, "Disenfranchised groups have had to adopt a double vision for survival; one of the political transformations of recent decades has been the realization that enfranchised groups [...] would do well to adopt that double vision for the survival of us all."[29] Hence, one of my approaches in the next section will involve an attempt to fathom the significance of double vision where Serao is concerned.[30]

SERAO'S COMMONEST LOCUS OF FEMALE FRIENDSHIP: THE HETEROSEXUAL LOVE RELATIONSHIP AND THE "LESBIAN SUBTEXT"

I shall now investigate the place and importance of female friendship in narratives which appear to focus on the romantic heterosexual bond. My analysis will centre, in varying degrees of detail, on four texts where there is no double: *Il paese di Cuccagna* (1891), *Storia di una monaca* (1898), *Tre donne* (1905) and *Mors tua* (1926).[31] These novels display a shift in Serao's representation of female friendship over the period of time they span. While none of them overtly hinges on one particular female friendship, the issue of female friendship looms large for many of the characters—sometimes larger than the heterosexual romantic relationships presented, or at least referred to. *Storia di una monaca* and *Tre donne* have as their background the developmental processes of female adolescents. Both of them describe interactions between female characters as well as between male and female characters. Most—but not all—of the female characters in these novels appear to be enacting the traditional female *Bildungsroman*, propelling themselves as fast as possible along the road towards their socially sanctioned goal, marriage; a minority aim at other roles in society, through either choice or force of circumstances. For instance, Chiarina Althan in *Storia di una monaca* deliberately shies away from the prospect of marriage, while Eva Muscettola chooses the alternative of convent life. Serao is arguably at her most interesting when her women characters are disappointed in love, because in that circumstance they must reassess their lives and re-evaluate all their other relationships. It is often at this stage that the primacy of the female tie is revealed. The other two texts differ from *Storia di una monaca* and *Tre donne* in that they concentrate on depictions of society fixed in times of crisis (*Il paese di Cuccagna* the poverty of Naples towards the end of the nineteenth century, *Mors tua* Italy as a whole under the impact of the First World War). Serao's concern here is not *specifically* focused on the romantic heterosexual relationship, though she does present it in different guises in the lives of different characters. The common denominator in all four texts, at least as far as this analysis is concerned, is their overwhelmingly positive depiction of female friendship, which is often posited as an alternative to the romantic heterosexual relationship.

Storia di una monaca foregrounds a group of female characters gathered together as a charitable sewing circle, and the subject of Serao's analysis is the friendships and animosities within the group. As I have indicated, most of these characters, including Eva Muscettola, the "monaca" of the title, initially see their future in terms of marriage. Chiarina Althan stands out among them as the only one to see marriage as a potentially stifling existence. The friendships within the group, however, are prominent from the beginning of the text, and contrary to the reader's expectations they are not eclipsed by marriage.

From the beginning of the narrative the friendships are nothing short of passionate. As early as page 3 the notion of a lesbian subtext comes to mind as Eva is described greeting her friend Tecla: "'O caro, caro il mio fidanzato' gridò da lontano Eva vedendo arrivare Tecla, 'sei puntuale come un giovanotto a un ritrovo!'" Although the tone here is clearly playful, the idea of an unusual female friendship is inevitably planted in the reader's mind. In fact I can think of no occurrence of such playful but sexual dialogue between women characters in novels either by the male writers by whom we know Serao was influenced or by other women writers of the period.

Serao covers her tracks very neatly, however, by immediately filling in Tecla's background of rivalry with another female character, Donna Maria, for the love of a male character, Carlo. This rivalry is not fully developed but it, too, has a strange quality. There are no scenes of jealousy on the part of either female character, indeed the attention of each focuses on the other rather than on the supposed object of her affections. Tecla discusses Donna Maria with her other friends rather more than she mentions Carlo. Whenever Carlo and both rivals encounter each other the focal point for each female character is the other woman. They calmly estimate each other's abilities in the struggle for their future, which hinges on a male character who is scarcely described: "'Siete molto forte, Tecla', mormorò donna Maria. 'Molto forte,' rispose costei quietamente" (page 94). Serao repeatedly compares the two women, often presenting them as mirror images of each other, but without developing this parallelism into a full use of the double. The denouement does not correspond to the classic close of the "double" story, but the parallels between the characters are carefully mapped: "Tecla Brancaccio aveva trascinato Carlo Mottola nella quadriglia [...] mentre donna Maria di Miradois, paziente, [...] ballava, li guardava, con uno strano sorriso sulle labbra. Anche Tecla sorrideva: alla luce si vedevano i dentini minuti [...] scintillare [...] mentre la bellissima bocca di donna Maria sorrideva profondamente" (pages 100–01). They are similar but complementary characters. Carlo functions as a prop facilitating Serao's analysis not of the heterosexual romantic element but of the relationship between the two female characters.

This seems strongly reminiscent—but obviously a rewriting—of earlier stories where the woman is purely an object of contention and the real interest lies in the battle between the two men: Serao changes the sex of the protagonists, with the male character as the object and the struggle between the female characters now the centre of the narrative interest. The *Decameron* and the *Heptaméron* are therefore, I think, significant precursors of this plot, with which Serao challenges the perspective of the male-centred text.

Tecla's marriage to Carlo is eventually presented not as a triumph of love but as a victory achieved by Tecla, and thus something which is defined, again, in relation not to the male and the female character but to the two women: "Ella, ostinata, ferrea, nella lotta con donna Maria di Miradois aveva vinto [...], aveva vinto penosamente, dolorosamente" (page 159). Serao presents the marriage itself in wholly negative terms; Carlo has embarked on it "di mala voglia" (page 159). Her success notwithstanding, Tecla's thoughts at the end of the novel are once more deflected from Carlo onto her female rival, with whom she feels a sense of unity despite their different perspectives: "Tecla, umilmente [...] pregava per i vinti come per i vincitori, per donna Maria di Miradois come per sé" (page 160). This is just one example in the novel of how Serao uses a passionate heterosexual relationship to cloak what is best described as a woman-centred awareness.

The case of Olga Bariatine in the same novel mirrors Tecla's in that here too Serao chooses as her apparent subject a relationship of heterosexual passion. Olga is presented as being in love with Massimo Daun. Yet this relationship, too, is fated to end in unhappiness. Unlike Tecla and many of the other female characters, Olga does not have a close friend: she is not part of an alternative female coupling. She is, however, one of the first of Serao's female characters to be part of a community of women that despite certain animosities is supportive, loving and passionate. Although all the other female characters have reservations about Olga's forthcoming marriage, they support her wholeheartedly, knowing that she is doing exactly what society requires of her.

There are possible echoes of Manzoni here: both Lucia and Gertrude were surrounded by friends before their projected marriage/taking the veil. If Serao echoes Manzoni, however, she also changes the focus. Manzoni is not especially interested in the gathering of "amiche e comari venute a far corteggio a Lucia":[32] his interest lies more in the Renzo–Lucia relationship. Nor does he build up a picture of the relationship between these female friends before the marriage/taking of the veil. *Storia di una monaca* retells some of the narrative of *I promessi sposi* from a different perspective. The scene where the friends congratulate Olga on her engagement has the air of an adolescent rite of passage. Serao focuses specifically on Eva's reaction to the forthcoming marriage, and Eva's prayers give the impression that the rite of passage will be an exceedingly difficult one: "La sposina chinava il capo arrossendo, tutta confusa, abbracciando le sue amiche che l'avevano circondata, avendo i lagrimoni sugli occhi; specialmente Eva [...], che le teneva un braccio al collo e le veniva ripetendo sottovoce, come se pregasse per lei: 'Iddio ti assista, Iddio ti assista, cara, cara, cara...'"

162   Chapter 4

(pages 29–30). Although Serao changes tone in the following pages, concentrating on the desirability of marriage for young women of Olga's class, the initial negative view of marriage inevitably colours the reader's perception of what follows.

What does follow for Olga is, predictably, negative. Serao charts her progress through fears of her fiancé's infidelity to dull resignation to an unhappy future. The climax of her story coincides with her marriage, which Serao describes in terms more appropriate to a funeral. As she leaves for her honeymoon all her female friends gather to say farewell, and Serao presents this scene as tragic. Olga is clearly leaving behind a community of love and affection and going into a partnership not of love (as one might expect) but of patriarchal domination. Serao first creates a sense of a caring female community: "Come Olga vide tutti quelli che l'aspettavano per salutarla e le mani amiche che le si tendevano [...], un tremore nervoso l'assalse [...] ma gli occhi le piangevano, la gola era soffocata dai singhiozzi. E man mano, ella si appartò con tutte quelle che erano state sue amiche, avendo con ognuna di loro una tenerezza [...] da scambiare" (pages 130–31). The use of tenses here effectively indicates that this is the end of an era, that the positive part of Olga's existence in a safe female community is over: "Erano state sue amiche" (page 131). It is paradoxically on her entry into marriage that she renounces all hope of a loving relationship. This is clearly revealed in an exchange between Chiarina and Olga, the latter now painfully aware of the consequences of her decision: "'Olga mia, la vita sempre serena, il cuore sempre innamorato,' le disse, piano, Chiarina Althan. 'Come è possibile, Chiarina?' rispose [...] con accento doloroso la sposina. 'Sii buona, sii buona, non ci pensare,' le soggiunse l'amica, toccandole la fronte, come per benedirla" (pages 136–37). Here again the element of ritual is strong, and the use of the verb *benedire* suggests images of the convent, that female community *par excellence*. On the heels of this verb comes the image of the patriarchy as exemplified in Olga's new husband: "Sulla porta Massimo Daun, al colmo del malumore, s'impazientava" (page 137). The most potent farewell described in this scene, however, is Olga's leavetaking from the sickly Angiolina Cantelmo. At this point the language is reminiscent of many descriptions of passion in novels of heterosexual romantic love: "Le due ragazze si guardarono un momento, un'occhiata così intensa e profonda che le labbra non trovarono altro da dire.

Angiolina teneva strette le manine di Olga nelle sue mani magre, quasi le volesse comunicare magneticamente le dolci cose che avrebbe voluto dirle" (pages 139–40). Even more reminiscent of the heterosexual romantic love relationship are Eva's last words to Olga, which Serao tellingly juxtaposes with the authoritative voice of Olga's husband: "'Ricordati che ti vogliamo bene, sempre, sempre: te ne voglio tanto Olga mia…' La campanella suonava: 'Olga, Olga' disse la voce secca e fischiante di Massimo" (page 141). The ellipsis adds to the force of the woman-centred subtext.[33]

Serao's treatment of Olga's move from a community of women into the state of marriage may be compared with a more general transition in women's fiction analysed by Annis Pratt. Pratt notes that women characters' attachment to the natural world is something they must leave behind on reaching adulthood, and argues: "The intensity of these moments [of enjoyment of nature] seems to increase in direct proportion to the imminence of the hero's young womanhood, comprehended as submission to the patriarchy" (*Archetypal Patterns in Women's Fiction*, page 22). This intensity is clearly present in Serao too as her characters approach marriage. If anything the shift is more revolutionary in *Storia di una monaca*, as marriage is represented as a negative transition into acceptance of the patriarchy. This submission to patriarchal society is emphasized by the ellipsis following Olga's last word in the novel (in reply to Massimo's call): "'Eccomi,' rispose lei ubbidendo…" (page 141).

Perhaps the most bizarre female friendship in this novel is located on the edge of the narrative, involving two minor characters, Giovanella Sersale and Felicetta Filomarino. Neither is capable of fitting into the wifely mould prescribed for them by society, Giovanella because she has been spurned by the man she loves, Felicetta for some mysterious reason that is never revealed. Serao describes this intense friendship in a manner calculated to arouse the reader's interest, and her emphasis on its oddity is designed to colour the reader's judgement of it: "Stavano sempre insieme, spesso avevano gli occhi rossi, una medesima malinconia le rodeva. Qual era dunque il segreto di Felicetta? Piú taciturna, piú riservata, ella non lo confidava, se non a Giovanella; e certo, nei loro colloqui solitari, esse piangevano insieme la loro gioventú sfiorita" (page 48). The friendship is abnormal, centres on exclusion from the dominant group, and is full of negative emotions. When the two characters reappear in Chapter 2, in the scene of a party on board a ship, she describes heterosexual couples in various poses—dancing, strolling arm-in-arm, standing looking out over the water. The couple in the sharpest relief, however, and deliberately differentiated from the others, is that of Giovanella and Felicetta, positioned like lovers: "Appoggiate alla ringhiera, come a un balcone, voltando le spalle alla gente, Felicetta Filomarino e Giovanella Sersale piegavano le teste nell'ombra, guardando la fosforescenza del mare" (page 86). Later in the same chapter they are again picked out and contrasted with the other characters. This time Serao is even more negative, seeming to regard them as sick or diseased: "Da capo il raggio scialbissimo erasi posato sul castello di prora, inondando di luce le due testine curve di Giovanella Sersale e di Felicetta Filomarino; e Giovanella nel pallore del suo volto emaciato, pareva quasi spettrale, Felicetta pareva quasi abbarbagliata, circonfusa di candore, entrambe corrose dallo stesso male" (pages 96–97). This "unhealthy" relationship is doomed to end: Giovanella enters into an affair with her former lover, who is now married to her sister, and for some reason this liaison cannot co-exist harmoniously with her relationship with Felicetta. The latter is still "la triste fanciulla che serbava gelosamente il suo segreto, rodendosi di dolore" (page 124), and Giovanella, while acquiring a temporary sense of calm (not happiness) in the affair with her brother-in-law, finishes in a situation exactly parallel to that of her former friend.

It seems, then, that this friendship runs counter to the other female friendships described in the novel: it appears to be an exaggeration of them, and on one level functions as a conventional reminder of the possible danger and impropriety inherent in intense female friendships. Here again, however, the subtext works to deconstruct the apparent warning message. By the end of the novel both characters envy Eva's fate of enclosure in a highly supportive all-female community. Giovanella is also consumed with envy at Eva's courage: "Oh Eva, lassú [...], era scampata dalla tempesta, era in salvo [...], ma lei, Giovanella, non poteva" (page 163). Felicetta's response parallels that of her former friend: "Come avrebbe voluto esser lei la monaca, Felicetta Filomarino" (page 181). The reasons proffered in the novel for this envy centre on Eva's detachment from a life of pain. She is presented as one who enters a different form of existence: one of death to the world, certainly, but one primarily constructed in opposition to the structure she leaves behind, that of patriarchal society.

All these bonds between female characters are extremely interesting and reveal much about Serao's attitudes (both overt and
covert) to the notion of female friendship. The denouement of
Storia di una monaca, however (Eva's decision to join the alternative
community of women), is conditioned most clearly by one particular bond, to which the novel pays considerable attention. Yet the
interaction between the characters concerned is confined to one
brief, poignant scene close to the end. This bond is the one on which
Chodorow focuses in her analysis of female psychology and to
which Abel gives central importance in her analysis of women's
friendship in modern literature: the bond between mother and
daughter.

The first character to refer to the formative influence of this
bond is Anna Doria, the spinster of the group, who has an entirely
negative view of the relationship.[34] Most interesting in her vituperat-
ive account, however, is her concentration on the mother's central
position as (positive or negative) emotional catalyst in the daughter's life: "Olga si marita subito e come vuole, perché non ci ha la
mamma: a noi le nostre mamme impediscono il matrimonio"
(pages 31–32). All the others reject this view of the mother as an
obstacle to their emotional lives: Serao describes them as "quasi
tutte scandalizzate" (page 32). Yet she goes on to vindicate Anna's
claim that this mother, at least, has blocked her daughter's emotional fulfilment, and indeed that the relationship has driven Anna
to the brink of insanity.

Nor does Serao restrict herself to depicting one case of a
suffocating mother–daughter bond: she gradually expands the
theme, introducing it into the story of the protagonist. Eva is
presented as the voice of reason, and gently reproves Anna after
the latter's frenetic outburst about her mother: "Le mamme nostre
ci amano, a loro modo: non sta in noi a giudicarle" (pages 37–38).
Anna's reaction, however, alerts the reader to the possibility that
there is something odd about Eva's relationship with her mother as
well: "E fai benissimo, tu, Eva', rispose malignamente Anna […].
Eva impallidí, tacque, ferita" (page 38). Serao later enlarges on
Eva's relationship with her family and clearly posits her familial
discontent as the reason for her total immersion in her relationships with her friends: "Quell' attività quotidiana […] soddisface-
va il bisogno di movimento e il sentimento di altruismo che era in
Eva, riempiva le sue giornate un po' vuote, un po' solitarie—la
madre apparente e sparente […], troppo giovane per la figliuola già

troppo grande—il padre che adorava ogni esercizio di sport [...], il fratello sempre in viaggio" (pages 44–45). Serao stresses that such superficial relationships are emotionally unfulfilling. It is natural, if we consider this scenario in the light of Chodorow's theory, that Eva should seek to fill the affective void in her life by gathering her women friends around her in an attempt to reconstruct the primary maternal bond—which is precisely what she does:

> Tutti questi l'amavano, Eva; madre, padre, fratello, ma a loro modo, negli intervalli di libertà che concedevano loro le passioni dominanti; e questo non bastava, non bastava al suo ardente bisogno di amore, alla sua vitalità esuberante. Cosí per isfogarsi, ella aveva messo su, col suo fuoco, con la sua fiamma di affetto, questa carità delle ragazze per i bimbi abbandonati. (pages 45–46)

Group activity is a substitute for an emotionally satisfying relationship, and a context in which, as we have seen, many emotionally rich female friendships are grounded.

Eva begins a heterosexual romantic relationship with Innico Althan, the brother of her close friend Chiarina. Yet this relationship does not interfere with her relationships with her female friends. In terms of emotion, however, the greatest insight we are given into Eva's feelings for her future fiancé is found in the bald statement, "Ella, in cuor suo, ammirava quel giovanotto" (page 67). This sentiment deepens only when Eva sees Innico in relation to her mother: his positive relationship with her mother endears him to her; it is as though she feels that through him she may succeed in becoming closer to the mother from whom she cannot get enough love. Serao's description of this focuses on Eva: "I suoi occhi e il suo spirito erano altrove, là [...] dove Innico Althan [...], tutto serio, parlava con donna Natalia Muscettola, la madre giovane di Eva. E in quel biancore di luce [...], nel cuore di Eva era nata, fluiva una novella, infinita, irremediabile tenerezza" (page 103). The reader may at first assume that this warmth is directed towards Innico only, but it becomes obvious that it centres on the combination of Innico and the mother figure, which Eva assumes to be an innocent coupling. As it becomes clear that her fiancé and her mother are spending time together, Eva's joy increases: "Eva sorrideva, tutta felice, tenendo d'occhio la porta per vedere se compariva sua madre e il suo fidanzato" (page 114).

Serao seems to bow to convention at the end of Chapter 3 when she has Eva express doubts about Innico's love for her, followed by standard exclamations of distress. The denouement, however, when considered in psychoanalytic terms and especially in the terms of Chodorow's argument, again subverts the idea of the primacy of heterosexual love. What Eva does here parallels her earlier actions in the novel. First, when not satisfied by her relationship with her family (particularly her mother), she organized a group of other women towards whom she could redirect her emotional demands. As this group has been forcibly splintered by the demands of society, mainly those of marriage, she now chooses a similar but pre-existing group which society is unlikely to penetrate, that of the convent. Her taking refuge there is a direct result of the further frustration of her emotional needs brought about by the affair between her mother and her fiancé. Although Serao never states by which character Eva feels more betrayed, the text contains indications which contradict what we might have expected. While Innico is absent from the last chapter, which describes Eva's profession, Eva's mother is present and is dwelt on by the author for the first time. Her posture is one of shame: "La duchessa [...] vestita di nero, teneva la faccia tra le mani, e pregava, o piangeva, o pensava" (page 148). It is soon apparent that an unbridgeable gap has opened up between mother and daughter: "Eva [...] si accostò a sua madre, ma non l'abbracciò, le baciò la mano: la duchessa aveva teso la faccia; ma si rigettò indietro, come pentita" (page 157). It is evident that Eva blames her mother for what amounts to a double betrayal, the most serious aspect of which must be the violation of the blood tie. Serao indicates as much later, when she comments that "la famiglia era distrutta da cima a fondo" (page 169).

The novel's closing scene, where Eva finishes taking her vows and enters the convent, runs counter to, and again subverts, the body of the chapter, which concentrates on how Eva's vocation amounts to a death. Serao now implies that by dying to society Eva has entered a new life, in a different world, a world of female community in the widest possible sense: "Eva si levò [...]. Il cardinale la benedisse e scomparve dal coro: le monache la baciarono [...]. La porticina fu richiusa, mentre la monaca, con le altre, orava: *Ego sum resurrectio et vita...*" (page 182). Eva is welcomed into this new community of women and it is clear that they conceive of their existence in terms not of death but of life. Serao, on the one hand, reiterates the view of contemporary society and, on the other, subverts it. The corroboration of society's view is insistent and repetitive, but the subtext remains no less challenging.

Storia di una monaca, then, questions any positive view of the accepted female vocation of marriage, and consistently stresses the primacy of the female tie. This serves to privilege the female friendships which parallel the heterosexual love relationships. It is also quite possible to argue for the existence of a lesbian subtext running parallel to the main plot.[35]

Tre donne is also a novel which deals with female adolescence, and thus provides an alternative to the male-oriented *Bildungsroman*. It has three female protagonists and one male protagonist. Its romantic heterosexual relationships centre on a single male figure, Don Francesco, while the variations hinge on the female protagonists. As Don Francesco is the focal point for the romantic dreams and aspirations of two adolescent female characters, one might expect the narrative to be filtered through his potentially unifying point of view. This, however, is not the case. Serao presents Don Francesco largely as an enigma, while using her authorial power to convey repeated criticism of his behaviour. The novel's psychological interest is concentrated in two of the three female protagonists, while the third provides an at first enigmatic parallel with Don Francesco himself.

In this novel Serao is concerned to identify the expectations of her adolescent female characters, and particularly to explore the extent to which those expectations centre on romantic love. Running parallel to her main theme is an investigation of the relationships between her female characters. This second theme moves beyond the bonds between young women to consider also the mother–daughter relationship. Here it would be misleading to argue for the existence of a lesbian subtext: there is no close female–female relationship which could be open to such a reading. What Serao does present here, however, is a further covert privileging of relationships between women, coupled with an overt denigration of the romantic heterosexual bond.

Much of the first part of the novel is devoted to describing the (largely negative) interaction, at a ball, between Donna Clara and Don Francesco. The latter is by turns gallant, flirtatious and authoritarian in his dealings with Donna Clara; she, in turn, is constantly irritated by him. In this opening section, however, equal space is devoted to exchanges between Donna Clara and Miss Daisy.

It is Clara who turns their conversation to marriage, and in the course of this discussion she adopts a tone in relation to Daisy that is both protective and commiserating: "O poverina […]! Gli uomini c'ingannano sempre, quando ci amano e quando non ci amano" (page 64). She also criticizes Daisy for dreaming of marrying for love, and reiterates a negative view of male–female relationships: "Gli uomini di adesso sono aridi come il sughero: non sanno nulla di passione e di romanzo. Tu rimarrai zitella" (page 65). She openly admits that she herself intends to marry for financial gain; in her view such a move is clearly analogous to promotion in social status. When accused by her friend of being unimaginative, however, Clara is quick to dismiss the charge: "'Sogno anch' io' disse la fanciulla bruna 'ma temo di mettere un nome ai miei sogni, temo che essi siano troppo belli e troppo indimenticabili, e mi rendano profondamente infelice'" (page 68). The novel manipulates the reader into supposing that such dreams revolve around Francesco and an ideal of romantic love. Yet there is a possible alternative explanation, based on an intense emotional attachment to women: "temo di mettere un nome ai miei sogni" is oddly reminiscent of "the love that dare not speak its name". Nor does the chapter's conclusion necessarily negate that explanation. While Serao here overtly tries to separate her characters she covertly unifies them by, again, having one mirror the other: "Si guardarono, affettuosamente come due amiche che si sono detto tutto, tenendo ognuna per sé il suo segreto" (page 70). In Chapter 3 it will be revealed that the secret is their mutual passion for Don Francesco; but I still suggest that a desire for an intense relationship with other women remains hidden in the subtext. Serao, however, chooses not to develop the relationship between these characters on any level of the text.

Chapter 2 has Don Francesco as its focal point. To him both Clara and Daisy write letters which express their emotions and reveal their state of mind. Clara writes to tell him of her impending marriage to—as she has predicted—a wealthy, elderly foreigner. Early in the letter her tone is matter-of-fact. The first note of bitterness creeps in not, as we might expect, in relation to Francesco but in relation to her ties with her mother. The letter foregrounds both the romantic heterosexual tie and the maternal–filial one.

The maternal–filial relationship is foregrounded first. In this first reference to her mother Clara posits the notion of sexual rivalry between mother and daughter: "Mamma è contenta, poiché il mio matrimonio e la mia partenza la tranquillizzano sul mio avvenire e le preparano una seconda gioventú, piena di libertà e piena di allegrezza: chi si rammenterà che donna Olimpia di Nerola, ha una figliuola maritata?" (page 80). This relationship is thus foregrounded as problematic in that it contains elements both of proper maternal concern and of apparent female rivalry.

Almost immediately afterwards the narrative focus is redirected to the heterosexual romantic relationship, which turns out to be no less problematic. Clara first asserts her passion for her addressee: "Io vi amo Francesco, cosí profondamente, cosí inguaribilmente, che soltanto nello scrivervelo la mia mano trema e un impeto di tenerezza mi soffoca il cuore. Io vi amo: voi lo sapete" (pages 82–83). This doomed love, Clara says, has almost led her to commit suicide. What has stopped her is the strength of that primary bond with the mother. At this point the mother–daughter relationship is presented much more positively. The focus on heterosexual love produces unity between mother and daughter: in effect, as the text makes clear, the bond with the mother leads the daughter to renounce the passionate heterosexual relationship. Clara goes to her mother in the depths of despair and is met with the most supportive reaction possible. Her mother is both emotionally and physically receptive to her, treating her like a baby. The one who gave her life insists that she retain it: "Mia madre [...] ha passato la notte con me, tenendomi le mani, baciandomi ogni tanto, accarezzandomi, piangendo con me. E ha cercato, in tutti i modi, di convincermi che le tragedie non risolvono nulla" (page 86). Clara's mother then questions her about Francesco's feelings for her and effectively points out that his romantic gestures are of no significance. She generalizes about men and their tendency to make empty romantic gestures, throwing a cold and practical light on the whole affair: "E cosí, dolcemente, senza rimproverarmi, ella ha levato alla mia vita ogni speranza di unione con voi: ed ella aveva ragione" (page 90). Eventually Clara fully accepts her mother's negative judgement of this romantic relationship and is persuaded to enter a loveless but financially advantageous union, which will pose no threat to the primary, female-oriented bond. The mother confesses that when young she found herself in a similar situation and, having chosen the practical solution, has not regretted it. This heightens the sense of unity between the two, and Clara soon comes to see her mother in a broader emotional light, as "la migliore amica" (page 94).

The narration of this scene takes up the greater part of the letter, and, while Clara ostensibly moves on to declare her undying love for Francesco, in fact she continues to muse firstly on her relationship with her mother, secondly on the female condition in general, and thirdly on the male–female relationship. She goes on: "Ripiglio in questo punto la lettera. Narrandovi la scena strana e appassionata fra me e mia madre una profonda emozione mi ha vinta, come da sé ancora innanzi, alla disperazione della figliuola, una buona mamma adorata facesse la suprema fra le confessioni. Ho dovuto alzarmi e vincere, passeggiando, pregando, l'impeto dei singhiozzi" (pages 96–97). The moment of unity with her mother has clearly been of great emotional significance for her, and this sense of unity leads her to lament the social restrictions on young women, which she sees as something divisive for the female sex as a whole: "Il silenzio e il riserbo e la compostezza e la freddezza, a cui siamo obbligate, noi ragazze—né, forse, potrebb' essere diversamente— ci isolano: e avendo l'apparenza di gentili bambole indifferenti, insensibili, noi viviamo profondamente, una vita interiore tumultuosa, spesso, che ci esalta" (pages 98–99). The loss of a potential female unity is regretted here, while the heterosexual relationship is seen in profoundly negative terms: "Come avete guastata la mia esistenza" (page 102).

The subtext of Donna Clara's story gives priority to the mother–daughter relationship, and clearly for Serao it functions in the same way as it would much later for Chodorow: it makes a happy heterosexual relationship impossible. Clara sees Francesco as inadequate precisely because he is not like her mother: he is less honest, understanding and physically responsive than the woman in her life.

To some extent the presentation of Daisy's story is conditioned by Clara's complaint that female friendship is constrained by the prescribed social behaviour for women. Despite fleeting moments of real affectionate closeness to Clara, Daisy is unable to envisage any object for her affections other than Don Francesco. Furthermore, she is still more circumscribed in her behaviour than Clara; she is the epitome of the reserved Englishwoman.

We learn from Daisy's letter to Francesco that she, like Clara, was conditioned to expect most in life from the heterosexual romantic relationship. Like Clara, too, she has been disappointed. This leads her to such a negative conclusion about the heterosexual romantic relationship, "l'amore è una illusione" (page 119)—and she is so devoid of alternatives—that she chooses to end her life. Unlike Clara, Daisy has no loving mother to sit and hold her hand: "Non avevo padre e madre" (page 121).

The third heterosexual romantic relationship in the novel is also presented negatively. In this relationship, unlike the other two, it is the female character who is in control and Don Francesco who is the supplicant. Donna Maria reacts to his "lettera voluminosa" with even greater indifference than he did to the letters he received from Clara and Daisy. In describing the coldness of her reaction Serao sees fit to define her with a masculine noun, underlining the fact that it is she who controls the relationship: "Ma il fiero giudice sdegnò la lettera, perché la tenne in mano, scherzandovi, senza aprirla" (page 151).

Donna Maria goes on teasing her suitor, and in the course of her teasing makes various pronouncements on how a romantic heterosexual relationship ought to be conducted. One of these, provoked by Francesco's use of the word *cattivo*, is, "Non si è mai abbastanza cattivi" (page 153). She also reveals the reasons for her negative response to Francesco's declarations of love: "Voi siete assai savio, Francesco, cosí savio che mi fate orrore" (page 155). This is the only time in the novel that Serao allows her character's guard to slip, and it suddenly becomes clear that Donna Maria is afraid of committing herself to the romantic heterosexual relationship into which Francesco wishes her to enter. Immediately after this slip Donna Maria resumes her usual mocking approach.

Serao's depiction of this relationship does not suggest that female friendship is important to Donna Maria. What she makes clear, however, is her character's wariness of the standard acceptable affective relationship for women of this class—the heterosexual romantic tie. Donna Maria affects scorn for Don Francesco, but when her guard slips we realize that her dominant feeling is fear of emotional entrapment, particularly at the hands of someone she knows to be cold in his relationships with others.

The overwhelming message for the reader in this novel is one of negativity in relation to the heterosexual romantic relationship.

Serao clearly sees it as destructive for women, as her female characters here either suffer because of their romantic attachments or fear they will suffer if they allow them to be formed. Men, on the other hand, are presented as potentially very cruel towards women—unless, of course, they are carefully kept at an emotional distance by the female character concerned. The only rewarding and supportive relationship in the text is one existing between women: that primary mother–daughter bond which is so frequently given such prominence in Serao's work. Serao's wish to privilege her female characters' point of view despite her use of a male protagonist is indicated by the title, *Tre donne*. This directs the reader's attention primarily to the three female characters involved with the protagonist, each of whom is resoundingly negative in her judgement on the male–female relationship. Yet Serao's title also covertly privileges the heterosexual relationship: this is, after all, a novel not about "tre donne" but about "quattro donne e un uomo". The centrality Serao gives the *three* women characters involved with the *one* male protagonist highlights the significance of the heterosexual relationship for the text. The fourth and perhaps most significant woman character is invisible in the title, and her role is firmly consigned to the subtext.

In *Il paese di Cuccagna* relationships with other women are presented as significant for all the major female characters. Here again there is no question of a true lesbian subtext, but the emotional bonds between female characters are privileged, and the privileging of female bonds always co-exists with a corresponding decrease in significance of the male–female romantic attachment.

The tales of Carmela and Maddalena, sisters in love with the same male character, Raffaele, provide a case in point. The two sisters' stories come to the same end: both are heartbroken and both, in effect, turn their backs on the male character and return to each other. Serao makes Raffaele invisible as she concentrates on the passionate relationship between the sisters; he is merely the instrument with which she explores their passionate love and essential loyalty to each other. The most dramatic demands of this relationship occur after Carmela has been accidentally shot. Maddalena arrives too late to prevent the duel, and Serao describes her reaction to her sister's wounding in the same terms as we would have expected if Raffaele had been wounded: "Si buttò nel gruppo, disperatamente, gridando, scostando le persone, gittandosi

alle ginocchia di sua sorella, avendo in quel gesto tutto l'abbando-
no di un dolore immenso" (page 460). Carmela's reaction is one of
shock and then of tender affection: "Aprí gli occhi e mostrò sulla
faccia un senso di doloroso stupore: con le deboli mani cercava
carezzare i capelli neri di Maddalena" (page 461). Carmela soon
realizes that Maddalena is there by design, and the first inkling of
who it is that has betrayed her causes her to react: "Un lividore si
era cosparso sulla faccia della ferita, udendo queste parole, e gli
occhi si erano sbarrati" (page 461). She harshly questions Maddalena, who breaks down: "E la mala donna si ributtò indietro, levò
le braccia al cielo e gridò: 'Sono un'assassina, sono un'assassina!'"
(page 462). Maddalena's passion is met quietly and angrily by her
sister: "Il volto di Carmela si fece terreo; sottovoce, borbottando,
come se piú la lingua non l'aiutasse, diceva anche lei: 'Assassina,
assassina'" (page 462). Clearly, the issue of betrayal here centres on
the relationship between the sisters, whose attention is focused
wholly on each other. Finally, Serao shows how Raffaele has
functioned as the stimulus for the breakthrough in the physical
relationship between the sisters. At the start of the novel physical
contact was obviously taboo ("Le due sorelle non si baciarono, non
si toccarono la mano", page 129); by the end of their tale this has
been broken down by their emotional closeness and by Carmela's
gesture of forgiveness: "La mano destra di Carmela, vagamente
cercò ancora qualche cosa, e finí per trovare la testa di Maddalena,
su cui si posò" (page 463). They subsequently form almost a tableau
vivant at one with nature: "la fisionomia della morta […] ormai
tranquilla: e silenziosamente curva, sotto quella mano perdonante,
la superstite: e tranquilla, silenziosa, la campagna, intorno" (page
463). The relationship is finally presented in a wholly positive light
now that the focus of each woman's attention is the other woman
rather than Raffaele.

The bond between Bianca Maria Cavalcanti and Antonio Amati is the only prominent heterosexual relationship in this novel
which Serao presents as having any positive qualities; and yet it too
fails. Ostensibly, this failure is a result of Bianca Maria's reluctance
to step outside the role of dutiful daughter and assert herself in the
face of her father's tyranny.[36] Yet the subtext suggests that the
emotional issues are rather more complex. There is in fact no
tangible difference between the ways in which the two male
characters, Marchese Cavalcanti (Bianca's father) and Antonio

Amati (her beloved), relate to her. Both love her, in their misguided ways. Her father tortures her mentally and demands total psychic and emotional commitment from her. Amati demands a parallel allegiance, and the only way in which Serao casts him in a more positive light than the patriarch is by having him appear to be genuinely concerned for Bianca's welfare—but then he is a doctor. Serao describes the two male characters in the same manner. She has the Marchese see his primary role as that of ruler of his household. When Bianca lies dying he initially refuses to let her see Amati. The language Serao gives him may only be described as authoritarian: "'No, no, no' urlò lui [...] 'egli non metterà mai piede qui dentro, finché io sono vivo'" (page 514). Amati, too, proves authoritarian in the face of his beloved's illness. When the Marchese finally agrees to send for him it is he who refuses to respond: "Ha letto la lettera... e ha detto che egli è troppo occupato, che la signorina aveva certo qualche altro buon medico" (page 519). And in case the reader does not fully see the parallel between the male characters Serao goes on to spell it out when she says of Amati: "Non osò fare rimproveri al marchese. Non aveva egli stesso, abbandonata la povera creatura [...]? Ambedue erano colpevoli, ambedue" (page 521). Both of them succeed only in tearing Bianca apart; neither offers her a viable mode of existence or the possibility of a beneficial relationship.

Bianca's response to the lack of alternatives in her emotional life is to focus all her emotional energy on another female character—one who is present in the text only through Bianca's consciousness—, her dead mother. It is to this shadow of a female character that she looks for understanding, and on her that she comes to depend. During her final illness she calls first and instinctively on this figure: "Ella aveva lungamente delirato, lungamente gridato, chiamando sua madre, mamma, mamma, come fa il fanciullo in pericolo" (page 510). As her illness progresses, she calls on Amati. But by the end, when she is close to death, it is once more on the mother figure that she focuses: "La delirante, con voce strozzata, chiamava sua madre [...], pregando la mamma che non la facesse morire" (page 528). Once more the mother–daughter bond is presented as more binding than the romantic heterosexual one.

The essence of *Il paese di Cuccagna*, then, is that it privileges female ties. All Serao's major female characters discover a relationship with at least one other woman which is supportive, positive and rewarding, while their heterosexual relationships remain the site of the mental, emotional and physical pain in their lives. Female friendship is valued more highly than the male–female relationship right across the class spectrum.

Mors tua, Serao's anti-war novel, is yet another text which systematically devalues the heterosexual relationship while privileging the supportive nature of female friendship. In each social group Serao presents several examples of fraught male–female involvements. In the aristocratic group the relationship between Barberina Moles and her husband Camillo is doomed to end dramatically in murder, while that between Magda and Mario Falcone is equally unhappy. Loreta Leoni, representative of the bourgeoisie, degenerates into prostitution after the failure of her relationship with Carletto. The lower-class marriage of Cesare and Mariuccia Pietrangeli founders on the separation caused by the war. Serao consciously and overtly compares these relationships by dealing with the representative members of each social group in different sections of each chapter. Clearly she intends to show once again the all-encompassing negativity of relationships between the sexes, and as usual she presents that negativity from the female point of view.

In this novel the supportive nature of female friendship and relationships between women is explored in the context of the group. The text opens with a group of women—a sewing group, as in *Storia di una monaca*—sitting and chatting together. Unlike the group described in the earlier work, this one consists of mature women. As a group they are clearly interdependent: it is to each other that they turn for support and advice.

Oddly, however, there is no instance of such support outside this middle-class group: the novel contains no aristocratic or lower-class equivalent. Nor does it contain any of the intense one-to-one female relationships which Serao depicted in her earlier works. Rather, she reverts to a more traditional presentation of rivalry between her female characters, such as that between Barberina Moles and Magda Falcone. There are no passionate female relationships in any social class. It is as though Serao is backing away from her previous stance and sanitizing the relationships between her female characters by considering them only within the context of a group.

One possible explanation for this careful revision of Serao's view of female relationships is suggested by Lillian Faderman's observation that "openly expressed love between women for the most part ceased to be possible after World War I."[37] Faderman contends that the popularization of the works of Krafft-Ebing, Freud and their respective followers introduced the notion of female homosexuality to the general public and made the presentation of an intense or passionate female same-sex involvement unacceptable in literature after 1914 and especially after 1920. Faderman identifies this concern with female–female relationships as originating in Germany and thence moving to both France and Italy (page 298). At the same time women's demands for independence increased after the First World War, during the course of which their lives had become less restricted in Europe as a whole, and, according to Faderman, "where women's demand for independence was the strongest and when it was most within their grasp, the conviction that female same-sex love was freakish or sick was at its most pronounced" (page 332). This led to something of a backlash against independent women in fiction, especially popular fiction, as Faderman demonstrates with reference to American and European writing. Serao may well have internalized elements of this backlash and hence avoided depicting the type of female relationship which had been so frequent in her earlier fiction. In *Mors tua* she refuses to deny the existence of friendship between women, and continues to privilege it over the heterosexual relationship; but she is extremely careful not to leave such female relationships open to what she would consider misinterpretation and hence seems to tone them down and situate them in a "harmless" group environment.

It is evident that between the early 1890s and the 1920s Serao's depictions of female friendship underwent a change. With this in mind it will be interesting to look in some detail at her earlier depictions of female friendship, and to consider how radical they are as compared to her later work. Equally important here are stylistic devices, such as the double, which give increasing complexity to her presentation of female friendship in her earlier writings.

THE HETEROSEXUAL LOVE RELATIONSHIP, THE LESBIAN SUBTEXT AND
THE FEMALE DOUBLE

In this section I shall consider the interaction between the double
and the female–female relationship, closely analysing two texts,
Cuore infermo (1881) and Fantasia (1883), and referring more briefly
to Addio, amore! (1890) and "La donna dall'abito nero e dal ramo di
corallo rosso"(1888).[38] Each of the three novels has a triangular
structure involving one male and two female characters (one
angelic, the other monstrous). The primary relationship in each
case, however, is not, as appears on the surface, the one between the
male and female characters, but that between the two female
characters, whom Serao also presents as doubles. In each novel
there is a strong attraction and understanding between the women
characters, though the degree of communication between them
differs. The fascination the female characters have for each other is
typical of the double relationship.[39] Yet the intensity inherent in this
fascination seems to lift these relationships beyond the literary
convention of the double and to indicate a romantic attraction or
involvement between the characters. The attachment is displayed
covertly in Cuore infermo and Addio, amore!, but overtly in Fantasia,
which is, I think, the only one of these novels which truly lends
itself to an interpretation based on a lesbian subtext. It is the only
one which presents an ongoing and developing relationship between its two female characters, so that the existence of such a
subtext is more easily verifiable.

One might begin by considering the possible reasons for Serao's
use of the female double (that is, a female first self mirrored by a
female second self). Her first use of it, in 1881, is roughly contemporary with its early use by many other women writers, such
as Charlotte and Emily Brontë (1874) and Mary E. Coleridge
(1896).[40] Why did so many women writers of that period feel a need
to confront the issue of duality? Male writers had been using the
device of the male double for some time, and one of its functions
appears to have been as a means of positing an alternative modus
vivendi. As Guérard says, "A strong feeling of sympathetic identification [of one character with another] may lead to a sense of
doubleness, an immobilizing recognition of the self one might have
been" (page 3). I suggest that nineteenth-century women writers,
because of the behavioural constraints imposed on them by soci-

ety, may have felt an even greater desire to explore this theme than their male counterparts. By using the double device women writers were able to create a more complete female character, splitting it into two very different characters, one socially acceptable, the other unacceptable. Clare Rosenfield, discussing the implications of the double in general, makes a point which adds credence to this idea: "The novelist who consciously or unconsciously exploits psychological doubles may either juxtapose or duplicate two characters, the one representing the socially acceptable or conventional personality, the other externalizing the free, uninhibited, often criminal self" (pages 3–4). And in a nineteenth-century context socially acceptable behaviour is far more circumscribed for women (and therefore often for the female characters created by the woman writer), than it is for men. That could account for the tendency to represent the free and uninhibited female self (the second self) as monstrous. Having stepped outside the boundaries of the conventionally feminine, this self mobilizes those aspects of the female which are unacceptable. The attraction of one self to the other is then explicable by the fact that, rather than existing as two separate characters, they function in many respects as one character split into two. Luce Irigaray has written of how feminine subjectivity expressed in literature gives rise to a set of stylistic and formal tendencies such as the use of double or multiple voices and open endings.[41] In a time of more rigid literary convention, I suggest that the double device served as an early expression of women writers' confusion about the issue of female subjectivity.

Indeed, it seems that the device of doubling (along with the inherent attraction of the two selves) is closely linked with the broader notion of female friendship as well as with the issue of self-definition. Cicero linked doubling, friendship and self-definition (in relation to men) when he described a friend as a second self: "Whoever is in possession of a true friend sees the exact counterpart of his own soul [...]. They can scarcely, indeed, be considered as separate individuals [...]. A true friend is no other in effect than a second self."[42] This applies to women writers' presentations of women's friendships in literature, but it also has a further basis in the psychological formation of the female child. According to Chodorow, women retain permeable ego boundaries because of their early closeness to their mothers: "Women situate themselves psychologically as part of a relational triangle in which their father and men are emotionally secondary or, at most, equal to their mother and women" (*The Reproduction of Mothering*, page 199). This pattern is repeated in the literary plots created by women writers, whence Serao's triangular structures presented entirely from the female perspective. Further, as Abel declares in relation to twenti-eth-century women writers, "Friendship becomes a vehicle of self-definition for women, clarifying identity through relation to an-other who embodies and reflects an essential aspect of the self" ("[E]merging Identities", page 416). Doubling, female friendship and self-definition may thus be linked in women's fiction; certainly all three issues are present in those of Serao's novels which I shall now discuss.

In *Cuore infermo* the relationship between Beatrice and Lalla holds most of Serao's interest, and from the beginning she invests it with an aura of mystery. From the moment the two characters first become aware of each other's existence, the motif of the double is evident. Each of them is presented as insatiably curious about the other. The normally reserved Beatrice avidly questions a friend about Lalla (pages 67–68) before Lalla's relationship with Marcello has even begun. Similarly, when Lalla first meets Marcello, she questions him keenly about Beatrice. The characters show a clear and carefully paralleled interest in each other. As Lalla's affair with Marcello progresses, the empathy between the two women grows. Interestingly, for both of them this empathy is partly based on fear, whereas in standard presentations of the double by male writers fear is normally an emotion restricted to the first self.

Lalla at first appears to pursue Beatrice, seeking opportunities to meet her and begging Marcello to allow her to attend the family church at the same time as his wife. Serao insists on Lalla's obsession with Beatrice: "Era lei la prima a pronunziare il nome di Beatrice, a condurre la conversazione su di lei, a interrogare minu-tamente, con insistenza, con un ardore implacabile, Marcello, su sua moglie. La mattina, ella scendeva nel parco, con la speranza di poterla incontrare" (page 175). The pursuit gradually becomes two-way, however, as Beatrice steels herself to encounter Lalla, with whom she must come to terms: she must face up to her other self. First Beatrice plays the piano loudly in such a way that Lalla, unlike Marcello, recognizes it as a form of pursuit and persecution; to underline the point Serao describes the music as threatening: "La musica dette in uno scoppio subitaneo, quasi imponesse loro silenzio [...]; il breve periodo di tranquillità [...] era scomparso" (page 181). Furthermore, Lalla reacts emotionally to the situation: "Non ti sembra un fatto molto grazioso, Marcello? Noi due sul balcone e Beatrice che veglia nella sua torricella e ci cruccia col suo lume; la fuggiamo, ella ci riprende colla sua musica" (pages 182–83). Yet despite this feeling of persecution Lalla reveals a definite empathy with her *alter ego*: "Udite, udite quanta malinconia in questo ritmo! [...] Tua moglie è triste, Marcello!" (page 182). Lalla here reveals her understanding of the change in character which the formerly austere, indifferent Beatrice has undergone as a direct result of her influence. Since Marcello does not grasp the emotional significance of Beatrice's music, he neither understands nor accepts Lalla's analysis. He thus stands outside the relationship between Lalla and Beatrice.

The same empathy between the two women is evident in the later scene where they meet at the house of Beatrice's friend Amalia. Lalla appears to be strongly attracted to Beatrice: "Guardava spesso Beatrice, sorridendole qualche volta, volgendo la testa dalla sua parte, come se volesse discorrere con lei" (page 205). Beatrice, too, is aware of the strong link between herself and Lalla, which she tries to rationalize by the suspicion that Lalla may be her half-sister, the child of her father and his mistress: "Una sola domanda si presentava molto chiara, tra la folla dei suoi pensieri. Ella chiedeva a sé stessa se Lalla d'Aragona non fosse la figlia della marchesa di Monsardo" (page 208). Serao never elaborates on this point, allowing the relationship between the doubles to remain ambiguous in this respect. On the one hand, the theme of blood-relationship corresponds to that of brother and half-brother common in the male writer's presentation of the double. On the other, it may well serve as a smokescreen to allay possible suspicions in the mind of the nineteenth-century reader as to the nature of the intense attraction between these two characters.

As Ann-Rosalind Jones points out, "Resistance to official discourses, the breaking of taboos and the exploration of homosexual or otherwise anti-patriarchal relationships are often perceived in the interstices of single texts or of collections of texts" (*Making a Difference*, page 99). It may be that Serao's use of the double here serves not only to open up the notion of the female quest for self, but also covertly to indicate the strength of bonds and attraction between those women who in the male writer's text are least likely to be either friendly or attracted to each other—those who are ostensibly in competition for the attentions of the same man.

The resolution of *Cuore infermo* corresponds closely to the standard resolution of the double theme, but again is doubly revealing in the female context. In the last scene where Beatrice and Lalla encounter each other they are for the first time described as physically similar. Both are weak, drawn and scarcely able to walk. The look that passes between them may be seen as one of recognition. Faced with the self which she has until now tried to deny but unable to bear the situation, Beatrice must die. Except as regards the sex of the protagonists, this denouement is perfectly described by a generalization of Keppler's: "In the vast majority of cases the harm done to the first self by the second is harm as catastrophic as harm can be. But also [...] it is not a harm which narrows him [...]; it may and usually does kill him at last, but it [...] compels self-awareness" (pages 194–95). In Serao's text a classically angelic female character is compelled to recognize her other self, her passionate and potentially monstrous essence. This recognition finally kills her, but her growth in self-awareness cannot be denied. It is only through relating to Lalla that Beatrice finally manages to express her emotions within the conventionally acceptable framework of her relationship with Marcello.

How far is it possible, then, to treat *Cuore infermo* as a lesbian novel, or at least a novel with a covert lesbian subtext? As Bonnie Zimmerman points out, "One of the most pervasive themes in lesbian criticism is that woman-identified writers, silenced by a homophobic and misogynistic society, have been forced to adopt coded and obscure language and internal censorship" (page 186). "Woman-identified" is a term borrowed by Zimmerman from Adrienne Rich, who uses it in connection with a primary identification with women by women, not as necessarily indicative of a lesbian sexuality. In that sense Serao is certainly a woman-identified writer, and the society in which she lived was certainly misogynistic, though critics such as Faderman would doubt that homophobia was omnipresent when Serao wrote her novel: in Faderman's view, it is only by the turn of the century that we see definite evidence of widespread discouragement of what she refers to as "romantic friendship" between women (page 238). It is possible that Serao's use of the double, while involving a broader and more sympathetic perspective on the angel/monster dichotomy in the literary presentation of the female character, and straining towards a more "realistic" presentation of self, also tended towards an evaluation of bonds between women as superior to bonds between women and men, and towards a realization of the possible physical attractions between women. *Cuore infermo*, however, may not be seen as an anatomy of a lesbian relationship: there is no real relationship between the female characters. It remains nonetheless undeniable that the power of the mere possibilities of their relationship is sufficient to overshadow the novel's heterosexual relationships completely.

The theme of attraction between women, touched on in *Cuore infermo*, is developed in *Fantasia*. Here Serao presents an actual relationship, which occupies a privileged position throughout the text. It involves the two female protagonists, Caterina and Lucia, and gives the novel its framework. The typically intense double relationship is present from the start as the narrative opens with a description of the deep friendship between the two characters as young girls. The significance of the friendship is drawn out through the symbolism which closes the novel, completing the frame.

The type of friendship described at the start of this novel is not a literary anomaly. There were many similar tales of infatuation and romantic attachment in girls' schools such as the *scuola normale* where Serao's plot is situated. The early stages of *Fantasia* are similar to the plot of Sarah Scott's *A Description of Millennium Hall* (1762).[43] Like Caterina and Lucia, Miss Melvyn and Louisa meet at boarding school and are devoted to each other. Miss Melvyn, like Caterina, marries a man who is unsympathetic towards her passion for her friend. In Sarah Scott's novel, however, the female characters' problems are conveniently resolved by the death of the churlish husband, which allows them to live happily together. Serao does not allow such soft options; she creates a far more complex plot.

Fantasia opens by presenting a gradual process of identification between the two girls. We are made aware of this from Caterina's point of view, as we are shown how her intense distress corresponds to her friend's emotional disturbance: "'Che hai, Lucia?' 'Nulla.' 'Dimmi, Lucia, hai dovuto soffrir molto? Soffri ancora?'" (page 23). (Such identification of one female friend with the suffering of the other is also present in *Millennium Hall*.) Lucia's pain culminates in a suicide attempt, from which the normally undemonstrative and unimaginative Caterina saves her: "Caterina la teneva stretta, affannando ma non lasciandola: Lucia si dibatteva con moti serpentini: le dette dei pugni, la graffiò, la morsicò" (page 24). This is the only point in the text where Caterina dares to oppose Lucia's will; it is clearly a matter of life and death for her as much as for Lucia. At this stage Serao is carefully building up her double motif.

The intense emotion in the novel is, as we might expect, not one-sided. Lucia, for her part, reveals a deep need of Caterina. On the last night they are to spend at school together, she mysteriously leads Caterina to the chapel and urges her to participate in an apparently odd ritual, which involves their swearing love and loyalty to each other for the rest of their days. Caterina is not forced to partake in this bizarre rite: she does so willingly. What Serao describes here amounts to a relationship exclusive of all others, the hallmark of which is its intensity. Lucia, as usual, takes control:

> "Ora noi che ci amiamo tanto ci dobbiamo separare [...]. Ci rivedremo presto? Non so. Vivremo di nuovo insieme, nell'avve-nire? Non so [...]. Ebbene, io ti propongo di vincere il tempo, la distanza, le cose, gli uomini, se si oppongono al nostro affetto. Di lontano, divise da tutto, se ciò accade, amiamoci come oggi, come ieri [...]. Lo prometti tu con un voto, con un giuramento?" "Con un voto, con un giuramento" ripetette Caterina, monotonamen-te, come un'eco. (page 38)

The language used here is like that typically used by most writers of the Romantic novel in depicting the heterosexual relationship. Serao's use of it to depict female friendship was not in itself revolutionary; indeed, its use for that purpose was quite common in women's writing, particularly in the eighteenth century. As Janet Todd points out, "Female friendship represented for most women simply a rapturous sentimental union, springing perhaps from fear of male aggression or neglect but fed primarily by yearning for a partner in sensibility, a confidante in literature" (*Women's Friendship in Literature*, page 360). Todd draws attention to what she terms the convention of ecstasy in eighteenth-century fiction. She also defines female friendship as "an historical phenom-enon, fed by and feeding into fiction" and employing "the lan-guage and dramatics of love" (pages 359–60). Serao was, then, clearly drawing on a specific literary tradition in her presentation of such scenes in this novel.

There is nevertheless something unusual—and something potentially dangerous—about these scenes. What is odd is the timing: by 1883 the tendency to depict such scenes in literature was no longer so prevalent, and they may well have seemed excessive to many readers. Indeed, as Faderman shows in her analysis of Zola's *Nana* (1880) and Daudet's *Sappho* (1884), where lesbianism was openly present it was seen as corrupt and evil. Faderman says, "The lesbian prostitutes that congregate in Laure's restaurant in *Nana* are vice-ridden, and their physical ugliness is a manifestation of their moral ugliness" (page 282). Faderman goes on to indicate that writers either revelled in this topic for its potential distastefulness, or generally avoided portrayals of intense friendships between women lest they be misjudged. Homophobia with regard to relationships between women, however, was not yet widespread. There can be no doubt that the incidence of such friendships in real life was still quite high; yet increasingly they were looked on with suspicion. Carl von Westphal had already questioned the normality of intense friendships between women in 1869;[44] and although, according to Faderman, his article did not circulate enough to have widespread public influence, works of writers who were inspired by him did. One of the latter was Havelock Ellis, whose 1897 study of sexual inversion included as an appendix a study by Obici and Marchesini conducted in the late nineteenth-century *scuola normale*.[45]

Obici and Marchesini draw clear parallels between intense friendships between women and what they refer to as love relationships, by which they mean heterosexual involvements. They summarize the characteristics of the former as follows: the extraordinary frequency with which, partly by means of subterfuges, the lovers exchange letters; the lovers' anxiety to see and talk to each other, to press each other's hands, to embrace and kiss; long conversations and longer reveries; persistent jealousy, accompanied by its many ploys and distinctive results; exaltation of the beloved's qualities; the lover's abnegation in overcoming all obstacles to the manifestation of her love; the awareness of doing something prohibited; the pleasure of conquest (Faderman, page 245). The authors conclude that about 60% of the girls studied had been actively involved in this kind of friendship. Ellis comments that the general cessation of such relationships, and indeed of such feelings for other women, on leaving school shows that there is no congenital abnormality in the women concerned. He and some of

Obici and Marchesini's interviewees are, however, more circum-spect when considering what damage may be done to the women concerned if this kind of friendship does not terminate at the appropriate time.

Serao's friendship with Cesare Lombroso (a disciple of Krafft-Ebing) implies that she cannot have been unaware of these trends.

Fantasia, then, describing such a relationship which does con-tinue beyond the boundaries of adolescence, must surely be one of the last narratives which could safely be written on this theme. Moreover, in the climate of the time it might well have seemed too overt in its celebration of female friendship were it not for its conclusion, which, as we shall see, again has a dual function.

In the novel's second section Serao repeatedly focuses atten-tion on the bond between the two female characters, to the ex-clusion of the heterosexual relationships. Caterina has married Andrea Lieti and, in keeping with her new surname, at first appears to be contented. In her husband's eyes she is the veritable "angel in the house". We are told that "l'incarico suo era di trovar saggio e onesto quanto suo marito faceva" (page 112), and this is indeed how she behaves, except in one vital area: she refuses to end her friendship with Lucia, whom Andrea initially dislikes (here again the plot is reminiscent of *Millennium Hall*). On one level Caterina, in preserving the friendship, is keeping the promise she made Lucia; but on another level she has already broken that promise by her marriage and her obvious adoration of her hus-band. This constitutes the first betrayal in the novel, and seems to provide Lucia's motivation for betraying Caterina in her turn. Lucia's response is consistent with the typical jealousy noted by Obici and Marchesini.

As Serao develops her double motif she reinforces the reader's perception of the intense bond between her characters. She does this in her presentation of Lucia, who has an uncanny intuition about the tragic outcome of her impending affair with Andrea: "Si staccò bruscamente, spaventata, stralunando gli occhi, vedendo una visione di terrore" (page 169). This would be implausible were she not so at one with Caterina that she is capable of predicting her actions. She is never unaware of her capacity to hurt her *alter ego*; nor, indeed, is Andrea, who to some extent understands the nature of the intense bond between the two women. In the scene where he discusses with Lucia his first physical advances towards her, he tells her that he has not mentioned this to Caterina. She responds, "Potevate dirglielo […] voi che l'amate tanto." When Andrea replies, "Se ne sarebbe doluta… e…", Lucia asks, "Per chi, doluta? Per voi, forse?", and Andrea explains, "No, per voi. Essa vi ama" (pages 129–30). Through this persistent questioning Serao conveys not only Andrea's understanding of the women's relationship but also Lucia's need to be reassured about Caterina's feelings for her. All this occurs at a time when the focus is ostensibly on the relationship between Andrea and Lucia.

The importance and full significance of the relationship between the two women is made absolutely clear in the final scene, where Caterina commits suicide. Serao presents Caterina's corpse in a symbolic posture: "Pareva diventata piú piccola, una bambina […]. E intorno alle mani terree, dalle dita violacee, azzurreggiava un rosario di lapis lazzuli, per metà spezzata" (page 274). In this closing sentence Serao twice implies both that Caterina blames Lucia for all that has happened, and that it is because of Lucia's betrayal, not Andrea's, that Caterina kills herself. She does this firstly by highlighting the central position of the broken rosary, given to Caterina by Lucia the day after they exchanged their vows of love and fidelity and thus a symbol of the unbreakable bond between them, and secondly by having Caterina return, in appearance, to a child-like state (childhood having been the stage at which she was closest to her other self).

The most striking difference between *Fantasia* and *Cuore infermo* lies in this direct causal relationship between the closeness of the two female characters and the eventual suicide of one of them. On the one hand, Serao is simply taking the double motif to what we have seen is its logical conclusion, in that she here illustrates the typical catastrophic damage done by the second self to the first. Yet on the other hand, by depicting such a stark conclusion Serao may be avoiding the potential charge of encouraging this type of relationship. Perhaps *Fantasia* ultimately negates its celebration of intense female friendship through Serao's use of the double and her ability to work elements of it into the plot of the cautionary tale. If, while flouting literary convention by daring to deal with this subject, she is protecting herself from censure through her melodramatic conclusion, such a strategy would accord with Faderman's observation that "on the Continent […] the perception of romantic friendship as a noble institution which society had no reason to discourage and every reason to encourage, was quite dead by the end of the nineteenth century" (page 294). Paradoxically, however, Serao's conclusion cannot weaken the intensity of the earlier depictions of the relationship between the female characters. It seems that Serao succeeded—in this one novel, at least—in conveying her view of the possibilities inherent in female relationships while simultaneously deflecting society's growing disapproval of such friendships. She successfully used a technique which might now be referred to as "lesbian realism: the adaptation of the conventions of the social and psychological novel to appraise bonds between women and demonstrate that such relationships are potentially of psychic and moral value".[46]

Fantasia must be the most revolutionary of Serao's writings in its exploitation of the double motif. In *Addio, amore!* her approach to the same motif shifts somewhat. Here her major achievement resides in her ability openly to unite her two female characters in confrontation with the supposed object of their respective affections. Once again the relationship between the two selves is particularly intense. Serao presents them as sisters, and thus on this occasion effectively negates the possible existence of a lesbian subtext. Rather, the double motif serves as a spur to the notion of female unity. Serao stresses that Laura and Anna share a single perspective on events; they function almost as one character. As Laura justifies her betrayal to Anna, Anna's fear of and anger against her sister disappear and she finds herself able to confront the male love object, Cesare Dias, who is the reason for the split between the two selves. In the course of that confrontation Serao, through Anna, places the blame squarely on the shoulders of the male protagonist, who has come between the two selves and denied them harmony. For the first time in Serao's work, a female character is permitted openly to criticize the actions of a male character (and Dias is an unusually strong figure in Serao's gallery of male portraits): "Tu sei veramente un uomo senza cuore e senza coscienza [...]; tu appartieni alla grande classe degli uomini putrefatti, tu mi fai ribrezzo e pietà, intendi?" (page 281).

In this novel, then, the use of the double facilitates the unification of the two female characters against the male character (and against his perception of them as diametrically opposed) in such a way that despite his strength he is practically negated. Faderman comments on the similar resolution of Edouard Bourdet's 1926 play *La Prisonnière*: "Once those female beings get together, man becomes the stranger, the enemy, powerless to separate them because there are no terms on which he can fight them" (page 348). Bourdet's play overtly warns men against female friendship and its dangers. Serao's novel reads more like a celebration of female solidarity: at no point does the reader sense any sympathy for the male character.

"La donna dall'abito nero e dal ramo di corallo rosso" is another of Serao's works in which the double is used. In this short story there can be no question of a relationship between the two female characters because in a sense they are literally one. For the only time in her fiction, Serao here uses the manifest (or overt, as opposed to the latent) double. A number of significant issues are raised through this. The one I wish briefly to examine centres on the duality experienced by women, which, through her use of the double, Serao presents as something imposed on them by men.

The very existence of the double in this story is brought about by the nature of the heterosexual relationship: it is the first self's relationship with the male character that calls the second self into being. Serao implies that the romantic male–female bond leads, for the female, to a sense of duality and ultimately of crisis.

The text's dramatic climax occurs during a love scene. It suddenly seems to the first self that her lover's words are addressed not to her but to another female figure (the second self) seated behind her; and so she accuses him of loving this ghostly female figure, whom she describes in detail and with repugnance. To her horror, he agrees, and says she has just described herself. He leads her to look at herself in a mirror, and the narrator describes what she sees: "Vidi nel cristallo una faccia smorta, consunta dall'età [...]. Vidi la sua figura, che era la mia figura; urlai come una bestia, 'Non sono pazza [...]; il fantasma si è messo nell'anima mia [...]; siamo due'" (pages 140–41). The act of looking in the mirror is frequently used in the literature of the double to symbolize a recognition of one's true self. Serao, however, by having the male character lead the female character to the mirror, and thus to a different perception of herself, appears to be claiming that woman is compelled to perceive herself, with distress, in the light of man's perception of her. As Gilbert and Gubar state, with reference to the artist's literary self-definition, which they say must precede self-assertion, "the woman writer acknowledges with pain, confusion and anger that what she sees in the mirror is usually a male construct [...], a glittering and wholly artificial shield" (*The Madwoman in the Attic*, pages 17–18).

Serao's use of the double fits well into such an analysis, centring as it does on the idea that woman is compelled, by man, to perceive herself in an-other light. Judith Kegan Gardiner has commented (on women writers generally, though she could have been thinking of Serao): "The woman writer uses her text, particularly one centring on a female hero, as part of a continuing process involving her own self-definition and her empathic identification with her character."[47]

The use of the double, then, allows Serao to explore the issue of female self-definition (including that of the woman writer, as we have seen in Chapter 3) and the whole area of relationships between women in overt juxtaposition to the heterosexual relationship. Her judgement of the male–female romantic bond is overwhelmingly negative. Her judgement of female same-sex relationships is problematic, hemmed in as it is by elements of the cautionary tale together with tragic and melodramatic turns of plot. On balance, however, the close female relationships she presents are, at least, sources of support and understanding, and certainly offer an inkling of the potential for passionate friendships between women. Serao was no stranger to intense female friendship. Her ties with both Eleonora Duse and Sibilla Aleramo were certainly intense (the former rather more so than the latter).[48] It appears that Serao, as well as giving and receiving support in these friendships, also experienced pain as a result of them, especially in the case of Eleonora Duse. The pain-pleasure dichotomy is reflected in the texts analysed in this and the preceding sections.

FEMALE FRIENDSHIP IN ISOLATION FROM THE HETEROSEXUAL BOND: ALTERNATIVE SOCIAL GROUPINGS

Given what I have said about Serao's presentation of female friendship when situated alongside her analysis of the heterosexual relationship, one might expect that when she considers women and girls in a group situation (school, home, workplace) she will be less constrained, and thus that her presentation of same-sex relationships within a group will contain more elements indicative of a lesbian subtext. In fact, however, while she is almost wholly positive in her presentation of female relationships within the group, there is arguably still more internal censorship at work in the short stories which I shall examine next.[49] The increasing suspicion with which such relationships were viewed during the period is again discernible in the pattern of her writing. In only two of her short stories, "Telegrafi dello Stato" (1885) and "Scuola normale femminile" (1886), does Serao deal with anything remotely resembling a passionate female relationship. Both are early works and both are confined to the years of adolescent girlhood, when, as we have seen, such relationships were common and (relatively) tolerated.

"Scuola normale femminile" is set in the same environment as *Fantasia*, written three years earlier. Serao's approach in the short story, however, is different from that adopted in the novel, as here the main focus of her attention is (as we saw in Chapter 3) the work which the pupils must do and the pressure placed on them by society. Other themes are nonetheless present, including that of female friendship. Serao no longer focuses on the importance of such bonds to the exclusion of all else, but is concerned to give her readers another realistic picture of the nature of female same-sex relationships within the environment of the school.

The Obici–Marchesini study mentioned earlier is categorical about the types of protagonists involved in passionate relationships in the *scuola normale*: "The relationship [...] generally exists between a boarder on one side and a day-pupil on the other. Notwithstanding [...] its apparently non-sexual nature, all the sexual manifestations of college youth circle around it, and in its varying aspects of differing intensity all the gradations of sexual sentiment may be expressed" (Ellis, page 243). Serao's short story opens with an equivalent explanation of such relationships: "La severissima ordinanza direttoriale proibiva qualunque rapporto fra convittrici ed esterne: ma appunto per questo, esterne e convittrici erano unite a coppie, a gruppi, cosí saldamente che nessun castigo poteva disunirle [...]; si erano stabilite amicizie ferventi che rasentavano la passione" (pages 952–53). Serao here explains such passionate relationships as a direct result of a natural sense of rebellion on the part of adolescent girls. Yet she does not shrink from portraying the extent of these passions.

Possibly the most significant relationships portrayed in the story are those between Caterina Borrelli (Serao's *alter ego* figure, who recurs repeatedly in her more youthful writings) and Amelia

Bozza and between Caterina and Annina Casale. This suggests that Serao herself may have had first-hand experience of the emotions she here deals with. At the start of the story Caterina is involved with Amelia Bozza in a relationship which Serao describes as passionate. The tone is, again, reminiscent of the romantic novel: "Si vedeva bene lo sguardo che Amelia Bozza, una convittrice del primo corso […], fissava su Caterina Borrelli, l'esterna del terzo corso […], e Caterina Borrelli girava fra le dita una rosa appassita che Amelia Bozza le aveva data, tre giorni prima" (page 953). Serao goes on to show that this kind of friendship is not unusual:

> Gabriella Defeo, una biondinetta del terzo corso, convittrice, voltava con affettazione le spalle a Carolina Mazza, una esterna […] con cui aveva litigato il giorno prima […]. Non cantava Artemisia Jacquinangelo […] perché Giuditta Pezza, esterna […], non le voleva piú bene; Giuditta Pezza sorrideva a Maria Donnarumma, ma invano […]. Di mano in mano passava una boccettina di odore che Clotilde Marasca aveva comperata per Alessandrina Fraccacreta, la bruttona sentimentale e civettuola. (page 953)

Such passions are clearly widespread, as is public knowledge of them within the community of schoolgirls as a whole. Serao is quite open about the depth of emotion involved in these liaisons: "Amelia Bozza […], passando innanzi a Caterina Borrelli, le aveva consegnato un biglietto: diceva *se non mi vuoi bene o impazzisco o muoio*" (pages 969–70). Again, the vocabulary is that of heterosexual love.

Serao, however, does not concentrate solely on the passions inherent in these relationships. The elements of female solidarity and support which we might by now expect to find are also present, particularly in the scenes between Caterina and Annina. This relationship is the most significant in the story because in the third chapter, where Serao reveals her characters' future, it is stated that both Caterina and Annina will go on to be "telegrafi dello stato", implying that their relationship (and no other) will continue after their schooling has finished. It is therefore the one liaison which, like that of Caterina and Lucia in *Fantasia*, might be considered harmful.

Oddly, however, Serao does not bring this relationship to any conclusion. In her earlier "Telegrafi dello Stato" she had already used the character Caterina Borrelli, but the friendship she had had there was with yet another female character, Annina Pescara. Clearly Annina Pescara/Casale is some kind of composite character functioning as the object of Caterina's affections. But in any case, as we shall see, the relationship in "Telegrafi dello Stato" is much weaker and less central to the story than the one in "Scuola normale femminile". Serao clearly did not wish her fiction to pursue the implications of the continuing liaison.

One further interesting area of "Scuola normale femminile" consists of cases where dislike exists between female characters. There are few such cases, but those female characters who are disliked are disliked universally. Serao suggests that the antipathy is at least partly due to physical appearance. The text contains two ugly characters, Isabella Diaz and Giustina Marangio, the former sympathetic in disposition, the latter antipathetic. (We have already encountered them in the preceding chapter.) Giustina is described as follows: "quella faccetta livida di vecchietta diciottenne, quella testolina viperea […]; non aveva amiche" (page 955). Isabella, another solitary character, is described thus: "In verità era cosí laida […] che faceva nausea" (page 980). Such presentations appear to be partly drawn from life. The Obici–Marchesini study included one eye-witness account which stated that of the 40% of female pupils who are not involved in same-sex passionate relationships, only half reject such affections while "the other 20 are excluded either because they are not sufficiently pleasing in appearance, or because their characters do not inspire sympathy" (Ellis, page 244).

In "Scuola normale femminile", then, Serao gives what appears to be a realistic picture of a possible relationship between adolescent females, together with a partial examination of the passions underlying it. Yet there is in this story a sense of a surface merely scratched. Even so, it is not true that—as Jeuland-Meynaud has suggested—Serao avoids describing physical contact between her characters. According to Jeuland-Meynaud, instances of physical contact in Serao's work, "all'infuori […] degli amplessi erotici […] dei quali c'è ben poco da dire […], concernono i diseredati della vita sociale condannati a condividere in troppi gli spazi angusti della miseria" (page 48). Jeuland-Meynaud does not consider the intense female relationships in Serao's fiction, and therefore presumably would not consider such liaisons in an erotic light. Yet the relationships in "Scuola normale femminile" clearly contain erotic elements, and Serao does not flinch from describing physical contact.

"Telegrafi dello Stato" is similar to "Scuola normale femminile" in that it concentrates largely on the work done by the characters and the expectations of their employers and society. Once again Serao considers the role of friendship in the group, but here its manifestations are weaker. I suggest that this is because she is concentrating on the gradual maturing of the female characters and here concerned to show how exclusive female friendships, although significant, are expected to become less passionate and less central to the "normal" girl's emotional happiness. Thus she presents a more socially acceptable version of female friendship, especially when this story is seen in harness with "Scuola normale femminile", as it was in 1886 when both were published in the collection *Il romanzo della fanciulla*.

Yet the transition Serao seems to be describing in these short stories—a transition from a female-centred adolescence full of passionate emotion to the environment of work and of adult (that is, heterosexual) passions—is not presented positively. The present existence of the female characters in "Telegrafi dello Stato", as well as their future, is depicted in a wholly negative light, through the filtering consciousness of the *direttrice*: "Levava la testa e guardava tutte quelle ragazze immobili [...] e non le sgridava piú, sentendo la mestizia di quelle lunghe ore fredde [...]: le nasceva in cuore una pietà profonda di loro, di sé medesima" (page 927). While there is an element of celebration of adolescent female passions in both *Fantasia* and "Scuola normale femminile", the need to put away such emotions is presented as painful. Annis Pratt writes about what she calls the "green world" in women's novels—the depictions of nature and their place in women writers' portrayals of female adolescence. She makes observations which I think apply, in Serao, to the adolescent female characters' experiences not of nature but of each other: "In most women's novels the green world is [...] something left behind or about to be left behind as one backs into the enclosure [...]. The intensity of these moments seems to increase in direct proportion to the imminence of the hero's young womanhood, comprehended as submission to the patriarchy" (*Archetypal Patterns in Women's Fiction*, page 22). Such, I think, is Serao's increasingly careful presentation of female friendship as a rite of passage from adolescence to womanhood—though it is a source always there to be tapped again by her characters as soon as the romantic heterosexual relationships into which they have entered inevitably let them down.

THE RELIGIOUS COMMUNITY

The only novel in which Serao focuses in any detail on the religious community and the life of the convent is *Suor Giovanna della Croce* (1901). Even here life within the walls of the convent furnishes the subject-matter only of the book's first section. Sections II–IV then move from the general to the particular, as Serao analyses how one religious woman copes with a transition from the secluded world of the convent to secular society.

Serao is openly critical, if only retrospectively, of the dissolution of the convents which began in Naples in 1860 as part of the secularization of the new Italian state.[50] Part of her justification for this appears to be the mental shift required of elderly nuns who had to move from an atmosphere of female solidarity into a harsh patriarchal society. Serao presents such a transition as rather cruel and ultimately near-impossible.

While elaborating her thesis Serao once again stresses the element of support in female relationships. From the beginning, an air of mutual aid pervades the life of the convent. The first glimpse we have of the elderly mother superior shows her "sostenuta da una suora piú giovane [...] che la guidava attentamente, misurando il suo passo su quello della vecchissima che a lei si appoggiava" (page 540). The use of the verbs *sostenere* and *appoggiare* here is striking: it captures the essence of the characters' life. The nuns also identify emotionally with their sisters' sufferings. At the moment when they are compelled to leave the convent, Serao focuses again on the mother superior: "A ognuna che passa la badessa suor Teresa di Gesú prova come una novella, piú acuta impressione di pena" (page 568). Serao implies that the support involved in these relationships is difficult to reproduce once the nuns are outside the exclusively female environment. Some of the nuns attempt to preserve their ties: "Suor Francesca [...] non avrebbe avuto pace, se non le fosse stato dato di ritrovare una sua sorella *sepolta viva*" (page 581). Yet Suor Francesca soon discovers that without the framework of the community even that is impossible—in fact, the narrator says, the very idea is too painful a reminder of what she is now missing. What Serao describes here is a late "submission to the patriarchy" (Pratt, page 22). Having refused to be bound by the laws of patriarchal society in adolescence (we might remember Eva's transition from one world to another in *Storia di una monaca*), these women are now forced into a late and painful submission by the agent of patriarchal society, the government.

On the other hand, it might be argued that the convent is equally subject to patriarchal rule—if not more so—, as a component of the patriarchal Roman Catholic Church. Serao's convent, however, functions autonomously on a day-to-day level, and any contact with the Church at large is in fact seen in a negative light. When the priest comes to inform the nuns that they must leave the convent they react negatively to the very sight of him. Indeed, they feel aversion to all men, including this one who symbolizes the power of the Church. As soon as the priest enters the nuns' chapel, "vi fu un rapidissimo movimento tra le monache, come di sgomento, come di pudore offeso: tutte, egualmente, si serrarono nel mantello nero, si strinsero il velo nero al viso" (page 542). Serao stresses that they all react in the same way. She goes on to indicate that the priest does not command respect. He is obtuse and quite incapable of understanding the group of women. As he suggests a date for their departure, Serao describes him mockingly: "Malgrado la sua limitata intelligenza, egli comprendeva che era quello l'ultimo colpo" (page 546). She takes pains to point out that the women are more intelligent than their supposed mentor, and undermines his very role as mentor, as it is to the mother superior, not the priest, that the nuns turn in their distress. The negativity of the nuns' reaction to the priest may be judged by comparing it to their reaction to the soldiers who come to eject them from the convent. Given the soldiers' role, the reader might well expect the latter reaction to be more extreme, but Serao uses the same vocabulary and describes the same type of reaction: "Le monache, vedendosi guardate, si stringevano anche piú dietro il seggiolone [...]; si serravano il mantello intorno la persona, si tenevano fermo sul volto il velo" (page 560). They react in the same way to representatives of both Church and state. Serao's repeated use of the verb *serrare* implies the nuns' desire to remain intact as a community; equally, on both occasions she stresses the significance of the veil as a means of retaining their integrity.

In *Suor Giovanna della Croce* Serao describes only one type of physical contact in relation to the enclosed group: the contact between the nuns and the mother superior as they leave the convent. Later in the text she emphasizes that such physical contact was not ordinarily permitted: "Le due monache [...] non si baciavano, non si toccavano la mano, poiché questi segni di affetto terreno sono proibiti, fra le suore" (page 582). This serves to contradict writers such as Diderot, who assume, as Janet Todd points out, that "female love flourishes when heterosexual love is denied—in convent, school, or harem" (*Women's Friendship in Literature*, page 322). Obviously Todd is here referring to sexual love. Even so, Serao's description of the leave-taking is undeniably full of physical passion. The mother superior is the focus of the characters' attention: "Tutte le monache [...] l'avevano circondata, piangendo [...], prendendole le mani, baciandogliele" (page 543). The scene is repeated several times in this section of the novel.

Undoubtedly, then, while portraying men as oppressive and alien to these female characters, Serao presents women as their only source of affection, comfort and support. When she goes on, in later sections of the novel, to describe the relationships Suor Giovanna has with others, they follow the same pattern. Men (the priests, the judge, the police—all clearly representatives of patriarchal society) are repressive and harsh towards her. It is with individual women (Donna Costanza, Maria Laterza and Concetta Guadagna) that she finds friendship; yet these friendships, although intense, are temporary because of the effect which men have on the lives of the women concerned. They are not a community, and it is men (again, representing patriarchal society) who dictate the tone of their lives. Donna Costanza's son fails his university examination in medicine and so she must move to a poorer area and out of Suor Giovanna's world; Maria Laterza loses her wits after the birth of her son and is imprisoned in the asylum; Concetta's lover abandons her and she too must return to a poorer existence. Suor Giovanna, in any case, would be unable to retain these friendships because she too has to leave the area when the state cuts her allowance. In this text at least, the patriarchy militates against communities of women and against women as individuals.

In her depiction of Suor Giovanna's life after she has left the convent Serao falls back on an old comparison, that of the convent with the brothel. She uses it differently, however, from her male predecessors and contemporaries. As Janet Todd points out, "Both brothel and convent are set apart for the transmission of special knowledge and both are exclusively female. But both are fantasies doubly ordered and structured by men: in the novels' society, men have created them, and their fictional creation is also a male affair" (page 80). In *Suor Giovanna della Croce* Serao takes at least the fictional creation of both realms temporarily out of male hands.

Her presentation of both with a series of studied parallels between them, using the point of view of the innocent Suor Giovanna, is effective. When the protagonist leaves the convent and goes to stay with her grasping sister she develops an attachment to the house opposite her window: "Suor Giovanna aveva finito per amare questa casa dirimpetto che aveva un aspetto cosí austero e cosí taciturno: le ricordava [...] il monastero [...] con le sue fitte gelosie" (page 575). The reader is alerted to the nature of the building from the start, through Serao's aside about the amusement of the sister and her niece at this fascination. The parallel is subsequently developed further, still using Suor Giovanna as a filter. She discusses her interest in the other building with Suor Francesca: "Dirimpetto, vedete, abitano persone silenziose e solinghe, che non ho mai viste [...]; mi sembra, talvolta, di esser ritornata a suor Orsola" (page 588). Serao builds up her character's identification with the other house, and it reaches a peak in the scene just prior to Suor Giovanna's discovery of the true nature of the place. As she is about to leave her sister's house to make her way in society, "ebbe un sospiro breve di rimpianto per quel vano di balcone [...]; quella casa muta e cieca, dirimpetto, aveva prodotto su lei un effetto di pace" (page 601). Suddenly she notices a young man waiting in the street below and senses that something is about to happen: "Cercò vincere quel desiderio di vedere e di conoscere" (page 603); but she fails. Hence she witnesses the murder of another man as he leaves the brothel, and her cry of terror alerts the brothel's occupants. One shock follows another as the house is dramatically revealed in its true light: "Le [...] donne erano in vestaglie vistose, [...] e sottane di seta [...] e calzate di seta nera: alcune discinte e spettinate" (page 605).

Serao's depiction of Suor Giovanna's response to this discovery is morally conservative, though in literary terms it serves to point out the contrasts, rather than the similarities, between the two exclusively female communities. It thus functions as a further

corrective to earlier literary parallels: "A malgrado la sua ignoran-
za […] ella comprese in un baleno, quanto vi era di sozzo, d'im-
mondo, di orrendo, in quello spettacolo; e, per la vergogna, per la
nausea, per l'orrendo, cadde indietro" (page 605).

Although no further comparisons are made between brothel
and convent, that is not the end of the theme in this novel: a mere
ten pages later Serao takes it up again on a more individual basis.
Suor Giovanna is compelled through poverty to sell her lacework,
and the only potential customer is a nobleman's mistress called
Concetta, who lives above her apartment. Suor Giovanna does not
wish to meet Concetta because she is both ashamed of her own
poverty and contemptuous of the girl's situation. In the end,
practically forced to approach Concetta by her friend, Donna
Costanza, she gives in. Serao describes her protagonist as initially
most unwilling to accept Concetta's friendliness: "Si sollevò, stese
la mano per prendere la mano della monaca e baciarla. Costei,
umilmente, la ritrasse" (page 611). But as Concetta goes on to tell
the story of her previous life in a brothel and her current precarious
existence, Suor Giovanna unexpectedly warms to her. She comes to
realize that the appropriately named Concetta Guadagno—rather
like the protagonist herself, Serao seems to suggest—is full of a
rather naïve faith. As the ex-nun leaves, "Questa volta, Concetta
Guadagno arrivò a prendere fra le sue manine bianche e molli […]
profumate […] la mano magra, rugosa di suor Giovanna […] e a
baciarla" (page 614). So the comparison is restated and the interpretation of both ways of life is sympathetic. Serao reinforces the link
between the two female characters when at the end of Section III
Concetta's lover leaves her, compelling her to return to the streets,
while Suor Giovanna is left homeless by the cut in her state pension.
Serao, then, acknowledges the link between the two female communities, convent and brothel, but not in the lascivious, voyeuristic
terms of those writers who had previously posited such a link.

Ultimately, Serao uses *Suor Giovanna della Croce* to show the
network of physical and emotional support which may exist between women. Equally, however, she analyses the intrusion of the
patriarchy both into the female community (of both types: it is an
act of male violence that disturbs the brothel) and into the lives of
individual female characters. From all points of view she judges
the patriarchy negatively, while the female community is presented as a positive alternative mode of existence. She also questions

the basis of the literary commonplace where the brothel and the convent are comparable female communities, and re-evaluates it in a new light.

From her earliest writings to her last Serao's presentation of female friendship is an important aspect of her work, though her manner of presenting it changes. She seems to have been increasingly aware of the negative interpretations often placed on the type of intense friendship she describes, and to have therefore resorted to various types of subterfuge and even self-censorship. From her use of the double motif, from the elements of what might be described as a lesbian subtext, from her increasing unwillingness fully to develop this theme, it is evident that a degree of unease colours her attitude towards it. As Janet Todd states in relation to eighteenth-century fiction, women writers use "a cluster of motifs which relate most obviously to the central romance but which achieve new meaning when analysed in the context of female relationships" (*Women's Friendship in Literature*, page 403). It is easiest for Serao to analyse female friendship while hiding her analysis behind a presentation of the romantic heterosexual relationship. When she sets her analysis in the context of groups of female characters, removed in some way from the world of men, she often lacks the courage to develop it fully, so that her portrayals of female friendship in such writings tend to be weaker, the relationships themselves being presented as less intense.

Serao must, however, stand as an exception to a generalization made by Janet Todd: "Women authors [...] left no truly successful image of female friendship in fiction" (page 379). Many of Serao's female friendships succeed, in that it is through them rather than through the "central romance" (Todd, page 403) that the characters develop. And Serao's female friendships are invariably more successful than her heterosexual romantic relationships: they are a source of strength and support for her women characters. To borrow Adrienne Rich's words, Serao strives to describe "the mutual confirmation from and with another woman that daughters and mothers alike hunger for, pull away from, make possible or impossible for each other" (*Of Woman Born*, page 218).

The element of the cautionary tale implicit in certain of Serao's elaborations of this theme functions, I think, primarily as a concession to society's increasing concern about such relationships. Given her friendship with Lombroso, Serao must have been aware of this trend and, as always, was careful not to present overtly in her fiction anything that would offend the society in which she lived. Perhaps because of the strategies she employs, Serao's novels of female friendship seem, on the whole, more positive than many more recent novels by women writers exploring the same theme. Annis Pratt's survey of such recent novels is somewhat negative: "Battles about dominance and submission, self-punishments, and despair before gender-norms characterize many novels of love and friendship between women—often resulting in excessively punitive denouements" (*Archetypal Patterns in Women's Fiction*, page 95). While elements of all this are present in Serao's novels, the moments of support and intensity and the generally positive presentation of love and friendship between women militate against the punitive denouements. It seems to me that the denouements are primarily a concession to the views of society, while also serving as a kind of expiation of guilt for Serao herself.

The guilt would arise from Serao's tendency to give primacy to female same-sex relationships rather than to male–female ones. In Alicia Ostriker's words, she wishes to explore "a [...] central set of preoccupations [concerning] female–female relationships and the relation of the female to suppressed dimensions of her own identity"—though she would not have expressed herself thus.[51] Part of her desire to explore such relationships is no doubt rooted in her own personal experience with another woman artist, Eleonora Duse. Her relationship with the actress was undoubtedly both passionate and supportive. Serao referred openly to their relationship of passionate friendship on several occasions. In an article published in *Il giorno* on 25 March 1904, for example, she wrote about "questo suo grande cuore che è uno dei suoi fascini, quasi pari, in seduzione, a quello della sua intelligenza".[52] The words are reminiscent of many descriptions of female characters in her fiction—and also echo once more the tone of the traditional romantic novel, but with a subversive element. Serao's experience of such friendships (this one outlived both her marriage and that of Eleonora Duse, as well as the latter's passion for d'Annunzio) may well have been at least partly instrumental in her concentration on love and friendship between women in her short stories, her novels and even her journalism.

In view of Serao's attention to this theme, and of the various ways in which she dealt with it, it seems to me that her presentation of female friendship is, in spite of herself, undeniably political, and that it functions as a challenge to certain institutions, including heterosexual marriage and patriarchal society as a whole. This is more obviously the case where it is possible to identify a lesbian subtext, yet even where none is in evidence Serao's narratives remain woman-centred. Their focus on women, and women's relationships with each other, is central. They challenge both the exclusive privileging of specific social institutions and narrative privileging of specific textual structures.

NOTES

1   D. P. Rotunda, *Motif-index of the Italian Novella in Prose* (Bloomington, Indiana University Press, 1942), p. 158.
2   D. P. Rotunda, *Motif-index*, shows, for instance, that in Bandello's *novelle* friends are chosen at the expense of mistresses.
3   D. P. Rotunda, *Motif-index*, gives the example of some of Sercambi's *novelle* as tales in which this bonding is central.
4   G. Boccaccio, *Decameron* [1349–51], edited by A. E. Quaglio, 2 vols (Milan, Garzanti, 1974), I, 406–10.
5   M. de Navarre, *Heptaméron* [1559], edited by M. François (Paris, Garnier, 1967), pp. 311–15.
6   G. Boccaccio, *Decameron*, II, 887–906.
7   M. de Montaigne, "De l'amitié" [1580], in his *Essais*, edited by M. Rat, 2 vols (Paris, Gallimard, 1962), I, 181–94. Of friendship Montaigne says: "A dire vray, la suffisance ordinaire des femmes n'est pas pour responde à cette conference et communication [...] ny leur ame ne semble assez ferme pour soustenir l'estreinte d'un nœud si pressé et si durable" (p. 185). He adds, "Ce sexe [...] par le commun consentement des escholes anciennes en est rejetté" (p. 185), revealing how friendships between women have a long history of exclusion from male texts.
8   G. Flaubert, *Madame Bovary* [1857] (Paris, Garnier-Flammarion, 1966).
9   This is true of *I Malavoglia* [1881] and *Mastro-don Gesualdo* [1890].
10   G. d'Annunzio, *Il trionfo della morte*, in his *I romanzi della rosa*, 2 vols (Milan, Mondadori, 1949), I, 651–1049; G. d'Annunzio, *La fiaccola sotto il moggio*, in his *Tragedie, sogni e misteri*, edited by E. Bianchetti (Milan, Mondadori, 1940), pp. 935–1064.
11   J. Todd, *Women's Friendship in Literature* (New York, Columbia University Press, 1980), p. 305. This wide-ranging study concentrates mainly on eighteenth-century literature but is nonetheless useful for any analysis of the theme's continuation into the nineteenth century.

12 One example of this is the relationship between Clarissa and Anna in Richardson's *Clarissa* [1747–48], where Anna's marriage coincides with Clarissa's death. Furthermore, male authors often describe what J. Todd, *Women's Friendship in Literature*, p. 132, defines as manipulative female friendship. Thus the phenomenon of female friendship is often presented in negative terms.

13 As is pointed out by E. Moers, *Literary Women* [1963] (London, The Women's Press, 1978), p. 67, marriage is of central importance to the plots of nineteenth-century women writers. Many nineteenth-century heroines have three possibilities: the right marriage, the wrong marriage and spinsterhood. The heroine's choice of one of these is what closes the text.

14 The importance of this bond for Serao, both in her own life and as represented in her fiction, has been analysed in Chapter 2.

15 E. Abel, "(E)merging Identities: The Dynamics of Female Friendship in Contemporary Fiction by Women", *Signs*, 6 (1981), 413–35.

16 N. Chodorow, *The Reproduction of Mothering: Psychoanalysis and the Sociology of Gender* (Berkeley, University of California Press, 1978).

17 Chodorow has been criticized by many feminist critics for, while recognizing the importance of friendship between women, simultaneously seeming to to devalue it. Chodorow's "solution" to women's relational difficulties with men consists of involving men in child-rearing to a greater extent, thus redressing the asymmetric organization of parenting and ultimately leading to a different process of ego-formation. Critics such as Pauline Bart have responded negatively to this "solution", accusing Chodorow of "reinforcing heterosexuality and the nuclear family": see P. Bart, "Review of Chodorow's *The Reproduction of Mothering*", in *Mothering: Essays in Feminist Theory*, edited by J. Trebilcot (Marsland, Rowman and Littlefield, 1983), pp. 147–52 (p. 147).

18 This idea found a form in the practice of *affidamento* in Italian feminist groups of the 1980s.

19 H. Deutsch, *The Psychology of Women*, 2 vols (New York, Greene and Stratton, 1944–45), I, 13.

20 See also my article "Angel vs. Monster: Serao's Use of the Female Double", *The Italianist*, 7 (1987), 63–89.

21 Indeed, while E. Abel, "(E)merging Identities", argues for the similarity of female friends involved in such relationships, J. Kegan Gardiner, "The (Us)es of (I)dentity: A Response to Abel on '(E)merging Identities'", *Signs*, 6 (1981), 436–42, finds that even the couples analysed by Abel hinge on difference and complementarity rather than on similarity. She points out that "the basic pattern in these novels is not of two equal friends but a pair of similar but differentiated women [...]. There is a constant interplay between sameness and difference between the two. Often the women are treated by others as the same but feel themselves to be different" (p. 437). I would go even further than Gardiner and say that elements of total opposition seem to be a prerequisite for the depiction of intense female friendship by women writers.

22 Serao is uninterested in the process of male self-definition, and the male friendships she presents are entirely superficial. Nothing in her writing comes close to the intensity of relationships between women. What C. Burke, "Gertrude Stein, the Cone Sisters and the Puzzle of Female Friendship", in *Writing and Sexual Difference*, edited by E. Abel (Brighton, Harvester, 1982),

pp. 221–43, says of Gertrude Stein seems to me to be equally applicable to Serao: "She felt that women's characters were most intensely moulded in same-sex involvements" (p. 221).

23   M. Jeuland-Meynaud, *Immagini, linguaggio e modelli del corpo nell'opera narrativa di Matilde Serao* (Rome, Edizioni dell'Ateneo, 1986), p. 131.

24   M. Serao, *Suor Giovanna della Croce* [1901], in her *Opere*, edited by P. Pancrazi (Milan, Garzanti, 1944–46), I, 533–674.

25   This terminology is borrowed from R. Rogers, *A Psychoanalytic Study of the Double in Literature* (Detroit, Wayne State University Press, 1972). The manifest double is obvious from the start of the text, while the latent double is one of whose existence the reader only gradually becomes aware and is never overtly identified as such.

26   *The Voyage In: Fictions of Female Development*, edited by E. Abel, M. Hirsch and E. Langland (Hanover, University Press of New England, 1983), p. 5.

27   A. Pratt, *Archetypal Patterns in Women's Fiction* [1981] (Brighton, Harvester Press, 1982), pp. 34–35.

28   A. R. Jones, "French Theories of the Feminine", in *Making a Difference: Feminist Literary Criticism*, edited by G. Greene and C. Kahn (London, Methuen, 1985), pp. 80–113 (p. 99).

29   B. Zimmerman, "What Has Never Been: An Overview of Lesbian Feminist Criticism", in *Making a Difference*, pp. 177–211 (p. 203).

30   A. Rich, *Of Woman Born: Motherhood as Experience and Institution* [1977] (London, Virago, 1991), p. 225, also uses the term "double vision" when she discusses the mother–daughter relationship, to define a perspective which is at once that of mother and daughter. It seems to me that this is precisely the perspective Serao strives to attain in many of the narratives to be discussed here.

31   M. Serao, *Il paese di Cuccagna* [1891], in her *Opere*, I, 105–529; M. Serao, *Storia di una monaca* (Catania, Giannotta, 1898); M. Serao, *Tre donne* (Rome, Voghera, 1905); M. Serao, *Mors tua* (Milan, Treves, 1926).

32   A. Manzoni, *I promessi sposi* [1840–42] (Milan, Mondadori, 1947), p. 61.

33   S. Dranch, "Reading through the Veiled Text: Colette's *The Pure and the Impure*", *Contemporary Literature*, 24 (1983) 176–89 (p. 177), has said in relation to Colette's work that "a subtext, consisting of the clearly stated unsaid, or more precisely of an inter-said [*inter-dit*: forbidden], is indicated through ellipsis and metaphor and constitutes a unifying matrix for what appears to be a loosely connected series of stories, *Le Pur et l'impur*." It seems to me that Serao also uses ellipsis in a way that is significant in relation to the subtext, but that, rather than indicating the existence of a subtext, it underlines what the reader has already gleaned from the subtext, the existence of which is no longer in question.

34   Serao's problematic presentation of motherhood was considered in Chapter 2. It is unusual for her to present an adult daughter so openly negatively disposed towards the figure of the mother.

35   For a fuller analysis of *Storia di una monaca* see U. Fanning, "Sentimental Subversion: Representations of Female Friendship in the Work of Matilde Serao", *Annali d'italianistica*, 7 (1989), 273–87.

36   A further analysis of the function of Bianca Maria will be undertaken in Chapter 5, as she is one of Serao's most important "gothic" characters.

37   L. Faderman, *Surpassing the Love of Men* (New York, Junction Books, 1981), p. 20.

38   M. Serao, *Cuore infermo* (Turin, Casanova, 1881); M. Serao, *Fantasia* [1883], in her *Opere*, ii, 5–274; M. Serao, *Addio, amore!* [1890] (Rome, Edizioni delle Donne, 1977); M. Serao, "La donna dall'abito nero e dal ramo di corallo rosso", in her *Fior di passione* (Milan, Galli, 1888), pp. 129–41.

39   The following studies consider the element of attraction and repulsion which forms an inherent part of the double relationship: R. Tymms, *Doubles in Literary Psychology* (Cambridge, Bowes and Bowes, 1949); *Stories of the Double*, edited by A. J. Guérard (Palo Alto, Stanford University Press, 1967); C. Rosenfield, "The Shadow Within: The Conscious and Unconscious Use of the Double", in *Stories of the Double*, pp. 313–22; R. Rogers, *A Psychoanalytical Study of the Double*; C. F. Keppler, *The Literature of the Second Self* (Tucson, University of Arizona Press, 1972).

40   Recent feminist criticism has drawn attention to the use of the female double in the works of nineteenth-century English and American women writers. E. Showalter, *A Literature of Their Own* [1977] (London, Virago, 1982), highlights the use of the device in the works of Charlotte Brontë and George Eliot. S. M. Gilbert and S. Gubar, *The Madwoman in the Attic: The Woman Writer and the Nineteenth-century Literary Imagination* (London, Yale University Press, 1984), also deal with the above writers, along with Jane Austen, Christina Rossetti, Elizabeth Barrett Browning and Emily Dickinson.

41   L. Irigaray, "Quand nos lèvres se parlent", in her *Ce sexe qui n'en est pas un* (Paris, Minuit, 1977), pp. 203–17, translated by C. Burke as "When Our Lips Speak Together", *Signs*, 6 (1980), 69–79.

42   Cicero, *Offices, Essays on Friendship and Old Age and Select Letters*, edited and translated by T. Cockman and W. Melmoth (London, Dent, 1930), pp. 179, 206.

43   S. Scott, *A Description of Millennium Hall* [1762] (New York, Bookman Associates, 1955). This text is analysed in detail by L. Faderman, *Surpassing the Love of Men*, pp. 103–09.

44   C. von Westphal, "Die Konträre Sexualempfindung", *Archiven für Psychiatrie und Nervenkrankenheit*, 2 (1869), 73–108, analysed in detail by L. Faderman, *Surpassing the Love of Men*, pp. 239, 241, 278, 279.

45   H. Ellis, *Studies in the Psychology of Sex: Sexual Inversion* [1897] (London, Heinemann, 1933); G. Obici and G. Marchesini, *Le "amicizie" di collegio: ricerche sulle prime manifestazioni dell'amore sessuale* [1896] (Rome, Dante Alighieri, 1898). My direct source is L. Faderman, *Surpassing the Love of Men*.

46   C. R. Stimpson, "Zero Degree Deviancy: The Lesbian Novel in English", in *Writing and Sexual Difference*, pp. 243–59 (p. 253).

47   J. Kegan Gardiner, "On Female Identity and Writing by Women", in *Writing and Sexual Difference*, pp. 177–91 (p. 187).

48   For an analysis of Serao's friendship with Eleonora Duse throughout her adult life see A. Banti, *Matilde Serao* (Turin, UTET, 1965). The triangular friendship between Serao, Duse and Aleramo receives some attention in *Sibilla Aleramo e il suo tempo: vita raccontata e illustrata*, edited by B. Conti and A. Morino (Milan, Feltrinelli, 1981).

49   These are M. Serao, "Telegrafi dello Stato" [1885] and "Scuola normale femminile" [1886], parts of her *Il romanzo della fanciulla*, in her *Opere*, i, 911–50 and 951–88.

50   See M. Jeuland-Meynaud, *La Ville de Naples après l'annexion, 1860–1915* (Aix–Marseille, Editions de l'Université de Provence, 1973), p. 303 for an analysis of anticlerical movements in the city.

51   A. Ostriker, "The Thieves of Language: Women Poets and Revisionist Myth-making", in *The New Feminist Criticism*, edited by E. Showalter [1985] (London, Virago, 1986), pp. 314–39 (p. 319).

52   M. Serao, "Quella che tace", in her *Opere*, II, 757–60 (p. 757).

Chapter 5

GOTHIC RE-VISIONS

The first novel to define itself as Gothic was Horace Walpole's *The Castle of Otranto*, published in 1764.[1] Many critics regard the Gothic novel's heyday as having been the 1770s, when the first woman novelist to attempt the genre was writing: Clara Reeve published *The Old English Baron* in 1771.[2] Yet the Gothic did not deteriorate or fall out of favour after its supposed peak: it went on to provide many novels, and to provoke much critical debate on its style and content from the 1790s into the nineteenth century.

One of the most ardent debates on the nature of the Gothic novel took place between Ann Radcliffe and Matthew "Monk" Lewis.[3] Radcliffe distinguished sharply between Terror-Gothic, of which she saw her own novels as examples, and Horror-Gothic, used by Lewis. In her article on the use of the supernatural she has her character Mr W say: "Terror and Horror are so far opposite, that the first expands the soul, and awakens the faculties to a high degree of life; the other contracts, freezes, and nearly annihilates them."[4] From this it may be seen that one of the major concerns of the authors of Gothic fiction was the effect of their writing on the reader. It is an extremely self-conscious literature.

One is struck by two aspects of the debate between Radcliffe and Lewis, and also of the earlier one between Reeve and Walpole. Firstly, the context in which the Gothic novel was being written and analysed was that of England. (Although Beckford's *Vathek* was written in German before being published in English, it has always been considered within the English context, as has Maturin's *Melmoth*.[5] Germany was the first Continental country to be receptive to the Gothic, and the Schauerroman soon flourished.) Secondly, both these literary debates took place between a male and a female exponent of the genre. A division of opinion and technique appears to be linked to the sexes of the authors. Walpole and Lewis wrote sensational Gothic novels, piling on the supernatural and horrific elements. Reeve and Radcliffe were frequently accused by their male critics of being too practical in their approach to the genre—of providing explanations for their (less frequent) uses of the supernatural. Already the seeds of two strains of Gothic were sown: that written by men and that written by women. Once I have established what the main motifs and constituents of the Gothic novel are, I intend to turn my attention to the genre known as "Female Gothic", and thence to Serao as an exponent of it.

As might be gathered from Ann Radcliffe's words quoted above, the Gothic novel was intent on inducing a sort of pleasurable fear in its readers. One could say it drew their attention to what might be termed the uncanny. Part of the problem in describing the Gothic novel's tone resides in the difficulty of defining the uncanny. Freud, I think, sheds some light on the Gothic novel's eerie atmosphere: he defines the uncanny as "in reality nothing new or foreign, but something familiar and old-established in the mind that has been estranged only by the process of repression".[6] The use of such motifs as incest and doubling in Gothic literature may be partly explained by Freud's theory. Indeed, he goes on to discuss the figure of the double as a specifically uncanny device, and says its uncanny quality "can only come from the circumstances of the 'double' being a creation dating back to a very early mental stage, long since left behind, and one, no doubt, in which it wore a more friendly aspect" (page 389). Freud sees literature as an especially effective vehicle for the uncanny, and analyses several German Gothic tales (by Hoffman and Hauff) in which the uncanny is skilfully used. He seems perturbed, however, by the power of the writer who deals with uncanny material; he resents the author's power in ordering his or her environment and thus the reader's perception of it. Above all, he dislikes uncanny tales which are presented as being grounded in reality: "He [the author] takes advantage, as it were, of our supposedly surmounted superstitiousness; he deceives us into thinking that he is giving us sober truth, and then after all oversteps the bounds of possibility" (page 405). Freud would presumably have felt more at home, then, with the tales of such writers as Walpole and Lewis, with unrealistic horror-Gothic. The crux of Freud's analysis, though, lies in his sense of being manipulated by Gothic writers. He says: "We order our judgement to the imaginary realities imposed on us by the writer, and regard souls, spirits and spectres as though their existence had the same validity in their world as our own has in the external world" (page 405). If, on the one hand, this sense of manipulation of the reader has led to such criticism as Freud's, on the other hand, in the nineteenth and twentieth centuries readers have increasingly reacted negatively to the Gothic because of its apparent remoteness from reality, its excess. Some modern readers do not like to suspend disbelief, and thus Gothic literature has often been seen—especially by literary critics—as dated escapism.

More recently, however, there has been renewed critical interest in Gothic novels, which have begun to be taken more seriously. Part of the new approach rests on the discovery that the Gothic is a genre which marries well with certain others, notably the Romantic and the Sentimental. This may well have been the mixture of Gothic and "reality" (in the sense of a recognizable, even domestic situation) to which Freud somewhat petulantly alluded. Robert Hume has seen the link between the Gothic and the Romantic as follows: "Gothic and romantic writing are closely related chronologically and share some themes and characteristics, such as the hero who is a guilt-haunted wanderer. Both have a strong psychological concern with interior mental processes."[7] It appears, then, that Gothic and Romantic writing are linked in their characterization and approach—so Gothic may not after all be so inconsequential as it seemed.

Elizabeth McAndrew, too, has recognized that the Gothic is not an entirely independent genre. She discusses the tone, structure and devices of the Gothic novel in relation to the Sentimental novel: "The Gothic novel, in making monstrosity the outward show of the terrible inner distortions of man's innate good nature into evil, is [...] an expression of the other side of the benevolist ideas reflected in the Sentimental novel. It forms a variant of the Sentimental genre, with related structures, forms and devices" (page 24). (It is perhaps no wonder, then, that duality and doubling are devices dear to the Gothic.) Juliann Fleenor agrees with McAndrew's findings,[8] while Mary Patterson Thornburg has based her analysis of *Frankenstein*, and her view of the Gothic, on the same theory. She writes of the Sentimental/Gothic myth: "The Gothic side of the myth represents an unconscious acknowledgement of the potency of [...] rejected elements, an unconscious need within the culture to deal with reality in its entirety [...]. Thus the Gothic is in a very literal sense *monstrous*; it is a warning to the sentimental, a demonstration of its own existence."[9] One is reminded of Freud's theory of repression of the once familiar, and struck by how the Gothic is a meta-narrative which comments on its own devices—such as the figure of the monster.

I accept that there are connections between the Gothic and the Romantic, and between the Gothic and the Sentimental. I am not convinced, however, that such connections are present to the same degree in all Gothic novels. Some novels might properly be called Domestic-Gothic or Sentimental-Gothic, and their effect might well be striking because of the links between genres—because of the elements of surprise to which Freud took exception. Other Gothic novels stand rather in the realm of the truly sensational, with exaggerated use of the supernatural and other Gothic devices. Serao wrote both types, as I shall show in due course.

Having posited a distinction between Gothic textual types, it remains to consider what elements of the Gothic may exist in both. In other words, what are the specific characteristics of Gothic fiction in whatever locus it situates itself? One major characteristic is the effect produced on the reader by *all* Gothic: it is, as I have said, a reader-identified genre. The writer deliberately induces an identification with the main characters on the reader's part; point of view is adeptly manipulated. As Thornburg says, "In every case the Gothic is distinguished by its lack of dependable distance—by the threat it poses to sentimental characters with whom readers are expected to identify" (page 40). Thornburg's point is that Gothic terror must credibly threaten the Sentimental universe in which the reader feels secure. Any reader may easily identify with the characters of the Gothic because the latters' ambiguous situation in society makes them accessible to all readers regardless of class or gender. As Ann Tracy points out, "Protagonists are frequently orphans, or they are foundlings or adopted, their family origins mysterious."[10] The Gothic traditionally has standard devices: "closed worlds, mediated narratives, ancient houses, dark villains and perfect heroines" (McAndrew, page ix). Incest is a frequent motif, sometimes a central theme; as McAndrew says, "the problem of evil is [...] presented as a psychological problem created in the ambience of the family" (page 12). Characters, in what I would define as the sensational Gothic novel, are, according to McAndrew, "like the characters of the Sentimental novels [...]; their physical appearance corresponds to their spiritual state" (page 12).

McAndrew, in fact, implies that this is the case in all Gothic novels, but I would restrict the observation to the more sensational Gothic, and it is often more noticeable in early Gothic than in that of the nineteenth and twentieth centuries. The motifs of the Gothic novel not already mentioned are numerous. They include all manner of dramatic devices, such as abduction, murder, confinement (in more than one sense in Female Gothic), death, deathbed agonies, dismemberment, secret passages, dreams, swoons, apparitions, deformed figures, insanity, the occult, seduction, atmospheric storms and mysterious voices.[11]

Certain changes, relevant to Serao's technique, were introduced in nineteenth-century Gothic novels. As McAndrew says, "Settings were changed from medieval to contemporary, a man's house turned out to be still his Gothic castle and his soul, already reflected in paintings and statues, began to look back at him from mirrors and, worse still, from his double, a living, breathing copy of himself" (page 7). In Serao's case, this man was often a woman, but the technique was similar. In the nineteenth-century Gothic text a sense of incoherence also occasionally surfaced. Masao Miyoshi, although discussing poetry, puts it well when he says, "Incoherent details were many times forcibly 'resolved' by the overall scheme, leaving a painful cacophony."[12] Again, the dual impulse of the Gothic text (on the one hand the reader is encouraged to identify with the characters, on the other s/he is confused by the plot) reflects its central concern with issues of unity and doubling.[13]

It is becoming clear that as Gothic literature developed in the nineteenth century it retained its sense of identification with the reader (and *vice versa*) and its concern with certain motifs and tones, while acquiring greater psychological awareness and textual self-consciousness. The crucial motifs in the Gothic literature of the nineteenth century (and, in Serao's case, of the early twentieth too) centre on issues of identity, duality, sublimated incest, illness and madness.

FEMALE GOTHIC

The term "Female Gothic" was coined in 1963 by Ellen Moers,[14] and has been used repeatedly in literary criticism since then, most notably by Juliann Fleenor, who adopted it as the title of a collection of writings on the subject. Moers's definition is unproblematic: "What I mean by Female Gothic is easily defined: the work that women writers have done in the literary mode that since the eighteenth century we have called the Gothic" (page 90). Although I do not agree that all women writers write "Female Gothic" while all male writers write a non-female variety, I think Moers drew attention to two important aspects of the Gothic: firstly, the large number of women novelists who worked in it, and secondly, an element in the genre that is somehow "feminine". She wrote, "To confront the long engagement of women writers with the Gothic tradition is to be reminded that its eccentricities have been thought of, from Mrs Radcliffe's time to our own, as indigenous to 'women's fantasy'" (page 100).

It is undoubtedly the case that the Gothic genre attracted mainly women novelists, and that, whereas with the passage of time male novelists relinquished the Gothic, women were not disposed to. As Moers points out, male writers in the nineteenth century

> succumbed to the prevailing anti-heroic, quiescent temper of the bourgeois century, and admitted, with whatever degree of regret or despair, that adventure was no longer a possibility of modern life. Latecomers to literature as they were, and still bedazzled with the strengths of feminine self-assertion, women writers of the nineteenth century were long reluctant to succumb to the ennui, the spleen, the *tedium vitae* of the *mal du siècle*. (page 131)

Yet, alongside historical reasons for the genre's prevalence in women's writing, there must be a further reason why women writers repeatedly chose to use the same motifs, the same plots, the same themes, tones and ideas.

It seems to me that certain elements of the Gothic struck a chord for women writers. I have already discussed the significance of the double motif for nineteenth-century women writers and for Serao in particular.[15] Margaret Homans suggests that the Gothic may be particularly suited to women writers because of its concern with literalization/literal meaning. The literal, she says, is traditionally classified as feminine, and the feminine, seen from the point of view of our masculine culture, is defined as elsewhere.[16] Hence the locus of the feminine (elsewhere) and the literal (which cannot be adequately inscribed in the literary text) is the same: both exist outside our cultural representations. The woman is traditionally the Other. This is seen in countless male texts (not least Gothic ones). According to Homans:

> The initial movement of the Gothic into the supernatural world is a grotesque attempt at addressing the barrier of dualism from the other direction, from the position of objective reality rather than from that of subjectivity. The Gothic mode did not originate with women writers, nor was it exclusively practised by women, but it may be that it is predominantly a female form because it lends itself so well to women's response to the cultural identification of "woman" with the literal. It could be that women write the Gothic where all sorts of literalizations occur [...] because they have been *excluded* from it and must continually confront and defend against accepting that exclusion. (page 259)

This is a problem that faces all women writers, and it does seem that some women writers have chosen to approach it through the eminently suitable mode of the Gothic. Homans does not discuss women writers' use of the double motif, but her analysis functions as a partial explanation of the anguish depicted in the woman's text wherever the double is present. She states that "the dualism of presence and absence, of subject and object and of self and other, structures everything thinkable, yet women cannot participate in it as subjects as easily as can men because the feminine self is on the same side of that dualism with what is traditionally other" (page 257). The double (one of the most widely used Gothic devices) is thus even more painfully relevant to women writers than to their male counterparts. As Sybil Korff Vincent says, "The Gothic novel is a literary representation of our innermost fears. What we fear so much is ourselves. Using Pogo's [a character in Margaret Atwood's *Lady Oracle*] words to describe the Gothic we see that 'we have met the enemy and she is us.'"[17]

In relation to the Gothic in general, I have already mentioned the prevalence of the orphan motif. In the Gothic fictions of women writers the significant parental absence is that of the mother. Gilbert and Gubar have identified Mary Shelley's monster as a motherless being and discussed its importance for her: "It begins to be plain that [...] the monster's motherlessness must have had extraordinary cultural and personal significance for Mary Shelley [...]; feelings of rage, terror, and sexual nausea, as well as idealizing sentiments, accrete for Mary and the monster around the eternal feminine image."[18] Ellen Moers saw *Frankenstein* as an after-birth myth: "The material in *Frankenstein* about the abnormal, or monstrous manifestations of the child–parent tie justifies, as much as does its famous monster, Mary Shelley's reference to the novel as 'my hideous progeny'" (*Literary Women*, page 99). On the one hand, then, the importance of the mother figure for the woman writer is clear; on the other, there is the woman writer's consciousness of herself as (potential) mother. (In Chapters 2 and 4 I have dealt with the importance of the mother figure for Serao, to whose writings these general points are eminently applicable.) Gothic heroines are on the whole motherless, as Eve Kosofsky Sedgwick has pointed out with reference to the Gothic novel: "Always for women, and very often for men, life begins with a blank. The mother, if known, has disappeared."[19] Claire Kahane, in her article on Flannery O'Connor,[20] discusses the "mother–daughter confusion of identity", and such confusion has been analysed by Nancy Chodorow from a psychoanalytical point of view.[21] Kahane is aware of how Female Gothic works as "the imaginative exploration of that confusion, the apprehensive testing of the problematic boundaries of female identity and its relation to power, sexuality and the maternal body" (page 243). The woman writer, then, uses the Gothic to explore her feelings towards mother-figures, and also towards the experience of motherhood itself. The pregnancy, birth and labour motifs in women's Gothic novels are of great significance. They are also important in terms of literalization, and Homans's ideas are useful again in this connection: "That women bear children and men do not is, after all, the simple origin of this complex and troubling tradition that associates women with the literal and with nature" ("Dreaming of Children", page 261).

In women's Gothic novels motherhood itself is associated with intense fear, often leading to insanity. As Fleenor says, "The drama of pregancy [...] leads to constriction, not freedom, madness not sanity, and monsters not symmetry" (*The Female Gothic*, page 16). This may be linked with Serao's equally negative presentation of sexual love: in the nineteenth century, love and marriage often led woman to the highly ambiguous role of mother or, as Barbara Hill Rigney says in relation to *Jane Eyre*, to the realization that "the price paid for love and sexual commitment is insanity and death, the loss of self."[22] In becoming a mother one becomes, in terms of the Gothic, other than oneself.

In this respect, then, Sybil Korff Vincent's definition of Female Gothic may be more useful than Moers's. Although the former has a twentieth-century writer in mind, her theory is equally applicable to earlier women practitioners of the genre: "The Female Gothic [...] is a category within the genre which specifically deals with female anxieties and conflicts from a female perspective [...]; it relates particularly to the female condition" ("The Mirror and the Cameo", page 155). The "pulp" Gothic thrillers of our own time retain this ability to express female fears about entrapment and heterosexuality, according to current sociological analysis.[23] Thornburg finds a similar function in modern science fiction: "Like Gothic literature, science fiction is [...] *monstrous* literature, it warns" (*The Monster in the Mirror*, page 132). Specifically, Gothic fiction warns women particularly of the dangers inherent in relationships with men. As Kay Mussell says, "The explicit warning about men, the specific if somewhat euphemistic story about the dangers of sexuality" (*Women's Gothic*, page 5) was much stronger in Gothic than in Romantic fiction. Indeed, if one bears in mind the scantily veiled warnings in Serao's Sentimental and Realist novels one might expect (and rightly so) that her Gothic novels will be less euphemistic about the dangers of sexuality than the above quotation suggests.[24]

The Gothic novel's setting also seems to have appealed especially to women writers. As Claire Kahane points out, "The heroine's exploration of her entrapment in a Gothic house—both she and it vulnerable to potential penetration—can be read as an exploration of her relation to the maternal body which she too shares, to the femaleness of experience, with all its connotations of power over, and vulnerability to, forces within and without" ("The Maternal Legacy", page 243). The whole location or, as Mussell puts it, world of Gothic fiction "could be defined as one in which life itself was precarious, and especially so for young women" (*Women's Gothic*, page 10). Gothic literature, then, functions as a cautionary tale for the woman reader (of whom the author is always conscious).

The Gothic provides the woman writer with a means of analysing her fragmented identity, the bond/bind of the mother figure and the dangers which heterosexual relationships hold for her. It also allows her to use one more figure, very prominent in the genre as a whole and especially relevant to her role as writer, that of the monster. As Karen Stein reveals, "In the Gothic mirror, the self is reflected in the extreme poses of rebel, outcast, obsessive seeker of forbidden knowledge, monster. Monsters are particularly prominent in the work of women writers, because for women the roles of rebel, outcast, seeker of truth, are monstrous in themselves."[25]

SERAO'S USE OF THE GOTHIC

My analysis of Serao's use of the Gothic is divided into two sections, the first dealing with her inclusion of Gothic features in novels otherwise identifiable primarily as Romantic or Sentimental, the second focusing on her treatment of what might be termed full-blown Gothic, in which increasingly unlikely and supernatural events accumulate. The first section will involve an exploration of four novels, while the second will offer an analysis of two novels and one short story.[26] By way of preamble, however, I propose to pick up a point made earlier in this chapter, where I saw the literary divisions between Walpole and Reeve and Radcliffe and Lewis as to some extent indicative of a split based on gender. It seems to me that the first group of texts to be discussed below embodies more the Reeve–Radcliffe–feminine type, while the second group adopts a use of the Gothic which could be more easily aligned with the Walpole–Lewis–masculine type. Bearing this distinction in mind, it is important to be aware that Serao, while in her later writings using the Gothic motifs common to the second type, still deals in detail there with issues of significance to women writers. One such theme, for example, which runs throughout her Gothic writings, is the exploration of the mother–daughter relationship. What she does in her later work, as I will show, is refashion the "masculine" Gothic mode—its inventions and concerns—to make it more relevant to women writers and their readers. In her earlier writings, too, she did not simply reproduce the conventions of a "feminine" mode of the Gothic genre but made significant changes in the use of certain motifs—specifically in the denouements of her novels.

It is difficult to be precise about what Gothic novels Serao had read. Many of the works with which I draw parallels and make contrasts in this chapter were not available to her in Italian, though the earliest Gothic novels certainly were. On the other hand, the later women's novels which I discuss were, with the exception of *Villette*, available to her in French. I think it likely that she did in fact know these works, but to be certain is impossible. The case of *Villette*, which I discuss later in this chapter, makes one wary of too much certainty on this issue, as there seems to be no way in which she could have read it, though it contains many of her themes, devices and concerns. The question of influence, then, must largely be left open.

DOMESTIC/ROMANTIC/SENTIMENTAL/REALIST/GOTHIC

The term "Domestic Gothic" was coined by Joan Lidoff, in a twentieth-century context.[27] I find it useful for Serao's cross-genre writing, because it draws attention to the characteristic setting of the Romantic/Gothic and Sentimental/Gothic—the family circle. Lidoff defines Domestic Gothic as a genre whose "settings and situations, characters and events, are realistic or nearly so". Further-more, she points out that it is not a genre which traffics in Gothic abductions, eerie remote houses and the like. Even so, "the narrat-ive is [...] pervasively coloured by the emotional and metaphorical excesses of a Gothic novel, dominated by the violent emotional forces that seethe beneath ordinary events" (page 111). Each of the novels I shall analyse in this section, *Cuore infermo*, *Addio, amore!*, *Fantasia* and *Il paese di Cuccagna*, matches this definition: all four present, in a sense, the Gothic subdued but liable to break out at any time.

One of the ways in which Serao departs somewhat from Gothic convention in these novels is by concentrating primarily on the emotional conflicts experienced by her female characters. Each of the female protagonists is prey to violent emotional upheavals and passions. Ann Tracy has already pinpointed the importance of passion in the restrained Gothic novel: "Especially for novelists who wish to avoid the more lurid effects achieved by demons and villains, passions play the role of demonic agents, treacherously internal" (*The Gothic Novel*, page 8). Yet in the Gothic novel the passions to which Tracy refers normally accrete around the male character, who is often both villain and hero. The focal point of Serao's interest is, characteristically, Other.

I find *Cuore infermo* (1881) and *Addio, amore!* (1890) alike in that they read primarily as Romantic novels, with traces of the Gothic relatively well hidden. *Fantasia* (1883) and *Il paese di Cuccagna* (1891) are somewhat different: each of them has more clearly definable Gothic intrusions, but while the former belongs to the

Sentimental genre the latter is on the whole a Realist work. Cross-genre infection is clearly rampant. Because of these distinctions between the works, I shall examine them in pairs.

In *Cuore infermo*, Serao's first novel, it is already possible to discover a number of Gothic motifs. There is, of course, a *doppelgänger*, though unusually it is female.[28] Seduction takes place, twice (Lalla seduces Marcello and so, later, does Beatrice). Presentiments and dreams form an important part of the representation of Beatrice's consciousness—she has an "uncanny" feeling that romantic love spells danger for her. Although Beatrice is not a spineless Gothic heroine (unlike, for instance, Emily St Aubert in Mrs Radcliffe's *Udolpho*, who is liable to faint at the drop of a lace handkerchief), she does lose consciousness on occasions, and suffers from a lingering illness, which leads to the Gothic scene of deathbed (in her case death-chair) agony. Atmospheric storms occur at the most turbulent moments of Beatrice's existence—most threateningly at the moment when she decides to reveal her love to Marcello. Lalla, meanwhile, carries the typically Gothic stigma of illegitimacy (as she may or may not be the child of Beatrice's father and his mistress).

Lalla, as the text's *femme fatale*, has elements of a particular type of Gothic female character.[29] As I showed earlier, she functions as a catalyst for Beatrice, compelling her to acknowledge the strength of her passions. Barbara Bowman identifies a similar stage in twentieth-century Gothic novels, seeing the *femme fatale* as significant in what she calls the Gothic novel's "identity sequence": "In the identity sequence, the heroine primarily interacts with the *femme fatale*, which means she interacts with a *femme fatale* who is both a character outside of herself and a part of her own nature."[30] Lalla's role as determinant of Beatrice's future is thus typically Gothic. Syndy McMillen Conger has also considered the relationship between these two Gothic types. Her analysis in part sketches the character-types with which Serao here deals. It also serves to pinpoint Serao's difference from the literary norm: "Balancing the frail, submissive paragon in early Gothic fiction is the dark, imperious, passion-ridden one, the *femme fatale*. She has the independence of spirit, the emotional vibrancy, the ingenuity and the moral fallibility the heroine often lacks, but she pays a price for these strengths. She is their victim. [...] Her last days and her death may be unquiet."[31] This quotation shows clearly how Serao deviates from yet another pattern: Beatrice is frail but never submissive.

Lalla is imperious and passion-ridden—but so too, we discover, is Beatrice. Lalla is not alone as a victim of the strengths she in fact shares with Beatrice. Indeed, it is Beatrice's unquiet last days and unquiet death that Serao presents. We might assume Lalla's end would be similar, but Serao chooses not to enlighten us on that point. Who, in the end, *is* the heroine of *Cuore infermo*? If one decides in favour of Beatrice, the decision is not unproblematic, given Serao's obvious concern for her *femme fatale*.

The other outstanding Gothic motif in *Cuore infermo* is that of the absent mother. Beatrice's mother is significant from the outset. Beatrice has resolved not to repeat her mother's story, but Serao shows that she is destined to replicate her mother before she can find, and paradoxically lose, herself in the mother. The same was true of an even earlier Gothic heroine, Emily St Aubert, as Nina da Vinci Nichols has observed. She writes of "Emily's preoccupation with her dead mother's identity, sought by the light of the novel's dangerous and suffering women. The need to 'find' her mother and thus herself seems a remarkable foreshadowing of modern state- ments about women's ailing condition."[32] I am not sure that I agree with the "ailing condition" part of this statement, but Nichols's analysis certainly hints at how important study of the fictional mother is for the fictional daughter in the Gothic novels of women writers.

The importance of Beatrice's mother is clear from the outset. On her wedding day Beatrice is frightened at the mention of her mother's wedding. The reason for her coldness to her husband is bound up with her view of her mother, as she angrily explains, under pressure, to her father. She begins by contrasting her mother's warm demeanour with her own cold one: "Ella è morta di una malattia di cuore [...]. Ebbene, quel povero cuore infermo, che batteva cosí irregolarmente, che si gonfiava di sangue o rimaneva immobile per momenti, quel cuore infermo amava fervidamente con tutte le sue forze, con una devozione cieca ed ostinata" (page 136). She goes on to say that she is afraid of being like her mother. Clearly, the mother figure functions as one which links love to death: "Se il germe del male è in me, non io volenterosa gli darò la facoltà di scoppiare; io non amerò, io non sarò inquieta, gelosa, io non soffocherò i miei dolori ed i miei lamenti [...]. Per lasciarmi vivere, lasciatemi tranquilla" (page 138). The language used here is as dramatic and Gothic as one could wish; and there is no doubt that the figure of the daughter is determined by that of the lost mother. Beatrice perceives the emotional demands made on her by her father (in symbolic place of her husband—a covert incest motif) as tantamount to self-destruction. As Barbara Hill Rigney says, "That social institution in which the self is most vulnerable because most intimate with another is, of course, marriage" (*Madness and Sexual Politics*, page 47). Beatrice embodies this fear of engulfment of the self in romantic love. She struggles to retain a view of her self as paramount. What Serao here transmits to the reader is what Rigney describes (in relation to *Jane Eyre*) as "the essentially feminist message that, whatever the sexual ethos, there is a danger of the loss of self when self-love and self-preservation become secondary to love for another" (page 28).

The setting in which Beatrice feels most threatened by her growing love for Marcello is typically Gothic. Serao describes a night when Marcello does not return home. It is late, the weather inclement. Beatrice fears that Lalla (her other self) is with Marcello and goes into the unfamiliar territory of Lalla's grounds to see if she can discover any trace of them. She cannot, and turns to go home: "In quel momento le parve che il cielo si capovolgesse, che il parco le turbinasse d'attorno; fu presa da un terrore sconfinato, terrore della notte, della solitudine, della tempesta, delle case vuote, del pericolo ignoto. Fuggí ansante, chinando il capo sul petto, soffocando le sue grida di dolore" (page 194). It is increasingly clear that she is "becoming" her mother: "Il petto pareva si dilatasse per poter capire quel palpito sfrenato che la soffocava" (page 196). The pain is the same, the attempt to stifle it the same. The kind of panic described here is similar to that commented on by Rigney ("she" being each female protagonist in the four novels Rigney analyses): "realizing […] that she has lost a self somewhere along the socially prescribed false selves which she has assumed, willingly or unwillingly, consciously or subconsciously. In panic at this realization, she searches for some rationale, some agent or helper to heal the divided self—a mother" (pages 121–22). Beatrice is literally losing her self in an unwilling love for Marcello, and literally turns to her mother in a last, desperate, unsuccessful attempt not to become her: "Andò a cadere presso il letto, sul tappeto, nei suoi abiti fradici, alzando verso il ritratto di Luisa Revertera le sue mani sanguinanti, e gridando con la voce del fanciullo disperato: 'Mamma mia, mamma mia!'" (page 195). According to Rigney (pages 122–23), most women writers allow the mother to function as a redemptive *doppelgänger* for the female protagonist. Serao does not: Beatrice cannot be saved by her dead mother. Becoming the same as her mother leads to her death—and the pregnancy motif concomitant with her illness, which I have already discussed, further underlines the fact that she is becoming the mother figure.[33] Motherhood and mothers are, according to this analysis at least, ambiguous loci of ideals and fears as much for Serao as they were for Mary Shelley in 1818.

The ambiguity which surrounds sexuality is as clearly visible in this text as that surrounding motherhood. Sexual awareness, specifically heterosexual awareness, is fraught with danger but presented as inescapable. It is clearly demanded by society, as is revealed by the number of comments various characters, including the paterfamilias, make on Beatrice's initial coldness towards Marcello. In one sense this is typical of the Gothic novel: as Thornburg says, "Pain itself, and the infliction of pain, are substitutes for—or heighteners of—sexual pleasure" (*The Monster in the Mirror*, page 24). In another sense it is typical of Female Gothic: it acts as a cautionary tale for the young female character or reader about the dangers and pains inherent in heterosexual love—at the same time reminding her that it is demanded by society. Strikingly, however, Serao fulfils her threats about the dangers of heterosexual love. Other Gothic authors somehow resolve the contradictions in their plots: Radcliffe's Emily St Aubert, for instance, marries and enters the blissful land of happy-ever-after. For Serao, as usual, marriage represents the start, or intensification, of her heroine's problems, and there is to be no way out.

Cuore infermo contains two further Gothic motifs worthy of brief comment. One involves the traditional city/country dichotomy, here represented, respectively, by Naples and Sorrento. The country locus is normally where the heroine's problems intensify (in the fully Gothic novel she would have been abducted to the country). This is true of *Cuore infermo*, as it is in Sorrento that Beatrice realizes she is losing her self and starting to turn into the mother, as detailed in the storm scene.

The other interesting motif is that of incest. I have already mentioned in an aside that Beatrice's father, in his probing questions about her feelings, symbolically replaces Marcello. More than that, he causes her to perceive an analogy between her relationship with Marcello and the unsatisfactory relationship which existed between her parents; the couples are overtly paralleled. Beatrice's metamorphosis into the mother therefore raises the spectre of

Marcello's potential metamorphosis into the father. Underlining this incest motif is the ambiguous status of Lalla. If she is Beatrice's half-sister then her relationship with Marcello is morally questionable. The fact that these hints of incest are no more than hints, and remain unresolved, indicates Serao's dawning awareness of the sexual relationships buried within the family. In all her Domestic Gothic novels (I use this as an umbrella term to cover all the genres represented in this section) she will continue to handle the theme of incest in a relatively covert manner. Her later, more overt, use of the incest motif is in one sense less revolutionary than her handling of it in these novels, as when she uses it in this context her readers, too, realize how much Gothic resides in the Domestic. It intrudes into a conventional setting and is therefore more shocking.

Addio, amore! is another Romantic novel with strong Gothic overtones. It has certain motifs in common with *Cuore infermo*. The two main female characters, Anna and Laura, are again orphaned; once again, these two characters are each other's doubles; adultery occurs here too (between Laura and Cesare, Anna's husband); seduction again twice takes place (Anna "seduces" Cesare and Cesare in turn seduces her sister). But certain formal Gothic motifs not employed in *Cuore infermo* are also introduced. The narrative structure and point of view alter in passages where the device of the letter is used (Anna writes long, persuasive letters, expressing her feelings, to both Giustino and Cesare). Serao thus encourages the reader to identify with Anna rather than any of the other characters. The figure of the Gothic libertine is introduced in the person of Cesare, who is morally condemned, overtly by Anna and covertly by Serao in her descriptions of him. (Serao will develop the libertine type later, in her fully Gothic works.) *Addio, amore!* is full of presentiments—Anna's about Laura's relationship with Cesare—; and it contains another device typical of the Gothic: the conventional warning against reading romantic novels (it is Anna in her youth who indulges in this pastime, and Cesare who censures her for it). There is also a suicide (Anna's, at the end), a further device common to Gothic novels, and present in many of Serao's Gothic and quasi-Gothic works.

The orphaned status of Anna and Laura is particularly important in this novel, for two reasons. On the one hand, Serao uses it to highlight the significance of the absent mother; on the other, it allows her to explore the incest motif more fully, though still covertly.

The figure of the mother is important to both female characters, particularly Anna. When they travel from Naples to their villa in Sorrento (here we see the same city/country dichotomy as in the earlier novel), they go first to their mother's room:

> Le due sorelle andarono immediatamente nella stanza della loro madre, quasi a sciogliere un voto [...]; portando dei fiori freschi, Laura [...] girava intorno [...] a fare, insomma, una rassegna di massaia accurata, Anna, invece, si era subito buttata sull'inginocchiatoio di legno scolpito [...] e innanzi alla Madonna della Seggiola, innanzi alla piccola e gentile miniatura di sua madre, aveva abbassato il capo sulle mani guantate. (page 151)

There are a number of significant features in this passage. Firstly, both characters have a strong need to communicate with the figure of the mother, albeit in different ways. It is as though they search for her when they enter the villa; one is reminded of Rigney's comment on the search for the mother who can heal the split in the self, in this case the Anna–Laura split. Secondly, the device of the miniature is important in Gothic fiction—and Serao's miniatures are always of, or related to, mothers. In the Gothic novel generally, they function as a means of identifying a member of one's family; often they are of the father. In her use of the miniature device Serao again draws attention to the importance for the daughter of the figure of the mother.

Later in the novel Serao uses the mother figure to provide a Gothic vision/hallucination. Immediately after Anna's acceptance of Cesare's proposal she goes to her mother's room, as though to communicate with her again:

> Ella fece il giro della stanza materna, dove era stato il nido di un puro e profondo amore che solo la morte aveva infranto e che forse, neppure la morte aveva infranto [...]; ella si sedette [...] innanzi alla piccola scrivania, dove, certo, sua madre si era seduta a leggere, scrivere, a pensare; e nascosta la faccia tra i fiori [...] testimoni dell'amor suo, anche ella pensò; [...] a un tratto, innanzi a sé, sul bianco capezzale guarnito di merletti, le sembrò di scorgere un delicato volto ovale e due occhi neri, pensosi, dolci, che la carezzavano, guardandola. Ella tremò, dalla testa ai piedi, a quella visione, fece tre passi e cadde con le braccia tese verso quel capezzale dicendo: "O mamma, mamma." (page 166)

In this passage the love between Anna and her mother (pure, deep and everlasting) is implicitly contrasted with the "love" coldly offered in the previous scene by Cesare Dias. It is also clear that Anna wishes to be like her mother, to do as she did; she imitates her movements and gestures. Finally, it seems that the spirit of the mother is called up before her eyes, producing precisely the same effect as in *Cuore infermo*: the character falls to her knees and calls on her mother. The emotion portrayed here is rather negative: it is overpowering, frightening and debilitating. It occurs at the same kind of moment as in *Cuore infermo*—at a time of crisis associated with romantic heterosexual love. It is as though, in both novels, the maternal figure acts as a vehicle of foreboding, a warning against the course the daughter is about to take. In this case heterosexual love is clearly devalued in the light of the powerful mother–daughter relationship. Serao thus uses Gothic techniques to achieve a rather un-Gothic result.

In *Addio, amore!* Serao does not overtly call attention to the incest motif, but it is difficult to avoid being conscious of it. Significantly, the supposedly deceased father of the female characters is scarcely mentioned: certainly he has no emotional significance for them, in direct contrast to the figure of the absent (deceased) mother. Yet there is one male figure around whom the affections of both Anna and Laura cluster. He is important to them, emotionally, pedagogically and erotically, as a source of security. Cesare Dias is, after all, their guardian—literally and symbolically the one who takes the place of the father. He is first referred to in the text (by Giustino, the initial object of Anna's passion) as "colui che dispone di te" (page 19); his function is unambiguously patriarchal. In age he is far removed from his wards: Anna, during her first passion, sees him as one who is "quasi vecchio" (page 20), and refers to "l'abisso che divide il mio carattere da quello di Cesare Dias" (page 28); figuratively speaking, this abyss could be the incestual abyss into which both Anna and Laura will fall. After Anna has run away to be with Giustino but found him unresponsive, Serao describes her return, at the end of Chapter 2, in terms of a reconciliation between father and daughter:

> L'uomo si avanzò verso la camera oscura e chiamò ancora, con la voce che tremava leggermente [...]. "Anna, dove sei dunque?" L'uomo [...] mostrava una bellissima fisionomia di persona quarantenne, contratta dall'agitazione, portò il lume di là, cercando con gli occhi la fanciulla. Essa udí e vide: con una volontà

immensa vinse il suo abbattimento, si levò, fece due o tre passi vacillanti e si abbatté ai piedi di Cesare Dias, dicendo: "Perdonatemi, perdonatemi…" […]; udí la voce di costui mormorare, per la prima volta impietosita: "Povera figliuola." E una forte mano sollevarla, poi posarlesi paternamente sui capelli. (page 50)

Serao here clearly shows that the relationship between her two characters is that of parent and child. It is immediately after this scene that Anna conceives a passion for her guardian/tutor/ father-figure, and that passion, illicit in every way, is to end in suicide. Serao's use of the incest motif may have led her to imagine the odd conditions—one might say restrictions—which she places on the Anna–Cesare marriage: "'Io non vi domando di amarmi: debbo amarvi io'. 'Voi non me lo chiederete giammai?' 'Giammai'. 'Promettetelo'. 'Lo prometto […]. Voi siete il padrone: disporrete della vostra vita e della mia'" (page 162). This relationship is not like a marriage: it is rather a union of two most unequal parties— as unequal as father and daughter in the world Serao depicts.

This does not exhaust the incest motif in the novel. After Anna and Cesare marry, the affair between Cesare and Laura begins. This liaison is doubly incestuous in that Laura not only stands in the same relation to Cesare as Anna does but is also his sister-in-law. Serao even refers to her ambiguously as his sister: "Anna, ogni volta che arrivava una lettera di Cesare dava i suoi saluti a Laura e le leggeva la parola cortese, che vi si trovava sempre per sua sorella: 'Grazie' diceva Laura, senz' altro" (page 209). In reference to this relationship, too, Serao avoids the word "incest" but not the concept. She uses circumlocutions in Anna's dialogue with Laura: "Devi coraggiosamente strapparti dall'anima questo impuro amore che la deturpa […]. Laura devi ricordarti che sei mia sorella, devi dimenticare Cesare" (page 261). As usual in the Gothic novel, incest is dramatically punished: Anna kills herself for her quasi-incestuous relationship, and Laura's tragic story unfolds in *Castigo*, the sequel to *Addio, amore!*[34]

The character of Cesare is even more complex than that of father-figure and object of incestuous passion: he is the first truly Gothic villain Serao created. Beatrice's father in *Cuore infermo* had something of the complex Gothic father-figure about him, at once giving and withholding love. Cesare mirrors him but is more fully developed. Cynthia Griffin Wolff has said that "in modern Gothics, the woman marries the demon lover."[35] Yet in this nineteenth-century novel, too, Anna chooses the "demon" lover (Dias) at the expense of the "chaste" lover (Luigi Caracciolo); in this respect, then, Serao prefigures modern Gothics. Anna experiences Cesare as demonic in her first flush of passion for Giustino: "È un uomo cattivo" (page 19). She perceives him as inhuman even in the throes of her passion for him: "pensando a quello che era il cuore di Cesare Dias: le parve di trovarsi innanzi a una montagna altissima di ghiaccio dal sentiero stretto e ripido che ascendeva fra due pareti di ghiacciai, nel bianco accecante della neve […] senza che raggio di sole arrivasse a disciogliere quella eterna neve" (page 126).

Dias is still more than this: he is something of a mesmerist. Only thus can his hold over Anna and Laura be fully explained. The language Serao uses in describing him underlines this aspect of his character. He is largely in control of his own emotions and highly manipulative of those of others. This is most clearly revealed in the seduction scene witnessed by Anna. Laura moves nervously away from him:

> Egli fissava Laura, di lontano, richiamandola a sé imperiosamen-te. Ella fece ancora qualche passo, esitando, vacillando, incerta, affascinata. Nella sua allucinazione, Anna avrebbe voluto, se avesse potuto parlare, muoversi, dare a Laura la forza di togliersi da quel fascino della passione, liberarla, e liberar sé stessa da quella magia. "Dio, Dio, dàlle la forza, dammi la forza" pregò ancora Anna, nel suo sogno, nella sua follia. Ma Laura non ebbe la forza di andar via. (page 244)

It is easy to see the duality of the two female characters: both are under his spell; both try to break away; Anna clearly links herself with Laura and tries to infuse her strength into her. Yet both are powerless against this mesmeric man. Dias corresponds to a type of character discussed at some length by Nina Auerbach, and which I shall return to in the next section.[36] Auerbach would define him as a Svengali/Dracula type. He is certainly one type of Gothic villain—and Serao will expand on the type in her full-blown Gothic novels. He offers, as Elizabeth McAndrew says of the typical Gothic villain, "a frightening vision of a world of relative moral values" (*The Gothic Tradition*, page 44).

Although Cesare Dias is one of Serao's most complex male characters, her primary interest nonetheless remains in her female characters, in the relationship between them and in their relation-ship with their mother. Interestingly, the importance of the mater-nal figure gradually fades as Cesare progressively increases his mesmeric hold over Anna and Laura. Clearly Serao—again— posits a diametric opposition between maternal love and hetero- sexual love. Anna, at the height of her despair, recognizes that she is fated to be unhappy in the latter: "Una forza arcana combatteva contro lei, contro ogni suo sforzo di passione. Nulla le sarebbe riuscito, giammai amando [...]; ella portava in sé, avvinghiata alla propria vita, quella fatalità" (page 268). This could be explained by reference to her prior and primary relationship with her mother. Ultimately, Anna (like Beatrice in *Cuore infermo*) becomes her mother, in death.

This novel, then, involves many of the same Gothic concerns as its predecessor, principally incest and the orphan. Again Serao makes these motifs particularly relevant to women through her use of the mother figure and the intensification of prohibitions sur- rounding heterosexual love. She also develops her style by creating the complex and very Gothic character Cesare Dias.

Fantasia does not contain a male character of the stature and complexity of Cesare Dias—perhaps not surprisingly, as it is an earlier work. Indeed it is more Sentimental than Romantic, partly because of its relatively Sentimental hero, Andrea, who equals neither the Duca di Revertera (Beatrice's father) nor Cesare Dias in Romantic stature. Caterina, too, is almost an archetypal Senti- mental heroine, submissive, passive and without either the intelli- gence, independence and passion of Beatrice or the passionate, imaginative nature of Anna. Serao may have been unable to resist creating one such character for, as Elizabeth McAndrew says, "A natural tendency to be victims makes the delicate characters of Sentimentalism suitable to be transported bodily into the cloudy world of Gothic fiction" (*The Gothic Tradition*, page 68). Yet Serao does not "transport" Caterina into the Gothic realm: she allows her to remain in the Sentimental world, bringing, instead, the Gothic to her in the person of Lucia, her vibrant *doppelgänger*. The novel's Gothic motifs include Caterina's orphan status (and the motherless status of Lucia, who is in effect orphaned by her sense of being distanced from her father), adultery between Andrea and Lucia following the former's marriage to Caterina, seduction (Lucia seduces Andrea) and a dramatic suicide, by Caterina, with which the text closes. As in *Addio, amore!*, letters prove important. Lucia is a writer of voluminous letters (mainly addressed to Caterina rather than the typical recipient of such missives, the male prot- agonist), which allow the reader some insight into the image of the self that Lucia projects. They are not confessional and emotional (as Anna's will be) but expressive and imaginative—works of art in themselves. Lastly, the text includes the conventional warning of the dangers inherent in reading novels, this time in the feverish atmosphere of the girls' school.

What differentiates *Fantasia* from the two novels considered before it, and what links it with *Il paese di Cuccagna*, is Serao's prolonged analysis of illness and madness and their relationship with femininity and creativity. These issues centre on Lucia, the text's *femme fatale*, who is far more violently ill and closer to insanity than any other female character of her kind in Serao's fiction. (Elsewhere the *femme fatale* is not such a powerful object of combined fear and pity.) From the early pages Lucia is hypersensitive to external stimuli. She faints at the least provocation: candles and incense, or scoldings from her teachers. This is a trait of the Sentimental heroine, but Lucia possesses no other characteristics of that figure. In fact the Sentimental heroine is Caterina, in all respects except her physical strength. What we have here, then, may be a *doppelgänger*-like exchange of characteristics.

An interesting facet of Lucia's character is her rather mystic nature. One of the novel's earliest scenes takes place in the school chapel. Here Lucia reveals an excessive mysticism which remains part of her character throughout the novel: "Vi fu un momento di silenzio, e si udí la voce affogata di Lucia Altimare che balbettava: 'Maria… Maria… Maria bella.' 'Preghi sottovoce, Altimare' avvertí la direttrice con una certa dolcezza. Il rosario ricominciò, senza interruzione […]. Lucia Altimare si era buttata giú, col capo sulla paglia, con le braccia cadenti, trasalendo" (page 7). This mystic type of character has been interpreted in a revealing way by William James, who suggests a psychological explanation, based on the mystic as a divided self responding not to God but to repressed guilt.[37] This sheds further light on Lucia as a double figure and helps to explain the fact that Serao continually highlights her attitude to religion—which often has a grotesque air.

Like Beatrice and Anna, Lucia is significantly at her weakest when she gives way to her love for Andrea. While a guest of Andrea and Caterina, Lucia has what appears to be an epileptic fit:

> Ella cadde per terra, in preda a una convulsione nervosa, come ne soffriva da fanciulla; si contorceva tutta, le braccia fendevano l'aria, la testa balzava sul pavimento […], le battevano i denti come per tremore febbrile, l'orbita scompariva sotto le palpebre

[…]. Quando poi la chiamava Andrea tutto il viso le si scomponeva, la convulsione aumentava di ferocia […]. Rinvenendo ella
pianse a dirotto, strappandosi i capelli, come se le fosse morto
qualcuno. (pages 216–17)

Although Serao here states that Lucia has been prey to such
convulsions for some time, earlier in the novel she has not been
seen experiencing any. It is interesting that Lucia's crisis worsens
when she hears Andrea's voice: it is as though she perceives him as
a threat. Her reaction, on recovery, indicates that she has lost
something, or someone: herself? Caterina? The fact that Serao
presents Lucia as epileptic reminds us that Freud writes in "The
Uncanny" of "the uncanny effect of epilepsy and madness". He
says that a person sees in these ailments "the workings of forces
hitherto unsuspected in his fellow-man but which at the same time
he is dimly aware of in a remote corner of his own being" (page
397). As Caterina is Lucia's double, we must assume that such
forces reside in her too. And since the two together form a composite female character, I think it is safe to assume from this passage in
Fantasia some relationship between heterosexual love and a threat
to female wholeness.

From the aesthetic point of view, Lucia's paroxysms can only
be seen as grotesque. Elizabeth McAndrew shows how the grotesque was used in the Gothic: "The grotesque was eminently suited
to embody the view of madness as demonic possession" (page 138).
She goes on to summarize Gothic authors' use of it: "In seeing evil
as a distortion of the natural being […] they presented it as working
like an alien force within the psyche and they portrayed the
character suffering such conflict as maddened by it" (page 158). We
are back to the notion of the division of the self, the split in the
psyche. I find McAndrew's use of the masculine pronoun in the rest
of this passage (not quoted here) significant. I think she uses it in the
collective sense, as often in her analysis, but I also find it hard to
think of other Gothic female characters who suffer such grotesque
manifestations of madness and illness as certain of Serao's. Lucia
is the most extreme of the type, even in Serao's *œuvre*. In most
Gothic writings the grotesque is reserved for monsters and male
characters. In extending its use to certain female characters Serao
clearly wishes to show how women are as much prey to conflicting
impulses as men are. This, I suggest, is part of her strategy to create
a more complex female character—a strategy I have analysed in
Chapter 1.

Lucia's grotesque acts reflect at least one literary precedent. Not coincidentally, I think, the character in question is called Lucy; she is found in Walter Scott's *The Bride of Lammermoor* (1819). Lucy Ashton is more violent than Lucia Altimare, but certain scenes in the two novels are similar. Having murdered her husband, whom she did not want to marry, Scott's character is described as follows: "her head-gear dishevelled; her nightclothes torn and dabbled with blood, —her eyes glazed and her features convulsed into a wild paroxysm of insanity".[38] The scene is similar to that of Lucia's epileptic fit, though Lucia's violence is entirely turned in upon herself while Lucy's is directed outwards towards a man— Showalter says that Lucy represents "female sexuality as insane violence against men" (*The Female Malady*, page 14). Serao's Lucia is more closely bound up with the self: violence against the self, self-revulsion. She represents a threat only to her self (and in this formulation I include Caterina). If Serao has borrowed something of Lucy she radically changes her function. Showalter goes on to consider the post-Scott use of the Lucy type; she mentions Donizetti's *Lucia di Lammermoor*, doubtless familiar to Serao and possibly the source of her Lucia. Showalter also refers to Flaubert's use of the Lucia figure in *Madame Bovary*, where he has Emma identify with the violent heroine on seeing a production of the opera (pages 15– 17). Lucienne Kroha has written on the relationship between *Madame Bovary* and *Fantasia*.[39] I suggest that *Madame Bovary* may also be a link between *Fantasia* and *Lucia di Lammermoor*, through Serao's conscious revisionary use of this grotesque Gothic heroine.

Lucy Ashton and Lucia Altimare have their successors too, though I think the type is more closely related to Lucy Ashton than to Lucia, because of the difference in function I have identified. The function of many of Lucy/Lucia's successors is to prey, physically, on men. The Gothic Lucy Westenra in *Dracula*—yet another Lucy— is a split personality, sweet by day, a predator by night.[40] In that she attacks others she is like Lucy, not Lucia, but in other respects she is more reminiscent of Lucia. Nina Auerbach summarizes her as follows: "Her penchant for somnambulism, trance, and strange physical and mental alterations, even before Dracula's arrival, would find her a place in either a romantic sonnet by Wilde or in Breuer and Freud's garland of female hysterics" ("Magi and Maidens", page 119). Interestingly, except for the reference to Dracula, these words would apply equally well to Lucia Altimare

and to Bianca Maria Cavalcanti. In spite of earlier and later ana-
logues, however, it seems to me that Serao's treatment of her
heroines remains unique in her insistence on seeing the crises
suffered as crises of identity: the character's violence turns in upon
the self, and the crisis is always provoked by the heterosexual
romantic relationship.

So much for Lucia. Serao's treatment of Caterina, for the most
part a typical Sentimental heroine, in some ways diverges from the
norm. One of the most interesting aspects of Caterina is her
restrained love for Andrea: in a sense, she is emotionally and
sexually withdrawn from him. In this Serao anticipates many
twentieth-century women novelists. Barbara Hill Rigney discusses
the emotionally withdrawn heroine, commenting on her primary
"desire for self-preservation". Caterina seems to have something
in common with Woolf's Mrs Dalloway, whose motivation, according to Rigney, is "the preservation of privacy and thus a hold on
ontological security, however tenuous" (*Madness and Sexual Politics*, page 121). From this point of view Caterina also mirrors
Beatrice in *Cuore infermo*. She senses a threat to the self (the unified
Caterina–Lucia self) emanating from Andrea, and therefore wards
him off.

The situation may be even more complex. Although there is no
overt incest motif in this novel, I suspect that the motif is covertly
present. The reader's first view of the relationship between Andrea
and Caterina is when the former returns from hunting, and the
scene is like that of a child greeting her father: "Andrea acchiappò
sua moglie per la vita, la levò come un bambino sul suo largo torace,
la baciò [...]. 'Sei venuto... sei venuto' mormorava lei, tutta ridente,
col pettine che le cadeva e certe macchie rosse che apparivano, vive
sulla pelle" (page 44). Apart from the word "bambino" (the image
is repeated several times in the text), we also have here the childish
Caterina whose comb slips from her hair and who reacts, on the
whole, like a child whose "daddy's gone a-huntin'". Never is the
relationship between Andrea and Caterina portrayed as one between equals. She fears his displeasure and his bad temper as a
child might those of an unpredictable father. In one scene Andrea
begins by scolding Caterina: "'Ti par bene farsi guardar dalla
gente? Farsi burlare?' Ella non rispondeva, gli occhi chinati, le mani
nascoste nel manicotto [...]; si mordeva le labbra, impallidiva, non
potendo piangere, non trovando un filo di voce per rispondere"

(page 77). Here she is like a child unjustly accused and unable to find the words to explain the situation to her angry father. The relationship is certainly both paternal and patriarchal in tone. As for Lucia (her other self), although her relationship with Andrea is more equal it is illicit. It is also possible that for Lucia Andrea takes the place of a caring father-figure, standing in for the indifferent father of her childhood. The incest motif, then, may partly explain both Caterina's reserve towards Andrea and the overpowering sense of prohibition surrounding the Lucia–Andrea relationship.

Another reworked Gothicism shapes the outcome of the Lucia–Caterina relationship. Charlotte Brontë, in a typical Gothic resolution, does away with Bertha Mason; as Karen Stein puts it, "The darker, monstrous, more sexual, angry self, Bertha, is killed in order that the more moderate, more controlled self, Jane, can live within the limitations imposed by society" ("Monsters and Madwomen", page 136). In *Fantasia* the opposite occurs: Caterina is sacrificed to the passionate Lucia. The same happens in *Cuore infermo*: Lalla lives while Beatrice dies. Serao seems to allow the more passionate, grasping side of her female doubles to go on while eliminating the more passive, angelic side. As noted earlier, she does not present the survivor's existence as in any way positive: it is blighted and tormented. Yet there is something of a new Gothic realism, and a challenge to convention and conventional morality, in the survival of the more vibrant side of the double.

Certain typically Gothic elements contribute to *Fantasia*'s structure. One of them is the city–country dichotomy (Naples–Caserta this time), with the country house (the more Gothic and unfamiliar locus) the scene of the Gothic events (such as Lucia's convulsions). The school, too, is a Gothic locus of strange events, such as attempted suicide, fainting fits, religious ecstasies and mysterious vows. It seems that Serao's school setting here functions in much the same way as George Sand's convent school in *Historie de ma vie*,[41] on which Ellen Moers comments as follows: "As a girl, George Sand was virtually incarcerated in a convent school [...], which in her autobiography she makes look very much like a Gothic castle: the sprawling old buildings, complicated passageways, mysterious garrets and subcellars and high walls" (*Literary Women*, page 131). Serao's *Fantasia* includes not just the Gothic castle setting but also Gothic events, so that her use of the convent school is similar to Brontë's use of the girls' school in *Villette*.[42] Both are clearly Gothic structures full of secrets.

It seems to me that the most interesting of all the novel's Gothic elements is its title, which virtually announces its nature. This is, of course, a novel about Lucia's imagination and Caterina's pragmatism, but, even more than that, the title *Fantasia* is a meta-textual comment. Ellen Moers defines the Gothic as a style in which "fantasy predominates over reality, the strange over the commonplace, and the supernatural over the natural with one definite auctorial intent: to scare" (page 90). *Fantasia* is a novel which certainly calls attention to its own fantastic elements and one where, in the end, the fantastic is allowed to predominate. Sibyl James says of the Gothic, "It is the satisfaction of the need for imagination and the component of psychological reality […] which accounts for the continuing power and popularity of the form."[43] It seems that in *Fantasia* Serao consciously meets both these criteria.

Il paese di Cuccagna is possibly the most interesting of Serao's forays into Domestic Gothic. It is, on the whole, a realistic portrayal of the existence of the whole spectrum of contemporary Neapolitan society. The stories of Carmela the *sigaraia*, Maddalena the prostitute and Luisella the unfortunate wife of the wasteful Cesare contrast sharply with the lives of the upper-class but impoverished Bianca Maria Cavalcanti and her father. The tone of the greater part of the novel—the analysis of the vice of the *lotto* and the resulting poverty—contrasts with the melodramatic pathos of Bianca Maria's story. In the latter sections of the novel, set apart from the rest in judiciously spaced chapters, the events are unmistakably Gothic.[44] The Gothic infects the realistic, but no critic has ever commented on the Gothic elements, which have been ignored in the general praise of this novel as Serao's *capolavoro*—a masterpiece of Realism.[45]

The Gothic motifs crammed into the appropriate sections of the novel include Bianca's deathbed agony, her vivid dreams, her physical weakness and illness manifested in the convenient swoons of the Sentimental/Gothic heroine, and her eerie presentiments. For the first time the Gothic miser appears in Serao's writing, in the person of Marchese Cavalcanti, Bianca's father (Serao will depict such a figure again in the fully Gothic *La mano tagliata*). Statues often played a significant part in Gothic novels, and the *Ecce Homo* in this novel is used to create one of the most Gothic scenes. Yet here Serao also inserts a touch of Comic Gothic: the statue, assumed to be a corpse, is drawn out of the Cavalcanti well. The situation turns back to melodrama, however, with Bianca's convulsive and violent response to what she first assumes to be murder and then sees as sacrilege. The typically Gothic escape route of seclusion in the convent is also used: it is one of Bianca's favourite fantasies, as a possible way out of her hellish Gothic existence.

The most significant Gothic elements in the novel, however, are much more complex than any of the above devices, which Serao employs in a relatively superficial and conventional manner. The three central Gothic ingredients, in the order in which I shall deal with them, are the incest motif, the motif of the (crucially) absent mother, and the supernatural/occult.

From its earliest depictions the relationship between Bianca Maria and her father is problematic and beyond the norm; and it becomes increasingly demanding and abnormal as the novel progresses. From the beginning the father tries to possess Bianca Maria, wishing her to use the mystical powers he believes she has to reveal the numbers of the *lotto*; and from the beginning she resists him. His response to her resistance can hardly be described as paternal: "'Ah, tu fingi di non capire?' gridò lui, già furioso. 'Tutte così queste donne, tutte una mandra di pecore, o pazze o egoiste [...]. Ingrate e perfide, le donne!'" (page 169); he equates his daughter with "all women". In almost the next breath he promises her luxuries to be purchased with his winnings, very much in the manner of a persuasive lover: "Ti voglio comperare una collana di perle, otto file di perle legate da un solo zaffiro e un diadema di brillanti" (page 170). Bianca Maria's reaction is revealing: "Nel cuore quella voce paterna le risuonava, nei consueti discorsi che gli sgorgavano ogni sera dall'animo troppo caldo, le risuonava con echi angosciosi, come un lento tormento." She sees her father's emotions as too passionate, and they are exceedingly painful to her. To some extent, however, and in spite of herself, she responds to him on a deeper level: "Quegli sfoghi di passione [...] facevano trasalire e sussultare la sua anima innamorata di pace e di silenzio" (page 171). Bianca Maria's pain may perhaps be interpreted in the light of Thornburg's view quoted earlier, as a substitute for, or heightener of, sensual pleasure.

Naturally, then, the greatest conflict between father and daughter is destined to centre not on the *lotto* but on the figure of Antonio Amati, who is to be the father's rival for Bianca Maria's affections. The conflict between the two male characters is apparent from Amati's entry onto the scene. Not surprisingly, perhaps, he resembles the Marchese: both are attractive, strong characters. Amati, however, is younger and a more legitimate object for Bianca's affections. After one of Bianca Maria's swoons, Amati, a doctor, is called to attend her and begins to comprehend that something odd is going on between father and daughter: "Non aveva udito che cosa avesse chiesto il padre alla figliuola, ma intese di nuovo sorgere il gran segreto della famiglia, vedendo la tenera e dolente occhiata di Bianca Maria. 'Non le domandate nulla' disse bruscamente il dottore a Don Carlo Cavalcanti. Il vecchio patrizio represse un moto di sdegno" (page 202). Overtly the father in fact torments the daughter with questions about any vision involving *lotto* numbers she may have had during her swoon. The subtext, however, especially with such dramatic vocabulary, suggests more than this: the Gothic "gran segreto della famiglia" is often incestuous.

Bianca Maria's relationship with Amati soon comes to resemble her relationship with her father. The following account of Amati with Bianca, for example, reads like an accurate portrayal of the Marchese and his daughter: "Erano soli, seduti uno di fronte all'altro, in un gran silenzio, intorno: si guardavano appena ma si parlavano come due anime che lungamente avessero vissuto insieme, nella gioia e nel dolore" (page 223). Amati becomes increasingly similar to the Marchese as his love for Bianca Maria develops: "La parola era detta [...] con la severa risoluzione di un uomo, ondeggiando dalle purissime linee dell'idillio alle violente prospettive drammatiche" (page 313). Amati here reveals a character with hidden depth equal to that of the Marchese. The ensuing conflict between the two male characters is only to be expected.

Serao hints at the depth of this conflict. She rejects the idea that it arises because they are characters with different ideals and different expectations of life, and goes on: "Forse la ragione dell'antipatia scambievole, della freddezza di Amati, della ostilità di Cavalcanti, era piú intima, piú profonda, piú misteriosa: forse nessuno di loro osava confessarla a sé stesso: infine, era un sospetto, una diffidenza, un'ostilità inconscia" (page 319). Although she does not elaborate on this one senses the importance of the subconscious: the mutual dislike is clearly based on rivalry for the possession of Bianca Maria.

This rivalry elicits a confused reaction from Bianca Maria, who loves them both but becomes increasingly aware that she will have to make a choice between them. Eventually she chooses her first love, her father. Indications that this will be so are scattered throughout the novel. For example, after an argument between the two men, which she has witnessed, her father leaves the room with the cryptic command: "Diglielo, diglielo quello che sai, te lo permetto, Bianca [...]. Narragli tutto" (page 328). Amati then interrogates her harshly: "'Non dovete dirmi qualche cosa? Vostro padre non ve lo ha consigliato, quasi imposto?' Ella trasalí. Il tono di voce di Amati era aspro. Non le aveva mai parlato cosí. E offesa da quell' asprezza, la sua anima si chiuse. 'Io non so niente' ella rispose, a voce bassa. 'Non ho nulla da dirvi'" (page 329). This is to be symbolic of their relationship. As Amati himself says to Bianca, "Presso vostro padre, presso voi, sono un qualunque intruso, che si mischia dei fatti vostri, senz' averne il diritto e senza risultato" (page 331). The family circle is closed to him. The figure of the father-lover constantly stands between the lovers: "Non riesciva loro di concentrarsi, di assorbirsi nel loro affetto profondo" (page 402). The Marchese becomes fixated on the conviction that his daughter must not marry: "Una volta che Margherita [the servant], in presenza di Cavalcanti, aveva accennato alle voci di matrimonio fra la marchesina e il dottore, il marchese era diventato una furia e aveva dato un tale urlo dicendo: *no!* che la cameriera si era turata le orecchie, spaurita" (page 406). Eventually Amati asks the Marchese for his daughter's hand. Predictably the latter refuses, in terms which are highly revealing. Amati claims he will raise Bianca from impoverishment, to which the Marchese replies, "'Io soltanto ho il dovere di arricchirla.' 'Vi ho detto che l'amo.' 'Nulla può agguagliare la mia tenerezza [...]. È un no, sempre un no, niente altro che un no. Non avrete la Marchesina Bianca Maria Cavalcanti', e sghignazzò diabolicamente" (page 246). The father claims that his bond with Bianca is the primary one, that she is his responsibility, and that his love for her is greater than Amati's; and Serao transforms him into a demonic figure.

Cavalcanti is, in a way, a more complex version of the Gothic father-figure discussed by Ellen Moers, who analyses the St Aubert/Montoni double in Radcliffe's *Udolpho* as "a father who is at one moment gentle, kind and indulgent, and the next moment is whisked off the stage to be replaced by the father who is severe, demanding, nasty and perverse" (*Literary Women*, page 135). Cavalcanti, too, embodies all these traits, but in one persona. This figure of the "bad father" is one which Serao will use again in her fully Gothic novels.

In the end it is Bianca Maria who rejects Amati, but she hides under her father's cloak to do so. The two men confront her and appeal to her to decide her own future, and she tells Amati, "Non ho nulla da dire […]. Non vi rifiuto: è mio padre che vi rifiuta" (page 428). Thus she aligns herself—indeed virtually identifies herself—with her father's will. Miyoshi's observation may be of some relevance here: "Given the time-honoured sense of the family as an extension of self, a larger self in a sense, the incestuous act becomes the moment for the self meeting with itself" (*The Divided Self*, page 11). This could explain Bianca's Gothic sublimation into the figure of the father which follows the above scene: "'La vostra figliuola è morta' ella mormorò, e aprendo le braccia, cadde indietro, riversa, livida, fredda, immobile" (page 430). She has died, in a sense, for and into the will of the father, and in so doing has become one with him. It is ultimately the covert incest motif which explains Bianca's greatest suffering and her death. The verb *peccare* is used many times in the novel in relation to her, and is always associated with a sense of dis-ease and pain. Amati once says to her: "'Voi non fate peccati…' […] tentando di scherzare. 'Non si sa' disse lei, gravemente" (page 223). The notion of sin pervades Bianca Maria's story.

In this novel Serao often uses the incest motif in a largely conventional way (finally punishing both father and daughter), though somehow it seems entirely to have escaped critics' notice. Where Serao here deviates from the norm, however, is in the importance she attaches to the figure of the absent mother. Usually the mother does not figure in such a tale of incest; here she is forever present in her absence.

In a sense, Bianca Maria spends the entire novel searching for her mother, of whom she is ever mindful and with whom she constantly compares herself. As Rigney might say, her search indicates a sense of division within herself, possibly exemplified in her wish to love both male characters. Nor can the Marchese escape the figure of his dead wife: "quella glaciale casa dove era morta di languore, di dolore, sua moglie, dove pareva ancora si aggirasse l'ombra mesta dell'estinta" (page 275). But the real "ombra mesta" of this Gothic dwelling is Bianca, who is in a way the incarnation of her dead mother.

While searching for her mother as a source of guidance, Bianca also fears her, which is consonant with the incest motif. Having overheard her father pray to her mother asking her to appear before his daughter (to give her the *lotto* numbers), she is intensely afraid. This precipitates one of the novel's most typically Gothic scenes: "Fuggí, tenendosi la testa fra le mani, con gli occhi chiusi; ma giunta nella sua camera, le parve udire come un profondo, triste sospiro dietro a sé, le parve che una lieve mano le si posasse sulla spalla; e folle di terrore [...] crollò [...] e giacque come morta" (page 180). Such a swoon is typically Gothic because it prevents the rather weak Sentimental heroine from facing what she is constitutionally unfitted for. In the usual Gothic tale, however, the "vision" precipitating such a terrified swoon does not feature the loving mother.

Yet Serao is clear about Bianca's dependence on the mother figure. The daughter resembles her mother in her role of Sentimental victim: "Dalla madre che aveva vissuto una vita dolente, ella aveva una squisita ma silenziosa sensibilità" (page 314). More significantly, the image of the dying mother has dictated her mode of existence thereafter: "Ah Bianca Maria rammentava, rammentava il volto di sua madre, morente cosí, fatta terrea da un pensiero roditore, inconsolabile, di dover morire cosí presto: e da questo ricordo indelebile, una gravità restava ancora e rendeva austera quella sua giovinezza e l'allontanava da tutti i desiderii, da tutte le aspirazioni, da tutte le civetterie di quella età" (page 315). She uses the image of the mother in a feeble attempt to convince her father to sanction her love for Amati: "Mia madre vi amava, e ve lo ha detto, ed era una dama pudica" (page 427). She thus tries to use her mother's love for her father to claim from her father her right to love another. Yet she also uses the mother figure as a justification for her renunciation of Amati: "Non posso fare altrimenti, mia madre mi maledirebbe dal cielo [...]; debbo ubbidire" (page 428). Clearly, here again the figure of the mother is one of conflicting ideals and ambivalence.

Eventually, like many of Serao's other heroines in Domestic Gothic, and later in full-blown Gothic novels, Bianca Maria becomes her mother, in character, outlook, role and appearance. In her Gothic deathbed agony she seems to sense her impending fusion with the figure of her mother: "Nelle lugubri convulsioni [...] ella aveva lungamente delirato [...], chiamando sua madre, *mamma, mamma*, come il fanciullo in pericolo, come il fanciullo che si perde" (page 510). While in the grip of these convulsions she entirely rejects her father: "Da dieci giorni lo scacciava dal suo letto, con lo sguardo e col gesto della mano" (page 513). The mention of the bed seems to confirm a rejection of the incestuous role which has caused her so much doubt and suffering. Her death itself is described in terms exactly mirroring those in which the mother's death was depicted. Neither wished to die so young: "Mamma, non voglio morire, non voglio, non voglio, mamma cara!" (page 528). It is interesting, too, that the long process of "becoming the mother" is preceded by a period of confinement in the father's house—confinement in the Gothic sense of imprisonment, but perhaps also in the metaphorical and peculiarly feminine sense of pregnancy.

Again, then, Serao stresses the significance of the mother figure for her female character. She portrays an especially ambivalent mother–daughter relationship and all the dangers inherent in the act of becoming the mother.

Lastly, I shall consider the significance of the occult elements in *Il paese di Cuccagna*. The occult arts are a topic dear to Gothic fiction, but this is the first of Serao's novels to deal with them. (She returns to them in *La mano tagliata*.) From the beginning it is clear that Bianca Maria's tale is set in metaphorically as well as morally murky waters. Cabalism is rife in her father's house.

For Bianca Maria the occult is a source of intense fear, which is itself typically Gothic. Sybil Korff Vincent defines this fear as an "attitude" of the Gothic novel: "the feeling of fear, the concept of multiple selves or no self, the search not for a 'they' but for an 'I'" ("The Mirror and the Cameo", page 153). We have already seen an example of it in Bianca's flight, where she is (perhaps) pursued by the figure of her dead mother. Bianca's fear is greater than that of the average Gothic heroine, because Serao gives her the role of "seer", through the agency of her insistent father: "'Come lo hai visto? Nella veglia? Nella dormiveglia? Nel sonno? Era una figura bianca, nevvero? Con le palpebre abbassate, ma sorridente? Che ti ha detto? Una voce debole debole, nevvero? […]' 'Mio padre, voi volete che io muoia' pronunziò ella, desolatamente" (page 277). The role is one she wishes to reject, but she is incapable of doing so. She has a typically Gothic vision: "Mi guarda… mi guarda fisamente… ha gli occhi cosí tristi, cosí tristi… mi guarda con pietà; perché mi guarda cosí, come se fossi morta?" (pages 282–83).

The context of this highly Gothic scene reveals, I think, the function of much of the occult in this tale. Bianca's father has stealthily entered her bedroom at night to induce these visions. He succeeds in provoking a strong physical reaction in his daugher—and in himself:

> Egli […] vibrava di gioia […]. Oppressa, affannata, Bianca Maria
> era scivolata dal petto di suo padre sui cuscini e si udiva il sibilo
> del suo respiro, si vedevano i suoi occhi brillare stranamente […];
> il marchese si tenea ritto presso il letto, spiando […] ogni gesto,
> ogni atto della sua figliuola […]. A un tratto, come per una scossa
> elettrica, le mani della fanciulla brancicarono convulsivamente la
> coltre: un riso rauco le uscí dalla strozza. (pages 281–82)

Overtly the scene is comprehensible as no more than what it ostensibly is: the father watches the agonizing daughter, who is in a visionary state. Yet the imagery is so strongly sexual and incestuous as to make it clear that in this novel the incest motif is linked with the occult. Both are hidden, both beyond the norm. This enables us to understand the unease characterizing Bianca's involvement with the occult: it is connected with the unease caused her by her emotionally incestuous relationship with her father. Her severe illness, bordering at times on insanity, is traceable to the same source.

Syndy McMillen Conger, discussing *Wuthering Heights*, writes about what she perceives as an unusual "intimate alliance between the Gothic heroine and the demonic or supernatural realm". She points out that "in earlier novels, the heroine moves apart from this world […]. She is a creature of the diurnal sphere" (page 102). *Wuthering Heights* was published in 1847, *Il paese di Cuccagna* in 1891; Serao may have read the English novel in the French version published in 1892—a year after *Il paese di Cuccagna* appeared. But her involvement of Bianca Maria in the supernatural realm is, I think, greater than Emily Brontë's of Catherine. Both heroines, on the other hand, have quasi-incestuous family relationships and both are motherless. Serao's success in linking the occult with the incest motif and with the motif of the absent mother (a much more powerful figure here than in Brontë's novel) is one of the most impressive achievements of this "Realistic" novel.

I find all four novels analysed in this section effective in their use of Gothic motifs. Part of their effectiveness resides, I think, in the fact that they mix genres in a manner which is often surprising—in other words, in their very nature as Domestic Gothic novels. Also effective, and potentially radical, are the ways in which Serao departs from Domestic Gothic norms. Much of her use of the Gothic centres on the negative elements of the heterosexual romantic relationship. As in other Gothic texts, this relationship is full of potential risks for the female protagonist, and gives rise to

various, apparently irrational, fears. Serao not only depicts potential risks, but also details actual risks, and thus shows these fears to
be rational. In three of these novels (*Cuore infermo, Addio, amore!* and
Fantasia) the marriage is allowed to take place, and it is after the
marriage that the real Gothic horror begins. The subtext of these
three works must be that marriage is potentially horrific. Where no
marriage takes place, in *Il paese di Cuccagna*, it is because the heroine
has a prior, more important, incestuous tie to contend with. This
too is horrific, and enough to call up supernatural manifestations.
In both cases the Gothic heroine cannot win.

Even so, the outlook is not wholly bleak. Serao's emphasis on
the potentially redemptive (if also frightening) aspects of the
mother figure allows her Gothic heroines some measure of hope. It
is essential for them to attain some comprehension of the mother
figure before they can achieve any sense of self. Yet to become the
mother is as dangerous as to become the lover/wife; and naturally
the former role often follows the latter.

Serao's depiction of hysteria in her heroines is in some respects
typically Gothic. It is possible that she was influenced in some
works by discussions of Freud's treatment of the topic, perhaps
through her friendship with Lombroso (though this is specula-
tion).[46] Like many women novelists studied by Showalter (*The
Female Malady*, pages 190–91), she went on to describe shell-shock
among her postwar male characters in much the same terms as
female hysteria.[47] As Showalter points out, "The hysterical soldier
was seen as simple, emotional, unthinking, passive, suggestive,
dependent and weak—very much the same constellation of traits
associated with the hysterical woman" (page 175). Serao shows the
same sympathy in her final novel for victims of male hysteria as she
does in her earlier writings for female victims of the same illness.[48]
The essential difference lies in her identification of causes: in her
view the War caused male hysteria, while society, especially its
male members, causes female hysteria.

Serao, then, takes Domestic Gothic to its logical conclusion.
Writers like Mrs Radcliffe, the Brontë sisters and George Eliot had
also depicted the female dilemma vividly in their novels, but had
stopped short of total condemnation of the heterosexual romantic
relationship. Instead they had taken refuge in a happy ending,
often irreconcilable with the novel's earlier dramas.[49] Serao does
not: she maintains the horror to the very end.

PURE GOTHIC

In this section my analysis will focus on those of Serao's works which may be described as wholly Gothic in setting, characterization and tone. They also contain more than the usual cluster of Gothic motifs uncovered in the previous section. The earliest of these wholly Gothic works is the short story "La donna dall'abito nero e dal ramo di corallo rosso", which has already come under scrutiny in Chapter 1. This is the most straightforward of the three works, partly because of its comparative brevity. Published for the first time in 1888 and again in 1890, it was written within the time-span of Serao's Domestic Gothic works.

The two novels are more problematic. The earlier of them, *Il delitto di via Chiatamone*, was originally published in instalments. It is a highly melodramatic, fully realized Gothic novel with a sting in the tail of the type we have come to expect from Serao. It has, however, been largely ignored by critics. *La mano tagliata*, de-scribed by Martin-Gistucci as a "roman fantastique",[50] is in some respects even more traditionally Gothic than any of its precursors: its denouement is certainly not what the reader would expect of Serao. It, too, has largely escaped critical attention; for the most part it is seen as one of Serao's more "embarrassing", feminine literary fiascos.[51]

One of the most problematic things about these novels appears to be their timing: *Il delitto di via Chiatamone* was published in 1908, *La mano tagliata* in 1912. Why was Serao still dealing with the Gothic in this period? Why, indeed, did she at this point use more Gothic conventions than ever before? Ellen Moers's theory may shed some light. Appropriately where Serao is concerned, Moers links the continuance and indeed growth of women's Gothic writing to the concept of the self: "The savagery of girlhood [a reference to Catherine's words in *Wuthering Heights*] accounts in part for the persistence of the Gothic mode into our own time; also the self-disgust, the self-hatred and the impetus to self-destruction that have been increasingly prominent themes in the writing of women in the twentieth century" (*Literary Women*, page 107). Serao could not entirely leave the issue of the self behind when she moved on from the Domestic Gothic: it continued to make its haunting presence felt in her fully Gothic novels.

Both these novels seem at times to revel in their Gothic nature, revealing themselves as Gothic with the turn of each page. *La mano tagliata* brazenly calls attention to its Gothic nature in its very title. As Freud said in his 1919 essay, "Dismembered limbs, a severed head, a hand cut off at the wrist [...] —all these have something peculiarly uncanny about them" (page 397). So in this novel we are dealing not just with the uncanny but with the "peculiarly un-canny"—in other words, pure Gothic.

Il delitto di via Chiatamone is at its most Gothic, and paradoxic-ally its most modern, in its confusing use of assumed names by different characters. The novelist plays a game of half-revelations with the reader, and hints at the "true identity" of various char-acters; in the end all is clarified. Miyoshi's comment on Shaw's *Arms and the Man* (1894–98), that it "demonstrates the absurdity of the mask and all attempts to hide the presumed true self from the world" (*The Divided Self*, page 331), is equally applicable to Serao's novel. Despite the final clarity the contradictions and complexities of the "true self" remain.

In essence both novels are wildly unlikely tales of abduction, murder and attempted murder, seduction and attempted seduction, with villains, heroes and detectives, and stereotypical feminine victims, offset by braver and more independent versions of them-selves. In these two texts Serao's characterization is in some ways more typically Gothic than we have seen in her Domestic Gothic work. Teresa, in *Il delitto di via Chiatamone*, is a natural Sentimental victim (to re-use McAndrew's formula) "transported bodily into the cloudy world of Gothic fiction" (*The Gothic Tradition*, page 68). The contrasting character is Anthonia. McAndrew's remark about Isabella and Matilda in *The Castle of Otranto* is equally applicable to Serao's pair of female protagonists: "They are [...] contrasted, one dark, lively, willing to risk action, the other a blonde descendant of the Sentimental heroine, very passive and very good" (page 69). It is fascinating to see how radically Serao makes use of these stereo-types in *Il delitto di via Chiatamone*, and how they mirror and interact with each other even though they do not meet (are not united) until the closing pages of this extremely long novel.

In both novels the Gothic villains are in some respects quite traditional. Both San Luciano in *Il delitto di via Chiatamone* and Marcus Henner in *La mano tagliata* have traits typical of the Gothic villain as defined by McAndrew: "The features of the Gothic villain [...] result in the compounding of good and evil in him, the creation of a mixed character, and a frightening vision of a world of relative moral values" (page 44). But Serao makes them more complex than this: they are hopelessly divided between good and evil. They are also both mesmeric figures.

"La donna dall'abito nero e dal ramo di corallo rosso", too, is interesting in its presentation of the male characters, all of whom, like the female character(s), are anonymous. One of them is definitely a Gothic villain, false and dramatic, intent only on seducing the heroine: "Egli divorato dal desiderio, ch'era vanità [...], fremeva di falso amore, e pregava e scongiurava, versava lagrime di dispetto" (page 134). He does seduce the heroine, but only with the aid of her passionate and somewhat degenerate double. The second male character who appears in the story seems to be a hero. He certainly represents the acme of male emotional sensitivity: "Mi amava veramente, con la lealtà spirituale delle anime elette" (page 138). In appearance, too, he is the heroic type: his face is "onesto e buono" (page 139). Yet the female character, although somehow debased and disgusted by the relationship with the "villain", is far more seriously threatened by her relationship with the hero. He it is who leads her to recognize that she *is* her degenerate double: "Mi condusse allo specchio [...]. Vidi la sua figura, che era la mia figura" (page 140). Then the downward, threatening spiral into madness begins for the female protagonist: the hero is in fact the villain of the piece. Because the villain is easily recognizable as such he is less threatening to the heroine's wholeness. In this respect "La donna dall'abito nero e dal ramo di corallo rosso" prefigures both *Il delitto di via Chiatamone* and *La mano tagliata*: the equivocal figure of the "hero" is a feature of Serao's pure Gothic works.

This story is pure Gothic in many respects. It centres on the question of the protagonist's identity: who is she? She is uncertain herself, and as the tale is told in first-person narrative the reader is also unsure of her character. This uncertainty is typical of pure Gothic. The motif of confinement, too, is introduced at the beginning of the story, which is at first told from inside a lunatic asylum. Here we have a trio of Gothic motifs: confinement, the hint of lunacy and a substitute for the Gothic castle (the asylum). Moreover, the *doppelgänger* figure, bound up as usual with the question of female identity, is ubiquitous.

It is the narrative structure which firstly defines the nature of this tale. As McAndrew points out,

> From the beginning the dream-like quality of Gothic tales is evoked through the narrative structure. The fact of a remote

world created through the method of narration interposes a mind between the reader and the tale. When the mind belongs to a character within the tale, the effect is intensified. It is the condition of such a story that the reader is told what the narrator thinks or has heard of or has seen to be what happened. (*The Gothic Tradition*, pages 200–01)

The world of this story is indeed remote: we are never told where the tale takes place. We know that part of the narrative is set in a city, with crowded streets and a theatre (page 133). Then there is a traditionally Gothic shift to the country: "Io passeggiava nella campagna trasalendo d'emozione per la maestà del fiume che se ne andava lento al mare" (page 135). Yet we are given no indication as to where, even in what country, the story is set. The mind interposed between the reader and the tale is not merely that of a character within the tale: it is that of a character who may be mad; our source is unreliable. The structure really is that of a dream, or at least of the unconscious, whence the plot's occasional incoherences. The tale's great *non sequitur* hinges on the identity of the man who is dying in the opening pages. We never discover who he is or where he fits in. We are told that the first time the narrator saw the "other" was when she was on her way to the deathbed of this man, described as "qualcuno che mi amava" (page 131). The next section begins, "Io non amava quell' uomo" (page 133), the implication at this point seeming to be that she did not love the dying man. She goes on, "Quell' uomo era un essere volgare e miserabile" (page 134). Then, apparently still with the same man in mind, she writes, "Ho tollerato due anni la menzogna, perché non mi amava" (page 137). She cannot be referring to the same character; yet no light is ever shed on the dying man's identity. The only explanation for this lies precisely in the narrative's dream structure; after the break in the text there must be a shift in the narrative consciousness. It is, to quote Miyoshi again, an instance of "incoherent details [...] forcibly 'resolved' by the overall scheme, leaving a painful cacophony" (*The Divided Self*, page 107).

In a way this structure is not unlike that of Brontë's *Villette*. Mary Jacobus says of Brontë's Lucy: "Her deliberate ruses, omissions and falsifications break the unwritten contract of first-person narrative (the confidence between reader and 'I') and unsettle our faith in the reliability of the text."[52] The same is true of the narrator in "La donna dall'abito nero e dal ramo di corallo rosso"—and we do not even know who she is.

The comparison between this tale and *Villette*, however, may be made on more than one level. At times the figure of the ghostly nun in *Villette* seems similar to the apparition of the eerie double in "La donna dall'abito nero e dal ramo di corallo rosso". Both appear at moments of passion or emotional significance in the heterosexual romantic relationship. Until the tragic end of Serao's short story both are seen only by the female protagonist. As Jacobus says of the nun, though she could have been referring to Serao's double figure, "Her uncanniness lies in unsettling the 'mirroring' conventions of representation […] and in validating Gothic and Romantic modes, not as 'discursive' and parasitic, but—because shifting, unstable, arbitrary and dominated by desire—as the system of signification which can most properly articulate the self" (page 51). In Serao's text the double appears at moments when the heroine's integral self is most at risk, and eventually, when the heroine becomes her mirror image, both "unsettles 'mirroring' conventions of representation" and indicates the disintegration of the self. This short story, like *Villette* as viewed by Jacobus, is a work "whose ruptures provide access to a double text and whose doubles animate, as well as haunt the fiction they trouble" (page 59). Strikingly, I have been unable to find any indication of direct influence of *Villette* on this short story: as far as I can tell, Brontë's novel was not translated into Italian or French in Serao's lifetime, and so she could not have read it.

The double in "La donna dall'abito nero e dal ramo di corallo rosso" also gives rise to depictions of (possible) madness. Thus an element of the grotesque, which fits well with the Gothic tone, is introduced into the narrative. Yet in this text madness may function in a particularly complex manner. Showalter has studied English women writers' representations of madness in the period 1920–60. She says: "These narratives provide the woman's witness so marginal or absent in the nineteenth-century discourse on madness; they give us a different perspective on the asylum, on the psychiatrist, and on madness itself; and they transform the experiences of shock, psychosurgery and chemotherapy into symbolic episodes of punishment for intellectual ambition, domestic defiance and sexual autonomy" (*The Female Malady*, page 210). Serao does not dwell for long on the punishments meted out to her female character for (maybe) being mad; but punishments they are. The character has not committed herself to the lunatic asylum: it is implied that the supposed hero has done that. "Chiamate un prete," she said (page

141), but he clearly chose to do otherwise. Serao shows that she does suffer: "In questa lunga agonia, io non posso morire" (page 129); and apparently she does not see herself as mad: "Non è vero che io sia pazza; io vivo, sento, ricordo e ragiono" (page 130). The litany of punishments is recited in a resigned voice: "È inutile la doccia sulla testa, il camerotto foderato di materassi, il bagno caldo, la sorveglianza continua" (page 130). For what is this character being punished? For her sexual independence, having two (possibly three) lovers? Or for having dropped her guard before the only one whom she (foolishly, Serao and the "other" would say) allowed herself to love? Is it that she has revealed to him her state of mind, her view of herself, and must pay for it? We can only surmise.

After all, in one sense the protagonist's behaviour is perhaps not all that peculiar. Showalter quotes a very interesting passage by the art historian John Berger: "A woman […] is almost continually accompanied by her own image of herself […]. From earliest childhood she has been taught and persuaded to survey herself continually. And so she comes to consider the *surveyor* and the *surveyed* within her as the two constituent yet always distinct elements of her identity as a woman."[53] Thus, as Showalter puts it, "A woman's psyche is split in two by her constructed awareness of herself as a visual object and her resulting double role as actor and spectator" (*The Female Malady*, page 212). This is, in effect, the process Serao describes throughout "La donna dall'abito nero e dal ramo di corallo rosso". At moments of romantic contact the protagonist is ever conscious of her self/other: "Io soffriva infinitamente piú di lui, io che vedevo la maga sedersi accanto a noi" (page 139). I conclude that Serao intends this anonymous female character, and her perception of self/other, to represent the experiences of the female psyche, especially in regard to heterosexual romantic involvement.

Moers suggests that "to give *visual* form to the fear of self, to hold anxiety up to the Gothic mirror of the imagination, may well be more common in the writings of women than of men." This is certainly what Serao does in her short story. Moers also offers a reason for her generalization, one which tallies with Berger's view: "Nothing separates female experience from male experience more sharply, and more early in life, than the compulsion to visualize the self" (*Literary Women*, page 107). This difference between women and men could, then, partly account for the punitive reaction experienced by the female character in this story when she voices her dual perception of her self: "L'altra non vuole andarsene, vuol vivere in me, così siamo due" (page 141). This is unacceptable to the "loving" hero and to society as a whole: "Ora mi dicono pazza" (page 137).

The perception of the self is finally achieved through the use of the mirror. As McAndrew says, "The devices of reflection, the mainstay of Gothic fiction from the beginning, continue to be its central feature" (*The Gothic Tradition*, page 155). Serao has her character look in the mirror, at the insistence of the "hero", and for the first time her two images of self coalesce: "Vidi la sua figura, che era la mia figura" (page 140). Yet this image is anything but reassuring. She is aware that beneath the image lies an-other reality. Miyoshi has pointed out that "for writers of the nineties [...] introspection, mirror-gazing, is a sanctioned activity. For the world, wear your mask; for a true glimpse of yourself, consult your mirror" (*The Divided Self*, page 311). This suggests, again, that the heroine's mistake lies in revealing to the hero a different self from what she knows her self to be. Serao's particular use of the mirror, with two gazers searching for the identity of one of them, is new. The double here is, as Jacobus has said of the nun in *Villette*, "the alien, ex-centric self which no image can mirror" ("The Buried Letter", page 51). No image can adequately reflect the truth of what the protagonist now knows to be her dual self, but patriarchal society and its representatives in the text—the lovers and the doctors—cannot comprehend this.

Jacobus's summary of the relationship between text and subtext in *Villette* cannot be bettered, I think, as a means of explaining the same relationship in "La donna dall'abito nero e dal ramo di corallo rosso". But when she writes of a "double ending" Jacobus gives a slightly different emphasis from that needed for Serao's text. She uses the term in a structural sense, whereas I would employ it in a figurative sense: "The double ending [...] reinstates fantasy as a dominant rather than parasitic version of reality, but at the same time suggests that there can be no firm ground; only a perpetual de-centring activity" (page 54). Serao's short story affirms the power of the Gothic to address the issue of self. It is therefore not surprising that Serao continues to exploit the Gothic in later novels.

Il delitto di via Chiatamone is typically Gothic, apart from anything else, in its length—615 pages.[54] It is divided into two parts, and was published in two separate volumes after originally appearing in serial form. In essence it is the tale of the illegitimate daughter of a duke (Teresa Gargiulo/Vargas) who, unknown to herself, is due to inherit a considerable fortune on her twenty-first birthday. The novel centres on the attempts of her cousin (Giorgio, Duca di San Luciano [Carlo Altieri]) first to murder her, then to seduce and marry her, so that he, instead, can inherit the money. Pitted against his satanic machinations are the efforts of Gennarino Esposito (a sailor enamoured of Teresa) and the reformed courtesan Anthonia d'Alembert/Antonietta Dugué, with the help of a lawyer, Giuseppe Rossi, the only party (except the reader) who has almost full knowledge of the situation. The forces of evil consist of 'Tore 'o Stuarto, a Neapolitan brigand, his mother Concetta Cardone and his brother Gaetanino.

The tale is set mainly in Naples, with occasional forays to Florence, and towards the end of Part II a typically Gothic shift from the city to a large house in the country, which functions very much as a Gothic castle. The house belongs to San Luciano, and there he imprisons Teresa, who is constitutionally incapable of finding her way about within its walls. Villa Merenda is a very effective prison for her, a truly Gothic dwelling: "L'appartamento era troppo vasto e deserto perché non le incutesse una certa paura. Di giorno ella cercava di impararne la divisione, aprendo tutte le porte; ma ella trovava sempre nuovi stanzini, nuove scalette, […] e non ci capiva piú nulla" (Part II, page 14). It is also the locus of some typically Gothic storms, which are especially threatening to Teresa now that she is fully in the clutches of San Luciano (believing him to be her devoted lover): "Tutte le porte stridevano. Nelle notti di temporale, villa Merenda pareva diventata il centro della bufera, ed ella batteva i denti nel suo letto, sotto le coltri" (II, 15). The first part of the novel has already had such storms occurring repeatedly in Naples. In typical Serao fashion, they are symbolic of the threat facing Teresa as she gradually succumbs to San Luciano's seduction. As she gives herself to him, swearing to be his for ever, Serao wrenches them apart with her pathetic fallacy:

> A un tratto un orribile fragore metallico risonò, secco, vicinissimo, con lungo rimbombo; un impetuoso colpo di vento schiuse la finestra, con uno scroscio di cristalli rotti, e ingolfandosi nella stanza spense il lume. Teresa, dato un grido tremendo di paura, si era rifugiata in un angolo della stanza, battendo i denti, con gli occhi chiusi […]. Carlo, interdetto all'oscuro, la chiamava, per sentire dove fosse. (I, 233–34)

It is ironic that Teresa flees from the storm and not from Carlo (the false identity her seducer has assumed). The threat represented by the storm will be wholly fulfilled in her wretched future with him.

As is suggested by the use of assumed names, identity is a crucial issue in this novel. Teresa believes herself to be Teresa Gargiulo, daughter of a poor Neapolitan worker, Francesco Gargiulo. In fact she is a *signora*, a Vargas, daughter of a nobleman who seduced her impoverished mother. Her identity does not concern her until she discovers that her lover, Carlo Altieri, is not the humble bank clerk she thought he was but the Duca di San Luciano, as he reveals to her when the "forces of good" threaten to uncover this first deceit of his towards her. The news provokes Teresa's first identity crisis, conveyed in a dialogue with her lover: "'Lo rammenti chi sei tu?' 'Lo rammento: una infelicissima figlia del popolo.' 'Ed io sono un duca di San Luciano, con tre o quattro altri titoli, sono Grande di Spagna: la distanza è enorme. Conosci tu il tuo nome?' 'Ahimé... non ne sono certa!'" (II, 38). Later she is temporarily reassured by the discovery of her true name and origin, which makes her feel the equal of San Luciano (by then her husband).

Identity is also important to Contessa Anthonia d'Alembert, who assumed this name because she thought it fitting for a wealthy courtesan. When she falls in love with Gennarino Esposito she wishes to return to her real self and former lifestyle as Antonietta Dugué, seamstress: "Veramente una vita di operaia faceva [...] Antonietta Dugué. Ella si alzava molto presto, [...] pettinava da sé i suoi magnifici capelli neri [...], parlava pochissimo [...], cuciva biancheria quasi tutto il giorno" (I, 293). Gennarino, however, persuades her to return to being the Contessa in order to help free Teresa from the clutches of San Luciano, who is in love with Anthonia d'Alembert. In the end, through Teresa's death Anthonia/Antonietta seems to incorporate Teresa's character with her own more vibrant self.

For Teresa the issue of identity is made more complex by the nature of her relationship with her mother. As usual, Serao dwells in detail on this relationship and on Teresa's own experience of motherhood. Like the typical Gothic victim, Teresa is orphaned by the time the novel opens. She is aware that her father's identity is shrouded in mystery and that her mother suffered greatly at his hands. Her mother gave her several obscure warnings about the future, intimating that her twenty-first birthday is of special significance. She also left her in possession of a sort of amulet bearing the

inscription "Temi il leone." (This is also the novel's subtitle.)
Eventually the reader learns that the "leone" is the crest of the San
Luciano family, who represent a threat to the unwitting Teresa.
When Teresa herself discovers this she begins, for the first time, to
make connections between her mother's life and her own: "Il mio
destino è simile al suo [...]. Ella è stata sedotta... ed io come lei [...].
Ella ha avuto una figliuola... ed io un figlio [...]. Io sono una
bastarda... e mio figlio che è? [...] Mia madre è stata abbandonata... ed io... ed io?" (II, 185). It is not coincidental that she makes
these connections when her position so closely mirrors her mother's.
(This is prior to her marriage to San Luciano.) Once again Serao
creates a character who "becomes" her mother.

During Teresa's "confinement" she is confined to Villa Merenda; after San Luciano has discovered that she is pregnant he spirits
her away. It is during this period that Teresa is at her sickliest. The
process of becoming a/her mother is particularly Gothic and
horrifying because of her pre-existing weakness due to the gunshot
wound (fired by 'Tore 'o Stuarto, under instructions from San
Luciano) which she sustained at the start of the novel. As may be
seen with hindsight, this wound is the first hint of an incest motif
in the novel. Thornburg says, "Incest is characteristically masked,
if it is masked at all, by the violent crimes of assault, murder, or
other violation" (*The Monster in the Mirror*, page 50). In *Il delitto di
via Chiatamone* the incest is at first masked and then openly revealed.
Teresa is constantly ill after this wound, and suffers several Gothic
deathbed agonies: firstly in the hospital after the gunshot wound
in her lung; secondly during childbirth; and finally at the moment
of her death after several shocks to her sensibilities, including the
revelation of the whole truth. The following is an example of the
typically Gothic tone in which childbirth is described: "Pallida,
stralunata, senza fiato nel suo debole petto oppresso, a ogni dolore
pareva che fosse per render l'anima. Ella gemeva sempre, ma ogni
tanto un grido straziante le usciva dalle labbra, lungo, irrefrenabi-
le" (II, 83). In childbirth Teresa nearly dies: after several pages of
Gothic description the doctor says, "Signor duca, non so come non
ha reso lo spirito!" (II, 87). Clearly, the birth of the child, the act of
becoming the mother, almost occasions a split in the self. As her
mother warned her, the direct cause of this is Teresa's relationship
with San Luciano.

One of the reasons for the disaster so avidly courted by Teresa
revolves around two Gothic motifs. The first is the discovery of a

lost relative, who in Gothic fiction normally restores the victim to her rightful place in society. The second is the incest motif. San Luciano, as Teresa's cousin, does not exactly involve her in an incestuous relationship, but Serao presents the liaison as though it were incestuous. She allows the reader to fear a close incestuous bond in Part I, where she repeatedly stresses that San Luciano forcibly reminds Teresa of her father, whom she saw once, when she was five. This familiarity is part of what attracts her to him. In Part I Serao covertly hints several times that San Luciano might be Teresa's brother: "Talvolta, silenziosamente, egli la baciava con un piccolo bacio breve e taciturno, con un bacio quasi fraterno" (I, 216). Sometimes she suggests a conflict in San Luciano and hints that it is caused by the incestuous nature of the relationship: "Carlo Altieri escercitava su lei una seduzione assoluta e travolgente. Tuttavia, egli non aveva l'aria di esercitarla né di volerla esercitare" (I, 217). The reader's anxiety grows as Serao continues to insist that this relationship is of a very close, incestuous nature: "Non sono io il tuo amico, il tuo fratello, il tuo sposo?" (I, 229), she has "Carlo" say. Serao eventually backs away from this strong incest theme by making San Luciano Teresa's cousin. Teresa, however, is as shocked as she can be when she finally discovers that she has married, and had a child by, such a close relative. Teresa's blindness, despite the hints she herself has been given, is one of the most irritating facets of her character. Thornburg is right when she says, "The Gothic heroine is a passive, pallid creature not so much because she is frail and helpless but because she is, necessarily, so blind to the dangers she courts that we suspect her blindness is deliberate" (page 43). It is the lawyer, Rossi, who breaks the news to her, when he comes to announce her inheritance on her twenty-first birthday: "'Oh, Giorgio, Giorgio, tu non mi avevi detto questo!' mormorava Teresa, ricadendo sulla sedia, come morta [...]; pendeva dalle labbra dell'avvocato, e il suo volto si scomponeva" (II, 261). Eventually she has a clear view of what has been her story and pronounces, "'Non mi resta che morire per te' [...] con voce cupa" (II, 265). This she obligingly does as a result partly of her weakness following pregnancy and partly of the shock at discovering the nature of her relationship with her husband. In other words, Serao here presents yet another Sentimental heroine who would have fared better had she avoided nurturing a romantic passion.

Much of what Ellen Moers has written about Female Gothic is applicable to this novel. We have here the bad father-figure of the

type Moers discusses: he is "absent" in the character of Francesco
Vargas, who abandoned his mistress and daughter and whose
attempt to make good the damage done to his daughter leads to her
eventual destruction; he is "present" in the figure of San Luciano,
who closely resembles him physically and repeats the father's
seduction and betrayal patterns in his relationship with Teresa.

Moers has summarized *Evelina* in a manner equally applicable
to, and very revealing of, *Il delitto di via Chiatamone*.[55] She sees it as
a Radcliffean-type novel which identifies the following dangers
awaiting the female protagonist: "masculine cruelty [...], restraints
on her freedom, all the way to actual imprisonment; [...] and, over
all, the terrible danger of slippage from the respectable to the
unrespectable class of womanhood" (*Literary Women*, page 136).
Teresa's greatest mistake is that of giving in to San Luciano; she no
longer has any power over him once she has surrendered to him.
She has, in a sense, erred in slipping from one class of woman to
another. So too has the character who functions as her double,
Anthonia/Antonietta. Anthonia can never have the love and respect of the "hero", Gennarino, because of her status as "fallen
woman". Gennarino begins by despising Anthonia's love and
devotion: "'Siete la piú infame fra le donne, ecco!' urlò il giovane."
Yet from the beginning Anthonia knows there is something that
links her with Teresa: "'E la tua Teresa anche!' gridò lei, col volto
presso a lui" (I, 210). Gennarino sees the two women as diametrically opposed: "la cara donna amata [...], la fanciulla dai bei capelli
biondi, di un biondo che formava un'aureola intorno alla bianca
fronte, dai begli occhi azzurri cosí casti e dolci, mentre i capelli di
Anthonia erano neri come la notte e i suoi occhi erano pieni di
mistero" (I, 202). One, for him, is the angel, the other the monster.
Serao, however, does not let him continue to see them in this light
for long: as soon as he discovers the nature of Teresa's relationship
with San Luciano she becomes in his eyes "un angelo caduto"
(II, 277).

The rest of the novel is taken up with his attempts to rescue
Teresa, inspired by pity for her. Anthonia becomes involved—
unwillingly at first—solely out of love for Gennarino. Soon, how-
ever, she is as obsessed as he is with liberating Teresa, her *alter ego*
(both women were poor seamstresses before their respective falls).
She even tries to enter Villa Merenda to inform Teresa of San
Luciano's plot against her, and risks her life in a battle of wits with
San Luciano intended to trap him into writing down the details of

"his" forthcoming inheritance. To achieve this she returns to the
life she has renounced, that of courtesan. Serao carefully delineates
Anthonia's growing bond with Teresa: "'Poveretta! Vi assicuro che
darei non so che, per vederla guarita e allegra!' esclamò Anthonia
con un vero slancio" (ii, 160). When all attempts to liberate the
captive have failed, she demands that San Luciano give Teresa into
her keeping, claiming that she is jealous of her: "'Voglio Teresa […].
Voglio Teresa domani' disse Anthonia, con la rigidezza di un
implacabile destino" (ii, 220–21). This too fails, but Serao uses the
scene to reveal the sense of kinship that Anthonia now feels with
her *alter ego*. In fact, she is allowed to see Teresa (to unite with her)
only as the latter lies dying, at the novel's close. With Gennarino
she approaches Teresa's bed. Both have "le facce stravolte" (ii, 283),
and Teresa's end is narrated as follows: "Malgrado tutte le lacrime
di Gennarino Esposito e d'Anthonia d'Alembert, ella morí" (ii, 284).
In a sense Anthonia, at the end of the novel, retains the best of both
female characters. She remains independent and wealthy without
returning to her Antonietta Dugué existence; she also retains a
(probably) unfulfilled and exalting love for Gennarino—clearly,
according to the novel's didactic element, the safest kind of devotion.

Most interesting in Serao's depiction of these two female characters is her presentation of how the one (Anthonia) exerts herself
to help the other self to escape male plots and structures (the
designs of San Luciano and Villa Merenda). It is equally significant
that Anthonia, in incorporating the character of Teresa, carefully
avoids Teresa's pitfalls: one character is an education for the other.
Hence, although Thornburg's summary of the typical Gothic characters fits this novel, Serao radically reworks the format by including the interesting character Anthonia and the denouement involving her. Thornburg says: "The hero and heroine of Gothic literature are good sentimental characters, carried to the inevitable
extremes sentimental literature does not show—the tamed masculine hero becomes the depleted male victim, the pure sentimental
heroine becomes the dying maiden, the murdered bride" (*The
Monster in the Mirror*, page 44). The "hero" description is applicable
to Gennarino. Teresa is, precisely, the "murdered bride", who dies
on the night of her incestuous wedding. By the manner in which
Anthonia exists, however, Teresa is redeemed.

The male characters in this novel are interesting for their roles
as *doppelgängers* (though this is developed only at the simplest

level). Gennarino and San Luciano both want Teresa; as soon as San Luciano possesses her, he begins to mistreat her, and at the same time Gennarino professes that he can no longer love her because she has "fallen" into San Luciano's clutches: "Io non sposerò mai Teresa […]. Ella ha peccato" (I, 216). Both characters are also involved with Anthonia, San Luciano professing to love her and Gennarino finally coming to prize her more than he originally thought possible. Gennarino is merely the "good", heroic version of San Luciano. As Thornburg points out, "The masculine ideal is […] represented by a less interesting character […], often […] a secondary character, the heroine's father, brother or the man who will save her from harm or ruin at the hands of the excessively masculine [character]" (page 32). Serao, however, does not allow Gennarino to "save" Teresa, partly, one assumes, because he is too weak a character to do proper battle with San Luciano, and partly because his "saving" Teresa would not allow the more interesting Anthonia to develop fully. Rossi, the lawyer, also functions as a double for San Luciano. This is obvious in the confrontation between the two—a veritable battle of wills—, where Teresa is reduced to a (literally) helpless onlooker.

San Luciano, as a Gothic villain, is a very interesting character. He is Faustian in that he is an over-reacher; he hungers after what is not his to take—Teresa / the money—, and for this he is punished. At the end of the novel he commits suicide: "Giorgio di San Luciano si era tirato un colpo al cuore […]; il suo terribile nemico si era ucciso" (II, 284). He is not the last of this type in Serao's Gothic fiction: Marcus Henner in *La mano tagliata* is even more Faustian. And San Luciano has more than this in common with Henner, in that he is something of a mesmerist, though here again not Henner's equal. As he makes love to Teresa for the first time he admits his role in her life, in a mesmeric manner: "In quel sogno era stata Teresa che aveva detto, con voce moribonda: 'Tu mi uccidi.' E […] ella aveva udito una strana voce, come lontana, ignota alle sue orecchie, dirle fra quell' incendio che la faceva agonizzare: 'Sì, voglio ucciderti'" (I, 237). So hypnotized is she by him that she never questions this. Indeed, Serao repeatedly shows that his hold over her is somehow abnormal, verging on the supernatural. Although Teresa is shocked by his actions, she is incapable of blaming him for anything: she dies expressing her forgiveness and wishing only that he had been honest with her from the start. Serao goes to some lengths, however, to make it clear that within San

Luciano there are two "natures" doing battle. He is usually one character with Teresa and quite another with Anthonia, though his guard sometimes slips and he permits each of them to glimpse his other self. In this inner self-division he is characteristically Gothic: "E se questi discorsi turpi di denaro lo avevano molto spoetizzato togliendogli l'illusione che mai Anthonia potesse amarlo per sé, *pure sollevavano in lui la parte peggiore*, dimostrandogli che infine con l'oro tutto si ottiene" (I, 73, my italics). Anthonia fathoms his character thus: "Che uomo siete voi? Che avete di nero, di tragico, di pauroso in voi? Io non vi conosco, ma v'intravedo" (II, 219). There is duality both within him and outside him, in the characters of Gennarino and Rossi.

There are still more Gothic elements in this novel, though since they are less significant for the present analysis I shall mention them only briefly. There are numerous descriptions of gory scenes, mainly following the shot which wounds Teresa; there are many dreams and presentiments, again attaching to Teresa (she ignores them, as a good, blind, Sentimental heroine should); there is the figure of the nun, Suor Marta di Gesú, who, however, rather than being eerily Gothic has the sole function of helping Teresa; and at the end of the novel Gennarino Esposito takes on the role of the wanderer: unable to find peace, he becomes something of a Youthful Mariner (the text frequently refers to him as "il giovane marinaio"). The function of the lower classes, represented by Concetta, Gaetanino and 'Tore, is typically Gothic. Thornburg points out that while in the Sentimental tradition the poor are blessed sufferers, in the Gothic tradition they aid the villain (page 43). The atmosphere of the novel as a whole is Gothically oppressive, and it is the child-like Teresa, with her sensitivity, who suffers from it. Her fears (of storms, silence, solitude and darkness) are explicable in Freud's terms as "elements in the production of that infantile morbid anxiety from which the majority of human beings have never become quite free" ("The Uncanny", page 407). In this respect Teresa represents all of us.

This novel, then, can be seen only as purely Gothic. Serao uses a plethora of stock motifs, devices and figures to weave a tale of terror. But she does more than this: she reworks the figure of the Gothic heroine by ultimately sacrificing Teresa to the stronger Anthonia. And all the terrors and threats she incorporates hinge again on the dangers inherent in the romantic heterosexual relationship for her female characters. Most interestingly of all, per-

haps, she holds the reader continually in suspense as to the outcome. The reader of traditional Gothic novels must expect a conventionally "happy" ending (in which, for instance, Teresa might
remain an invalid, but would not die: she might marry Gennarino—who could overcome his scruples were he not San Luciano's
super-ego—and live a peaceful, uneventful life). Serao has Rossi,
Anthonia and Gennarino hint continually at the prospect of a
"happy" ending, of "saving" Teresa; they are full of confidence. Yet
at the same time she subverts this by allowing the reader no
illusions as to the strength of San Luciano's hold over Teresa and
the depths of his evil. It is repeatedly stated that she probably
would not leave him even if she knew the whole truth (as, indeed,
she must at a subconscious level). Serao ultimately frustrates the
conventional "happy" ending, leaving the reader with a most un-
Gothic *open* ending. This is not just a tale of terror: it is, more than
anything, a cautionary tale. Having, importantly, restored Anthonia to a life of independence and luxury, Serao leaves her readers
to construct their own ending. In the closing paragraph she *asks*
what became of Gennarino and Anthonia: "Si commosse, forse, il
cuore di Gennarino Esposito? Vissero essi insieme, felici, o si
divisero per sempre? Chi sa! I grandi amori vanno alla vita e vanno
alla morte, egualmente!" (II, 287). The tone is above all one of
warning. Hence, although Serao expresses many pious sentiments
in this novel (particularly about Anthonia, "la donna che si era
redenta per l'amore": II, 286), the overall thrust is towards a positive
evaluation of Anthonia's return to independence, and towards a
warning to her (and the reader) that love is full of danger. It is, I
think, a fascinating denial of perhaps the most dependable part of
the Gothic novel, its denouement.

La mano tagliata is another late, typically Gothic novel, and
another tale in which the issue of identity is of crucial importance,
the mother has great significance for the daughter's definition of
self, and *doppelgängers* proliferate. The occult arts are more significant here than in any of Serao's earlier novels, while Marcus Henner
is one of the most complex Gothic male characters Serao ever
created: he is simultaneously the mesmerist, the scientist, the
Gothic monster and the Wandering Jew.

In essence, this is the tale of a rather exotic Jewish family: Mosé
Cabib and his wife Miriam/Sara (later Maria). Miriam, when
young, has an affair with a young Christian, Jean (Jehan) Straube,
which results in the birth of a child, Rachele. The adultery is

unknown to Mosé, who accepts that Rachele is his daughter. Great complications in this family's existence originate in the person of Marcus Henner, a doctor and mesmerist who successively falls in love with both Maria and Rachele. His power over Mosé is such that he persuades him to entrust his wife to him; thereafter she is his prisoner until released by Roberto Alimena, who has come into possession of her severed hand (severed to release her from a particularly dangerous mesmeric trance) and resolved to find its owner. Henner, meanwhile, has attempted to gain power over Rachele, who happens to be in love with Roberto's friend, Ranieri Lambertini. He has succeeded only in separating her from her lover, whom she wrongly believes to have been unfaithful to her. Rachele has taken refuge in a convent, and is about to be professed when she receives a letter from the mother she had thought dead, asking her to return to Lambertini, who truly loves her. This she does. Maria, though, has since been killed by Henner, who then proceeds to kill himself. The novel is long (434 pages) and tortuous, and the above summary gives only the most basic outline of the narrative.

The narrative structure, too, is complex. The novel begins with a third-person description of the character of Roberto Alimena and the manner in which he finds the severed hand (Henner left it behind in a railway compartment they shared). It then proceeds somewhat in the manner of a detective story, as with Ranieri's help Roberto discovers more about Henner and Maria. The tale of Rachele runs parallel to that of Roberto and is also told in third-person form. As the plot thickens, first-person narrative is used in letters, correspondence being the main form of communication between Roberto and Ranieri. Other letters, too, tell other parts of the story: Maria's to Rachele, for instance; Roberto's to his scientist friend, Silvio Amati, and Amati's letters to him, which clarify the nature of the "mano tagliata"; and finally, Marcus Henner's own suicide tome, which explains all his actions and motives. The narrative, then, is basically concentric, and thus effectively retains the Gothic atmosphere as described by Elizabeth McAndrew: "The medieval setting was soon abandoned for a contemporaneous one [...] as if to bring home the depicted evil to the reader's own time. When the tale is no longer set in the distant past, a system of 'nested', concentric narration maintains the illusion of a strange world, isolating a symbolic landscape within the ordinary 'world'" (*The Gothic Tradition*, page 48). This narrative structure also allows the reader to piece together the elements of the narrative only gradually: for much of the novel the reader is no less in the dark than any of the protagonists. Serao allows the reader to share the point of view of different characters in turn. At first we identify with Roberto, then with Rachele, then with these two in turn again; towards the end of the novel we share Ranieri's confusion as we too become privy to the information contained in Roberto's letters; finally, we are required to share Marcus Henner's point of view, though Serao seems to have reservations about asking us to do so. The one character whose point of view we never share is Maria: she exists mainly in the narratives of others (Roberto, Henner's servant John, Henner himself), and we are never allowed to see fully inside her mind. She remains something of an enigma, though a power-fully drawn character.

Four dwelling-places described in the text could be defined as typically Gothic. One of these is the convent of the "Sepolte vive" in Naples, which Rachele (Grazia) enters after her disappointment in love. Serao uses terms of Gothic enclosure to describe it: "Pronunziata una volta i voti sacri, non uscivano piú [...]. Non era neppure a traverso la grata, come in altri conventi di clausura, che avveniva la conversazione, ma a traverso il muro. Un colpo al muro e vi si applicava l'orecchio: le voci arrivavano fioche e sorde, stranissime" (page 187). The second Gothic building is the house of Contessa Loredana (who is in league with Marcus Henner to murder Lambertini and have the blame ascribed to Roberto Alimena, thus getting rid of both his rivals). This is described in a letter from Roberto to Amati: "Un sol fanale illuminava il piccolo viale [...]; tutto il giardino restava, quindi, in ombra. Ho bussato e il cancello mi si è schiuso avanti, aperto per incanto come nelle case delle maghe" (page 222). The atmosphere here is that of the uncanny, and of impending doom. The third Gothic locus is a public house by the docks in London: "La taverna aveva l'aspetto di un sotterraneo e il fumo delle pipe, gli aliti e non so quale bruma venuta dal fiume, ne rendevano piú strano e piú pauroso l'aspetto" (page 275). Again there is a sense of something negative and threatening in this odd setting (where Roberto and the quintessentially English detective, Dick Leslie, have arranged a rendezvous with Henner's servant, John). The most Gothic structure of all is the Henner household in London. Here we have all the traditional Gothic trappings, such as hidden doors and secret passageways:

Marcus Henner introdusse una chiavettina in un fregio di legno,
ad altezza di uomo, nella sua libreria e un pezzo di questa si aprí,
come una porta: egli sparve colà dentro e alle sue spalle la falsa
libreria si richiuse. Egli si trovò nell'anticamera di un vasto e
sontuoso appartamento [...]; attraversò una serra a cristalli [...].
Poi penetrò in una stanza da letto, anche essa deserta [...]. Attese
un minuto e poi si accostò a una parete, sollevando una portiera
che la ricopriva; vi era una piccola porta, dietro. Tentò la mani-
glia, ma la porticina resistette, come se fosse chiusa a chiave.
(pages 171–72)

I find this paragraph interesting for at least two reasons. Firstly,
the setting, a house in London. Many of the earliest English Gothic
novels were set in Italy, the exotic, strange location *par excellence*. In
a sense Serao here turns the tables: her remote, exotic Gothic
location is London. (To some extent she may be continuing the
fascination of both French and Italian writers with what Mario Praz
calls "le vice anglais".)[56] Still more interesting, perhaps, is the way
in which enclosure works in this novel. Maria is a Gothic victim,
kept prisoner by Henner, yet she exerts more control over her
environment than he can. He wishes her to be kept in the outer
bedroom described in this passage, instead of which she has
moved into a further enclosure: she has created an alternative
prison for herself—and *she locks him out*. She is an unusual Gothic
heroine, and much stronger than her predecessors, in her ability to
control her environment and her relationship with her captor.

This strength is a characteristic shared by mother and daughter. Although both are pursued and tormented by Henner, and
ultimately held in enclosed spaces, neither is a Sentimental Gothic
victim. Both react to their persecutor in the same way. Rachele, in
fact, finds the strength to repulse Henner through her relationship
with her mother, which exists only in the two characters' subconscious minds. Rachele has been told that her mother is dead, yet
she only half-believes it. Like other Serao heroines, Rachele possesses a miniature of her mother, and she carries on a constant
dialogue with it: "Il ritratto di Sara Cabib era vecchio di una
quindicina di anni e molto scolorito: ma gli occhi conservavano una
vivace espressione dolce e fiera nello stesso tempo, e pareva che la
guardassero. 'Madre, madre mia, se tu vivi, vieni a me!'" (page 67).
As with many of Serao's other Gothic heroines, Rachele's request
is Gothically granted:

A un tratto, nell'ardore di quella preghiera, a Rachele Cabib parve che quel ritratto scolorito avesse uno sguardo *vivo*, negli occhi: parve che su quella bellissima e pallida bocca fiorisse un sorriso *vivo*. E parve, proprio le parve, che una voce, una voce *udita altra volta* non una voce propriamente, ma un soffio, *a lei noto*, di voce, le dicesse "Eccomi". La fanciulla gettò un grido e cadde riversa, svenuta. (page 68; italics mine)

This faint is atypical of Rachele. She loses consciousness only once again in the novel, and that incident also centres on the mother figure (Henner tells her he knows where her mother is, but refuses to tell her the place). The mother figure is the one which provokes her greatest crises, yet she is equally the source of her strength. Rachele rejects Henner on the grounds that her mother "mi ha parlato, in sogno" (page 129). It is this link between mother and daughter that Henner, master of the occult, finds most threatening. To Henner's horror, it has existed only since he began to pursue Rachele: "'Sempre che voi avete voluto infliggermi il tormento e la vergogna del vostro amore *ella* è venuta. Ella mi ama, Marcus Henner, e vi odia, mia madre!' 'Voi delirate, Rachele Cabib!' esclamò il maestro, non dominando la sua commozione" (page 130). The link between mother and daughter is so strong that Henner can gain access to the mother only by speaking to her about the daughter. In the final chapter the reader discovers that what Maria has been constantly writing is a type of diary-letter addressed to her daughter; it is a "herstory".

Part of Rachele's drama lies in the fact that she is ignorant of her story and her mother's. From the beginning she senses a barrier between herself and her father. She has an insatiable curiosity about the past: "'Parlami del passato, parlami', e si chinava con ansietà sul vecchio, quasi a beverne le parole [...]. 'Padre, tu non sai se mia madre è morta?' ella gridò, in preda a uno strano terrore [...]. 'Tua madre è seppellita in un piccolo cimitero di Germania' disse, a voce bassa, Mosé Cabib [a] lei, diventata glaciale, a un tratto, sentendo che la verità le sfuggiva" (pages 56–57). Her identity is bound up with her mother, and literally unconnected with the man she knows as her father.

The problem of identity is temporarily and superficially resolved for Rachele when she enters the convent and becomes Suora Grazia. Several times Serao hints that this new identity is transient by retaining both names for her character: "Rachele Cabib ovvero suora Grazia" (page 200), "suora Grazia, cioè Rachele Cabib" (page

200), "Rachele Cabib, ossia suora Grazia" (page 201), "suora Grazia
la novizia, che aveva lasciato in monastero il nome di Rachele
Cabib" (page 330). This enclosure, or (we might say) confinement,
in the convent is in a sense a prelude to Rachele's becoming the
mother. Both mother and daughter are confined for a long time. On
her release Maria manages to contact her daughter, and Rachele
too is "released". At the end of the novel she is "Rachele Cabib, piú
bella, piú giovane" (page 434). Like her mother, she left enclosure
for love. Yet we know that her mother was killed because of her
love for Roberto, and although Henner is gone it remains difficult
for the reader to accept the novel's supposedly happy ending.
Rachele's "release" is contemporaneous with her discovery of her
identity and her past, but these discoveries are quite tragic. The
romantic close ("Mia madre mi ha scritto di venire a te, di amarti
fedelmente, sino allo morte. Eccomi!": page 434) has been preceded
by so much melodrama and tragedy that it is impossible to accept
it at face value. It is also noticeable that Rachele is (again) acting on
her mother's instructions: she is still in the process of becoming her
mother. The reference to "morte", too, sounds oddly at variance
with this traditional ending, itself unusual in Serao's fiction.

Another typically Gothic feature of the novel is Serao's use
(overuse?) of the *doppelgänger* motif. It seems obvious from what I
have said about Maria and Rachele that they are doubles—in
similar situations, with similar reactions, and with subconscious
links—; indeed they are the novel's most fully realized doubles.
Serao also uses a complex set of doubles in delineating her male
characters. It is clear from a relatively early stage that Roberto, who
loves Maria, and Ranieri, who loves Rachele, are doubles, thus
making a neat parallel with the duality of the female characters.
Serao introduces the duality between Roberto and Ranieri as
follows. From the time he discovers the severed hand Roberto is
conscious of being followed, and when he meets Ranieri the latter
confides to him: "'Da che amo Rachele, sono seguito, pedinato,
perseguitato; ma due o tre volte ho avuto delle liti, per la via; ma
sono assediato da mendichi, da facchini, da fattorini...' 'Dite sul
serio?' mormorò Roberto, colpito da grande meraviglia, notando la
strana coincidenza" (page 101). Both have seen the man they know
to be their tormentor, Henner: "'Il mio rivale, il mio persecutore, è
gobbo, magro, con gli occhi verdi' asserí Ranieri. 'Che dite?' gridò
Roberto" (page 104). From then on the two characters are set in a
typical double relationship, with a tremendous sense of unity

between them. Ranieri is stabbed, and Roberto is blamed for the attack by all except Ranieri himself. Finally, Ranieri recovers and Roberto is cleared. Each pursues the object of his affections, but it is only through the medium of the Roberto–Maria unit that Ranieri can reach Rachele.

The novel contains a further doubling which at first is not so easily seen: that of Henner and Roberto. Both love Maria Cabib, both are, in different senses, attached to her hand, each hates and fears the other. This doubling, which is much darker and more Gothic than those identified above, is first suggested by the troubled scene of the attack on Ranieri at Contessa Loredana's home. It is Roberto who discovers Ranieri's inert form after the stabbing, and Roberto whom the police suspect of the deed, the weapon used being his. Generally, a cloud of doubt hangs over Roberto's retelling of the event in his letter to Amati: "È sempre il mio pugnale, quello che è stato trovato nella ferita di Ranieri Lambertini, sono sempre io, che sono stato trovato disteso sul suo corpo […]; lo stesso Lambertini non ha saputo e potuto dire nulla sul tentato assassinio di quella notte, egli non ha visto niente, è stato aggredito alle spalle, non sa da chi" (page 242). This leads Roberto to formulate a theory about his relationship with Henner, which makes sense only as an explanation of the double motif which Serao will go on to develop: "Questo atroce malfattore domina la mia vita. Or dunque un legame terribile mi unisce a quest' uomo ed io debbo assolutamente cercarlo, conoscere il suo segreto, annientare la sua potenza, uccidere forse quest' uomo […]; una lotta corpo contro corpo, anima contro anima, è sorta tra me e questo assassino" (page 243). Thus Roberto's pursuit of Henner is not simply intended to discover the owner of the severed hand: it is intimately bound up with Henner himself. In fact, it is only by taking Maria away from Henner (and, in so doing, leading her to her death) that Roberto manages to drive him out of hiding, bring him onto his own territory and finally discover the secret of his existence as he has vowed to do. The novel therefore centres on this relationship as much as on any other.

Roberto often frames his relationship with Maria in terms of hers with Henner. In one of his letters to her he says: "Dio, Dio, che cosa gli farò mai, io, a questo scellerato, a questo boia, per punirlo del suo efferato delitto, quale tortura inventerò io per farlo soffrire mille volte di piú, di quello che voi, povera anima, avete sofferto?" (page 267). In fact, Roberto's dependence on Maria, as revealed in the same letter, mirrors Henner's: "Non mi abbandonerete mai, ecco tutto. Siete una buona cristiana e non condurrete un'anima alla disperazione. No. No. Lo so bene che non mi lascerete mai!" (page 269). In a sense, what he proposes is the mirror image of the existence Maria has had with Henner: she is not to be allowed to leave either of them. Even Roberto's behaviour before he "frees" Maria from Henner's house is reminiscent of Henner's when he took her from Mosé Cabib. Roberto prepares his luggage and "vi uní quello femminile, tutto ciò che può essere necessario a una donna, in viaggio: della roba fine ed elegante, che egli scelse con cura speciale, come può fare un innamorato" (page 300). We have already seen the room Henner prepared for Maria in his London home with precisely the same motivation. Maria herself has scornfully listed his cares for her: "Io non dormo nelle stanze principesche che tu mi prepari, io mi contento di una cella monacale; io non indosso le stoffe di velluto e di seta che tu mi doni, mi basta una veste di lana bianca" (page 181). The two male characters, then, behave in the same way. It is hardly surprising that after Maria's death and Henner's suicide Roberto sees that he has nothing to do but wait for death to come to him too. Between those two events he has a reason for living, to kill Henner, his *alter ego*; but in that he is frustrated.

If Roberto and Henner are doubles, why does Maria respond so differently to them? Part of the answer lies in her relationship with her daughter: whereas Henner keeps her from Rachele, Roberto promises to take her to her (but, significantly, never does). Serao shows that this is uppermost in Maria's mind when she leaves Henner's house. Roberto, in his letter to Ranieri, narrates: "'È vero che voi mi condurrete da ma figlia?' ella mi chiese […]. 'Sí, o signora' le risposi io […]. 'Andiamo, signore' ella mi disse senz' altro" (page 359).

Another part of the answer lies in Henner's monstrous nature. The motifs of monstrosity and deformity are both prominent and problematic in Gothic writings by women. Moers points out that monsters were popular Gothic motifs from early Gothic writing onwards: "Distortion of scale was the first visual effect employed by Gothic novelists in creating monsters […]: well before Frankenstein's outsize monster, Walpole had filled *The Castle of Otranto* with spectres of giant stature" (*Literary Women*, page 101). What is interesting is the way in which women writers adapted the theme of monstrousness, as well as the fact that they have used it up to the present day, as Moers points out: "Women writers have […] continued to make monsters in the twentieth century, but not so often giants or animaloid humans as aberrant creatures with hideous deformities" (page 108). Serao certainly makes Henner monstrous, both physically and in temperament: *mostro* is the word most frequently used to describe him in the novel. Yet he is also a *maestro*, a leader of his people. This is the crux of the depiction of his character. Serao herself has a dual attitude towards him. On one level she hates and despises him (as do her female protagonists); on another she understands and pities him. Her attitude is reminiscent of Mary Shelley's towards her monster, whom she hates and yet pities.[57] Both writers allow their monstrous creations to speak for themselves, which is how we can sense their sympathy.

Serao allows many characters to refer to Henner as a monster. Maria does so in a moral sense, reproaching him for allowing her former lover to think her dead (when in fact she was in a hypnotic trance): "Tu, tu, mostro, gli facesti vedere che io era morta" (page 180). When Ranieri and Roberto speak of him they both concentrate on his deformity. Most significant of all, perhaps, as an indication of Serao's early self-alignment with the view expressed by most of her protagonists, is the title she gives to Chapter 4: "Sulla traccia del mostro". Again we are reminded of *Frankenstein*, and particularly of Victor's pursuit of the monster.

Paradoxically, Serao's sympathy for Henner comes across most clearly in his account of his own self-disgust: "Ho commesso un orribile delitto. Ho ucciso una donna debole, inerte e indifesa […]. E il mio delitto si è compiuto in una maniera tanto atroce, che al solo pensarvi, i capelli si rizzano sul mio capo seminudo, e l'agghiacciato sudore del rimorso ne bagna le radici" (page 392). Like Mary Shelley's monster, Henner has killed a woman because of her love for his rival. Also in a manner reminiscent of Shelley's monster, Henner identifies the elements of his monstrous nature: "Sono gobbo, calvo, brutto, sporco: faccio paura agli uomini, ribrezzo alle donne" (page 396). Like Frankenstein's monster, what he lacks is love. His servant tells him he is respected and feared, but Henner's refrain is, "Ma non m'ama nessuno!" (page 161). This is highly reminiscent of Shelley's monster, whose refrain is, "I am solitary and abhorred" (page 130). He too craves love: he begs Frankenstein to create a bride for him, whereas Henner spends most of his existence trying to compel Maria and/or Rachele to love him. Both fail, eliciting only extreme negative responses. Shelley's monster speaks in the same tone as Henner: "Who can describe their horror and consternation on beholding me?" (page 135).

It is this sense of self-disgust and isolation that seems to provoke Serao's sympathy for her character (and, indeed, Shelley's for hers). The sympathy is detectable in the closing pages of Henner's letter: "Sono un vinto, sono un misero, sono la più miserabile creatura del mondo, l'ultimo verme della terra. Non mi piangerà nessuno [...]. Abbastanza, da me mi odio e mi disprezzo" (page 430). The conflict inherent in Henner—his duality—is another reason for the author's sympathy; he refers to "questo sangue dove ardeva la fiamma di un uomo giovane e bello mentre io era un mostro di bruttezza" (page 430). Inside, he is Roberto; outside, unfortunately for him, he is Henner.

Serao's sympathy for Henner is further evinced by the fact that he is not the novel's only deformed character: Maria, after all, is the one with the "mano tagliata". It might be said that Henner and Maria have their deformity in common. Interestingly, Henner effects the dismemberment (in itself typically Gothic) not in an attempt to harm Maria, nor even to make her conscious of his deformity: it is presented as his only choice when he has put her into a hypnotic trance so deep that only a severe physical shock will return her to normal existence. This event, too, is narrated in his letter and causes him to suffer torment:

> Nella notte atroce che dedicai a questa opera terribile, io ho visto imbiancare gli ultimi capelli che rimanevano sul mio cranio deforme, e non ho mai provato nella mia vita uno schianto simile, come quando [...] io vidi sotto i miei occhi recidere il braccio sinistro di Maria [...]; al grido di belva, colpita mortalmente, che uscí dal petto della mia povera vittima, si uní un grido straziante, il mio. (page 421)

This allows Serao to present Henner in the semi-sympathetic light typical of the Gothic villain. As McAndrew stresses, typical Gothic villains "suffer the torments of the damned while committing their nefarious deeds because they must battle with themselves to commit them and must also repress their own feelings. Yet the reader is invited to feel with and for them in the rending conflicts from which they suffer" (*The Gothic Tradition*, page 82). Part of the reason for Serao's sympathy/identification with Henner resides, no doubt, in the tendency of the woman writer to identify with what is abnormal and monstrous, because of her view of herself as such.[58] Furthermore, it is clear that although Serao presents Henner sympathetically towards the end of the novel she does not expect her readers to accept that presentation. This is exemplified in Ranieri Lambertini's reaction to the letter: "Contro quel morto lo teneva un'ira cosí truce, che nessuna corrente di pietà arrivava a temperare" (page 433). Yet again, Serao cannot resist a last, piteous portrait of her Gothic villain: "E cosí, nella morte come nella vita, il grande ipnotizzatore, l'uomo che aveva piegato innanzi a sé tutte le volontà salvo una, e che aveva posseduto tutto nella vita, salvo l'amore di una donna, non arrivava ad ispirare pietà, neanche con la grandezza della sua espiazione" (pages 433–34). This, however, is not quite true: he certainly inspires pity and sympathy in his creator.

The character of Marcus Henner leads us back to Mary Shelley's novel in another, very important, respect. The picture of him standing over Maria, suffering as her arm is severed, reminds one forcibly of the scene where Victor Frankenstein creates his monster:

> It was already one in the morning, the rain pattered dismally against the panes […]; by the glimmer of the half-extinguished light, I saw the dull yellow eye of the creature open […]. How can I describe my emotions at this catastrophe […]? […]. Breathless horror and disgust filled my heart. Unable to endure the aspect of the being I had created, I rushed out of the room. (page 57)

Both scenes are set in a laboratory at night; both involve work on an apparently lifeless being; both are concerned with giving life to this being; both provoke the horror of the giver of life. *Frankenstein*, as I pointed out earlier, has been seen as a birth myth, and it is possible to apply that interpretation, loosely, to this section of Serao's novel too. Yet what seems more interesting here is the way in which Henner is in one respect the monster but in another the Victor Frankenstein figure—the scientist, the Faustian overreacher.

The monster Henner creates is himself. And he creates it through his interest in the occult, in science and in mesmerism: "Mentre mio padre m'iniziava agli studi practici di medicina e io seguiva gli studi scientifici, in età ancora giovanissimo, con una precocità straordinaria, mia madre m'iniziava allo studio delle scienze occulte" (page 397). In a manner reminiscent of Victor Frankenstein's studies, "Io sono passato a traverso la vita, senza vederla, studiando sui libri e sulle erbe, interrogando tutte le sorgenti dell'esistenza, conoscendo i segreti della scienza e dell'ipnotismo" (page 398). In this respect Henner conforms to a certain Gothic character-type: he is like Faust, Frankenstein and Jekyll, whose "studies tend towards 'the mystic and the transcendental'", as Miyoshi says of Dr Jekyll (*The Divided Self*, pages 297–98). Elizabeth McAndrew has described the Gothic manifestations of the intellect and the physical thus: "Throughout the tales featuring grotesques, artists, scientists and the intellect itself are brought into some kind of conflict with the demons of the physical, the creatures from underground or from the mental below-ground of characters and readers alike. The figures of the intellect, however, also appear frighteningly ambiguous and shifting" (page 173). The analysis squares well with *Frankenstein, Dr Jekyll and Mr Hyde* and a host of other Gothic works. Serao stands somewhat apart from that tradition in her depiction of the negative traits of the intellect and of the body incorporated into one character. Henner represents both the intellect and the grotesque monster.

A significant aspect of Henner the monstrous mesmerist is the fact that he is a travelling mesmerist. He visits Russia, Italy, France and England to treat his patients (sometimes to heal them and sometimes, as we shall see, to manipulate them). His origins are German. He is, indeed, a Wandering Jewish mesmerist.

The theme of the Wandering Jew reminds us again of Frankenstein. The following is Miyoshi's summary of George Eliot's *The Lifted Veil*,[59] which he considers in relation to *Frankenstein*: "Many incidents in the story are traceable to Mary Shelley: the friendship of the scientist and the poet, the revivification, the Faustian Devilcompact, the Wandering Jew, the hero's isolation, and the locale itself, all are *Frankenstein* motifs" (page 232). Much of this is equally applicable to *La mano tagliata*. Roberto's friendship with Amati is fundamentally a friendship between a scientist (Amati) and a poetic type (Roberto—see his love letters to Maria); the revivification I have already pointed out; and both Henner and Roberto are noticeably isolated.

Where I think Serao diverges slightly from Mary Shelley is precisely in her use of the figure of the mesmeric Wandering Jew. It is Henner's mesmerism that distinguishes him from others of his type and allies him, in particular, with the mesmeric male "character". Nina Auerbach has undertaken a complex and interesting study which is extremely useful for linking the type of the mesmerist and the Wandering Jew. Her specific topic is "incarnations" of women in the 1890s:

> In a key tableau of the nineties, we see first, as we often do, not women, but men; three men lean hungrily over three mesmerized and apparently characterless women, whose wills are suspended by those of the magus/monsters.The looming men are Svengali, Dracula and Freud; the lushly helpless women are Trilby O'Farrell, Lucy Westenra and (as Freud calls her) "Frau Emmy von N, aged 40 from Livonia". ("Magi and Maidens", page 113)

Such a type, too, is Marcus Henner, as we see him trying to hypnotize Maria: "Dicendo queste cose il gobbo aveva negli occhi verdi e nella voce tanto imperio, tanto fluido di dominazione, che un genio infernale pareva sprizzasse dal suo sguardo e dalle sue parole. Distesa, tutta bianca nelle sue vesti, Maria, inerme, indifesa, subiva tutto il fascino malvagio di quell' uomo terrible" (page 184). This passage certainly links Henner to the Svengali/Dracula literary type, but what about Freud? Auerbach defends her view of Freud as a mythic, mesmeric figure:

> As a mere mortal and historical figure, Freud might seem out of place in this preternatural company, but in his case history of Frau Emmy von N [...] there is delicious magic in his use of hypnosis [...]; he revels in a psychic appropriation that is quite Svengali-like: "I made it impossible for her to see any of those melancholy things again [...] by removing her whole recollection of them, as though they had never been present in her mind. I promised her that this would lead to her being freed [...] from the pains all over the body." (pages 113–14)[60]

Auerbach continues: "The virtually limitless powers he arrogates to himself in this initial amalgam of science, myth and magic give him access to our mythic pantheon" (page 114). Serao presents Henner in precisely the same light as Freud presented himself: Henner is here seen with an English patient of his, Elisa Jackson: "'Ve ne andrete via convinta di non avere nessun male.' 'Va bene.' 'Se durante i due giorni in cui dovrà durare l'obbedienza, vi viene in mente di esser malata, scaccerete questo pensiero.' 'Sí'" (page 170). In my view it is no accident that we see Henner only with women as subjects for his hypnosis. Statistically, women were more likely to receive such treatment; and, as we see in Freud's

Studies on Hysteria,[61] they were also its subjects in literature and psychoanalytical writings.

In that Henner is a mesmeric Wandering Jew, Henner and Freud are, in essence, even closer than Henner and Svengali or Dracula. Serao may not consciously have intended Henner to be a Freudian type, but the connections are difficult to escape.

A further similarity between Henner, Svengali, Dracula and Freud is the role of women in their dramas. Auerbach gives a surface description of these female characters: "All selfhood [is] suspended as [they] are invaded by the hyperanxious and culturally fraught male/master/monster." Yet, paradoxically, great powers are granted to these women characters: "The victim of paralysis possesses seemingly infinite capacities of regenerative being that turn on her triumphant mesmerizer and paralyse him in turn" (page 114). Auerbach shows that Trilby and Lucy become the stronger characters in their respective tales, and that Freud's patients walk out on him ("Dora", for example) or show themselves capable of "amazing and empowering transformations" (page 124). Henner's victims, too, either elude him (Rachele) or overcome him (Maria). At the end of the hypnosis session with Maria mentioned earlier, just when it seems she is most in Henner's power:

> Avvenne una cosa terribile. Quel corpo abbandonato al sonno ipnotico, vinto da una fascinazione terribile, diventato lo schiavo di quel corpo dagli occhi verdi, quel corpo che era suo, di cui egli poteva fare quel che voleva [...], si levò, di scatto, parve piú alto, fantomatico, nelle vesti bianche. E gli occhi di quell' ipnotizzata si spalancarono, grandi, vitrei, senza sguardo. Ella gridò, avendo superato il fascino: "No, assassino!" E Marcus Henner [...], diventato un cencio [...], cadde a terra, lungo disteso, con le braccia aperte, piangendo sulla sventura. (page 186)

In Serao's work too, then, the strength of the female character seems greater than that of the male mesmerist. This is further suggested in Henner's letter, with which the novel closes: "Per lei io muoio [...], quella innocente mi ha colpito, morendo" (page 430).

It is nonetheless clear that Serao dislikes and distrusts the figure of the male mesmerist. Henner, because of his loneliness, has no scruples about seducing any of his patients under hypnosis, as we have seen him try to do with Maria. This is the level on which Serao most clearly detaches herself from Henner: "Quando erano sveglie, mi guardavano disgustate e sgomente [...]. Però, quando io comandava di dormire, esse dormivano [...]; allora morendo di rabbia, di crepacuore, io *comandava* una di esse [...] comandava di amarmi [...] e io la possedeva" (page 396). This is a very Gothic seduction with the added complication of the mesmeric theme.

Many of Henner's negative qualities are associated with Serao's broadly anti-Semitic stance in this novel. The Jewish–Christian conflict is expressed particularly in the two female characters, Rachele and Miriam/Sara, who change their names, their religion and their identities—one suspects so that their creator may openly sympathize with them. Her descriptions of the ghetto, seen through Rachele's eyes, are coloured by the most pronounced stereotypically anti-Semitic tone possible: "Ella odiava il Ghetto e la sporcizia ebrea" (page 59). It is not coincidental that Maria's "father", Mosé, is the novel's Gothic miser: he is a committed Jew, horrified to think of his daughter's conversion to Christianity. The typical warning on the danger of novel-reading for young women is here transmuted into a warning about the danger that for a young Jewish girl lies in reading a book expressing Christian ideology, *I promessi sposi*.

Yet we have seen how, almost in spite of herself, Serao identifies with Marcus Henner. If her views are so anti-Semitic, why should this be the case? She could be aware that, as Ernesta Pellegrini has said, "la condizione ebraica si fa [...] metafora e anticipazione di un destino comune."[62] This is applicable in several ways. The Jew, like the monster in Gothic literature, is isolated. Pellegrini highlights this when she mentions the significance of "il mito novecentesco di Ulisse, dell'ebreo errante, dello straniero".[63] Henner is both a Wandering Jew and a strange foreigner. Pellegrini goes on to consider "quel senso di smarrimento e di mostruosa alienazione" (page 1019) which characterizes Jews who have left their environment behind. Henner, who returns to his ghetto only sporadically, certainly suffers from literally monstrous alienation. He even cries out in despair, "Ahi, non avessi mai lasciato il mio paese natio!" (page 400). His sense of isolation is overpowering. The notion of duality which, as we know, is essential to Serao's view of the self, especially when that self is a woman writer, also seems to be consciously part of the mentality of the Jewish people, and hence particularly suitable for her purposes here. Pellegrini discusses the "elemento ebraico, nello sdoppiamento implicito di una personalità frantumata fra etica pubblica e etica privata, fra

desiderio di assimilazione e volontà di affermare e proteggere la
propria identità" (page 1021). The terms seem particularly applicable to Serao's view of herself as a monstrous exception to the
rule.[64] It is not surprising, then, that there should be so many
doubles in this tale of a supremely split personality, a personality
that clearly attracts Serao's censure and dislike as well as her
admiration, understanding and sympathy: on one level, in fact,
Marcus Henner may function as a representation of Serao herself
(destined, according to Pellegrini's theory, to become a representative of the human condition over the next twenty years or so).[65]

On a much more basic, structural level, the mere fact that
Marcus Henner is a Wandering Jew allows Serao a variety of
settings for her novel, and also gives Maria, despite her imprisonment, a certain freedom of movement. Maria becomes the type of
travelling heroine described by Moers: "the woman who moves,
who acts, who copes with vicissitude and adventure". Writing
about Mrs Radcliffe's characters, Moers says, "In the power of
villains, her heroines are forced to do what they could never do
alone" (*Literary Women*, page 126). The same is true of Serao's
(much later) female characters.

La mano tagliata encompasses most of Serao's previously used
Gothic motifs, but also introduces Gothic characters and devices
with which she had not previously dealt, such as the Wandering
Jew, the physically grotesque monster and the concentric narrative
structure. In this novel Serao also further plumbs the depths of the
occult. It seems to me that she uses all these devices in a manner
which continues to reflect her perception of her role as a woman
writer. In *La mano tagliata*, too, she finally sheds the Sentimental
heroine and replaces her with two heroines who are much stronger
and more independent in character.

As often in Serao's fully Gothic works, there are inconsistencies
in the narrative. At one point after her dismemberment Maria is
seen to have two hands. Roberto, in his letter to Ranieri, remarks on
this, and promises an explanation, though it never materializes.
The reader can only assume that Henner, with his Frankenstein-
like gifts, has made an "arm" for her—but we do not know this, and
are thus left Gothically perplexed. The other major inconsistency
centres on Maria's Jewish name: Rachele tells us that she was Sara
before becoming Maria; Henner, in his letter, says she was Miriam.
What are we to believe? And what is the significance of this
difficulty in naming?

The difficulty of naming characters, and of characters' naming themselves, colours all three of Serao's fully Gothic works: the protagonist of "La donna dall'abito nero e dal ramo di corallo rosso" is anonymous; Teresa Gargiulo is really Teresa Vargas; Anthonia D'Alembert is really Antonietta Dugué, though in the end she rejects this identity; Miriam/Sara Cabib is really Maria Cabib; Rachele Cabib is Grazia Straube, but eventually chooses to retain her original identity. It seems that the question of naming is entirely bound up with the concept of identity. (There are, as we have seen, many splits in character.) Questions are posed as to *who* particular characters actually are. In a sense the issue of uncertain identity is the basis of the Gothic trap—and one which Serao exploits to the full. In her wholly Gothic novels she is in fact concerned not just with the nature of female identity, as was the case in her Domestic Gothic writing; here she analyses male identity too (for example, Carlo Altieri is San Luciano, and there are many male doubles).

Yet despite Serao's interest in her male characters the general thrust of her fully Gothic works is essentially the same as that of her Domestic Gothic ones. Without exception, there are warnings in all these texts about the nature of the romantic heterosexual relationship and the danger inherent in it for the female character. In none of these novels is there a positively presented male–female relationship. Even the "good" male characters, the "heroes", are bad. Gennarino in *Il delitto di via Chiatamone* passes stern moral judgements which make him an inflexible character and thus potentially dangerous to both Teresa and Anthonia. Maria's relationship with Henner in *La mano tagliata* is one of implacable hatred and disgust on her part—and she survives it despite all its potential dangers. It is her love relationship with Roberto that leads to her final destruction: only when she responds to his passionate, possessive love is she most in danger. She survives fifteen years in Henner's captivity but only two months in Roberto's. Hence the "happy ending" of *La mano tagliata* (the only one of these novels to have one) is essentially suspect. If Rachele "becomes" her mother in leaving her enclosed space to love Ranieri, while we can only speculate on the result our speculations cannot be positive. I think the most striking element of Serao's Gothic stories is their unrelenting pessimism, their uncharacteristically extreme warnings to their female readers.

THE GOTHIC CONCLUSION

Serao's works, then, are unmistakably Gothic in many respects, sometimes in setting, and always in the emotions portrayed. Syndy McMillen Conger enumerates some of these classic elements in her essay on *Wuthering Heights*, referring to "emotions central to the Gothic experience, melancholy, desire and terror" and to "names [which] evoke that sense of vague threat so pervasive in the Gothic world" ("The Reconstruction of the Gothic Feminine Ideal", page 91). These are present from *Cuore infermo* to *La mano tagliata* and in all the works analysed in this chapter. Wherever Serao uses the trappings of the Gothic novel, she always retains its nightmare quality.

What she reneges on is its essentially predictable fairy-tale ending. She is not the only woman writer to do this. Isak Dinesen does it once, in *The Monkey*,[66] as Sibyl James points out: "The emphasis at the end [...] falls not on marriage but on [...] mutual understanding gained [...]; this marks another of Dinesen's shifts in the use of the Gothic, since no marriage actually takes place" ("Gothic Transformations", page 152). Dinesen, however, wrote *The Monkey* eight years after Serao's death. Serao is unusual not only in refusing to end her Gothic tales with marriage (even *La mano tagliata* does not actually end thus) but in either warning against marriage or using marriage as a springboard for the most Gothically terrifying elements of her narrative.

Serao, then, rejects a Sentimental conclusion to her Gothic novels (even to her Sentimental Gothic novels). She rejects, too, the creation of typically Sentimental heroines, making her Gothic heroines increasingly independent and assertive. The process culminates in *La mano tagliata* with the strong-willed characters Rachele and Maria: doubles, yes, but neither is weak. In a way, all Serao's Domestic Gothic and fully Gothic novels seem to reiterate and develop the theme recognized by Ellen Moers and George Sand's editors in Sand's *Consuelo*: "The whole of *Consuelo* appears today [...] to reflect George Sand's ambition to provide [...] a *Bildungsroman*, a novel of formation and apprenticeship to life equivalent to Goethe's *Wilhelm Meister*—only 'the hero would not be Man, but Woman.'"[67] By the time she reached her fully Gothic phase Serao seems to have succeeded, somewhat paradoxically, in helping her heroines to develop: there are no female suicides here. The role of victim seems rather to have passed to the male: both San

Luciano (*Il delitto di via Chiatamone*) and Marcus Henner (*La mano tagliata*) kill themselves.

What Serao shows in her Gothic writings (the vulnerability of the self, especially within the institution of marriage) is, in effect, the subject-matter of Barbara Hill Rigney's *Madness and Sexual Politics in the Feminist Novel*. In that very perceptive study, Rigney analyses the writings of Charlotte Brontë, Virginia Woolf, Doris Lessing and Margaret Atwood. Brontë is, in a sense, the heroine of European feminist critics because of the complexity of her view of female identity and the manner in which she deals with "women's issues". The others are also seen as trail-blazing, modern women writers. I find it interesting that an analysis of Serao's writings should dovetail so neatly with Rigney's analysis of the works of her chosen authors. That Serao reads, in many respects, like a feminist contemporary of Lessing and Atwood is astounding.

Serao is the writer described by Judith Jeffrey Howard as an "anti-feminist who viewed the world through her perception of her proper role as a woman".[68] I would argue, instead, that Serao was very aware of woman's "proper" sphere in her day—and of its dangers and pitfalls for woman's sense of self.

Serao uses the Gothic, one of the most conventional literary forms imaginable, as a vehicle for radical ideas. It is a form in which she synthesizes her views of the heterosexual romantic relationship (and the Sentimental novel), her attitude towards the role of the mother and her presentation of the divided self.

NOTES

1   H. Walpole, *The Castle of Otranto* [1764] (London, Scholertis Press, 1929). It was published in Italian (London, 1795) and was probably known to Serao.

2   C. Reeve, *The Old English Baron* [1771] (Oxford, Oxford University Press, 1967). I can find no reference to an Italian translation of this novel accessible in Serao's lifetime, but she may have read it in the 1787 French version.

3   Ann Radcliffe wrote *The Mysteries of Udolpho* [1794] (London, Routledge, 1903), which was translated into Italian in 1863 (Milan, Ferrario), so that Serao may well have read it, and *The Italian* [1797] (London, Folio Society, 1956). Serao may also have read Matthew Lewis's *The Monk* [1795] (London, Gibbings, 1913), which had appeared as *Il frate* (Milan, Guglielmini, 1861).

4   A. Radcliffe, "The Supernatural in Poetry", *New Monthly Magazine*, new series, 16 (1826), 145–50 (pp. 149–50). The Radcliffe–Lewis and Reeve–Walpole debates are detailed in E. McAndrew, *The Gothic Tradition in Fiction* (New York, Columbia University Press, 1979).

5   W. Beckford, *Vathek* [1786] (Oxford, Oxford University Press, 1970); C. Maturin, *Melmoth the Wanderer* [1820] (Lincoln, Nebr., University of Nebraska Press, 1963), written and mainly set in Ireland.

6   S. Freud, "The Uncanny" [1919], in his *Collected Papers* (London, Hogarth Press, 1925), pp. 369–407 (p. 394).

7   R. D. Hume, "Gothic vs. Romantic: A Revaluation of the Gothic Novel", *PMLA*, 84 (1969), 282–90 (p. 288).

8   J. Fleenor, "Introduction" to *The Female Gothic*, edited by J. Fleenor (Montreal, Eden Press, 1983), pp. 3–28 (p. 9).

9   M. K. Patterson Thornburg, *The Monster in the Mirror: Gender and the Sentimental/Gothic Myth in "Frankenstein"* [1984] (Ann Arbor, UMI Research Press, 1987), p. 4.

10   A. B. Tracy, *The Gothic Novel, 1790–1830: Plot Summaries and Index to Motifs* (Lexington, University of Kentucky Press, 1981), p. 5.

11   A. B. Tracy, *The Gothic Novel* is a storehouse of Gothic motifs. The ones I mention here are those most relevant to my discussion, that is, those most used by Serao.

12   M. Miyoshi, *The Divided Self: A Perspective on the Literature of the Victorians* (London, University of London Press, 1969), p. 107.

13   Such cases of incoherence are not the norm in Serao's Gothic works, but do surface occasionally, as I shall show later.

14   E. Moers, *Literary Women* [1963] (London, The Women's Press, 1978).

15   See Chh 1, 2 and 4, as well as my article "Angel vs. Monster: Serao's Use of the Female Double", *The Italianist*, 7 (1987), 63–89.

16   M. Homans, "Dreaming of Children: Literalization in *Jane Eyre* and *Wuthering Heights*", in *The Female Gothic*, pp. 257–79 (p. 257).

17   S. Korff Vincent, "The Mirror and the Cameo: Margaret Atwood's Comic/ Gothic Novel, *Lady Oracle*", in *The Female Gothic*, pp. 153–63 (p. 155).

18   S. Gilbert and S. Gubar, *The Madwoman in the Attic: The Woman Writer and the Nineteenth-century Literary Imagination* [1979] (London, Yale University Press, 1984), p. 244.

19   E. Kosofsky Sedgwick, "The Character in the Veil: Imagery of the Surface in the Gothic Novel", *PMLA*, 96 (1981), 255–70 (p. 261).

20   C. Kahane, "The Maternal Legacy: The Grotesque Tradition in Flannery O'Connor's Female Gothic Novel", in *The Female Gothic*, pp. 242–56 (p. 243).

21   N. Chodorow, *The Reproduction of Mothering: Psychoanalysis and the Sociology of Gender* (Berkeley, University of California Press, 1978). In the previous chapter I used Chodorow's methods and insights to show the importance of the mother–daughter relationship in Serao's novels.

22   B. Hill Rigney, *Madness and Sexual Politics in the Female Novel: Studies in Brontë, Woolf, Lessing and Atwood* [1978] (Madison, WI, University of Wisconsin Press, 1980), p. 16. *Jane Eyre* was probably known to Serao in its 1904 translation (Milan, Treves), though she may well have read the French version of 1854.

23   N. N. Holland and L. F. Sherman, "Gothic Possibilities", *New Literary History*, 8 (1977), 279–94, referred to in K. Mussell, *Women's Gothic and Romantic Fiction: A Reference Guide* (Westport, CT, Greenwood Press, 1981), p. 155.

24   See my conclusion to Ch. 1.

25   K. F. Stein, "Monsters and Madwomen: Changing Female Gothic", in *The Female Gothic*, pp. 123–37 (p. 123).

26 The first four novels are *Cuore infermo* (Turin, Casanova, 1881), *Addio, amore!*
    [Naples, Giannini, 1890] (Rome, Edizioni delle Donne, 1977), *Fantasia* [Turin,
    Casanova, 1883], in M. Serao, *Opere*, edited by P. Pancrazi, 2 vols (Milan,
    Garzanti, 1944–46), ii, 5–274, and *Il paese di Cuccagna* [Milan, Treves, 1891], in
    M. Serao, *Opere*, i, 105–529. The three works in the second group are "La
    donna dall'abito nero e dal ramo di corallo rosso" in M. Serao, *Fior di passione*
    (Milan, Galli, 1888), pp. 129–41, *Il delitto di via Chiatamone* [Naples, Perrella,
    1908] (Florence, Salani, 1979) (Parts i and ii) and *La mano tagliata* [Florence,
    Salani, 1912] (Florence, Salani, 1919).

27 J. Lidoff, "Domestic Gothic: The Imagery of Anger in Christina Stead's *The
    Man Who Loved Children*", in *The Female Gothic*, pp. 109–23.

28 See Chh 1 and 4 for my analysis of this figure.

29 See Ch. 1 for my analysis of Lalla as *femme fatale*.

30 B. Bowman, "Victoria Holt's Gothic Romances: A Structuralist Inquiry", in
    The Female Gothic, pp. 69–81 (p. 73).

31 S. McMillen Conger, "The Reconstruction of the Gothic Feminine Ideal in
    Emily Brontë's *Wuthering Heights*", in *The Female Gothic*, pp. 91–106 (p. 95).

32 N. da Vinci Nichols, "Place and Eros in Radcliffe, Lewis and Brontë", in *The
    Female Gothic*, pp. 187–206 (p. 193).

33 See Ch. 2 for my discussion of how Beatrice's illness resembles a pregnancy,
    complete with strange predilections, weakness, the overpowering largeness
    of the house (a standard representative of the female body), increased
    physical beauty, changes of mood, and finally the contractions accompany-
    ing her death.

34 M. Serao, *Castigo* (Turin, Casanova, 1893).

35 C. Griffin Wolff, "The Radcliffean Gothic Model: A Form for Feminine
    Sexuality", in *The Female Gothic*, pp. 207–23 (p. 214).

36 N. Auerbach, "Magi and Maidens: The Romance of the Victorian Freud", in
    Writing and Sexual Difference, edited by E. Abel [1980] (Brighton, Harvester
    Press, 1982), pp. 111–31.

37 W. James, *Varieties of Religious Experience* (London, Longman's and Green,
    1907), referred to by E. Showalter, *The Female Malady* [1985] (London, Virago,
    1987), p. 227.

38 W. Scott, *The Bride of Lammermoor* [1819] (London, Dent, 1964), p. 323.

39 L. Kroha, "Matilde Serao's *Fantasia*: An Author in Search of a Character", *The
    Italianist*, 7 (1987), 45–63.

40 B. Stoker, *Dracula* [1897] (London, Hutchinson, 1978).

41 G. Sand, *Histoire de ma vie* [1854–55] (Paris, Gallimard, 1970).

42 C. Brontë, *Villette* [1853] (Oxford, Blackwell, 1931).

43 S. James, "Gothic Transformations: Isak Dinesen and the Gothic", in *The
    Female Gothic*, pp. 138–52 (p. 141).

44 These chapters are: Ch. 3, "In casa Cavalcanti: il convegno dei cabalisti";
    Ch. 4, "Il dottor Amati"; Ch. 9, "Le visioni di Bianca Maria"; Ch. 11, "Idillio
    e follia"; Ch. 15, "Il sacrilegio: il bel sogno d'amor svanisce"; Ch. 20 (the last
    chapter), "Bianca Maria Cavalcanti". From these chapter titles, we may see
    that more than a quarter of the novel concentrates on the strange goings-on
    in the Cavalcanti family, and the Gothic nature of many of the titles is
    obvious.

45 A. Banti, *Matilde Serao* (Turin, UTET, 1965), p. 164, for example, sees the novel
    as a document of social realism.

46 S. Freud, *Studies on Hysteria* [1895] (London, Hogarth Press, 1955). Since this work was not translated into either Italian or French in Serao's lifetime, she could not have been directly familiar with it.

47 "Immediately after the war [...] women novelists appropriated the theme of shell-shock, and fixed it in the public mind" (E. Showalter, *The Female Malady*, p. 190).

48 M. Serao, *Mors tua* (Milan, Treves, 1926).

49 Readers have often been puzzled, for instance, by the denouements of *Jane Eyre* and *Wuthering Heights*. I would argue that part of the reason for this lies in the incomplete working out of these novels' Gothic elements.

50 M. G. Martin-Gistucci, *L'Œuvre romanesque de Matilde Serao* (Grenoble, Presses Universitaires de Grenoble, 1973), p. 587.

51 One study does briefly consider both novels: T. Pinto Wyckoff, *Realism and Romanticism in the Presentation of Female Characters in the Works of Matilde Serao* (unpublished PhD dissertation, University of Washington, 1983; Ann Arbor, University Microfilms, 1984). Wyckoff regards *La mano tagliata* as an attempt to reproduce the Gothic horror of the Romantic age, but does not see *Il delitto di via Chiatamone* in the same light. She describes both novels as weak (p. 279). This analysis is, I think, inadequate. One fascinating article has appeared on the second of these novels: N. Harrowitz, "Matilde Serao's *La mano tagliata*: Figuring the Material in Mystery", *Stanford Italian Review*, 7 (1987), 191–204.

52 M. Jacobus, "The Buried Letter: Feminism and Romanticism in *Villette*", in *Women Writing and Writing about Women*, edited by M. Jacobus [1979] (London, Croom Helm, 1986), pp. 42–61 (p. 43).

53 J. Berger, *Ways of Seeing* (Harmondsworth, Penguin, 1972), pp. 46–47.

54 For an analysis of this novel as a typical example of Serao's use of the Gothic genre, see U. Fanning, "Serao's Gothic Revisions: Old Tales Through New Eyes", *The Italianist*, 12 (1992), 32–42.

55 F. Burney, *Evelina* [1778] (Oxford, Oxford University Press, 1982).

56 M. Praz, *The Romantic Agony* [1933], translated by A. Davidson (London, Oxford University Press, 1954), Appendix I (pp. 413–33).

57 M. Shelley, *Frankenstein* [1818] (Oxford, Oxford University Press, 1980). This novel was not published in Italian before or during Serao's lifetime, but would have been available to her in French (Paris, Girand, 1854).

58 K. F. Stein, "Monsters and Madwomen", points out that in Gothic fiction the self is reflected in the figure of the monster especially in the works of women writers.

59 G. Eliot, *The Lifted Veil* [1859] (London, Macmillan, 1982).

60 Auerbach's quotation ("Magi and Maidens", pp. 113–14) is taken from J. Breuer and S. Freud, *Studies on Hysteria*, translated and edited by J. Strachey [1895] (New York, Basic Books, 1957), p. 61.

61 The introduction to E. Showalter, *The Female Malady* offers a concise summary of the position of women both as actual patients and as subjects of psycho-analytical literature.

62 E. Pellegrini, "Ebraismo ed europeismo nella Toscana degli anni Trenta", *Il ponte*, 38, x (31 Oct. 1982), 1017–51 (p. 1020).

63 E. Pellegrini, "Ebraismo ed europeismo", p. 1017. Sartre, to whom Pellegrini refers, discussed the plight of the Wandering Jew in his *Réflections sur la question juive* (Paris, Gallimard, 1954). He saw the displaced Jewish figure in the literature of the early twentieth century as a character reflecting the

situation of mankind as a whole, a figure with no sense of belonging, whose public and private images of himself are different.

64   N. A. Harrowitz, *Anti-semitism, Misogyny and the Logic of Cultural Difference: Cesare Lombroso and Matilde Serao* (Lincoln, Nebr., University of Nebraska Press, 1994), pp. 110–32, offers an interesting reading of this text, in which she sees the Jew functioning as marginalized Other for Serao, as well as a repository for her critique of patriarchy.

65   Whether or not Loria, for instance, borrowed from Serao for his "atmosfera notturna di un'umanità in lutto […] certi gobbi dalla vita distorta" (E. Pellegrini, "Ebraismo ed europeismo", p. 1029) is difficult to ascertain. There is, however, considerable overlap between Marcus Henner and certain of Loria's characters, "rappresentati […] da una deformità fisica che ne fa dei predestinati dell'esistenza obliqua dei 'sospetti'" (p. 1031).

66   I. Dinesen, "The Monkey", in her *Seven Gothic Tales* (London, Putnam, 1934), pp. 109–220.

67   E. Moers, *Literary Women*, p. 129, referring to the Introduction to G. Sand, *Consuelo* [1842–43], edited by L. Cellier and L. Guichard (Paris, Garnier, 1959).

68   J. Jeffrey Howard, "The Feminine Vision of Matilde Serao", *Italian Quarterly*, 71 (1975), 55–77 (p. 55).

SELECT BIBLIOGRAPHY

WORKS BY MATILDE SERAO

Addio, amore! [1890] (Rome, Edizioni delle Donne, 1977)
All'erta, sentinella! [1889] (Milan, Galli, 1896)
Castigo (Turin, Casanova, 1893)
Cuore infermo (Turin, Casanova, 1881; Florence, Salani, 1914)
Dal vero [1879] (Milan, Baldini and Castoldi, 1905)
Evviva la guerra! (Naples, Perrella, 1912)
Fantasia [1883], in M. Serao, *Opere*, edited by P. Pancrazi, 2 vols (Milan, Garzanti, 1944–46), II, 5–274
Fior di passione (Milan, Galli, 1888)
Gli amanti (Milan, Treves, 1894)
"Guerra ai ladri" [1904], in M. Serao, *Napoli*, edited by G. Infusino (Naples, Quarto Potere, 1977), pp. 167–71
Il delitto di via Chiatamone [1908] (Florence, Salani, 1979)
Il giornale (Naples, Perrella, 1906)
Il paese di Cuccagna [1891], in *Opere*, I, 105–529
Il romanzo della fanciulla [1884] (Milan, Treves, 1886)
Il ventre di Napoli (Milan, Treves, 1884)
La ballerina [1899], in *Opere*, I, 3–101
La conquista di Roma [1885], in *Opere*, II, 277–514
"La donna dall'abito nero e dal ramo di corallo rosso", in *Fior di passione*, pp. 129–41
La Madonna e i santi nella fede e nella vita (Naples, Trani, 1902)
La mano tagliata [1912] (Florence, Salani, 1919)
La virtú di Checchina [1884], in *Opere*, I, 863–908
Le amanti [1894] (Naples, Perrella, 1907)
"L'epistolario di Gustave Flaubert", in W. de Nunzio Schilardi, *Matilde Serao giornalista* (Bari, Milella, 1986), p. 164
Mors tua (Milan, Treves, 1926)
Napoli [1906], edited by G. Infusino (Naples, Quarto Potere, 1977)
"O Giovannino o la morte", in *All'erta, sentinella!*, pp. 307–66
Pagina azzurra (Milan, Quadrio, 1883)
Parla una donna (Milan, Treves, 1916)
Piccole anime [1883] (Naples, Libreria Economica, 1907)

Preghiere (Milan, Treves, 1921)

"Quella che tace", in *Opere*, II, 757–60

Ricordando Neera (Milan, Treves, 1920)

"Scuola normale femminile" [1886], in *Opere*, I, 951–88

"Silvia", in *Dal vero*, pp. 285–306

Storia di due anime [1904], in *Opere*, I, 675–799

Storia di una monaca (Catania, Giannotta, 1898)

Suor Giovanna della Croce [1901], in *Opere*, I, 533–674

"Telegrafi dello Stato" [1885], in *Opere*, I, 911–50

"Terno secco", in *All'erta, sentinella!*, pp. 123–79; also in *Opere*, I, 991–1024

Tre donne (Rome, Voghera, 1905)

Vita e avventure di Riccardo Joanna [1887], in *Opere*, II, 517–740

"Votazione femminile", in *Pagina azzurra*, pp. 54–66

OTHER PRIMARY SOURCES

Aleramo, S., *Una donna* [1906] (Milan, Feltrinelli, 1982)

Austen, J., *Persuasion* [1818] (Oxford, Oxford University Press, 1926)

Balzac, H. de, *Albert Savarus* [1842], in his *Œuvres complètes*, 40 vols, edited by M. Bouteron and H. Longnon (Paris, Conard, 1912–50), III, 1–107

Balzac, H. de, "Devoir d'une femme", in his *Scènes de la vie privée* [1837] (Paris, Gallimard, 1976), pp. 52–83

Balzac, H. de, *La Cousine Bette* [1846] (Paris, Garnier, 1962)

Balzac, H. de, "La Fille aux yeux d'or", in his *Œuvres complètes*, XXXVIII, 55–123

Balzac, H. de, *Le Lys dans la vallée* [1836], in his *Œuvres complètes*, XXV, 1–262

Balzac, H. de, *Une Fille d'Eve* [1838–39] (Paris, Garnier, 1965)

Beckford, W., *Vathek* [1786] (Oxford, Oxford University Press, 1970)

Boccaccio, G., *Decameron* [1349–51], edited by A. E. Quaglio, 2 vols (Milan, Garzanti, 1974)

Brontë, C., *Jane Eyre* [1847] (London, Norton, 1987)

Brontë, C., *Shirley* [1849] (Oxford, Blackwell, 1931)

Brontë, C., *The Professor* [1857] (Oxford, Oxford University Press, 1987)

Brontë, C., *Villette* [1853] (Oxford, Blackwell, 1931)

Brontë, E., *Wuthering Heights* [1847] (London, Cape, 1932)

Burney, F., *Evelina* [1778] (Oxford, Oxford University Press, 1982)

Capuana, L., *Giacinta* [1889] (Milan, Treves, 1930)

Cicero, *Offices, Essays on Friendship and Old Age and Select Letters*, edited and translated by T. Cockman and W. Melmoth (London, Dent, 1930)

d'Annunzio, G., *Giovanni Episcopo* [1891], in his *Prose di romanzi* (Milan, Mondadori, 1953), pp. 337–94

d'Annunzio, G., *Il trionfo della morte* [1894], in his *I romanzi della rosa*, 2 vols (Milan, Mondadori, 1964–68), I, 651–1049

Deledda, G., *Romanzi e novelle*, edited by N. Sapegno (Milan, Mondadori, 1971)

Diderot, D., *La Religieuse* [1770] (Paris, Gallimard, 1966)

Dinesen, I., "The Monkey", in her *Seven Gothic Tales* (London, Putnam, 1934), pp. 109–220

Eliot, G., *Adam Bede* [1859] (London, Dent, 1930)

Eliot, G., *Daniel Deronda* [1874–76] (London, Chatto and Windus, 1971)

Eliot, G., *Felix Holt the Radical* [1866] (Oxford, Oxford University Press, 1988)

Eliot, G., *Romola* [1862–63] (Harmondsworth, Penguin, 1980)

Eliot, G., *The Lifted Veil* [1859] (London, Macmillan, 1982)

Eliot, G., *The Mill on the Floss* [1860] (London, Dent, 1972)

Eliot, G., *Middlemarch* [1872] (Oxford, Oxford University Press, 1988)

Flaubert, G., *L'Education sentimentale* [1869] (Paris, Flammarion, 1985)

Flaubert, G., *Madame Bovary* [1857] (Paris, Garnier–Flammarion, 1966)

Flaubert, G., *Salammbô* [1862] (Paris, Garnier, 1961)

Gaskell, E., *Cousin Phyllis* [1863], in her *The Complete Works*, edited by A. W. Ward, 8 vols (London, Smith and Elder, 1906), VII, 1–109

Gaskell, E., *Cranford* [1851] (London, Ward Lock, 1912)

Gaskell, E., *Mary Barton* [1848] (London, Smith and Elder, 1892)

Gaskell, E., *Ruth* [1853] (Oxford, Oxford University Press, 1985)

Gaskell, E., *Sylvia's Lovers* [1863] (London, Smith and Elder, 1892)

Gaskell, E., "The Old Nurse's Story" [1852], in her *The Complete Works*, III, 422–45

Gaskell, E., "The Poor Clare", in her *My Lady Ludlow and Other Tales* (London, Smith and Elder, 1892)

Gaskell, E., *Wives and Daughters* [1865] (London, Lehmann, 1948)

Hardy, T., *Tess of the d'Urbervilles* [1891] (Oxford, Clarendon Press, 1983)

Invernizio, C., *Cuore di madre* (Florence, Salani, 1918)

Lewis, M., *The Monk* [1795] (London, Gibbings, 1913)

Manzoni, A., *I promessi sposi* [1840–42], edited by G. R. Ceriello (Milan, Mondadori, 1947)

Marivaux, P., *Marianne* [1731–41] (Paris, Garnier, 1963)

Maturin, C., *Melmoth the Wanderer* [1820] (Lincoln, Nebr., University of Nebraska Press, 1963)

Montaigne, M. de, "De l'amitié", in his *Essais,* edited by M. Rat, 2 vols (Paris, Gallimard, 1962), I, 199–226

Navarre, M. de, *Heptaméron* [1559], edited by M. François (Paris, Garnier, 1967)

Neera [collected works and criticism], edited by B. Croce (Milan, Garzanti, 1942)

Patmore, C., *The Angel in the House* (London, Bell, 1885)

Radcliffe, A., *The Italian* [1797] (London, Folio Society, 1956)

Radcliffe, A., *The Mysteries of Udolpho* [1794] (London, Routledge, 1903)

Radcliffe, A., "The Supernatural in Poetry", *The New Monthly Magazine*, new series, 16 (1826), 145–60

Reeve, C., *The Old English Baron* [1771] (Oxford, Oxford University Press, 1967)

Sand, G., *Consuelo* [1842–43], edited by L. Cellier and L. Guichard (Paris, Garnier, 1959)

Sand, G., *Histoire de ma vie* [1854–55] (Paris, Gallimard, 1970)

Sand, G., *Indiana* [1832] (Paris, Delmas, 1948)

Sand, G., *Lélia* [1883] (Paris, Garnier, 1960)

Scott, S., *A Description of Millennium Hall* [1762] (New York, Bookman Associates, 1955)

Scott, W., *The Bride of Lammermoor* [1819] (London, Dent, 1964)

Shelley, M., *Frankenstein* [1818] (Oxford, Oxford University Press, 1980)

Staël, Madame de, *Delphine* [1802] (Paris, Editions des Femmes, 1981)

Stoker, B., *Dracula* [1897] (London, Hutchinson, 1978)

Verga, G., *Eva* [1873], in his *Opere*, edited by L. Russo (Milan, Ricciardi, 1965), pp. 1–88

Verga, G., *I Malavoglia* [1881], in his *Opere*, pp. 175–404

Verga, G., "La lupa" [1880], in his *Opere*, pp. 835–72

Verga, G., *Mastro-don Gesualdo* [1890], in his *Opere*, pp. 497–800

Verga, G., *Nedda* [1874], in his *Opere*, pp. 89–113

Walpole, H., *The Castle of Otranto* [1764] (London, Scholertis Press, 1929)

Zola, E., *Germinal* [1885], in his *Œuvres complètes: Les Rougon-Macquart*, 5 vols (Paris, Cercle du Livre Précieux, 1960–67), III, 1131–1591

Zola, E., *L'Assommoir* [1877], in his *Œuvres complètes*, II, 371–796

Zola, E., *La Terre* [1887], in his *Œuvres complètes*, IV, 363–811

Zola, E., *Le Docteur Pascal* [1893] (Paris, Charpentier, 1893)

Zola, E., *Le Ventre de Paris* [1873] (Paris, Livre de Poche, 1969)

Zola, E., *L'Œuvre*, in his *Œuvres complètes*, IV, 9–362

Zola, E., *Nana* [1880], in his *Œuvres complètes*, II, 1093–1485

Zola, E., *Une Page d'amour* [1878], in his *Œuvres complètes*, II, 797–1092

SECONDARY SOURCES

Abel, E., "(E)merging Identities: The Dynamics of Female Friendship in Contemporary Fiction by Women", *Signs*, 6 (1981), 413–35

Aleramo, S., "Appunti sulla psicologia femminile italiana" [1910], in *La donna e il femminismo: scritti 1897–1910*, edited by B. Conti (Rome, Editori Riuniti, 1978), pp. 133–58

Armstrong, N., and L. Tennenhouse, *The Ideology of Conduct: Essays on Literature and the History of Sexuality* (London, Methuen, 1987)

Aron, J. P., *Misérable et glorieuse: la femme du XIXᵉ siècle* (Poitiers, Fayard, 1980)

Arslan-Veronese, A., *Dame, droga e galline: romanzo popolare e romanzo di consumo tra '800 e '900* (Padua, CLEUP, 1977)

Auerbach, N., "Magi and Maidens: The Romance of the Victorian Freud", in *Writing and Sexual Difference*, pp. 111–31

Banti, A., *Matilde Serao* (Turin, UTET, 1965)

Barański, Z. G., "The Power of Influence: Aspects of Dante's Presence in Twentieth-century Italian Culture", *Strumenti critici*, new series, 1 (1986), 343–76

Beer, G., *George Eliot* (Brighton, Harvester Press, 1986)

Beizer, J. L., *Family Plots: Balzac's Narrative Generations* (London, Yale University Press, 1986)

Benjamin, J., *The Bonds of Love: Psychoanalysis, Feminism and the Problem of Domination* (London, Virago, 1988)

Berger, J., *Ways of Seeing* (Harmondsworth, Penguin, 1972)

Bertoni Jovine, D., *Storia dell'educazione popolare in Italia* [1954] (Bari, Laterza, 1965)

Borie, J., *Zola et les mythes* (Paris, Seuil, 1971)

Bowlby, R., *Still Crazy after All These Years: Women, Writing and Psycho-analysis* (London, Routledge, 1992)

Bowman, B., "Victoria Holt's Gothic Romances: A Structuralist Inquiry", in *The Female Gothic*, pp. 69–81

Burke, C., "Gertrude Stein, the Cone Sisters and the Puzzle of Female Friendship", in *Writing and Sexual Difference*, pp. 221–43

Buzzi, G., *Invito alla lettura di Matilde Serao* (Milan, Mursia, 1981)

Calder, J., *Women and Marriage in Victorian Fiction* (London, Thames and Hudson, 1976)

Caldwell, L., *Italian Family Matters: Women, Politics and Legal Reform* (London, Macmillan, 1991)

Caldwell, L., "Reproducers of the Nation: Women and the Family in Fascist Policy", in *Rethinking Italian Fascism: Capitalism, Populism and Culture*, edited by D. Forgacs (London, Lawrence and Wishart, 1986), pp. 110–42

Chianesi, G., *Storia sociale della donna in Italia, 1800–1980* (Naples, Guida, 1980)

Chodorow, N., *The Reproduction of Mothering: Psychoanalysis and the Socio-logy of Gender* (Berkeley, University of California Press, 1978)

Cixous, H., "La Jeune Née", in *Diacritics*, 7 (1977), 64–69

Cixous, H., "The Laugh of the Medusa", in *New French Feminisms: An Anthology*, edited by E. Marks and I. de Courtivron [1981] (Brighton, Harvester Press, 1986), pp. 245–64

Corona, D., *Donne e scrittura* (Palermo, La Luna, 1990)

Czyba, L., "Misogynie et gynophobie dans *La Fille aux yeux d'or*", in *La Femme au XIXᵉ siècle: littérature et idéologie*, edited by R. Bellet (Lyon, Presses Universitaires de Lyon, 1978), pp. 139–49

Czyba, L., *Mythes et idéologie de la femme dans les romans de Flaubert* (Lyon, Presses Universitaires de Lyon, 1983)

Davidson, C. N., and E. M. Broner, *The Lost Tradition: Mothers and Daughters in Literature* (New York, Frederick Ungar, 1980)

da Vinci Nichols, N., "Place and Eros in Radcliffe, Lewis and Brontë", in *The Female Gothic*, pp. 187–206

De Caro, G., *Matilde Serao aneddotica* (Naples, Berisco, 1977)

De Donato, G., "Donna e società nella cultura moderata del primo Ottocento", in *La parabola della donna*, pp. 11–96

De Grazia, V., *How Fascism Ruled Women: Italy 1922–1945* (Berkeley, University of California Press, 1992)

Delamont, S., *The Sociology of Women* (London, Allen and Unwin, 1980)

de Nunzio Schilardi, W., "L'antifemminismo di Matilde Serao", in *La parabola della donna*, pp. 277–305

de Nunzio Schilardi, W., *Matilde Serao giornalista* (Bari, Milella, 1986)

Deutsch, H., *The Psychology of Women*, 2 vols (New York, Greene and Stratton, 1944–45)

Dickenson, D., *George Sand: A Brave Man—The Most Womanly Woman* (Oxford, Berg, 1984)

Dranch, S., "Reading through the Veiled Text: Colette's *The Pure and the Impure*", *Contemporary Literature*, 24 (1983), 176–89

Eagleton, M., *Feminist Literary Theory: A Reader* (Oxford, Blackwell, 1986)

Eco, U., *Tre donne intorno al cor: Carolina Invernizio, Matilde Serao, Liala* (Florence, La Nuova Italia, 1979)

Ellis, H., *Studies in the Psychology of Sex: Sexual Inversion* [1897] (London, Heinemann, 1933)

Faderman, L., *Surpassing the Love of Men* (New York, Junction Books, 1981)

Fanning, U. J., "Angel vs. Monster: Serao's Use of the Female Double", *The Italianist*, 7 (1987), 63–89; revised version in *Women in Italy*, pp. 263–92

Fanning, U. J., "Matilde Serao", in *Italian Women Writers: A Bio-bibliographical Sourcebook*, edited by R. Russell (London, Greenwood Press, 1994), 386–94

Fanning, U. J., "Sentimental Subversion: Representations of Female Friendship in the Work of Matilde Serao", *Annali d'italianistica*, 7 (1989), 273–87

Fanning, U. J., "Serao's Gothic Revisions: Old Tales through New Eyes", *The Italianist*, 12 (1992), 32–41

Fanning, U. J., "Writing Women's Work: The Ambivalence of Matilde Serao", *Italian Studies*, 48 (1993), 62–70

Ferguson, M. A., "The Female Novel of Development and the Myth of Psyche", in *The Voyage In*, pp. 228–43

Finucci, V., "The Search for the Mother in G. d'Annunzio's *Il piacere*", *Journal of the Association of Teachers of Italian*, 47 (Summer 1986), 4–17

Foster, S., *Victorian Women's Fiction: Marriage, Freedom and the Individual* [1985] (Totowa, Barnes and Noble, 1986)

Freud, S., *On Sexuality* (Harmondsworth, Penguin, 1981)

Freud, S., *Studies on Hysteria* [1895] (London, Hogarth Press, 1955)

Freud, S., "The Uncanny" [1919], in his *Collected Papers* (London, Hogarth Press, 1925), pp. 369–407

Fucini, R., *Napoli a occhio nudo* (Florence, Le Monnier, 1877)

Furst, L., *All is True: The Claims and Strategies of Realist Fiction* (Durham, NC, Duke University Press, 1995)

Furst, L., *Realism* (New York, Longman, 1992)

Gérin, W., *Charlotte Brontë* [1967] (Oxford, Oxford University Press, 1987)

Ghidetti, E., *L'ipotesi del realismo: Capuana, Verga, Valera e altri* (Padua, Liviana, 1982)

Ghirelli, A., *Napoli italiana: la storia della città dopo il 1860* (Turin, Einaudi, 1977)

Gibson, M., *Prostitution and the State in Italy, 1860–1915* (New Brunswick, Rutgers University Press, 1986)

Gilbert, S., and S. Gubar, *The Madwoman in the Attic: The Woman Writer and the Nineteenth-century Literary Imagination* [1979] (London, Yale University Press, 1984)

Gisolfi, A. M., *The Essential Matilde Serao* (New York, Las Americas, 1968)

Griffin Woolf, C., "The Radcliffean Gothic Model: A Form for Feminine Sexuality", in *The Female Gothic*, pp. 207–23

Guidacci, A., *La donna non è gente: l'esistenza emarginata delle più oppresse* (Milan, Rizzoli, 1977)

Gusdorf, G., *L'Homme romantique* (Paris, Payot, 1984)

Harrowitz, N. A., *Anti-semitism, Misogyny and the Logic of Cultural Difference: Cesare Lombroso and Matilde Serao* (Lincoln, Nebr., University of Nebraska Press, 1994)

Harrowitz, N. A., "Matilde Serao's *La mano tagliata*: Figuring the Material in Mystery", *Stanford Italian Review*, 7 (1987), 191–204

Hellman, J. A., *Journeys Among Women* (Oxford, Blackwell, 1987)

Hill Rigney, B., *Madness and Sexual Politics in the Feminist Novel: Studies in Brontë, Woolf, Lessing and Atwood* [1978] (Madison, WI, University of Wisconsin Press, 1980)

Hirsch, M., "Spiritual Bildung", in *The Voyage In*, pp. 23–49

Hirsch, M., *The Mother–Daughter Plot: Narrative, Psychoanalysis, Feminism* (Bloomington, Indiana University Press, 1989)

Holland, N. N., and L. F. Sherman, "Gothic Possibilities", *New Literary History*, 8 (1977), 279–94

Holmes, G., *The "Adolphe Type" in French Fiction in the First Half of the Nineteenth Century* (Quebec, Naaman, 1977)

Homans, M., *Bearing the Word: Language and Female Experience in Nineteenth-century Women's Writing* (London, University of Chicago Press, 1986)

Homans, M., "Dreaming of Children: Literalization in *Jane Eyre* and *Wuthering Heights*", in *The Female Gothic*, pp. 257–79

Hume, R. D., "Gothic vs. Romantic: A Revaluation of the Gothic Novel", PMLA, 84 (1969), 282–90

Humm, M., *Feminist Criticism: Women as Contemporary Critics* (Brighton, Harvester Press, 1986)

Infusino, G., *Matilde Serao tra giornalismo e letteratura* (Naples, Guida, 1981)

Infusino, G., *Matilde Serao: vita, opere, testimonianze* (Naples, Polisud, 1977)

Irigaray, L., "Quand nos lèvres se parlent", in her *Ce sexe qui n'en est pas un* (Paris, Minuit, 1977), pp. 203–17; translated by C. Burke as "When Our Lips Speak Together", *Signs*, 6 (1980), 69–79

Jacobus, M., *Reading Woman: Essays in Feminist Criticism* (London, Methuen, 1987)

Jacobus, M., "The Buried Letter: Feminism and Romanticism in *Villette*", in *Women Writing and Writing about Women*, pp. 42–61

James, S., "Gothic Transformations: Isak Dinesen and the Gothic", in *The Female Gothic*, pp. 138–52

James, W., *Varieties of Religious Experience* (London, Longman's and Green, 1907)

Jeffrey Howard, J., "The Feminine Vision of Matilde Serao", *Italian Quarterly*, 71 (1975), 55–77

Jeuland-Meynaud, M., *Immagini, linguaggio e modelli del corpo nell'opera narrativa di Matilde Serao* (Rome, Edizioni dell'Ateneo, 1986)

Jeuland-Meynaud, M., *La Ville de Naples après l'annexion, 1860–1915* (Aix–Marseille, Editions de l'Université de Provence, 1973)

Jones, A. R., "French Theories of the Feminine", in *Making a Difference*, pp. 80–113

Kahane, C., "The Maternal Legacy: The Grotesque Tradition in Flannery O'Connor's Female Gothic", in *The Female Gothic*, pp. 242–56

Kaplan, C., "Pandora's Box: Subjectivity, Class and Sexuality in Socialist Feminist Criticism", in *Making a Difference*, pp. 146–77

Kaplan, C., *Sea Changes: Culture and Feminism* (London, Verso, 1986)

Kaplan, E. A., *Motherhood and Representation: The Mother in Popular Culture and Melodrama* (London, Routledge, 1992)

Kegan Gardiner, J., "A Wake for Mother: The Maternal Deathbed in Women's Fiction", *Feminist Studies*, 4 (1978), 146–65

Kegan Gardiner, J., "On Female Identity and Writing by Women", in *Writing and Sexual Difference*, pp. 177–91

Kegan Gardiner, J., "The (Us)es of (I)dentity: A Response to Abel on '(E)merging Identities'", *Signs*, 6 (1981), 436–42

Kemp, S., and P. Bono, *Italian Feminist Thought* (Oxford, Blackwell, 1991)

Keppler, C. F., *The Literature of the Second Self* (Tucson, University of Arizona Press, 1972)

Klopp, C., *Gabriele d'Annunzio* (New York, Twayne, 1988)

Korff Vincent, S., "The Mirror and the Cameo: Margaret Atwood's Comic/Gothic Novel, *Lady Oracle*", in *The Female Gothic*, pp. 153–63

Kosofsky Sedgwick, E., "The Character in the Veil: Imagery of the Surface in the Gothic Novel", PMLA, 96 (1981), 255–70

Krakowski, A., *La Condition de la femme dans l'œuvre d'Emile Zola* (Paris, Nizet, 1974)

Kristeva, J., *Desire in Language: A Semiotic Approach to Literature and Art* (Oxford, Blackwell, 1980)

Kroha, L., "Matilde Serao's *Fantasia:* An Author in Search of a Character", *The Italianist*, 7 (1987), 45–62

Kroha, L., "Neera: The Literary Career of a Woman of the Nineteenth Century", *Yearbook of Italian Studies*, 5 (1983), 77–101

Kroha, L., "The Early Matilde Serao: An Author in Search of a Character", in her *The Woman Writer in Late Nineteenth-century Italy* (New York, Mellen, 1992), pp. 99–122

La parabola della donna nella letteratura italiana dell'Ottocento, edited by G. De Donato (Bari, Adriatica, 1983)

La voce che è in lei: antologia della narrativa femminile italiana tra '800 e '900, edited by G. Morandini (Milan, Bompiani, 1980)

Le Play, F., *Les Ouvriers européens*, 2 vols (Paris, Imprimerie Impériale, 1855–78)

Levin, H., *The Gates of Horn: A Study of Five French Realists* (New York, Oxford University Press, 1963)

Lidoff, J., "Domestic Gothic: The Imagery of Anger in Christina Stead's *The Man Who Loved Children*", in *The Female Gothic*, pp. 109–23

Livi Bacci, M., *Donna, fecondità e figli: due secoli di storia demografica italiana* [1977] (Bologna, Il Mulino, 1980)

Lombroso, C., *La donna delinquente, la prostituta e la donna normale* (Turin, Loescher, 1893)

Lombroso, G., *Il pro e il contro (riflessioni sul voto alle donne)* (Florence, Associazone Divulgatrice Donne Italiane, 1919)

Lovell, T., *Consuming Fiction* (London, Verso, 1987)

Lucente, G. L., *Beautiful Fables: Self-consciousness in Italian Narrative from Manzoni to Calvino* (Baltimore, Johns Hopkins University Press, 1986)

McAndrew, E., *The Gothic Tradition in Fiction* (New York, Columbia University Press, 1979)

McMillen Conger, S., "The Reconstruction of the Gothic Feminine Ideal in Emily Brontë's *Wuthering Heights*", in *The Female Gothic*, pp. 91–106

Mack Smith, D., *Italy: A Modern History* [1959] (Ann Arbor, University of Michigan Press, 1969)

Making a Difference: Feminist Literary Criticism, edited by G. Greene and C. Kahn (London, Methuen, 1985)

Marks, E., and I. De Courtivron, *New French Feminisms* (Brighton, Harvester Press, 1981)

Marmo, M., *Il proletariato industriale a Napoli in età liberale (1880–1914)* (Naples, Guida, 1978)

Martin-Gistucci, M. G., *L'Œuvre romanesque de Matilde Serao* (Grenoble, Presses Universitaires de Grenoble, 1973)

Meredith Maxfield, C., *"Valorose donne": The Emerging Woman in the Nineteenth-century Novel* (unpublished doctoral dissertation, Cornell University, 1977)

Merry, B., *Women in Modern Italian Literature* (Townsville, James Cook University, 1990)

Meyer Spacks, P., *The Female Imagination: A Literary and Psychological Investigation of Women's Writing* (London, Allen and Unwin, 1976)

Michel, A., *Le Mariage chez Honoré de Balzac: amour et féminisme* (Paris, Les Belles Lettres, 1978)

Miles, R., *The Female Form: Women Writers and the Conquest of the Novel* (London, Routledge, 1987)

Miller, J., *Women Writing about Men* (London, Virago, 1987)

Miller, K., *Doubles: Studies in Literary History* (Oxford, Oxford University Press, 1985)

Miller, N. K., "Arachnologies: The Woman, the Text, and the Critic", in *The Poetics of Gender*, edited by N. K. Miller and C. G. Heilbrun (New York, Columbia University Press, 1986), pp. 270–95

Miller, N. K., "Emphasis Added: Plots and Plausibilities in Women's Fiction", PMLA, 96 (1981), 36–48; also in *The New Feminist Criticism*, pp. 339–61

Mitchell, J., *Psychoanalysis and Feminism* (Harmondsworth, Penguin, 1974)

Miyoshi, M., *The Divided Self: A Perspective on the Literature of the Victorians* (London, University of London Press, 1969)

Modleski, T., *Loving with a Vengeance: Mass-produced Fantasies for Women* (New York, Routledge, 1988)

Moers, E., *Literary Women* [1963] (London, The Women's Press, 1978)

Moi, T., *Sexual/Textual Politics: Feminist Literary Theory* (London, Methuen, 1985)

Monteith, M., *Women's Writing: A Challenge to Theory* (Brighton, Harvester Press, 1986)

Mothering: Essays in Feminist Theory, edited by J. Trebilcot (Marsland, Rowman and Littlefield, 1983)

Mozzoni, A. M., *La liberazione della donna* [1864–92] (Milan, Mazzotta, 1975)

Mussell, K., *Women's Gothic and Romantic Fiction: A Reference Guide* (Westport, CT, Greenwood Press, 1981)

Nozzoli, A., *Tabú e coscienza: la condizione femminile nella letteratura del Novecento* (Florence, La Nuova Italia, 1978)

Obici, G., and G. Marchesini, *Le "amicizie" di collegio: ricerche sulle prime manifestazioni dell'amore sessuale* [1896] (Rome, Dante Alighieri, 1898)

Ojetti, U., *Alla scoperta dei letterati* (Milan, Dumolard, 1985)

Olsen, T., *Mother to Daughter to Mother* (London, Virago, 1985)

Ostriker, A., "The Thieves of Language: Women Poets and Revisionist Mythmaking", in *The New Feminist Criticism*, pp. 314–39

Pascale, V., *Sulla prosa narrativa di Matilde Serao* (Naples, Liguori, 1989)

Patterson Thornburg, M. K., *The Monster in the Mirror: Gender and the Sentimental/Gothic Myth in "Frankenstein"* [1984] (Ann Arbor, UMI Research Press, 1987)

Pellegrini, E., "Ebraismo ed europeismo nella Toscana degli anni Trenta", *Il ponte*, 38, x (31 October 1982), 1017–51

Pennisi Badalà, G., *La donna nella vita pubblica: studio critico* (Acireale, Donzuso, 1905)

Perugi, G., *Educazione e politica in Italia, 1860–1900* (Turin, Loescher, 1978)

Phillips, A., *Divided Loyalties: Dilemmas of Sex and Class* (London, Virago, 1987)

Pieroni Bortolotti, F., *Femminismo e partiti politici in Italia, 1919–1926* (Rome, Editori Riuniti, 1978)

Pinto Wyckoff, T., *Realism and Romanticism in the Presentation of Female Characters in the Works of Matilde Serao* (unpublished doctoral dissertation, University of Washington, 1983; Ann Arbor, University Microfilms, 1984)

Pratt, A., *Archetypal Patterns in Women's Fiction* [1981] (Brighton, Harvester Press, 1982)

Praz, M., *La carne, la morte e il diavolo* (Milan, La Cultura, 1930)

Rasy, E., *Le donne e la letteratura* (Rome, Editori Riuniti, 1984)

Ravera, C., *Breve storia del movimento femminile in Italia* (Rome, Editori Riuniti, 1978)

Reed, W. L., *Meditations on the Hero: A Study of the Romantic Hero in Nineteenth-century Fiction* (London, Yale University Press, 1974)

Rich, A., *Of Woman Born: Motherhood as Experience and Institution* [1977] (London, Virago, 1991)

Ridge, G. R., *The Hero in French Romantic Literature* (Athens, GA, University of Georgia Press, 1959)

Rogers, R., *A Psychoanalytic Study of the Double in Literature* (Detroit, Wayne State University Press, 1972)

Rosenfield, C., "The Shadow Within: The Conscious and Unconscious Use of the Double", in *Stories of the Double*, pp. 313–22

Rosmini, A., *Filosofia del diritto* [1841–45], 2 vols (Naples, Lauriel–Rossi Romano, 1856)

Rotunda, D. P., *Motif-index of the Italian Novella in Prose* (Bloomington, Indiana University Press, 1942)

Ruthven, K. K., *Feminist Literary Studies: An Introduction* (Cambridge, Cambridge University Press, 1984)

Santoro, A., *Narratrici italiane dell'Ottocento* (Naples, Federico and Ardia, 1987)

Sartre, J-P., *Réflexions sur la question juive* (Paris, Gallimard, 1954)

Sayers, J., *Mothering Psychoanalysis* (Harmondsworth, Penguin, 1991)

Schor, N., *Breaking the Chain: Women, Theory and French Realist Fiction* (New York, Columbia University Press, 1985)

Schor, N., *Reading in Detail: Aesthetics and the Feminine* (London, Methuen, 1987)

Schor, N., *Zola's Crowds* (Baltimore, Johns Hopkins University Press, 1978)

Scott, J. W., and L. A. Tilly, "Women's Work and the Family in Nineteenth-century Europe", in *The Family in History*, edited by C. E. Rosenberg (Philadelphia, University of Pennsylvania Press, 1975), pp. 146–78

Showalter, E., *A Literature of Their Own* [1977] (London, Virago, 1982)

Showalter, E., *Speaking of Gender* (London, Routledge, 1989)

Showalter, E., *The Female Malady: Women, Madness and English Culture* [1985] (London, Virago, 1987)

Sibilla Aleramo e il suo tempo: vita raccontata e illustrata, edited by B. Conti and A. Morino (Milan, Feltrinelli, 1981)

Stein, K. F., "Monsters and Madwomen: Changing Female Gothic", in *The Female Gothic*, pp. 123–37

Stevenson, A., "Writing as a Woman", in *Women Writing and Writing About Women*, pp. 159–77

Stimpson, C. R., "Zero Degree Deviancy: The Lesbian Novel in English", in *Writing and Sexual Difference*, pp. 243–59

Stoneman, P., *Elizabeth Gaskell* (Brighton, Harvester Press, 1987)

Stories of the Double, edited by A. J. Guérard (Palo Alto, Stanford University Press, 1967)

Stubbs, P., *Women and Fiction: Feminism and the Novel, 1880–1920* (Brighton, Harvester Press, 1979)

Sullerot, E., *Histoire et sociologie du travail féminin* (Paris, Gonthier, 1968)

Taricone, F., and B. Pisa, *Operaie, borghesi, contadine nel XIX secolo* (Rome, Carucci, 1985)

Tench, D., "Gutting the Belly of Naples", *Annali d'italianistica*, 7 (1989), 287–99

The Family in Italy from Antiquity to the Present, edited by D. Kertzer and R. Saller (London, Yale University Press, 1991)

The Female Gothic, edited by J. Fleenor (Montreal, Eden Press, 1983)

The Feminist Encyclopedia of Italian Literature, edited by R. Russell (Westport, CT, Greenwood Press, 1997)

The Kristeva Reader, edited by T. Moi (Oxford, Blackwell, 1986)

The Lonely Mirror: Italian Perspectives on Feminist Theory, edited by S. Kemp and P. Bono (London, Routledge, 1993)

The (M)other Tongue: Essays in Feminist Psychoanalytic Interpretation, edited by S. Nelson Garner et al. (New York, Cornell University Press, 1985)

The New Feminist Criticism: Essays on Women, Literature and Theory, edited by E. Showalter (London, Virago, 1986)

The Voyage In: Fictions of Female Development, edited by E. Abel, M. Hirsch and E. Langland (Hanover, University Press of New England, 1983)

Todd, J., *Feminist Literary History: A Defence* (Oxford, Polity Press, 1988)

Todd, J., *Women's Friendship in Literature* (New York, Columbia University Press, 1980)

Tondeur, C., *Gustave Flaubert: Critique* (Philadelphia, Benjamin's, 1984)

Tracy, A. B., *The Gothic Novel, 1790–1830: Plot Summaries and Index to Motifs* (Lexington, University of Kentucky Press, 1981)

Tseelon, E., *The Masque of Femininity* (London, Sage, 1995)

Tymms, R., *Doubles in Literary Psychology* (Cambridge, Bowes and Bowes, 1949)

Villari, P., "La scuola e la questione sociale", in his *Le lettere meridionali ed altri scritti sulla questione sociale in Italia* (Florence, Le Monnier, 1878), pp. i–xx

Warner, M., *Alone of All Her Sex: The Myth and Cult of the Virgin Mary* (London, Picador, 1976)

Watt, G., *The Fallen Woman in the Nineteenth-century English Novel* (London, Croom Helm, 1984)

Weedon, C., *Feminist Practice and Poststructuralist Theory* (Oxford, Blackwell, 1987)

White Mario, J., *La miseria di Napoli* (Florence, Le Monnier, 1877)

Women and Italy: Essays on Gender, Culture and History, edited by Z. G. Barański and S. W. Vinall (London, Macmillan, 1991)

Women Writing and Writing about Women, edited by M. Jacobus [1979] (London, Croom Helm, 1986)

Wood, S., *Italian Women's Writing, 1860–1994* (London, Athlone Press, 1995)

Woolf, D., *The Art of Verga: A Study in Objectivity* (Sydney, Sydney University Press, 1977)

Woolf, V., "Professions for Women" [1931], in her *The Death of the Moth and Other Essays* (London, Hogarth Press, 1942), pp. 236–38

Woolf, V., *The Common Reader* [1925] (London, Hogarth Press, 1929)

Writing and Sexual Difference, edited by E. Abel [1980] (Brighton, Harvester Press, 1982)

Zimmerman, B., "What Has Never Been: An Overview of Lesbian Feminist Criticism", in *Making a Difference*, pp. 117–211

INDEX OF REFERENCES TO SERAO'S WORKS

INDEX OF NAMES